T0214586

Lecture Notes in Computer Science   11153

Commenced Publication in 1973
Founding and Former Series Editors:
Gerhard Goos, Juris Hartmanis, and Jan van Leeuwen

More information about this series at http://www.springer.com/series/7409

Cesare Pautasso · Fernando Sánchez-Figueroa
Kari Systä · Juan Manuel Murillo Rodríguez (Eds.)

Current Trends in Web Engineering

ICWE 2018 International Workshops
MATWEP, EnWot, KD-WEB, WEOD, TourismKG
Cáceres, Spain, June 5, 2018
Revised Selected Papers

 Springer

Editors
Cesare Pautasso (iD)
Faculty of Informatics
University of Lugano
Lugano, Switzerland

Fernando Sánchez-Figueroa (iD)
Quercus Software Engineering Group
Universidad de Extremadura
Cáceres, Spain

Kari Systä (iD)
Tampere University of Technology
Tampere, Finland

Juan Manuel Murillo Rodríguez (iD)
Escuela Politécnica
Universidad de Extremadura
Cáceres, Spain

ISSN 0302-9743 ISSN 1611-3349 (electronic)
Lecture Notes in Computer Science
ISBN 978-3-030-03055-1 ISBN 978-3-030-03056-8 (eBook)
https://doi.org/10.1007/978-3-030-03056-8

Library of Congress Control Number: 2018959427

LNCS Sublibrary: SL3 – Information Systems and Applications, incl. Internet/Web, and HCI

This Springer imprint is published by the registered company Springer Nature Switzerland AG
The registered company address is: Gewerbestrasse 11, 6330 Cham, Switzerland

Preface

ICWE aims to promote research and scientific exchange related to Web engineering, and to bring together researchers and practitioners from various disciplines in academia and industry in order to tackle emerging challenges in the engineering of Web applications and associated technologies, as well as to assess the impact of those technologies on society, media, and culture.

This volume collects the papers presented at the workshops co-located with the 18th International Conference on Web Engineering (ICWE 2018), held during June 5–8, in Cáeres, Spain. In the tradition of previous ICWE conferences, the workshops complemented the main conference, and provided a forum for researchers and practitioners to discuss emerging topics, both within the ICWE community and at the crossroads with other communities. As a result, we accepted the following five workshops, whose papers included in this volume underwent a rigorous peer-review process and were presented on June 5, 2018.

- First International Workshop on Maturity of Web Engineering Practices (MATWEP 2018)
- Second International Workshop on Engineering the Web of Things (EnWoT 2018)
- 4th International Workshop on Knowledge Discovery on the Web (KDWEB 2018)
- International Workshop on Engineering Open Data (WEOD 2018)
- First International Workshop on Knowledge Graphs on Travel and Tourism (TourismKG 2018)

The objective of the MATWEP workshop (five papers) was to provide an open discussion space combining solid theory work with practical on-the-field experience in the Web engineering area.

EnWoT 2018 (five papers) focused on various themes all the way from engineering the Internet of Things (IoT) with Web technologies to addressing the challenge of delivering a liquid user experience from the standpoint of multi-device software engineering and end-user development.

Finally, KDWeb 2018 (five papers) focused on the field of knowledge discovery from digital data, with particular attention for advanced data mining, machine learning, and information retrieval methods, systems, and applications.

The focus of the WEOD 2018 workshop (three papers) was to present the latest research on practical engineering approaches (a) to design and develop means for promoting the consumption of open data and (b) to design and develop composition mechanisms that help in combining open data sources.

The goal of TourismKG 2018 (13 papers) was to raise awareness of the importance of knowledge graphs in the travel industry and discuss their usage, challenges, enhancement, and ways of commercial exploitation.

We would like to thank all the workshop organizers for their excellent work in identifying cutting-edge and cross-disciplinary topics in the rapidly moving field of

Web engineering, and organizing inspiring workshops around them. A word of thanks also to the reviewers, for their meticulous work in selecting the best papers to be presented. Last, but not least, we would like to thank the authors who submitted their work to the workshops and all the participants who contributed to the success of these events.

July 2018   Cesare Pautasso
Fernando Sánchez-Figueroa
Kari Systä
Juan Manuel Murillo Rodríguez

Contents

1st International Workshop on Maturity of Web Engineering Practices (MATWEP 2018)

1st International Workshop on Maturity of Web Engineering Practices (MATWEP 2018)

Francisco José Domínguez Mayo[1], José González Enríquez[2],
Nora Koch[2], and Esteban Morillo Baro[3]

[1] University of Seville, Seville, Spain
fjdominguez@us.es
[2] IWT2 Group, University of Seville, Seville, Spain
{jose.gonzalez,nora.koch}@iwt2.org
[3] Servinform, S.A., Seville, Spain
emorillob@servinform.es

Abstract. Knowledge transfer and adoption of software engineering approaches by practitioners is always a challenge for both academia and industry. The objective of the workshop MATWEP is to provide an open discussion space that combines solid theory work with practical on-the-field experience in the Web Engineering area. The topics covered are knowledge transfer of Web Engineering approaches, such as methods, techniques and tools in all phases of the development life-cycle of Web applications. We report on the papers presented in the edition 2018 and the fruitful discussion on these topics.

Keywords: Web engineering · Methods · Techniques
Tools · Knowledge transfer · Industrial environment

1 Introduction and Motivation

The First International Workshop on Maturity of Web Engineering Practices (MATWEP 2018) was held in conjunction with the 18th International Conference on Web Engineering (ICWE 2018) in Cáceres (Spain) on June 5th 2018. The motivation for this initiative stands in the aim of building a better bridge from theory to practice, from academia to industry.

The focus of this first workshop and future editions of MATWEP is the analysis and discussion on positive experiences and difficulties that arise in the construction of such bridges. The goal is to show the lessons learned in the knowledge transfer process. This way it promotes to obtain feedback from practitioners for improving Web Engineering techniques, methods and approaches developed in research-intensive environments.

2 Presentations

During the first edition of the workshop five papers were selected for presentations at the workshop; three of them were selected to be published in these proceedings. We hope you find these papers useful reading material.

The first paper describes how the Navigational Development Techniques (NDT) - an MDWE methodology - was applied to manage the test phase of a real-world case study, part of the ADAGIO project. L. Morales et al. show the advantages of the automated generation of test cases improving the quality of the final product, and how the feedback obtained will serve to improve the NDT-tools to reduce the computational cost of generating tests from complex functional requirements.

The second paper written by A. Kravchenko, R. R. Fayzrakhmanov, and E. Sallinger focuses on different representations of web pages, and introduces BERYL, a novel framework and language, which consolidates a rule-based approach with machine learning. The rule-based approach is used for feature engineering and pattern recognition, while machine learning is used for classification based on the inferred features. The evaluation of BERYL help to identify some main points as feedback, and which can direct future work, such as the integration of a common framework for describing topology and various spatial relations, and the possibility of selecting the most relevant machine learning algorithm.

In the third paper E. Falzone, and C. Bernaschina present a MDD approach which organizes the model transformation rules and the code architecture in a way that preserves the manual modifications of the code defined outside the model-and-generate cycle, such as the code defining the look and feel of the user interface and the connection to the required service endpoints. They report on the experience using the MDD approach in the development of web and mobile applications for an energy demand management project, and the generation of game versions from IFML models, in which both the presentation code and the code for connecting the game to a back-end cloud platform were added manually.

For further information and material, such as the presentations slides, please visit the MATWEP 2018 website: http://www.iwt2.org/matwep2018/.

3 Discussion

The very fruitful discussion round during the last workshop session focused on the difficulties of the knowledge transfer and the different possibilities to make the adoption of new techniques, methods, and tools more successful in an industrial environment.

Difficulties were mentioned, such as the costs of the development of tools and their maintenance, as well as the provision of training courses and tool documentation. The question was posed, if the role of academia is to implement such tools, or instead should limit itself to develop new techniques and methods, eventually providing prototypes, that could be adopted by tool providers.

4 Acknowledgement

The organization of this workshop has been supported by the POLOLAS project (TIN2016-76956-C3-2-R) of the Spanish Ministry of Economy and Competitiveness, and the investigation plan VPPI of the University of Seville.

We like to express our gratitude to the authors and presenters for the well-prepared presentations, all the workshop participants for their questions and comments, the MATWEP Program Committee that did a great job reviewing the submitted papers, and the ICWE 2018 Organizing Committee for their excellent support.

5 Program Committee

Miguel Angel Barcelona, Everis Spain, Spain
Antonia Bertolino, ISTI-CNR, Italy
Marianne Busch, BMW, Germany
Olga De Troyer, Vrije Universiteit Brussel, Belgium
Piero Fraternali, Politecnico di Milano, Italy
Javier Gonzalez-Huerta, Blekinge Institute of Technology, Sweden
Andrés L. Martínez Ortiz, Google, The Netherlands
Eva-Maria Schön, IWT2 Group, University of Seville, Spain
Gustavo Rossi, LIFIA-F. Informatica, UNLP, Argentina
Adel Rouz, Fujitsu Laboratories Europe, UK
Carlos Torrecilla-Salinas, IWT2 Group, University of Seville, Spain
Fernando Sánchez, Universidad de Extremadura, Spain
Jörg Thomaschewski, University of Applied Sciences Emden/Leer, Germany
Cesar Wagener, Getronics, Spain
Marco Winckler, Université Nice Sophia Antipolis (Polytecj), France

Intelligent Code Generation for Model Driven Web Development

Emanuele Falzone(✉) and Carlo Bernaschina

Dipartimento di Elettronica, Informazione e Bioingegneria, Politecnico di Milano,
Piazza L. Da Vinci, 21, 20133 Milano, Italy
emanuele.falzone@mail.polimi.it, carlo.bernaschina@polimi.it

Abstract. Model Driven Development requires proper tools to derive
the implementation code from the application models. However, the use
of code generation tools may interfere with the software development and
maintenance practices, because most state-of-the art tools are incapable
of preserving manual modifications to the code when the implementation
is regenerated from the models. In this paper, we present an approach
which organizes the model transformation rules and the code architecture
in a way that preserves the parts of the code that are defined outside the
model-and-generate cycle, such as the code defining the look and feel of
the user interface and the connection to the required service endpoints.

Keywords: Model Driven Development · Code generation
Agile development

1 Introduction

Model Driven Development (MDD) is the branch of software engineering that
advocates the use of *models*, i.e., abstract representations of a system, and of
model transformations as key ingredients of software development. Developers
use a general purpose (e.g. UML[1]) or domain specific (e.g. IFML[2]) modeling language to specify systems under one or more perspectives, and use (or build) suitable chains of *transformations* to refine the models into a final product (e.g. executable code). Abstraction is the far most important aspect of MDD. It enables
developers to validate high level concepts and introduce details, which increase
complexity, later in the process. In the *Forward Engineering* approach details
are introduced via model transformations, which iteratively refine the model
eventually getting to the final product. After each model change, the process is
reiterated to produce a new version. Model to Model (M2M) and Model to Text
(M2T) transformations are tailored to achieve this goal. Transformations can be
grouped into two groups: **(I) Model Enhancement.** The model is enhanced by
the introduction of details that are fixed, or easily derivable from the model itself

---

[1] http://www.uml.org.

[2] http://www.omg.org/spec/IFML/1.0/.

© Springer Nature Switzerland AG 2018
C. Pautasso et al. (Eds.): ICWE 2018, LNCS 11153, pp. 5–13, 2018.
https://doi.org/10.1007/978-3-030-03056-8_1

with fixed rules. An example is a M2M transformation in the Entity Relationship domain which maps hierarchies into equivalent entities and relationships. **(II) Model Specialization.** The model is refined by introducing details specific for a target platform (e.g. system, language, ...). This is obtained via a M2M or M2T transformation having a high-level source meta-model and a platform specific target meta-model. An example is a M2T transformation that maps a state machine representing GUI interactions to the source code of a specific GUI framework. In this work we focus on model specialization.

Transformations should map each valid source model into one valid target model deterministically. When the target meta-model has a higher expressive power two scenarios are possible: **(I) Exploitation.** The transformation exploits the expressive power of the target meta-model to express in higher detail the concepts defined in the source model. An example is a M2M transformation that defines the semantics of a language by mapping it to a more expressive and well defined one, like in [7], where Statecharts are used to define the semantics of WebML, and in [5], where Place Chart Nets (PCN) are used to describe the semantics of IFML. If the target meta-model (Statecharts, PCN) is more expressive than the source model (WebML, IFML), all the valid models that cannot be produced have no practical usage for the specific purpose of the transformation. **(II) Ambiguity.** More then one valid target model is a possible output candidate for the M2T transformation. The developer is responsible of directing the transformation to take a decision among the possible alternative outputs. An example is a M2T transformation that generates a GUI implementation from an application model [4]; many visual representation can be produced, by taking different assumptions on layout and styling. The model does not contain the information required to generate fine grained styling details.

While it is not always possible to uniquely assign a transformation to one of the two groups, the fuzziness introduced by the ambiguous transformation scenario are the most interesting, and the main motivation of this work. Fuzziness arises from abstraction itself. The high-level description can ignore details that are not uniquely inferable. A *Forward Engineering* approach requires such unknowns to be solved by enhancing both meta-model and transformations to remove uncertainties and maintain a unidirectional flow. This approach can lead to loss of abstraction and diminishes the benefits of the MDD methodology. User Interfaces (UI), and in particular web based ones, are a relevant example of this situation. While abstraction simplifies reasoning about the application structure and the high-level interaction, low-level details such as layout, sizing, colors or gestures can completely change the final user experience. For special domain applications a compromise can be achieved with approaches like the one implemented in commercial tools (e.g. WebRatio[3]), where the high-level model can be marked with ad hoc attributes allowing the M2T transformation to properly select a presentation template. While this approach has been successfully adopted in the industry, it introduces a layer of complexity that can easily demand more work than manual coding for application with highly specific

---

[3] http://www.webratio.com/.

presentation requirements. In this paper, we discuss an alternative approach, which relaxes the assumptions of *Forward Engineering* enabling the manual introduction of details (e.g. styling) in the generated code, while simplifying the resolution of conflicts between the generated code and manual changes through the use of good practices in coding and development work-flows.

The paper is organized as follows: Sect. 2 surveys model-based and text-based approaches for the evolution of textual final products and current trends on coding practices for web applications; Sect. 3 presents a novel approach for the mitigation of the effects of fuzziness in M2T transformations; it uses as running example a M2T transformation generating the source code of a web application from an IFML model, while it has been implemented using the AgiLe MOdel Transformation framework (ALMOsT.js [3]) the approach is generic and can potentially be applied to every M2T transformation language; finally, Sect. 4 draws the conclusions and gives an outlook on future work.

2   Related Work

Model to text transformations can have deep impact on an MDD work-flow. Various approaches and tools have been proposed to enhance them. Given the template-based nature of such transformations, complexity can easily arise, especially during maintenance.

Various approaches and tools have been proposed to enhance or replace M2T transformations. In [6] the automatic production of code generators from interpreters has been proposed avoiding the need for M2T transformations. In [13] a polymorphic approach has been presented, showing how modularization and dynamic invocation of templates can reduce complexity and simplify maintenance. Complexity can arise from changes in both source meta-model and target technologies. In [11] an approach to simplify M2T transformation evolution after a meta-model change is discussed. In [8] a survey of possible approaches to organize model transformations is conducted, showing the effects of moving rapidly evolving aspects of the architecture from the M2M transformations to the M2T transformations and even outside of the MDD work-flow in a manually coded abstraction layer; the study focused on SQL queries. Model and Text co-evolution has been proposed as a way to simplify M2T transformations. In [2] a bidirectional M2T transformation approach based on Triple Graph Grammar (TGG) has been proposed. The Abstract Syntax Tree (AST) representation of the target language is used in a bidirectional M2M transformation defined via TGG. The AST is structured with particular attention to supporting extra chunks of text that can be introduced during manual modifications, but are not directly managed by the transformation. In general, solving text level co-evolution with model level approaches can reduce complexity, at the cost of defining a parser specific for the target language. In [9] a trace based framework for change retainment has been proposed, which could be potentially applied in this scenario. Increasing the complexity of M2T transformations can drastically increase computation time. In [14] manual and automatically generated signatures (small, efficiently computable proxies to the final text) are exploited to increase the performance of the MDD pipeline.

Conflict Resolution at text level has been studied for a long time. Version Control Systems (VCS) like Git[4], Mercurial[5] or SVN[6] need to manage conflict resolution, in particular if working in a distributed environment. Coarse grained/language agnostic [12] or fine grained/language specific [6] automatic resolution approaches can be applied, leaving the manual intervention of the developer as a fall-back.

Separation of Concerns. In Web Applications, UI development demands a sharp division between structure (HTML) and style (CSS) for easy adaptation to various devices and clients capabilities [10]. Complexity of UI layout and styling is shifted from HTML, which describes the structure and semantics of the content, to CSS. While this scenario enables advanced use-cases, in practice it may not achieve a real separation of concerns in all cases. To obtain advanced layout and styling, the CSS rules become dependent on the HTML structure, which increases complexity, maintenance cost, and code duplication.

In the past years, coding practices shifted towards an effective compromise between separation of concerns and development costs. Modern CSS frameworks, such as Bootstrap[7], Zurb Foundation[8], Materialize CSS[9], and many others, have shown how sharing layout concerns between HTML and CSS layers can enhance re-usability and eventually reduce development time. The same trend can be seen in the field of Mobile Applications with Framework7[10], Flutter[11] and many others. This compromise blurs the line between structure and styling making more and more difficult for M2T transformations to avoid conflicts at code level.

3   An M2T Based Hybrid Automatic and Manual Approach for Web Application Development

We propose a two steps approach to M2T transformations, which leverages both MDD and manual coding, aiming at the reduction of maintenance costs. We use as running example a code generator for web applications presented in [4], which applies forward engineering via a M2T transformation from an high-level IFML description of an application into a working prototype.

---

[4] http://git-scm.com/.
[5] http://www.mercurial-scm.org/.
[6] http://subversion.apache.org/.
[7] http://getbootstrap.com/.
[8] http://foundation.zurb.com/.
[9] http://materializecss.com/.
[10] http://framework7.io/.
[11] http://flutter.io/.

3.1 Requirements

We focus on agile development methods, such as SCRUM [15], which commands developers to create minimum viable products rapidly and evolve them via frequent iterations (sprints). As a reference usage scenario, we imagine a software team, who decides to exploit MDD in its development, by progressively introducing requirements and freely experiment with the generated code in order to enhance the user experience. Not all members of the team have a profound knowledge of the MDD pipeline and each member contributes to the project based on his role and expertise. Under the above mentioned drivers, the requirements of the proposed methodology can be summarized as follows: **(1) Model and Text Co-Evolution.** It must be possible to introduce new functional requirements at model level and in parallel to modify directly the code-base, e.g., to improve performance and/or styling. Changes applied to the generated code must be preserved after model change and implementation regeneration. **(2) VCS Support.** The evolution of the project must be trackable using preexisting VCSs.

3.2 Intelligent Code Generation

The structure of the code generated by M2T transformations influences its maintainability. It should adhere to specific, possibly preexisting, best practices and coding styles, to facilitate code maintenance and conflict resolution. The possible aids can be divided in two main categories.

Project Structure. Modularization and separation of concerns improve software maintainability. In the web domain, approaches for code and markup modularization, such as CommonJS[12], Asynchronous Module Definition (AMD)[13] and Web Components[14], have been so successful to influence such standards as ECMAScript 6 [1] and HTML5 [16]. Splitting the generated code both logically (components, modules, . . .) and physically (files and folders) helps achieve both model and text co-evolution and VCS support: it is easier for VCSs to identify the updated files and for humans to contextualize and solve conflicts. Similarly to *protected areas* in Acceleo[15], a well structured project can automatically concentrate manual editing to specific areas of the code (e.g. GUI, service endpoints, . . .) and leave the majority of the generated code untouched (e.g., code devoted to orchestration, routing, . . .).

Coding Style. When files can be thoroughly affected by both model changes and manual editing languages, specific approaches can be applied. Modern languages give to developers freedom over many non functional aspects of the code. White-spaces and new-lines, identifiers names, order invariant statements can lead to really different appearance, which retain the same semantics. Making both developers and M2T transformations follow the same coding conventions

---

[12] http://wiki.commonjs.org/wiki/Modules.
[13] http://github.com/amdjs/amdjs-api.
[14] http://www.webcomponents.org/.
[15] http://www.eclipse.org/acceleo/.

can help to address requirement #1, reducing friction between developers and automatically generated code, as if the code generator were just another member of the team. Common VCSs, such as Git, apply text based conflict resolution algorithms [12], many of which are line based. Coding conventions can be enhanced in order to facilitate such procedures. Some examples are: splitting statements that can be possibly effected by both model changes and manual coding;

```
<!-- The class field is possibly effected by manual changes while the
     data-bind field can be changes by the generator. -->
<div class="list-item" data-bind="text: fields['title']"/>
<!-- Splitting the tag in two avoids conflicts on the same line. -->
<div class="list-item"
    data-bind="text: fields['title']"/>
```

facilitate the insertion of new code without affecting nearby lines.

```
// Introducing a new item will mark the entire line as changed
var items = ['item1', 'item2'];
// Introducing a new items will not mark the entire array as changed
var items = [
    'item1',
    'item2', // The comma simplifies the insertion of new lines
];
```

Given the language-specific nature of code organization practices, we will not enter into further details.

3.3   Conflict Resolution Strategy

Manual editing of the generated code (requirement #1) inevitably produces conflicts, which are not different from the ones that arise from a classic VCS based distributed work-flow (requirement #2). Different developers work at the same time starting from different versions of the same code-base. Each developer needs to synchronize its local copy of the repository with the central one, solving potential conflicts that arise, before the changes are accepted. The code generator can be treated as yet another developer, who applies changes on an outdated repository. We will just consider conflicts that arise on the source code, we will ignore concurrent changes on the model. The work-flow can be organized as follow: (1) The initial model is constructed and the code generator is run the first time. This revision of the source code G_1 (1st Generated) is sent to the central repository. (2) A developer introduces a new manual change, starting from G_1, producing revision M_1 (1st Manual change) which is sent to the central repository. (3) Concurrently, another developer introduces a new manual change, also starting from G_1. During synchronization possible conflicts are identified and solved producing M_2 (2nd Manual change) which is sent to the central repository. (4) A change at model level is applied and the code generator is run again. By applying this new version on top of G_1 the generator is comparable to the second developer. During synchronization possible conflicts are identified and solved, by reapplying all the deltas introduced by each revision. Two new revision are sent to the central repository; G_2 containing the generated code and $M_{1,2}$ reintroducing the manual changes of M_1 and M_2 over G_2.

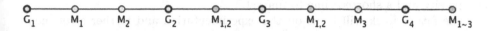

Fig. 1. Revisions history.

Figure 1 shows the revision history resulting from various reiterations of the proposed approach. The developer always sees a central repository, which is aligned with all the changes manually introduced. The code generator can be considered as a developer always out-of-sync who applies changes on top of the latest G_i revision. The introduction of an artificial, purely generated, M_i revision has the unwanted side effect of polluting the history with highly redundant code decreasing the benefits of a VCS system (requirement #2). The proposed approach schema can be enhanced to reduce this effect. The list of files effected by a model change is generally small compared to the whole code-base. It is possible to exploit this characteristic to reduce the impact of G_i and $M_{1\sim j}$ revisions by concentrating on the files that are actually effected. After code generation, conflicts are addressed on a per file base. Each project file can be in 4 possible states: (1) The file was not part of the code-base (effect of a constructive change in the model). It is added in the G_i revision as a newly created file. (2) The file was created in a G_i revision but is not part of the generated code anymore (effect of a destructive change in the model). It is removed from the code-base and the changes applied to it in any M_j or $M_{1\sim j}$ revision are discarded. (3) The file was created in a G_i revision and it is not changed. It can be skipped and the current state of the file is preserved. (4) The file was created in a G_i revision and it is changed. Synchronization will start from the latest G_i revision in which it is contained. All the changes applied after G_i, both in M_j or $M_{1\sim j}$ revisions, are reapplied and manual interventions is requested if automatic resolution fails. The file is added to the current G_i revision and the version after the resolution of the conflicts is added to the current $M_{1\sim j}$ revision.

4   Discussion and Future Work

This paper presented an approach for model and text co-evolution with particular attention in conflicts prevention and conflict resolution via VCS work-flows.

The approach is being used in the MDD development of web and mobile applications[16] for a energy demand management project, in which multiple editions of a energy awareness game are produced in rapid sprints, to support a user-centric design cycle in which stakeholders contribute to the design of applications. The described approach has been applied to the generation of game versions from

---

[16] http://play.google.com/store/apps/details?id=com.eu.funergy.

IFML models, with a hybrid approach [4], in which both the presentation code and the code for connecting the game to a back-end cloud platform are added manually. While the described transformation architecture introduced extra conflicts resolution time after each model iteration it was compensated by a lower complexity and a shorted time to market.

The future work will focus on the experimentation and further assessment of the proposed approach in the industry, with two scenarios: companies that do not yet use MDD in their practices, to understand if introducing MDD without the disruption of existing development practices lowers the reluctance of traditional developers towards modeling; companies already applying in-house domain specific models and code generation techniques, to understand the added value of a mixed approach between MDD and manual coding.

Acknowledgments. This work has been partially supported by the European Community, through the H2020 project enCOMPASS (Grant #723059).

References

1. ECMAScript 6. http://www.ecma-international.org/ecma-262/6.0/
2. Anjorin, A., Lauder, M.P., Schlereth, M., Schürr, A.: Support for bidirectional model-to-text transformations. ECEASST (2010)
3. Bernaschina, C.: ALMOsT.js: an agile model to model and model to text transformation framework. In: 17th International Conference on Web Engineering, ICWE (2017)
4. Bernaschina, C., Comai, S., Fraternali, P.: IFMLEdit.org: model driven rapid prototyping of mobile apps. In: 4th IEEE/ACM International Conference on Mobile Software Engineering and Systems, MOBILESoft@ICSE (2017)
5. Bernaschina, C., Comai, S., Fraternali, P.: Formal semantics of OMGs interaction flow modeling language (IFML) for mobile and rich-client application model driven development. J. Syst. Softw. **137**, 239–260 (2018)
6. Birken, K.: Building code generators for DSLs using a partial evaluator for the Xtend language. In: Margaria, T., Steffen, B. (eds.) ISoLA 2014, Part I. LNCS, vol. 8802, pp. 407–424. Springer, Heidelberg (2014). https://doi.org/10.1007/978-3-662-45234-9_29
7. Comai, S., Fraternali, P.: A semantic model for specifying data-intensive web applications using WebML. In: Proceedings of the first Semantic Web Working Symposium, SWWS 2001 (2001)
8. García, J., Dìaz, O., Cabot, J.: An adapter-based approach to co-evolve generated SQL in model-to-text transformations. In: Jarke, M., et al. (eds.) CAiSE 2014. LNCS, vol. 8484, pp. 518–532. Springer, Cham (2014). https://doi.org/10.1007/978-3-319-07881-6_35
9. Goldschmidt, T., Uhl, A.: Retainment policies - a formal framework for change retainment for trace-based model transformations. Inf. Softw. Technol. **55**(6), 1064–1084 (2013)
10. Hall, C.A.: Web presentation layer bootstrapping for accessibility and performance. In: Proceedings of the International Cross-Disciplinary Conference on Web Accessibility, W4A (2009)

11. Hoisl, B., Sobernig, S.: Towards benchmarking evolution support in model-to-text transformation systems. In: Proceedings of the 4th Workshop on the Analysis of Model Transformations Co-located with the 18th International Conference on Model Driven Engineering Languages and Systems, MODELS (2015)

12. Horwitz, S., Prins, J., Reps, T.W.: Integrating non-interfering versions of programs. In: Conference Record of the Fifteenth Annual ACM Symposium on Principles of Programming Languages (1988)

13. Kövesdán, G., Asztalos, M., Lengyel, L.: Polymorphic templates: a design pattern for implementing agile model-to-text transformations. In: 3rd Workshop on Extreme Modeling Co-located with ACM/IEEE 17th International Conference on Model Driven Engineering Languages & Systems, XM@MoDELS (2014)

14. Ogunyomi, B., Rose, L.M., Kolovos, D.S.: Property access traces for source incremental model-to-text transformation. In: Taentzer, G., Bordeleau, F. (eds.) ECMFA 2015. LNCS, vol. 9153, pp. 187–202. Springer, Cham (2015). https://doi.org/10.1007/978-3-319-21151-0_13

15. Schwaber, K., Beedle, M.: Agile Software Development with Scrum, 1st edn. Prentice Hall, Upper Saddle River (2001)

16. World Wide Web Consortium (W3C): HTML5. https://www.w3.org/TR/html5/

Applying Model-Driven Web Engineering to the Testing Phase of the ADAGIO Project

L. Morales$^{(\boxtimes)}$, S. Moreno-Leonardo, M. A. Olivero,
A. Jiménez-Ramírez, and M. Mejías

Computer Languages and Systems Department, University of Seville,
Avenida Reina Mercedes, s/n, 41010 Seville, Spain
{leticia.morales,sara.moreno,miguel.olivero,
andres.jimenez}@iwt2.org, risoto@us.es

Abstract. The Model-Driven Engineering (MDE) has been used in recent years to promote better results in the development of Web Applications, in the field that has been called Model-Driven Web Engineering (MDWE). One of the advantages of applying MDWE is that it offers a solution to reduce the cost of the tests without affecting their quality execution. This paper presents the application of a MDWE methodology (Navigational Development Techniques, NDT) that provides support for all the phases of the lifecycle of a software project development proposing transformations between these phases, to manage the test phase of a real-world case study named ADAGIO. This project, among other goals, proposes the development of a web application whose main objective is to offer researchers the possibility of integrating and consolidating heterogeneous data sources, showing a unified vision of them, allowing to simplify the search task in different repositories as well as the relationship between the sources found.

Keywords: Model-Driven Web Engineering · NDT · Early Testing
Web application

1 Introduction

Model-Driven Engineering (MDE) offers the advantage to support automation, as the models can be automatically transformed from the early stages of development to the final ones. Therefore, MDE enables automating tasks involved in software development, such us testing tasks [1]. The process of software development involves a series of activities in which the chances of a human error is high (mistakes can happen in the beginning of the process, in which the objectives can be inadequately specified, as well as during later steps) [2]. In this context, trying to find errors in the earliest stages of development, would greatly help to reduce the costs of the total computation of the project, showing errors before they appear.

Model-Driven Testing (MDT) [3], increases the level of automation, automating not only the execution of system tests, but also their design. System tests are generated automatically from a software product model. This results in a repeatable and rational

© Springer Nature Switzerland AG 2018
C. Pautasso et al. (Eds.): ICWE 2018, LNCS 11153, pp. 14–21, 2018.
https://doi.org/10.1007/978-3-030-03056-8_2

basis for testing the product, ensuring the coverage of all its behaviors, and allowing the tests to be directly linked to the requirements.

In the Web Engineering and Early Testing IWT2 research group, where this research has been carried out, we have spent years working on the Model-Driven Web Engineering (MDWE) [4] paradigm. From this research, the Navigational Development Tools (NDT) [5] methodology was born, including a very important pillar based in MDT. This paper presents a real-world case study of validation about the application of the automatic system tests generation that NDT proposes in a concrete scenario: the ADAGIO Project.

The remainder of this paper is organized as follows: Sect. 2 presents some related work based on Model-Driven proposals that aim to automate the generation of system tests, Sect. 3 describes the ADAGIO project is being developed based on two main pillars: MDE and NDT. Section 3 presents the ADAGIO project. Section 4 describes how the system tests generation proposed by NDT methodology has been applied into the ADAGIO project. And finally, Sect. 5 summarizes a set of conclusions and future works.

2   Related Work

There are a great variety of proposals that are based in methods for generating system tests. Next, some related work is presented.

Anand et al. [6] proposed the following classification for MDT for modeling notations: scenario-oriented, state-oriented and process oriented notations. The first one, directly describe the sequences of input and output between the System-Under-Test (SUT) and its environment. Usually, they are based on sequence charts, activity charts or use case diagrams although textual variations have also been proposed. This technique is generally simpler than other ones because a scenario is very similar to a test case. However, the system tests generation are not final system tests because it is needed to perform a test selection and to define the input parameters. The second one describes the SUT by its reaction on an input or output in a given state. As result, the models state is evolved and an output maybe produced. This technique may be expressed as diagrammatic or textual form. The last modeling notation describes the SUT in a procedural style, where inputs and outputs are received and sent as messages on communication channels. The approach that has been used in this paper is focused in scenario-oriented notations. In this sense, some related work to generate automatic system tests using this technique are presented.

Nogueira et al. [7] offer a strategy for the automatic generation of system tests of parameterized use cases templates. This approach considers a natural language representation that mixes control and state representation, which can be used to select particular scenarios during test generation. Kumar et al. [8] propose a model to generate an activity flow table (AFT) from an activity diagram converting it to activity flow graph (AFG). By using activity coverage criterion, authors generate the test paths through traversing the AFG. Finally, the system tests from these paths are generated. Olajubu et al. [9] presented a Model to Text (M2T) transformation language for test case generation from requirement specifications expressed in a Domain Specific Language (DSL).

Gutiérrez et al. [10] introduce a systematic process based on the Model-Driven paradigm to automate the generation of functional system tests from functional requirements, defining a set of metamodels and transformations and a DSL. Marín et al. [11] show a model-based testing technique that automatically generates abstract system tests from conceptual models used in Model-Driven Development (MDD) and a model-based testing technique that automatically generates concrete system tests in Java and C#, reducing the testing effort in MDD projects environments. Elalloui et al. [12], propose an improved version of a previous work where they implemented an algorithm that took as input user stories, and automatically generate UML sequence diagrams. In this improved work, authors automatically generate the system tests applying Model to Model (M2M) and M2T transformations through the use of AndroMDA, an open source MDA Framework. Usaola et al. [13] show a method to describe generic test scenarios by means of regular expressions, whose symbols point to a System Under Test (SUT) operation.

3   Background: The ADAGIO Project

The Analytics Data Aggregated Geolocation Open (ADAGIO) project, is funded by the center for industrial technological development (Centro para el Desarrollo Tecnológico Industrial, CDTI), public business entity of the Ministry of Economy, Industry and Competitiveness of Spain. This initiative is launched by the consortium of the IWT2 research group of the University of Seville and Servinform S.A. company.

The vision of the ADAGIO project is to develop of a web application that combines strategies of Big Data and Machine Learning in areas of treatment of geotagged data from diverse and heterogeneous data sources, to generate knowledge, starting from Open Data information already available. The generic goals of this project are:

- Facilitate research and data processing.
- Obtain geotagged populations that fit predefined criteria.
- To enable the performance of statistical analyzes and correlations of these populations.

ADAGIO functional model (Fig. 1) proposes 4 main modules: (i) download and catalog of data sources, (ii) the entity reconciliation process, (iii) administration and management of the data sources, and (iv), exploitation of the information through a web application.

This paper focuses on the fourth module. The main goal of this module is based the creation of queries by users of the system, in a language as natural and high level as possible, applying supervised Machine Learning and Text Mining techniques, with the aim of extracting hidden knowledge from the data sources previously processed in the other modules. The functionalities that this module will offer are: user authentication, data exploitation, automation of the import into the system of the data sources that have been identified at the beginning of the project and finally, the data sources will be available for their exploitation and accessible for future queries working as a unique data source thanks to the automation of the import process.

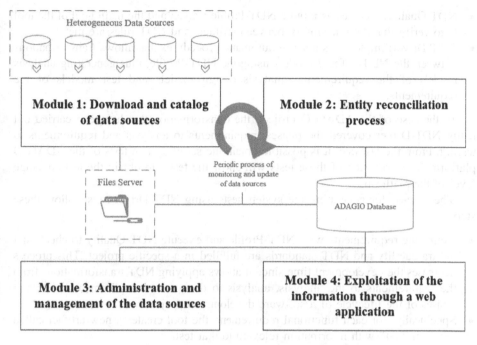

Fig. 1. ADAGIO functional model.

4 Model-Driven Web Engineering in the ADAGIO Project

Navigational Development Techniques (NDT) is a methodological approach oriented to Web Engineering [5]. NDT defines a set of metamodels for every phase of the life cycle of software development: the feasibility study phase, the requirements phase, the analysis phase, the design phase, the implementation phase, the testing phase, and finally, the maintenance phase.

Nowadays, NDT is a complete framework named "NDTQ-Framework" that provides support for all the phases of the lifecycle of a software project development and proposes automatic transformations between these phases. NDTQ-Framework proposes six groups of processes that have been defined on the basis of the life cycle of NDT although its terminology has referenced the standards ISO 12207 [14]. These processes are: development, software maintenance, testing, software quality, management and security.

NDT-Suite [15] is a set of tools that allow a software engineer to apply the NDTQ-Framework in a business environment. NDT-Suite is composed of 5 main tools: NDT-Profile, NDT-Quality, NDT-Driver, NDT-Prototypes, NDT-Glossary. The three more important are:

- NDT-Profile: this tool defines all the profiles that have been created to instantiate the metamodel proposed by NDT in the Enterprise Architect (EA) case tool. Profiling these metamodels, it is possible to use each NDT artifact easily.

- NDT-Quality: receives as input a NDT-Profile project and the main goal of the tool is to verify that the traceability between artifacts and NDT rules are met.
- NDT-Driver: implements a set of automatic procedures that allows transformations between the NDT-defined models using the NDT-Profile, thus generating analysis models of the requirements, analysis design models and test models of the requirements.

In the case of the ADAGIO project, the transformation that has been carried out using NDT-Driver covered the phases: requirements to analysis and requirements to testing. From the last one, it is possible obtain the set of system tests of the ADAGIO platform. The execution of these tests will allow the tester to obtain the test coverage level of the platform.

The process for generating the system tests using NDT-Driver must follow these steps:

- Define the requirements with NDT-Profile and execute NDT-Quality to check that the traceability and NDT standards are fulfilled in a specific project. This process decreases the development time since it allows applying NDT transformations from the requirements to the analysis, analysis to design, and requirements to testing phases of the lifecycle of a software development project.
- Specifically, for each functional requirement, the tool creates a new artifact called "System Test" with information relevant to that test.
- Subsequently, the different tests that have been generated from the definition of the functional requirements are associated to each artifact. The functional requirements are based on activity diagrams, so the NDT-Driver generates a test for each possible path that exists in the diagram between the initial and the end activity.

Left side of Fig. 2, shows how the functional requirement "RF-01. System Login" of the ADAGIO platform has been defined through the use of the EA tool. It is possible to see that it is highlighted in red color, one of the possible paths of the activity diagram considering it as one of the tests generated for the ADAGIO platform. Right side of Fig. 2 shows one of the specific tests generated for this functional requirement.

Once all the system tests considered relevant have been obtained, it is possible to generate a Test Plan through the use of the NDT-Report tool. This tool defines a template for the description of each of the tests automatically generated. This template includes the definition of the system tests in two different ways: a table that describes the name, version, date of creation, authors, relationships, description and pre and post conditions of the test, and the other one, where the activity diagram of the test is defined, which shows all the activities that the tester must perform to carry out the test satisfactorily.

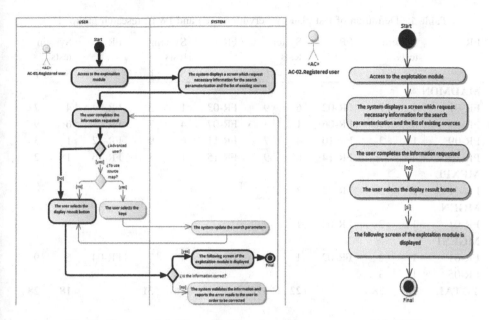

Fig. 2. Use case definition with EA and system test generated by NDT.

4.1 Results

As mentioned before, NDT methodology has been used, first, for defining the requirements and analysis phase of ADAGIO project, and second, for generating the system tests of that project.

After performing the requirement and analysis phases of the ADAGIO project, a total of 25 functional requirements (FR) were defined. The definition of the Test Plan of the web platform was defined in two ways: (i) by Servinform S.A. company and (ii), by IWT2 research group using NDT.

As possible to note in Table 1, where results of the number of system tests generated by each group are showed, the total number of system tests generated by IWT2 (136) are quite higher than the ones generated by Servinform S.A. (76), increasing considerably the system testing coverage level.

In addition, with the aim of rising the automation level of the Test Plan execution, it was used Selenium tool [16]. With this tool, authors achieved to reduce notably the cost of executing the Test Plan for each iteration.

5 Conclusion and Future Work

This paper has presented how a Model-Driven Web Engineering methodology (NDT) has been applied to a real world project called ADAGIO.

NDT has been used to define the requirement and analysis phase of the ADAGIO project, and, in addition, for generating and managing the test phase of this project. The definition of the requirements and analysis phase ended with a total of 25 functional

Table 1. Definition of test plan by Servinform (S) and IWT2 research group (I)

FR	System tests		FR	System tests		FR	System tests		FR	System tests	
	S	I		S	I		S	I		S	I
MADMON											
FR-01	4	7	FR-02	6	9	FR-03	1	3	FR-04	4	7
FR-05	6	9	FR-06	1	3	FR-07	4	7	FR-08	6	9
FR-09	1	3	FR-10	4	7	FR-11	6	9	FR-12	1	3
FR-13	4	7	FR-14	6	9	FR-15	1	3	FR-16	1	2
MEXPL											
FR-01	2	5	FR-02	3	7						
MGEN											
FR-01	1	2	FR-02	1	2						
MGEST											
FR-01	1	2	FR-02	1	2	FR-03	4	7	FR-04	6	9
FR-05	1	3									
TOTAL	**20**	**38**		**22**	**39**		**16**	**31**		**18**	**28**

requirements. From these functional requirements, both, Servinform company and IWT2 research group, developed a Test Plan for the testing phase of the project. As mentioned before, NDT takes the activity diagram that defines each functional requirement to generate the different system tests. In this sense, the coverage level of the Test Plan will be the 100%.

Table 1 of Sect. 4, shows that Servinform company defined a total of 76 system tests and IWT2, a total of 136, increasing a bit more than the 44% of the ones created by Servinform. Thus, it is possible to conclude that the use of NDT for this project has served for improving the quality of the final product.

Finally, future works encompasses different tasks such as: (i) improve NDT-Driver to reduce the computational cost of generating tests from complex functional requirements and (ii), improve NDT-Driver to define a process that let automatically generate selenium tests based on the requirements specification allowing to reduce the cost of reviewing and instantiating the test plan.

Acknowledgment. This research has been supported by the POLOLAS project (TIN2016-76956-C3-2-R) of the Spanish Ministry of Economy and Competitiveness, the VPPI of the University of Seville and the ADAGIO Project (P106-16/E09).

References

1. Garcia-Garcia, J.A., Enriquez, J.G., Garcia-Borgonon, L., Arevalo, C., Morillo, E.: A MDE-based framework to improve the process management: the EMPOWER project. In: Proceedings of the 2017 IEEE 15th International Conference on Industrial Informatics, INDIN 2017 (2017)
2. Enríquez, J.G., García-García, J.A., Domínguez-Mayo, F.J., Escalona, M.J.: ALAMEDA ecosystem: centering efforts in software testing development. In: Quality Control and Assurance-An Ancient Greek Term Re-Mastered, vol. 1, pp. 155–172 (2017)
3. Dai, Z.R.: Model-driven testing with UML 2.0. In: Computer Science at Kent, pp. 179–187 (2004)
4. Brambilla, M., Cabot, J., Wimmer, M.: Model-driven software engineering in practice (2012)
5. Escalona, M.J., Aragón, G.: NDT. A model-driven approach for web requirements. IEEE Trans. Softw. Eng. **34**, 377–394 (2008)
6. Saswat, A., et al.: An orchestrated survey of methodologies for automated software test case generation. J. Syst. Softw. **86**, 1978–2001 (2013)
7. Nogueira, S., Sampaio, A., Mota, A.: Test generation from state based use case models. Form. Asp. Comput. **26**, 441–490 (2014)
8. Jena, A.K., Swain, S.K., Mohapatra, D.P.: A novel approach for test case generation from UML activity diagram. In: 2014 International Conference on Issues and Challenges in Intelligent Computing Techniques, pp. 621–629 (2014)
9. Olajubu, O., Ajit, S., Johnson, M., Turner, S., Thomson, S., Edwards, M.: Automated test case generation from domain specific models of high-level requirements. In: Proceedings of the 2015 Conference on Research in Adaptive and Convergent Systems, RACS, pp. 505–508 (2015)
10. Gutiérrez, J.J., Escalona, M.J., Mejías, M.: A model-driven approach for functional test case generation. J. Syst. Softw. **109**, 214–228 (2015)
11. Marín, B., Gallardo, C., Quiroga, D., Giachetti, G., Serral, E.: Testing of model-driven development applications. Softw. Qual. J., 1–29 (2016)
12. Elallaoui, M., Nafil, K., Touahni, R.: Automatic generation of TestNG tests cases from UML sequence diagrams in Scrum process. In: IEEE International Colloquium on Information Science and Technology (CiSt), pp. 65–70 (2017)
13. Usaola, M.P., Romero, F.R., Aranda, R.R.-B., Rodriguez, I.G.: Test case generation with regular expressions and combinatorial techniques. In: 2017 IEEE International Conference on Software Testing, Verification and Validation Workshops, pp. 189–198 (2017)
14. Jones, A.: ISO 12207 Software life cycle processes? Fit for purpose? Softw. Qual. J. **5**, 243–253 (1996)
15. García-García, J.A., Escalona, M.J., Domínguez-Mayo, F.J., Salido, A.: NDT-Suite: a methodological tool solution in the model-driven engineering paradigm. J. Softw. Eng. Appl. **7**, 206–217 (2014)
16. Selenium: Selenium website documentation. RA-MA Ed. Accessed Feb 2018

Web Page Representations and Data Extraction with BERyL

Andrey Kravchenko[✉], Ruslan R. Fayzrakhmanov, and Emanuel Sallinger

Department of Computer Science, University of Oxford,
Wolfson Building, Parks Road, Oxford OX1 3QD, UK
{andrey.kravchenko,ruslan.fayzrakhmanov,
emanuel.sallinger}@cs.ox.ac.uk

Abstract. The web contains a huge amount of data, which can be primarily accessed with the use of web data extraction technology. With increasing complexity of the web development stack and the source code, a web page visual representation rendered by the browser is often the only source reflecting the semantics, functional role, and logical structure of elements. Thus, modern automatic approaches typically target visual cues and structures (e.g., DOM and CSSOM) constructed by the web browser. In this paper, we briefly analyse different representations of web pages, generic approaches, and introduce BER$_y$L, a novel framework and language, which can consolidate two "worlds", two main approaches: the rule-based approach and machine learning. The rule-based approach is used for feature engineering and pattern recognition, whilst machine learning is used for classification based on the inferred features. This is achieved through three stages including (1) feature computation, pattern construction, and application, (2) machine learning, and (3) refinement.

Keywords: Web data extraction · Reasoning · Machine learning

1 Introduction

Huge volumes of data on the web serialised in heterogeneous formats can be acquired with the use of web data extraction technology. This technology can navigate and analyse web pages, transforming unstructured relevant data into structured data, which can be stored in a database. Web data extraction programs can take as input different forms of web page representation from the HTML source code to the structures rendered within the browser (i.e. DOM and CSSOM [1]). With a rising complexity of web technology and the source code, the rendered state of a page and its visual cues become the main source on which data extraction is applied. This is related to many aspects such as invocation of JavaScript, transforming data on a page, AJAX, asynchronously enriching the page with additional content, and the increasing complexity of the source code.

This work is supported by the EPSRC programme grant EP/M025268/1.

C. Pautasso et al. (Eds.): ICWE 2018, LNCS 11153, pp. 22–30, 2018.
https://doi.org/10.1007/978-3-030-03056-8_3

For example, sometimes retailers and meta-search engines use session-specific, automatically generated, and obfuscated HTML ids and classes, which often makes approaches based on XPath inapplicable. Moreover, web pages are made for human consumption, and visual representation is the target form, which consistently reflects domain-specific information and entities. Different types of elements on a page and their attributes are distinguished by their various visual features encoded in the layout, colours, font styles, and so on. The consistency and intelligibility are typically ensured by using a specific palette of visual design patterns, which repeat on each page from the same domain. Some web objects can have conventional representations[1], be it a web forum post, a navigation menu, or a flight search form. The use of visual cues thus often leads to more precise and more robust wrappers.

Analysis of a web page's visual features can be implemented through the automatic rule-based reasoning [4,12]. For example, there is a rule in the DIA-DEM [8,9] knowledge base, which, in simplified form, says the following: *The closest text chunk below or above an input field on a web page is (with high probability and in absence of better information) the explanatory label of this field.* Approaches, alternative to those using automatic reasoning, utilise machine learning (ML) to learn all necessary ranges of parameters reflecting intrinsic and relative features of elements [11,13,21]. In certain cases, it is impossible to define the best set of features and patterns with the use of qualitative information to identify desired objects on a web page. Thus, we believe that reasoning and ML should be used together to achieve better results. This was confirmed in [14,15].

In this paper we analyse different forms of web page representations on which web data extraction can be applied, methods of data extraction, and introduce BER_yL with its holistic approach leveraging benefits of automatic reasoning and ML for more effective identification of *web blocks* (i.e. logically consistent elements). The novelty of our approach is that we try to tailor feature sets for different web blocks by application of declarative programming to feature extraction. We propose a modular approach combined with the use of Datalog-based BER_yL language to construct complex reusable features and patterns. We integrate ML for learning unknown parameters and use constraints encoded in the BER_yL language for getting rid of incorrect classifications.

BER_yL achieves high precision and recall, with the overall F_1 score above 90% for identifying headers, footers, sidebars, and next links [15].

2   Web Page Representations and Data Extraction

This section gives an overview of different web page representations. In Fig. 1 we outline different well-known tools and techniques. We distinguish three main web page representations: source code, tree, and visual.

The **source code** of a page written in X/HTML or XML is a marked text, which can reflect structural characteristics of the content. Most of the relevant

---

[1] Examples of design patterns can be found at http://www.welie.com.

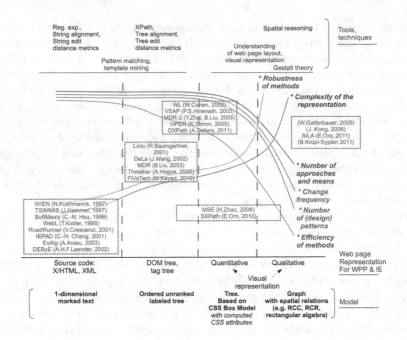

Fig. 1. Tools and techniques applied for different web page representations

data extraction techniques are based on regular expressions and string alignment with string edit distance metrics utilised [3,6]. A **tree structure** is typically presented by a DOM tree or a tag tree (usually modelled as an ordered unranked labelled tree) based on the source code. DOM tree is an internal representation of a web page within the browser. For interactive web applications (with JavaScript and AJAX), which can dynamically change the DOM tree, the analysis of the tree structure produced by the browser is more relevant. Most of the well-known approaches that operate on this representation are distinguished by using XML techniques (e.g. XPath), tree alignment, and tree edit distance [4,10,18]. A **quantitative visual representation** is usually utilised together with a tree representation. Therefore, it is usually represented as a tree enriched with data acquired from the CSSOM [1] computed by the browser engine [17,21]. A **qualitative visual representation** is typically modelled as a graph, which reflects a set of elements of different types with different relations defined on this set. The relations specified for the rendered web page are mainly spatial relationships between page elements, such as topology (e.g. based on RCC), distance and direction (e.g. based on RCR) expressed qualitatively [2]. The analysis of the rendered page mainly boils down to the analysis of its spatial characteristics and has a direct relation to spatial reasoning [12,16,20,22].

As it is symbolically depicted in Fig. 1, complexity of the web page representation increases from the source code to the qualitative visual representation, however robustness of methods greatly rises for the qualitative visual representation. We confirm this tendency by the fact that visual representation is the natural form of information representation for the human being. Therefore, methods operating on this view often reflect and simulate processes, which the human being uses, e.g. analysis of relative spatial allocation of elements including their size, colour, and typographical characteristics for the rendered page. This representation is not as semantically diverse as others. It is also important to mention the Gestalt theory [16, 22], which studies the peculiarities of human perception. From the source code to the visual representation, the graph of robustness is also related to the change frequency and number of corresponding design patterns. The source code and DOM tree are prone to greatly more frequent changes compared to the visual representation. Furthermore, the number of various visual design patterns and corresponding ways of spatially arranging information objects is greatly less than the set of various ways of coding them.

A representation can be chosen based on the task and the type of information to be extracted or analysed. For example, the source code and DOM tree (or tag tree) are best for the web data extraction from pages, which change relatively seldom, have relatively simple structures (e.g. the source code reflects the structure of web objects), or have regularities in their structures, which can be mined, and reflect features of the object to be extracted (e.g. pages from the Deep Web generated with a specific template from the back-end database). Approaches based on source code and tree structures, without executing JavaScript, are typically highly efficient in contrast to those requiring full-fledge rendering. The source code and DOM tree are well-studied, have corresponding standards, and plenty of various approaches and tools. Rendered pages are considered if the source code has a high complexity, and the analysis of spatial configuration or visual characteristics is required, e.g. for table recognition, product list extraction, or web page segmentation. With the growing complexity of pages' source code and the web development stack, web data extraction community has recently focused mainly on the visual representation with the application of approaches from AI, ML, and NLP.

From the viewpoint of web object identification for unseen web pages and different domains, the qualitative visual representation is the most adequate and semantically rich representation. However, in case of continuous, repetitive web data extraction more basic representations (e.g. the source code or tree) for the sake of a low runtime and resource consumption should be considered. To bridge this gap, visual-clue based wrappers can be automatically transformed into fast wrappers. Successful examples of such combined approaches are demonstrated by the DIADEM system [9], generating OXPath expressions as fast wrappers, and FastWrap [8], extracting data on the level of HTTP interactions and preserving the data extraction quality of the original wrapper. In a similar way, BER_yL data extraction workflow can be used in automatic construction of fast wrappers.

In spite of the fact that there are various approaches to extracting data from rendered pages, we strongly believe that some aspects have been overlooked. These include a uniform approach to feature engineering for automatic generation of relevant features and synergy of AI and ML. The former enables an automatic contraction of complex features and patterns to be identified on a web page, whilst the latter allows to unite automatic reasoning over computed features and identified patterns with ML for building more robust classifiers.

3 Web Data Extraction with BERyL

BER$_y$L (**B**lock classification with **E**xtraction **R**ules and machine **L**earning) is a Datalog-like language and a system for web data extraction [14,15].

3.1 BERyL Workflow

The overall BER$_y$L workflow consists of three main phases: (**1**) *feature computation*, (**2**) *machine learning based web block classification*, and (**3**) *refinement* with a holistic approach.

BER$_y$L has a Firefox browser integrated and can access all internal structures of a rendered web page, such as DOM tree and CSSOM [1] with computed CSS attributes. Thus, in **Phase 1**, the system has the tree and quantitative visual representations of a page. With the use of the BER$_y$L language, an expert can convey a concise declarative program to pick only relevant features from the rendered web page and with automatic reasoning construct more complex features and patterns, including the qualitative visual. With access to different web page representations, various approaches mentioned in Sect. 2 can be applied. The output of this program is a set of predicates, which enrich page elements with features relevant to web block classification (e.g. "vertically aligned elements") or semantic roles (e.g. "navigation menu" or "main content"). If there is no obvious pattern for a block to be extracted, and its semantic role therefore cannot be easily identified with the use of logical rules, the BER$_y$L system switches to the next phase.

Phase 2 classifies web blocks with the use of a ML classifier trained on web pages enriched with information obtained from Phase 1. This phase is needed in case it is impossible to find a universal pattern for an object to be identified and extracted, or if there are continuous parameters with a priory unknown ranges (e.g. the width range for navigation menu elements). Otherwise, labels obtained from Phase 1 can already represent desired blocks. Furthermore, it is often the case that there are many potential features, which can be used to characterise a specific object. However, only a few might play a major role in uniquely distinguishing this block type from all others. Hence, for BER$_y$L, a machine learning (ML) approach can tackle these challenges: given a training set with features computed in Phase 1, a selected classifier can learn both ranges and relevant features.

Phase 3 resolves issues of classifications, which can be caused by either a limited set of provided features or a small training set. This is achieved through a *holistic approach* to web block classification in which individual web block classifications are considered in the context of the entire page, and a set of constraints is imposed between these classifications with a greedy algorithm for conflict resolution [14]. Such constraints are defined with a set of rules written in

<figure>
visual proximity   left of visually   (left, top)

vertically aligned ↕ For sale To rent House prices New homes Commercial Overseas Invest Move Agents Discover

(right, bottom)
</figure>

Fig. 2. An example of a navigation menu (www.zoopla.co.uk)

BER$_y$L. Consider for example the constraint that states: a header cannot overlap with a footer and vice versa.

3.2   The BERyL Language

As a language, BER$_y$L extends Datalog with safe and stratified negation, aggregation, arithmetic, and comparison operators, denoted as Datalog$^{\neg,Agg,ALU}$ [15]. The usual restrictions apply, i.e. all variables in a negation, arithmetic operation, aggregation, or comparison must also appear in some other (positive) context. Further, there may be no dependency cycles over such operators. The BER$_y$L language also uses a number of syntactic extensions to ease the development of complex rule programs. The most important ones are *namespaces*, *parameters*, and the explicit distinction of *output predicates* – final semantic labels assigned to web page elements. All other intensional and extensional (facts) predicates are thus temporary predicates, and only used to compute target output predicates. To execute a BER$_y$L program, the system converts it into a Datalog program, which can be run in one of the existing reasoners, such as DLV or Vadalog [5].

BER$_y$L is a declarative approach to feature engineering and extraction. It (i) allows us to simplify the definition of new features through the employment of existing features or relation definitions and to learn new features by automatically finding the right combination of parameters for relation instantiations. (ii) Datalog is fast and widely used [19]. (iii) It is also much easier to learn Datalog predicates automatically than to learn procedural language programs [19], which is likely to come in useful in the large-scale block classification when we have to infer new features automatically. In other cases that require the use of efficient libraries and data structures or intense numerical computation (e.g. features acquired from image processing), we employ a procedural approach for feature extraction implemented through Java. In contrast to our previous approach, WPPS [7], which has an object-oriented API with an underlying reasoning engine, with BER$_y$L language it is possible to write concise and at the same time expressive programs. However, BER$_y$L currently lacks rigorous formalisms, such as RCC and two-dimensional interval relations, which are integrated into WPPS.

For the sake of demonstration, we introduce a basic synthetic example for horizontally-oriented navigation menus (see Fig. 2). An example BER$_y$L program is listed below.

```
 feature::horSeq(R,X,Y) ⇐ relation::descendant(R,X,D),
2   relation::descendant(R,Y,D), param::maxDepth(D),
    relation::sameDomLevel(X,Y),
4   relation::visNeighbourLeftOf(X,Y), param::vertAligned(X,Y).
  relation::visNeighbourLeftOf(X,Y) ⇐ RightX ≤ LeftY,
6   css::box(X,_,_,RightX,_), css::box(Y,LeftY,_,_,_).
    param::proximity(X,Y).
8 relation::visProximity(X,Y) ⇐ X ≠ Y,
    css::box(X,LeftX,TopX,RightX,BottomX),
10  css::box(Y,LeftY,TopY,RightY,BottomY),
    RightX + DHor ≥ LeftY, RightY + DHor ≥ LeftX,
12  BottomX + DVert ≥ TopY, BottomY + DVert ≥ TopX,
    param::dH(DHor), param::dV(DVert).
```

In this program, we define a navigation menu with the predicate horSeq as a set of pairs of elements, which are descendant of the same DOM element R with a maximum depth D (lines 1–2) and are from the same DOM level (line 3). Furthermore, these elements are horizontally oriented, such that each of the neighbouring elements are close to each other (visNeighbourLeftOf), and they are vertically aligned (vertAligned, line 4). The feature, horSeq, is an *output predicate* and is inferred based on data extracted from the DOM tree (e.g. descendant) and computed CSS attributes (e.g. box in other related BER_yL rules) of the rendered web page. All output predicates are denoted by the BER_yL-specific feature namespace, whilst all auxiliary predicates used to compute this feature are denoted by the relation namespace.

Atomic parameters, which get instantiated with concrete values, such as the parameters DHor, DVert, and D, as well as template predicates, which get instantiated with concrete predicates during the runtime, such as proximity, are denoted with the param namespace. In this example, proximity is instantiated with the visProximity relation (predicate for vertAligned is omitted due to the space constraints). This dependency is reflected in the BER_yL framework with additional constructs. Such instantiation of parameters between dependent components reflects the principle of BER_yL's *modular approach*.

The *(component-based) modular approach to feature engineering* is a key aspect of BER_yL. It allows an expert to construct complex features and patterns based on other features and patterns. Thus, components are fragments of BER_yL code that can be combined to allow for modular definition of complex features that we want to extract. Components can have different types (e.g. we distinguish between rule-based components that are mapped to Datalog programs and procedural components that are mapped to fragments of Java code). Components can also have parameters attached to them, which can either be (i) atomic parameters, e.g. font size, (ii) sequential parameters, e.g. a list of DOM tags we want to consider for analysis, or (iii) higher-level parameters that can link to other components within the definition of a given component.

If atomic parameters (e.g. DHor or DVert) cannot be specified by an expert, they can be learned in Phase 2 with the use of ML. Regarding our example, we should ensure that the navigation menu is in the upper part of a web page, on top of the main content. It can be corrected in Phase 3 with additional constraints assigned to elements classified as navigation menu, e.g. that a navigation menu cannot overlap with the main content area of the page. This can be expressed as follows (X and Y are DOM nodes):

```
constraintViolation::navMenuMainContentOverlap(X,Y) ⇐
2   cls::navMenu(X),cls::mainContent(Y),relation::overlap(X,Y).
```

4   Conclusion

BER$_y$L is a unique Datalog-based language and a system for feature engineering and web data extraction, which utilises capabilities of both automatic reasoning and machine learning. With its holistic approach, it evaluates the classified data with the whole web page structure in mind to eliminate erroneously selected web blocks. It has access to all the models rendered by the web browser and can construct more complex reusable features and relations in a declarative fashion.

In this paper we have discussed different web page representations, their applications, and how BER$_y$L can leverage these representations for the task of web block classification. A synthetic example of extracting a navigation menu has been presented. During the evaluation of BER$_y$L we have identified main points that can direct future work.

In particular, an integration of a common framework for describing topology and various spatial relations, e.g. with the use of RCC and and RCR, can be a useful instrument to simplify the process of describing complex spatial patterns and features and ensure its consistency. Due to the fact that BER$_y$L is a universal framework for extracting data of arbitrary complexity, there should be a possibility of selecting the most relevant machine learning algorithm. To further ease the process of feature engineering and allow domain experts with no prior knowledge of declarative programming to work with the system, BER$_y$L can be extended with a GUI. Since BER$_y$L is a general feature engineering framework, it can therefore be extended for other areas that need complex and easily extendible feature sets.

References

1. CSS Object Model (CSSOM). W3C Working Draft, 17 March 2016
2. Aiello, M., Pratt-Hartmann, I., van Benthem, J.: Handbook of Spatial Logics. Springer, Dordrecht (2007). https://doi.org/10.1007/978-1-4020-5587-4
3. Arasu, A., Garcia-Molina, H.: Extracting structured data from web pages. In: Proceedings of ACM SIGMOD 2003, pp. 337–348 (2003)
4. Baumgartner, R., Frölich, O., Gottlob, G.: The lixto systems applications in business intelligence and semantic web. In: Franconi, E., Kifer, M., May, W. (eds.) ESWC 2007. LNCS, vol. 4519, pp. 16–26. Springer, Heidelberg (2007). https://doi.org/10.1007/978-3-540-72667-8_3

5. Bellomarini, L., Gottlob, G., Pieris, A., Sallinger, E.: Swift logic for big data and knowledge graphs - overview of requirements, language, and system. In: Tjoa, A.M., Bellatreche, L., Biffl, S., van Leeuwen, J., Wiedermann, J. (eds.) SOFSEM 2018. LNCS, vol. 10706, pp. 3–16. Springer, Cham (2018). https://doi.org/10.1007/978-3-319-73117-9_1
6. Chang, C., Lui, S.: IEPAD: information extraction based on pattern discovery. In: Proceedings of WWW 2001, pp. 681–688 (2001)
7. Fayzrakhmanov, R.R.: WPPS: a framework for web page processing. In: Wang, X.S., Cruz, I., Delis, A., Huang, G. (eds.) WISE 2012. LNCS, vol. 7651, pp. 800–803. Springer, Heidelberg (2012). https://doi.org/10.1007/978-3-642-35063-4_70
8. Fayzrakhmanov, R.R., Sallinger, E., Spencer, B., Furche, T., Gottlob, G.: Browser-less web data extraction: challenges and opportunities. In: Proceedings of WWW (WebConf. 2018), pp. 1095–1104 (2018)
9. Furche, T., et al.: DIADEM: thousands of websites to a single database. PVLDB 7(14), 1845–1856 (2014)
10. Kayed, M., Chang, C.: FiVaTech: page-level web data extraction from template pages. IEEE Trans. Knowl. Data Eng. 22(2), 249–263 (2010)
11. Kohlschütter, C., Fankhauser, P., Nejdl, W.: Boilerplate detection using shallow text features. In: Proceedings of WSDM 2010, pp. 441–450 (2010)
12. Kong, J., Zhang, K., Zeng, X.: Spatial graph grammars for graphical user interfaces. ACM Trans. Comput. Hum. Interact. 13(2), 268–307 (2006)
13. Kordomatis, I., Herzog, C., Fayzrakhmanov, R.R., Krüpl-Sypien, B., Holzinger, W., Baumgartner, R.: Web object identification for web automation and meta-search. In: Proceedings of WIMS 2013, p. 13. ACM (2013)
14. Kravchenko, A.: BERyL: unified approach to web block classification. Ph.D. thesis, University of Oxford (2015)
15. Kravchenko, A.: BERyL: a system for web block classification. Trans. Comput. Sci. 33, 61–78 (2018)
16. Krüpl, B., Herzog, M., Gatterbauer, W.: Using visual cues for extraction of tabular data from arbitrary HTML documents. In: Proceedings of WWW 2005, pp. 1000–1001 (2005)
17. Luo, P., Fan, J., Liu, S., Lin, F., Xiong, Y., Liu, J.: Web article extraction for web printing: a dom+visual based approach. In: Proceedings of DocEng 2009, pp. 66–69 (2009)
18. Miao, G., Tatemura, J., Hsiung, W., Sawires, A., Moser, L.E.: Extracting data records from the web using tag path clustering. In: Proceedings of WWW 2009, pp. 981–990 (2009)
19. de Moor, O., Gottlob, G., Furche, T., Sellers, A. (eds.): Datalog 2010. LNCS, vol. 6702. Springer, Heidelberg (2011). https://doi.org/10.1007/978-3-642-24206-9
20. Oro, E., Ruffolo, M., Staab, S.: SXPath - extending xpath towards spatial querying on web documents. PVLDB 4(2), 129–140 (2010)
21. Spengler, A., Gallinari, P.: Document structure meets page layout: loopy random fields for web news content extraction. In: Proceedings of DocEng 2010, pp. 151–160 (2010)
22. Xiang, P., Yang, X., Shi, Y.: Web page segmentation based on gestalt theory. In: Proceedings of ICME 2007, pp. 2253–2256 (2007)

2nd International Workshop
on Engineering the Web of Things
(EnWoT 2018)

2nd International Workshop on Engineering the Web of Things (EnWoT)

Cáceres, Spain, 5 June 2018, in conjunction with the
18th International Conference on Web Engineering

Preface

The original goal of the World Wide Web was to serve as a platform for presenting digital content. Now, a few decades later, the Web is evolving to a platform where the worlds of the physical and the virtual meet. A growing number of Web-based services extend human abilities for social interaction and collaboration. The standard connectivity technologies foster this evolution for the rest of the things. From a software development perspective, the world of computing is shifting from the era of single device computing to a new era where literally every thing is Internet-connected and programmable. It is only logical to conclude that the Web will continue to evolve opening all new opportunities, challenges, and research questions for the Web engineering community.

Web of Things is the general term used for describing all the approaches of connecting physical things to the World Wide Web. At the moment, Web-based systems development is evolving from traditional centralized client-server based architectures towards more decentralized multi-device architectures in which people use several Web-enabled client devices, and data is stored simultaneously in numerous devices and cloud-based services. This paradigm shift will dramatically raise the new challenges for the device interoperability, implying significant changes for software architecture as well. On the other hand, this shift also opens new opportunities where the Web-based technologies enable the software to roam liquidly from one device to another without any hassle; The goal of many WoT applications is therefore that the software can follow the user to enable seamless interaction with the IoT devices where ever they go.

The 2nd International Workshop on Engineering the Web of Things was arranged to present the latest research and to discuss software engineering and development in this new exciting era of computing. The workshop was held on June 5th, 2018 in conjunction with the 18th International Conference on Web Engineering (ICWE 2018) in Cáceres, Spain. The workshop focused on various themes all the way from engineering the Internet of Things (IoT) with Web-based technologies to the user experience from the standpoint of multi-device software engineering and end-user development.

After the peer-review process, 5 papers were selected to be presented at the workshop. The papers covered various aspects of engineering the Web of Things and developing multi-device software:

The 1st paper was "Towards Distribution Options in the End-User Development of Multi-device Mashups" by Oliver Mroß and Klaus Meißner from Technische Universität Dresden. The paper presented the authors' ongoing work for providing assistance in the end-user development of multi-device mashups (MDM) by recommending distribution options for available devices, their capabilities, and other resources to augment the user-driven mashup development.

The 2nd paper was "Towards Dynamically Programmable Devices Using Beacons" by Alejandro Pérez-Vereda, Daniel Flores-Martín, Carlos Canal, and Juan M. Murillo from the University of Malaga and the University of Extremadura. The paper describes the use of beacons to dynamically download and execute scripts on smartphones for updating the virtual profiles with context information, and instructions to trigger actions for the devices.

The 3rd paper was "Architecting Self-Adaptive Software Systems" by Anni Huuhtanen, Niko Mäakitalo, and Tommi Mikkonen from the University of Helsinki. The paper studies four different self-adaptive software approaches and evaluates their usage in different contexts. As a result, the paper concludes that a general solution should combine aspects from all the studied approaches.

The 4th paper was "A Modular Pill Dispenser Supporting Therapies at Home" by Paolo Buono, Fabio Cassano, Alessandra Legretto, and Antonio Piccinno from the University of Bari "Aldo Moro." The paper describes a device for the management of pills according to the user's therapy, with the Internet of things (IoT) devices and by allowing users to manage the pill dispenser by themselves. The paper also presented the results of user studies conducted with the prototype.

The 5th paper was "Towards a Runtime Verification Approach for the Internet of Things Systems" by Maurizio Leotta, Davide Ancona, Luca Franceschini, Dario Olianas, Marina Ribaudo, and Filippo Ricca from the Università di Genova. The paper described an approach for runtime verification to IoT systems with a formal specification describing the expected behavior of the system and the definition of appropriate input scenarios.

We are grateful to the Program Committee members for their work on the paper review and selection process. We would also like to thank all the authors and workshop participants for the interesting discussions.

Marina Mongiello
Niko Mäkitalo
Francesco Nocera
Diego Pérez Palacin
Tommaso Di Noia
Eugenio Di Sciascio
Vito Bellini
Luca Riccardi

Organization

Program Committee

Jesper Andersoon	HassoLinnaeus University, Sweden
Marco Autili	University of L'Aquila, Italy
Simona Bernardi	Universidad de Zaragoza, Spain
Stefano Bistarelli	University of Perugia, Italy
Antonio Bucchiarone	Fondazione Bruno Kessler, Italy
Radu Calinescu	University of York, UK
Rafael Capilla	Universidad Rey Juan Carlos, Spain
Giuseppe Desolda	University of Bari, Italy
Ivano Malavolta	Vrije Universiteit Amsterdam, The Netherlands
José Merseguer	Universidad de Zaragoza, Spain
Raffaela Mirandola	Politecnico di Milano, Italy
Henry Muccini	University of L'Aquila, Italy
Elisa Nakagawa	University of São Paulo, Brazil
Liliana Pasquale	Lero - The Irish Software Engineering Research Centre, Ireland
Luigi Patrono	University of Salento, Italy
Patrizia Scandurra	University of Bergamo, Italy
Romina Spalazzese	Malmö University, Sweden
Ronny Siebes	Vrije Universiteit Amsterdam, The Netherlands
Maria Spichkova	RMIT University, Australia
Danny Weyns	Katholieke Universiteit Leuven, Belgium
Sungwon Kang	Korea Advanced Institute of Science and Technology, Republic of Korea
Eva Kühn	Vienna University of Technology, Austria
Uwe Zdun	University of Vienna, Austria

Towards Distribution Options in the End-User Development of Multi-device Mashups

Oliver Mroß$^{(\boxtimes)}$ and Klaus Meißner

Faculty of Computer Science, Technische Universität Dresden, Dresden, Germany
{oliver.mross,klaus.meissner}@tu-dresden.de

Abstract. In recent years several approaches addressed the development of applications for multi-device environments. Due to the mobility of devices, the volatile availability of their resources, e.g., limited battery life or communication quality, and changing user requirements, the application developer cannot anticipate every situation, e.g., new or leaving devices, their capabilities and interaction resources, at the application's design time. Hence, end-users should be able to create and customize multi-device applications at run time. Available solutions already provide user-centered development tools, but they are not sufficient and lack intelligent assistance to offer possible design options, in particular in terms of the application's distribution. In this paper, we present our ongoing work to provide assistance in the end-user development of *multi-device mashups* (MDM) by recommending distribution options with respect to available devices, their capabilities and resources to ease the user-driven mashup development. Furthermore, we investigate the use of aggregation rules and composition ranking rules to rate distribution options regarding their quality properties and their context fitness, e.g., when the MDM is used at home or in an automotive environment.

Keywords: Multi-device applications · Multi-device mashups
Mashups · Distribution options · End-user development

1 Introduction

With the increasing availability of web-enabled (mobile) devices and the paradigm shift towards the Web of Things (WoT) [9,12] the Web has become the ubiquitous platform for a new type of applications, in which several devices and their capabilities are combined and used together simultaneously according to the application domain. Following the *mashup* approach in [9], such multi-device applications are build by composing devices and their services on the application layer via Web APIs hiding heterogeneous platforms and service implementations. Device services are connected with each other using Web communication protocols as well as standard media types [2]. We call such applications *multi-device mashups* (MDM) that are associated with new challenges in their development

© Springer Nature Switzerland AG 2018
C. Pautasso et al. (Eds.): ICWE 2018, LNCS 11153, pp. 35–48, 2018.
https://doi.org/10.1007/978-3-030-03056-8_4

process. Considering the *heterogeneity* and *volatile availability* of mobile devices and their capabilities or limited resources, e.g., energy capacity, developers cannot anticipate every situation at the application's run time during its design phase. Furthermore, it is impossible to meet the changing user requirements without having a concrete understanding of the current situation an application is used in. Hence, strictly separating the design and run time leads to limited and inflexible applications. Accordingly, end-users without programming knowledge and limited experiences in adaptation cases should be supported to create/modify MDM at run time.

To the best of our knowledge, available *end-user development* (EUD) tools for multi-device scenarios lack concepts to guide users by providing hints or design options regarding the current usage context, e.g., presenting possible or most likely needed adaptation rules with respect to available device features. Furthermore, users should understand the consequences of each recommended design option on the application quality. This is illustrated in the following scenario. In a smart home environment the user wants to create a MDM to control the house's heating system depending on his/her position in the house. To this end, a *guidance system* presents several design options considering resources and capabilities of the smart home and its devices. Figure 1 presents an overview of the scenario.

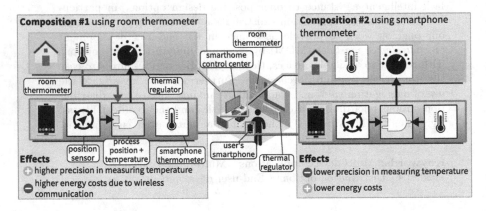

Fig. 1. Overview of several composition options in smart home scenario

The first option (left-side) wires together following software components encapsulating devices or digital processes: the user's smartphone indoor positioning sensor, the digital thermometer and the control interface of the thermal regulator within the smart home and a software component executed by the smartphone processing the user's position and room temperature to control the thermal regulator. Another design option (right-side) encompasses an alternative composition. Instead of using the room thermometer, the smartphone's build-in thermometer is wired together with the indoor positioning sensor and the processing component to control the thermal regulator. Both design options are associated with different *effects* on the application's precision and energy demands. To highlight the effects of each distribution option, mechanisms are needed that provide users with information on probable application states.

The *contribution* of this paper is a new architecture of the proposed end-user guidance system based on novel meta-models to ease the user-driven development by recommending *distribution options* context-sensitively to create/modify MDMs at run time. In addition, distribution options are rated semi-automatically considering their effects on the application quality and context suitability to assist end-users in choosing optimal design decisions, generally making the development process more transparent. Moreover, distribution options provide solutions to the problem of adapting black-box components in the context of dynamically distributing composition fragments between heterogeneous devices and their platforms. In our approach, we address the problem by replacing mashup components with functional alternatives but usable on the target device. The remaining of this paper is structured as follows. In Sect. 2 we discuss related work. Subsequently, in Sect. 3 we introduce fundamentals of our approach and characterize relevant aspects of the user-driven development of MDM. Furthermore, we present novel meta-models for distribution options and quality aggregation rules. Afterwards, we present the overall architecture of the end-user guidance system in Sect. 4 and explain relevant features to assist end-users during their development process based on the distribution options concept. Finally, in Sect. 5 we draw conclusions from our approach and discuss future work.

2   Related Work

In the EUD domain of Internet of Things (IoT) applications, different metaphors and programming styles can be distinguished [15]. On the one hand, *graphical mashup editors* abstract devices, their services, UI elements or application logic as visual components that are wired together by experienced developers or end-users, such as Node-RED[1] or glue.things [11]. Moreover, approaches such as AppInventor[2] or openHAB [7] are using EUD tools based on the *jigsaw puzzle metaphor*. As discussed in [5,6], such approaches are mainly suitable for experienced developers knowing fundamental programming concepts. They do not provide solutions to the problem that end-users lack experiences in modifying applications in continuously changing multi-device environments. Not only using a suitable metaphor is sufficient, but additional assistance is required. On the other hand, *rule-* and *language-oriented toolkits* [4,6,8] target end-users without programming experiences to create multi-device applications. For instance, Coutaz and Crowley present the AppGate approach [4] that supports end-users in the specification of smart home applications by syntax-oriented rule suggestions. This allows end-users to create *event-condition-action* (ECA) rules exploratively, but they have to anticipate application scenarios initially. This is

---

[1] https://nodered.org/.
[2] http://www.appinventor.org/.

difficult for inexperienced end-users. In this context, we assume that predefined applications as well as context information (e.g., usage history, preferences etc.) can be used to recommend design options.

In the domain of *mashup* applications, Daniel and Matera consider in [5] assistance capabilities as dimension for EUD mashup tools. They present quality-aware and pattern-based component recommendation features to reduce the burden in the development of mashups. Our approach is based on similar models to specify component interfaces and compositions, but goes beyond the single-device paradigm assumed in [5]. Although the model-based recommendation may be adopted to MDM, it lacks meta-model concepts on the component and composition layer to specify distributed composition fragments, for example, component descriptors are missing context requirements to derive potential target devices. However, we consider the quality aware recommendation as solution to the problem that end-users are not able to anticipate the effects of recommended adaption options. In our approach, quality-aware recommendations should estimate quality properties of the multi-device mashup and provide an insight to the likely future application state.

In the previous approaches, the application's distribution state and its adaptation is not taken into account explicitly, but this is of particular interest in the case of dynamic multi-device environments. In the research domain of distributed mashups, end-users are able to control the UI distribution at run time. For instance, the MultiMasher approach of Husmann et al. [10] supports the EUD of distributed mashups and allows to distribute and synchronize arbitrary web UI elements across several devices. However, due to the focus on the discovery and distribution of visual web UI elements, the integration of "headless" services such as web or device services without an UI is limited. Moreover, MultiMasher and other EUD approaches [8,14] in the distributed UI (DUI) research domain lacks assistance capabilities that consider context properties, e.g., target device resources. Thus, they are not able to draw the user's attention to the consequences of distribution state changes on the application quality. Thus, user-driven UI redistribution activities may result in error-prone application states, e.g., when mashup components are migrated to low-resource devices. In our approach, we address this problem of insufficient user experiences in dealing with UI redistribution activities by calculating quality properties at the (distributed) composition layer. Mashup quality properties can be used to rank design options or filter out critical ones.

In summary, there are already approaches to support the EUD of multi-device applications, but they lack concepts to guide end-users during the development considering the following problems: (a) the end-users' limited abilities to foresee potential situations in the multi-device environment, e.g., volatile device resources, and (b) the end-users' insufficient experiences in creating or adapting MDMs at run time as well as (c) the users' missing capabilities to anticipate adaptation effects on the application quality.

3 EUD of Multi-device Mashups

In this section, first we outline fundamentals of our approach and aspects of the user-driven development of MDM. On this basis, we explain concepts regarding distribution options of multi-device mashups. Moreover, since users should be able to evaluate them and to understand their effects on the application's quality, we present a new meta-model for specifying rules to aggregate quality properties of MDM context-sensitively. Finally, we discuss the process of providing distribution options as possibilities to design or adapt MDM by end-users at run time.

3.1 Fundamentals

In our approach, a *multi-device mashup* consists of several *black-box components* that are loosely coupled together and are distributed across several devices at run time. The mashup's composition, its data flow relations and its distribution state are specified in the *conceptual, communication* and *distribution model* respectively as entities of the same *mashup composition model*. Further details regarding the composition meta-model are described in [13].

Each mashup component may encapsulate web services, application logic, UI elements or device features and adheres to the Semantic Mashup Component Description Language (SMCDL) [16] providing the following concepts to specify the component interface: *properties, events, operations* and *capability* descriptions. In addition, domain ontology concepts are referenced in order to specify data and functional semantics as well as context requirements, e.g., relevant sensors or software APIs. Context requirements are used to determine a component's executability regarding device profiles.

3.2 EUD as Decision-Making Process

We consider the distributed runtime environment of MDMs as a *proactive assistant* guiding end-users by providing useful design options with respect to the usage context (devices, user profile or environment). Users act as *decision-makers* with regard to the application's structure, functionalities and their distribution based on design options provided by the system. Thus, *observability, traceability* and *comprehensibility*, as introduced by Coutaz [3], are relevant aspects of the end-user development of MDM.

Observability: This aspect implies to have an overview of included components, their features, data flow relations and their distribution. Based on this information, users are able coordinate their design decisions.

Traceability: This aspect addresses the need to understand why an adaptation is relevant in the current situation. For instance, the critical battery level of a smartphone is the cause of the application's redistribution. This requires to *present the adaptation's cause*. Due to the different relevance of distinct adaptation causes, not every design option has the same importance from an application's perspective. In the previous example, the mashup's redistribution caused by a critical battery level is more relevant in comparison to the addition of optional mashup components when new devices become available at the same time. This requires *prioritizing distribution options.*

Comprehensibility: Since, there could be multiple adaptations per situation, users should be able to comprehend the effects on the application's quality for each design option. In this context, the challenge is the multi-dimensional nature of the mashup quality concept and its context dependencies. For instance, the lifespan and responsiveness of an MDM depends on available energy resources and the current workload of each device. This results as requirement for *distributed quality aggregation* features that consider the static and dynamic nature of mashup quality properties.

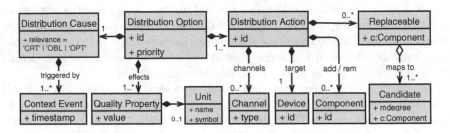

Fig. 2. Overview of the adaptation option model

3.3 Distribution Options Meta-Model

Considering the previous requirements, we specified the meta-model of *distribution options*, as presented in Fig. 2. Primarily, it supports the dynamic integration and distribution of composition fragments (single/multiple components and data flow channels) in the context of MDM. It does not address UI layout or styling adaptations or modifications on the component interface layer (e.g., reconfigure state or non-functional properties). Several *distribution options* are the result of a context-sensitive composition redistribution algorithm. Algorithm details are beyond the scope of this paper. The redistribution is triggered by generic or domain-specific *event-condition-action* (ECA) rules. They are integrated as (a) preinstalled generic rules of the MDM runtime environment or are (b) specified by users *implicitly* using domain-specific *mashup templates* or (c) *explicitly* using authoring tools, such as described by Ghiani et al. [8]. Each distribution option is caused by a *context event*, for instance, the change of device resources or environmental conditions. It is described as *distribution cause* associated with a *relevance* attribute. From the application's perspective, a context change has a specific relevance. On one hand, it can be *critical* in the case of existential device resources, such as limited energy or network bandwidth. On the other hand, there can be *obligatory* or *optional* distribution causes. A distribution option is obligatory in terms of the mashup's life cycle when it loads an application and its substantial functionalities. It is optional in such cases when further composition fragments may be integrated, e.g., when new devices become available and UI components could be replicated for flexibility purposes or to support multi-user scenarios. Moreover, a distribution option may be associated with multiple *quality properties*. They are the predicted effects on the application's quality. An example is the estimated energy-consumption as described in Sect. 1. Considering quality properties of distribution options, users are able to evaluate each option subjectively. However, they are also ranked objectively regarding their "context fitness". We discuss this in more detail in Sect. 4. Finally, a distribution option comes with the integration, removal or replacement of composition fragments. Thus, it has several *distribution actions*. Each action addresses a *target device* and is associated with components to be added, removed or replaced. The latter aspect is especially important for UI migration scenarios using heterogeneous devices. In the example of a smartphone's low battery, a distribution option is provided to migrate UI components between a smartphone and a tablet or desktop PC. Since, not every mashup component can be executed on any device, due to missing I/O-capabilities, platform APIs etc., we assume there are functional alternatives, which are usable in the context of the target device instead. Hence, each distribution action may encompass additional component replacement activities as "sub-adaptations in the adaptation". Component replacements are modeled using the *replaceable* item. Each item maps a source component to alternative *candidates*, whereby each candidate is executable on the action's target device. Here, we consider several component alternatives to support higher flexibility in future use cases. For instance, when presenting an option to migrate UI components, power users can choose from several alternatives regarding their quality, e.g., cheap vs. high-efficient components. In case of novice users, the best matching candidate (derived by its matching degree with respect to the source component) is selected automatically.

3.4   Aggregation Rules

The *comprehensibility* aspect implies to support end-users in rating their design decisions and therefore to increase the transparency of the user-driven development process. This leads to the requirement for a *distributed mashup quality aggregation mechanism* that should address the following challenges: (i) Each application quality property has its specific aggregation function. For instance, the estimated application lifespan is the minimum of device-specific lifespans. (ii) An application quality property depends on static or dynamic quality features of components distributed on heterogeneous and dynamically available devices. (iii) Dynamic quality properties may depend on specific context information. For instance, the application's usability depends on user language skills, which are specified as part of the user profile. It may be provided either by a device and its platform, by a web service or not at all. (iv) During the recommendation of distribution options, each estimated quality property value is a forecast regarding the mashup's future state. Therefore, the resulting quality value is error-prone and its estimation should to be precise as possible, even under condition of noisy data as in the case of the application's energy-consumption. With regard to these challenges, in our approach application quality properties are derived using generic or domain-specific *quality aggregation rules*. Generic rules are an integral part of the MDM runtime environment. Domain-specific ones can be added by the user dynamically using authoring tools that are beyond the scope of this paper. In Fig. 3a the *meta-model of aggregation rules* is presented, which we explain afterwards.

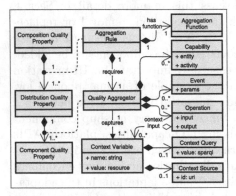

(a) Aggregation rule meta-model

```
{ id: "usability", aggfunc: { technology:"java",
    code:"de.mmt.documa.aggregation.Usability"
  },
  aggregator: { ...,
    variables: [{
      name:"skills",
      source: "http://example.com/uprof/s?query=",
      query: { type: "sparql", value: ''' ...
        PREFIX u: <http://example.com/uprof#>
        SELECT ?lang WHERE {
          ?user a u:User; u:speaks ?lang.
          ?lang a u:Language.
        }'''
      }
    },...],
    interface: [{
      type: "operation",
      input: [{type:"vref",name:"skills"},...],
      output: {type:"qp:usability"}
    },...]
  }
}
```

(b) Sample usability aggregation rule

Fig. 3. Overview of the aggregation rule model

The meta-model is based on the assumption that every *composition quality property* is calculated using a corresponding *aggregation rule*, which is related to a single *aggregation function*. The latter is specified as source code reference and results in the quality value at the application layer. Moreover, an application quality property depends on the same quality feature of each distributed sub-composition executed by its associated device. In the meta-model, each device-specific quality property at the local composition level is represented by the *distribution quality property* concept. In relation to a device the latter concept results from the aggregation of local *component quality properties*. Analogous to the *aggregation function* at the application level, the *quality aggregator* calculates the *distribution quality property* by considering the same component quality features as well as the usage context that may influence the quality as discussed previously in the estimated run time example. Due to the dynamic availability of heterogeneous devices and the property-specific nature of aggregation rules, *quality aggregators* should be integrated in the application context dynamically as individual software components responsible for the acquisition of quality-related context information. Hence, their interface elements (*events, properties, operations* or *capabilities*) are described as part of the aggregation rules. After they were integrated on each client at the application's run time, quality aggregators do not directly interact with application components, and they are not visible from the end-user's perspective. Considering the context-dependency aspect of quality properties, quality aggregators may access platform-specific APIs or external *context sources* (e.g., social networks) to retrieve relevant information, e.g., the consumption of energy resources or the user profile. In the case of using external context information by querying remote web services, the rule author can specify the aggregator's operation signature and hereby specify *context variables* as input parameters. This is illustrated in the example in Fig. 3b. Context variables can be resolved either by the client-side runtime or by any *context source* on the web using its associated *context query*.

After presenting basic concepts to support the user-driven development of MDM, in the next section we will focus on actors as well as key features in the overall *distribution options recommendation* system.

4   Recommendation of Distribution Options

In this section, we present the overall architecture of the *MDM assistance system* (MAS) guiding end-users during their development process based on the *distribution options* concept.

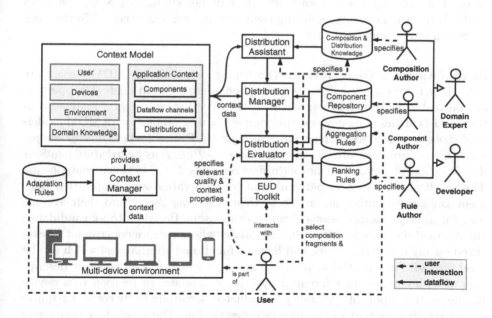

Fig. 4. Overview of the distribution options recommendation architecture

As presented in Fig. 4, we distinguish following actors: *Composition authors* model entire MDM or *distribution patterns* based on the concept of *co-occurence patterns as introduced by Chowdhury et al.* [1]. Distribution patterns are frequently used composition fragments annotated with distribution knowledge, e.g., the data flow between a remote control component used on mobile devices and a video player executed on a presentation device (e.g., smart TV etc.). **Component authors** design and implement application logic, UI elements or device services as mashup components as well as their interface descriptions using web technologies and domain-specific ontologies. **Rule authors** specify generic or domain-specific adaptation, aggregation and ranking rules. The latter rank arbitrary compositions (incl. *distribution options*) with respect to their usage context. For instance, distribution options that contain voice I/O features are ranked higher when the user enters her car together with her mobile devices. **Users** with domain knowledge and no programming expertise develop or configure MDM using EUD tools provided by the client-server runtime environment.

Features of the MAS are the following, which we explain in more detail afterwards: (i) Based on predefined or automatically derived composition and distribution knowledge, the MAS recommends distribution options at run time to integrate or distribute composition fragments semi-automatically. (ii) Moreover, the effects of distribution options are calculated automatically in terms of quality properties on the application layer. As result, users can filter out undesired adaptations or may easier coordinate their design steps. (iii) Next, the MAS ranks distribution options regarding their current "context fitness". To this end, users can reuse predefined *ranking rules*.

Semi-automatic Distribution. Developing or modifying MDMs, users are guided by recommended distribution options derived from context properties, e.g., available devices and their features. The *distribution assistant* matches context model entities (e.g., devices, environment or user profiles) with MDM models or *distribution patterns*, each specified as tuple $(\mathcal{C}, \mathcal{P}, \mathcal{D}, \mathcal{F})$ where several *components* $C_i \subseteq \mathcal{C}$ are associated to *context properties* $P_j \subset \mathcal{P}$ as *distribution* relations $d \in \mathcal{D}, d(C_i, P_j)$. Set $\mathcal{F}$ specifies *data flow* relations $f \in \mathcal{F}$ between components. The result of the "context-pattern" matching operation are composition fragment *candidates* ranked according to their *matching degree* and their average user rating of previous sessions given by other users. Based on top-k candidates, the *distribution manager* filters out candidates whose components cannot be executed on any registered device and have no functional alternatives, which can be used instead. For this, the *distribution manager* examines the interface description of each component referenced by every candidate. In relation to a device profile, each component's usability is evaluated according to its context requirements specified as part of the interface description. The result is a *component usability matrix* that includes valid component-device, component-alternatives or alternative-device pairs. Afterwards, the *distribution manager* calculates the *distribution graph* G_D that represents devices D, components C and component alternatives C' as vertices V_D, V_C and $V_{C'}$ respectively. Further, for each valid component-device or component-alternative pair there is an edge $E_{(C,D)}$ or

$E_{(C,C')}$ connecting corresponding vertices. Based on graph G_D, the *distribution manager* derives further redistribution options that are considered as optional distribution recommendations per candidate. Finally, the *distribution manager* creates at least a *distribution option* for each candidate. At this, every *distribution* unit $d \in D$ of a candidate results in a *distribution action* accordingly (cf. Fig. 2).

Distribution Rating. In this step, the *distribution evaluator* tries to calculate quality properties for each *distribution option* provided by the *distribution manager*. First, the *distribution evaluator* retrieves valid aggregation rules by matching *quality aggregator* interface elements of each rule (cf. Fig. 3a) with currently available device profiles. The latter result from the *target* devices of the distribution options (cf. Fig. 2) together with directly registered devices of the application context, e.g., the owner device. If every *target* device either provides appropriate *device services* or there are mashup components with compliant interfaces, and they can be executed on the *target* device regarding their context requirements, the aggregation rule is considered as valid. In summary, the *distribution evaluator* filters out usable rules. Second, each valid aggregation rule results in a corresponding quality property at the application layer. To this end, for each rule following sub-processes are performed: (a) In the context of the current rule, for every target device a *quality aggregator* instance is created and integrated on the client-side runtime environment. Further, the *aggregator instance* calculates the quality property on the local composition layer of the associated device as described in Sect. 3.4. (b) Afterwards, locally aggregated quality properties are sent from each target device to the central *distribution evaluator*. Here, they are used as input to the rule's *aggregation function*. The result of its application is a quality value at the application layer. (c) Finally, the calculated quality value of the current aggregation rule is assigned to the distribution option. In summary, each valid aggregation rule of every distribution option result in a corresponding quality value, which users may perceive as guidance to choose desired distribution options.

Context-Sensitive Ranking. Since each distribution option may be related to several quality properties, there is no general solution to rank distribution options regarding distinct user preferences. Therefore, our approach is based on the following solutions: First, users may rank distribution options interactively according to common quality properties and their values. Second, distribution options are ranked automatically considering their quality properties and "context fitness". The first solution has to be supported on the EUD toolkit's UI layer, e.g., representing distribution options and its quality values in tabular form as well as providing interactive sorting features. Regarding the second solution, the MAS provides *context-specific ranking rules*, which are specified by experts or are predefined as part of mashup templates. For instance, when distribution options are recommended in an automotive environment, those that provide voice I/O capabilities are preferred and thus ranked higher. A corresponding example rule is presented in Fig. 5.

```
{
  when: {
    match: ''' ...
      prefix e: <http://example.com/docudma/env#> .
      ask { ?env a e:Environment;
      owl:sameAs(e:Automotive). }
    '''
  },
  select: {
    type:"complex", op:"OR", children:[
      { type:"cmp", caps:[{ a:"ac:out",e:"m:voice"}],...},
      { type:"cmp", caps:[{ a:"ac:in" ,e:"m:voice"}],...}]
  }, rating: 4.5
}
```

Fig. 5. Sample ranking rule

With help of the *when*-clause, valid *ranking rules* are determined in consideration of the current context model by the *distribution evaluator*. The *select*-clause specifies necessary composition fragments and their capabilities. As shown in Fig. 5, composition patterns can be represented as combination of logical OR and AND statements to specify alternative and necessary component capabilities respectively. The rule's *rating* value is assigned to the distribution option when context and composition conditions are fulfilled. Here, we assume a five-point rating scale. Moreover, several *ranking rules* are applied to each distribution option and the mean rank per option is calculated from the mean quality value and the average context rating. Finally, the distribution options are sorted automatically according to their rank in descending order and are presented to the end-user by the EUD toolkit.

5   Conclusion and Future Work

Due to the mobility and limited resources of devices, developers (incl. end-users) of multi-device applications have to cope with the problem of dynamic context changes. In this context, we argue it is not sufficient to specify adaptation rules at design time only or at run time. Developers, especially end-users, cannot anticipate every situation at design time or are able to perform needed adaptations at run time, e.g., when a control device falls short on energy resources. Thus, they should be guided by an intelligent assistant to create/adapt applications at run time. To address this challenge, we introduced the concept of *distribution options* to modify MDMs dynamically. However, the limitations of our approach are (a) its dependence on predefined distribution, composition and rule models, the lack of assistance for (b) functional testing of resulting MDM and (c) detailed configuration of distribution options. Considering the first limitation, the quality of distribution options result from available applications, distribution patterns or rules. In this context, we assume that expert developers or the runtime administrator are responsible for sufficient quality that comes with a substantial initial effort. But this may be compensated by the community of expert users. Second, distribution options are intended as supplemental design recommendations in association with a graphical mashup editor end-users may apply to create or modify MDMs. Currently it lacks testing capabilities for distribution options that require a sufficient infrastructure to simulate multi-device scenarios and virtual devices based on user requirements. In this context, additional research is needed. Moreover, we question whether non-technical savvy end-users are not overwhelmed by such simulation capabilities as well? The last limitation addresses missing features to adjust distribution options in more detail, e.g., assigning events of a remote control component executed on a smartphone to another video playback feature executed on a smart TV. This might be of interest for power users. However, this comes with the need to track modifications to recalculate their effects on the application quality. Here, further investigations are needed.

In our future work, we focus on a wizard-like EUD toolkit to capture user requirements more precisely and to specify the application's distribution state based on abstract and distributable device capabilities. This allows to derive suitable composition fragments and distribution options more precisely and enables end-users to control recommended design options even more actively.

Acknowledgments. The work of Oliver Mroß is funded by the European Union and the Free State of Saxony within the EFRE program.

References

1. Chowdhury, S.R., Daniel, F., Casati, F.: Recommendation and weaving of reusable mashup model patterns for assisted development. ACM Trans. Internet Techn. **14**, 21 (2014)
2. Ciortea, A., Boissier, O., Zimmermann, A., Florea, A.M.: Responsive decentralized composition of service mashups for the internet of things. In: Schneegass, S., Schmidt, A., Michahelles, F., Kritzler, M., Ilic, A., Kunze, K. (eds.) IOT, pp. 53–61. ACM (2016)
3. Coutaz, J.: Meta-user interfaces for ambient spaces. In: Coninx, K., Luyten, K., Schneider, K.A. (eds.) TAMODIA 2006. LNCS, vol. 4385, pp. 1–15. Springer, Heidelberg (2007). https://doi.org/10.1007/978-3-540-70816-2_1
4. Coutaz, J., Crowley, J.L.: A first-person experience with end-user development for smart homes. IEEE Pervasive Comput. **15**(2), 26–39 (2016)
5. Daniel, F., Matera, M.: Mashups - Concepts, Models and Architectures. Data-Centric Systems and Applications. Springer, Heidelberg (2014). https://doi.org/10.1007/978-3-642-55049-2
6. Desolda, G., Ardito, C., Matera, M.: Empowering end users to customize their smart environments: model, composition paradigms, and domain-specific tools. ACM Trans. Comput.-Hum. Interact. **24**(2), 12:1–12:52 (2017)
7. openHAB e.V. Foundation: openhab: Empowering the smart home, December 2017. https://docs.openhab.org/addons/uis/habmin/readme.html

8. Ghiani, G., Manca, M., Paternò, F.: Authoring context-dependent cross-device user interfaces based on trigger/action rules. In: Holzmann, C., Mayrhofer, R. (eds.) MUM, pp. 313–322. ACM (2015)

9. Guinard, D., Trifa, V., Wilde, E.: Architecting a mashable open World Wide Web of Things. Technical Report 663, Institute for Pervasive Computing, ETH Zurich, February 2010. http://www.vs.inf.ethz.ch/publ/papers/WoT.pdf

10. Husmann, M., Nebeling, M., Pongelli, S., Norrie, M.C.: MultiMasher: providing architectural support and visual tools for multi-device mashups. In: Benatallah, B., Bestavros, A., Manolopoulos, Y., Vakali, A., Zhang, Y. (eds.) WISE 2014. LNCS, vol. 8787, pp. 199–214. Springer, Cham (2014). https://doi.org/10.1007/978-3-319-11746-1_15

11. Kleinfeld, R., Steglich, S., Radziwonowicz, L., Doukas, C.: glue.things: a mashup platform for wiring the internet of things with the internet of services. In: WoT, pp. 16–21. ACM (2014)

12. Mathew, S.S., Atif, Y., Sheng, Q.Z., Maamar, Z.: The web of things - challenges and enabling technologies. In: Bessis, N., Xhafa, F., Varvarigou, D., Hill, R., Li, M. (eds.) Internet of Things and Inter-cooperative Computational Technologies for Collective Intelligence. Studies in Computational Intelligence, vol. 460, pp. 1–23. Springer, Heidelberg (2013). https://doi.org/10.1007/978-3-642-34952-2_1

13. Mroß, O., Meißner, K.: Towards user-centered distributed mashups. In: Proceedings of the 2014 Workshop on Distributed User Interfaces and Multimodal Interaction. DUI 2014, pp. 11–14. ACM, New York (2014)

14. Nebeling, M.: Xdbrowser 2.0: Semi-automatic generation of cross-device interfaces. In: Mark, G., Fussell, S.R., Lampe, C., schraefel, M.C., Hourcade, J.P., Appert, C., Wigdor, D. (eds.) CHI. pp. 4574–4584. ACM (2017)

15. Paternò, F., Santoro, C.: A Design Space for End User Development in the Time of the Internet of Things. In: Paternò, F., Wulf, V. (eds.) New Perspectives in End-User Development, pp. 43–59. Springer, Cham (2017). https://doi.org/10.1007/978-3-319-60291-2_3

16. Radeck, C., Blichmann, G., Meißner, K.: Estimating the functionality of mashup applications for assisted, capability-centered end user development. In: Majchrzak, T.A., Traverso, P., Monfort, V., Krempels, K.H. (eds.) WEBIST (2), pp. 109–120. SciTePress (2016)

Towards Dynamically Programmable Devices
Using Beacons

Alejandro Pérez-Vereda[1]([⊠]), Daniel Flores-Martín[2], Carlos Canal[1],
and Juan M. Murillo[2]

[1] University of Malaga, Malaga, Spain
apvereda@uma.es, canal@lcc.uma.es
[2] University of Extremadura, Badajoz, Spain
{dfloresm, juanmamu}@unex.es

Abstract. With the grow of the Web of Things, lots of devices are being
connected to the network. Many of these devices require human interaction
when using them. In a desirable scenario, technology should allow to automatically adapt the behavior of these devices to the needs and expectations of
their users. To this extent, in previous work we proposed the Internet of People
model to automatically develop virtual profiles of people stored in their
smartphones. However, in order to build a complete virtual profile with information about the user's environment and context, we need also the contribution
of these surrounding devices. Our goal is to develop a framework in which users
and smart devices are integrated seamlessly and in real time, allowing programmatic adaptation and update of both virtual user profiles and surrounding
devices. As a proof of concept, in this paper we propose the use of beacons to
dynamically download and execute in the smartphone scripts for updating the
virtual profile with context information, and trigger actions both in the smartphone and the devices. This way, we take a first step to an effective Programmable World, in which everyday objects connected to the network can be
programmatically adapted to their users.

Keywords: Web of Things · Internet of Things · Internet of People
People as a Service · Programmable world · Virtual user profiles
Beacons

1 Introduction

In the last two decades, the Internet has been mainly seen as a way of connecting
people, and estimations say that nowadays over half of the world's population is online
[12]. However, the network is currently evolving to face a new challenge: the integration of myriads of objects in what has been called the Internet of Things (IoT) [6].
By 2020 there will be 50 to 100 billion devices connected to the Internet [17]. Indeed,
hardware advances come with the creation of new chips to include in almost every
device, enabling the development of *smart* things, capable of interacting with each
other and with the people who use or are just near them. Most of these things rely on

WWW standards for providing an interface to control and update their behavior, constituting an enormous Web of Things (WoT) [8].

Although this is not yet a problem, in a near future with huge amounts of connected devices, configuring how these smart things should work will be a serious burden for their users. For instance, someone can configure the timetable of her home heating system to reduce its energy consumption, but if something in her schedule changes, it would be necessary to update the timetable manually. This can be done with one device, but when someone interacts with dozens of smart things everyday, this task becomes a nightmare. To avoid this situation, we require solutions which consider users' context and preferences, permitting smart things to automatically and dynamically adapt their behavior to their users.

A number of research works aim to gather and process the contextual information of users in order to build comprehensive virtual profiles [5, 10]. Among them, previous work of the authors of this paper consisted in developing a model, called People as a Service (PeaaS) [7], that takes advantage from the pervasive presence of smartphones and the wide range of sensors they include to gather information about their owners, and use it for building and maintaining a virtual profile of each individual.

However, these virtual profiles cannot be completed using only the information acquired by the smartphones themselves. They need to interact with other smart devices in their surroundings in order to achieve more precise results. For instance, a smartphone virtual assistant will suggest using the public bike service of a city to go to a certain place, only if it interacts with the nearby bicycle stations to learn whether there are bikes available.

Moreover, this interaction between user profiles and connected things cannot be reduced to the exchange of data. In their roadmap to a programmable world [19], the authors advocate for a swift from today's data-centric IoT systems to a network in which smart objects are truly programmable. Hence, we must develop general solutions in order to dynamically update both virtual profiles and the behavior of smart things in a programmatic way.

According to all this, our goal is to use people's virtual profiles for dynamically adapting the behavior of the smart devices they will use daily. In particular, we aim to develop a programming framework that offers a wide range of interaction possibilities between connected devices and people, based on their virtual profiles. In this paper we take a first step towards this goal by presenting a solution in which beacons are used to enrich the contextual information in the smartphones, even being able to dynamically program updates of the virtual profiles and to trigger different actions.

We have chosen beacons for our proof of concept as these small and simple signal emitting devices can be deployed anywhere, while other smarter devices can detect them and trigger actions from their presence. This way, beacons are a great tool to transfer context-aware behavior to any connected device.

Indeed, beacons are the devices typically used in Google's Physical Web[1]. This is an open technology whose goal is to enable quick and seamless interactions with

---

[1] Physical Web: https://google.github.io/physical-web/.

physical objects and locations by receiving a URL linking to their web pages. However, our goal goes one step further typical Physical Web examples, as we will show.

The structure of this paper is as follows. Section 2 discusses the state of the art and some related works found in the recent literature. Next, Sect. 3 introduces our proposal and presents the architecture of the programming framework, together with the technologies that support it. In Sect. 4 we develop a proof of concept to show the main features of our proposal. Finally, Sect. 5 presents the conclusions and briefly discusses future work.

2 Related Work

The WoT offers new opportunities of orchestrating different devices to build complex systems [13]. However, as smart things are getting more presence in people's everyday lifes, this orchestration becomes a challenge. In this sense, Ambient Intelligence has emerged as a discipline for making everyday environments sensitive and responsive to people's needs [15].

If we focus on programming techniques for adapting software behavior to its context, Software Engineering approaches like Dynamic Composition [4] or Context-Oriented Programming [9] have already addressed this issue. They make it possible for developers to write a set of behaviors for a given entity, which will apply one of them depending on its external context. Although these techniques provide a certain degree of flexibility, so many variables would need to be considered during the development phase and hardwired within the code of the applications, such as user moods and preferences, those of the people around, etc. In practice, this makes it too hard to build a truly adaptable and proactive application for the WoT. The behavior and actions to take in a given situation should come up from an inference process starting off the actual context and preferences of the user.

Indeed, many recent research works agree on giving support to the WoT by means of a paradigm focused on the people [18, 20]. As mentioned before, in this paper we present a programming framework inspired by PeaaS, a mobile computing architecture that promotes empowering smartphones by giving them a key role in inferring, storing and sharing virtual profiles with personal information about their users. PeaaS is based on the Internet of People [16], a social computation model promoted by the authors of this paper that combines the IoT with people-related information to make it proactive and responsive to its users.

Many of the proposals described in the works mentioned above are related with user location. Smartphones include GPS sensors to get latitude and longitude measures outdoors, while alternative techniques [11] have been proposed to address fine-grained indoor positioning, in particular, beacons [1, 3]. In this work, we go one step forward mere positioning, and we use beacons and smartphones' Bluetooth capabilities to programmatically interact with the virtual profile stored in the smartphone.

As already mentioned, the Physical Web is based on beacons sharing the URL of a web page or application. Then, services on the smartphone, such as Google Chrome or Nearby Notifications, scan for and display these URLs after passing them through a proxy. However, we go one step further the Physical Web, as we don't use beacons just for showing web pages providing contextual information to the user, but to establish a programmatic mechanism of interaction with the virtual profile in the smartphone, being able to modify both the information stored and the behavior of all the devices involved in the communication.

3 A Programming Framework for Real-Time Context Adaptation

In this section we describe the main technical features of our proposal. It relies on the use of beacons and Bluetooth Low Energy[2] (BLE) capabilities of smartphones to make them dynamically run scripts containing fragments of behavior for interacting with the virtual profile stored in them, either for updating it, for adapting the behavior of smart devices to the context of the users present in a given situation, or for both. First, we briefly discuss beacons and BLE, and then we present the details of our programming framework.

3.1 Beacons and Bluetooth Low Energy

Beacons are small devices that broadcast BLE packets allowing nearby receiving systems to determine fine-grained indoor position or to trigger some other location-related action. BLE packets can vary in size from 10 to 47 bytes and consist of several fields [14]. One of them is the Protocol Data Unit (PDU) field, which is divided in two parts: A Header and a Payload. The Header contains information about the type of the PDU out of different options included in the BLE standard, and it also indicates the length of the Payload part. The Payload represents the information actually transmitted by the beacon. In our case, it contains the URL of an online script file, a piece of code to be executed in the smartphones which detect it. For that, we use Google's open source Eddystone-URL beacon format[3] in which the Payload contains a 16 bytes field for encapsulating an URL. The format also provides some tools to shorten the URL by encoding different structures and domains like "http://www." or ".com" in one single byte.

For beacon detection, we use the Android Beacon Library[4]. This API allows mobile phones to act both as transmitters and receivers of beacon signals following the BLE standard. This way, we do not actually need physical beacons for experimenting with our proposal, but standard smartphones can be used as virtual beacons, while others act as receivers. Moreover, these virtual beacons are mobile, which allows to envision a wider range of scenarios.

---

[2] Bluetooth 4.0. Core. https://www.bluetooth.com/specifications/adopted-specifications.

[3] Google's beacon platform. https://developers.google.com/beacons/overview.

[4] Android Beacon Library: https://altbeacon.github.io/android-beacon-library/index.html.

3.2 Architecture of the Proposal

Our goal is to develop a programming framework that: (i) makes easier the dynamic update of the user's virtual profile, adding some new appreciation to better describe their situation (i.e. the devices that can be detected in the nearby) and, the other way round, (ii) allows to adapt the behavior of connected devices involved in a certain situation (in a first step, just beacons), in order to trigger some actions related with the new information available from the users, such as their habits and preferences. This way, both virtual profiles and smart devices can be updated in a programmatic way, and the experience learnt will be available for the future services or devices the user interacts with.

The architecture of our proposal is shown in Fig. 1. First, beacons (in fact, smartphones acting as virtual beacons) broadcast by BLE a URL pointing to a script file with the behavior we want the smartphone to execute (1). A smartphone in the nearby receives the BLE signal, and access the URL, downloading the script from a server (2). Then, the script is run by the smartphone, updating the virtual profile stored in it (3). Additionally, the instructions of the script may also indicate how to update the server's file (4), changing this way the behavior associated to the beacon.

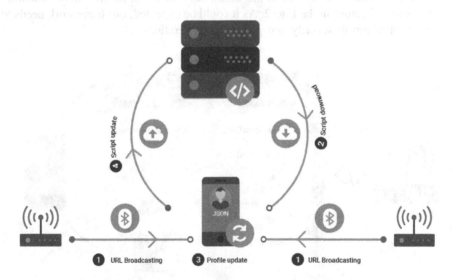

Fig. 1. Dynamic programming framework.

For the virtual profiles, we build on our previous work, and follow the PeaaS approach already mentioned in preceding sections. PeaaS endows the smartphone with the capability of storing, updating and of course sharing a virtual profile of its owner. Hence, the smartphone becomes a proxy or interface of its user with the rest of the world, in particular smart devices in the environment, allowing negotiating interactions with them in a seamless way [2]. The virtual profile can be seen as a timeline with the habits, actions and relations of the user. From the raw data collected along the day by its sensors or through user's actions, the smartphone infers the movements of its owner and the situations in which she is involved, and place them in the timeline. For instance, virtual profiles may store information about the people we meet along the day. For that, our smartphone and those of these people must detect each other, adding the corresponding information to both profiles. This information may also include the role of each individual (e.g. a shop seller, a caregiver, etc.) and can be used to infer patterns of accompaniment.

Virtual profiles are written in JSON, which is an open and easily extensible format, and stored in the phone with Couchbase Lite[5], which offers NoSQL database storage for smartphones. Couchbase provides native APIs for iOS, Android and.NET. With these APIs we can map database documents to a native object model, work directly with JSON structures, or both. It is important to clarify that the profile of an user is only stored in her smartphone.

Finally, for running the script we use BeanShell[6], a simple Java interpreter that allows runtime upload and execution of code. A typical script states instructions for querying and/or updating a virtual profile, and probably some other actions, such as notifications to the user, etc. BeanShell scripts are just pieces of code, not complete classes, and they may make reference to external variables, which act as parameters.

All these components are run in the smartphone as it can be seen in the software components architecture in the Fig. 2. As it could be expected, our framework needs to pay special attention to security and privacy considerations.

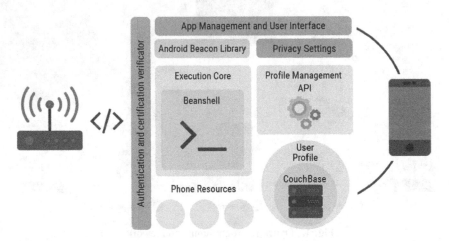

Fig. 2. Software components architecture

With respect to security, the main concern is for sure downloading code from an unknown device and executing it in the user's smartphone. Hence, our framework

---

[5] Couchbase Lite: https://www.couchbase.com/products/mobile.
[6] BeanShell: http://www.beanshell.org/.

includes a certification or authentication layer facing the detection of new devices. This layer can be based on certificates or a reputation system, allowing the smartphone to decide whether it has detected a trustful emitting device. Additionally, we do not allow the script to execute in the smartphone risky actions as for instance a system call, nor to freely update the user profile. This is solved by providing a Profile Management API through which interacting with the virtual profile.

Privacy concerns are addressed by privacy settings which only let the smartphone to share selected aspects of the information contained in the profile. Again, these settings are taken into account by the Profile Management API, when trying to access or to modify the data contained in the profile.

4 Validating the Proposal as a Treasure Hunting

In order to better illustrate our proposal and assess its viability, we have developed a proof of concept consisting in a treasure hunting game. Players have to find a final prize following hints hidden in treasures along their way. These treasures are represented by beacons. Each beacon has an associated script (Fig. 3) that adds to the player's virtual profile a hint to find the next treasure (lines 3–5), showing also a notification to the user (l.6). In addition, the script makes the smartphone to update the beacon file with the player's name and a timestamp (l.9–11); this way, we are able to inform future finders of the participants that have got the treasure in advance (l.12). Finally, when a player finds all the hints, a notification would be displayed telling that she has won the game (not shown in the figure), and the location of the prize. The variable mgmt references the Profile Management API mentioned in the previous section implementing methods for querying and updating the profile and some other utilities. The script is actually available in the shortened URL in line 1 below.

Accordingly, the virtual profile of a player consists of treasures and hints that have been acquired when the player passed near one of the beacons. Figure 4 shows the virtual profile of a user who has already got the first two treasures:

```
1  String URL = "https://goo.gl/pzuDuu";
2  if (mgmt.count("\"Treasure_Find_Game\" : \"treasure\"") == 1) {
3      mgmt.append("Treasure_Find_Game", "\"treasure\": {
4          \"value\": \"Treasure 02, Search the way\",
5          \"hint\": \"It seems that the NORTH face is the best way\"}");
6      mgmt.notify("It seems that the NORTH face is the best way");
7      String name = mgmt.get("\"Treasure_Find_Game\" : \"name\"");
8      Calendar now = Calendar.getInstance();
9      mgmt.upload(URL, "mgmt.notify(\"player " + name
10         + " already got this hint at " + now.get(Calendar.HOUR_OF_DAY)
11         + ":" + now.get(Calendar.MINUTE) + "\")"); }
12 mgmt.notify("player Carlos already got this hint at 12:35");
```

Fig. 3. Sample script for Treasure #2 (excerpt).

```
{... "Treasure_Find_Game": {
  "playerID" : "fn00004",
  "name" : "Alejandro",
  "treasure": {
    "value": "Treasure 01, The Beginning",
    "hint": "As in a climbing, you have to start from the ground"},
  "treasure": {
    "value": "Treasure 02, Search the way",
    "hint": "It seems that the NORTH face is the best way"}} ...}
```

Fig. 4. Virtual profile (excerpt).

Finally, for running the game we have developed a very simple Android application which scans for beacons, and downloads and runs the corresponding scripts, updating the virtual profile in the smartphone. In fact, all the treasure-hunting behavior is confined in the scripts, and the same Android application would be used for any other testing scenario we may develop.

5 Conclusions and Future Work

In previous works [7, 16], we advocated for using smartphones in order to infer virtual profiles of people with their daily activities and routines. These profiles would be one key element to a world in which technology works for the people and adapts to their needs automatically [2]. The objective is creating a seamless interface between people and their WoT environment in the Programmable World era [19]. With all this in mind, our medium-term goal is building a framework that allows programmatic update/adaptation of both user virtual profiles and surrounding connected devices. An important advantage of this approach is the development easiness intrinsic to itself as we only need one generic application for every interaction. What occurs during the interaction depends only on the scripts.

In this work, we present an initial step towards this goal. As a proof of concept, we have used beacons, as they are simple, cheap, and easy to deploy devices. However, beacons are not a key element of the proposal, and they can be replaced by any other smart device, probably presenting a more elaborate behavior. We leave this for future work.

Indeed, we use smartphones acting as virtual beacons. This also opens the possibility of using the programming framework for new collaborative scenarios in which smartphones and other smart devices can "talk", exchanging information among them, and reach common objectives.

Obviously in a framework such as the one we are proposing, authentication, trustworthiness, and security are crucial issues. We have developed a preliminary version of the API being the only way of interacting with the smartphone and the profile persuading the script of executing non-allowed actions or modifying the profile without any control. Further development will probably imply that scripts would not be written in a general-purpose Java dialect, but in a high-level language with primitives for interacting with virtual profiles in the smartphone, and a few other functionalities, such as push notifications. Also, it is important to know in each moment with who the smartphone is interacting, as we have different trustworthiness levels depending on the person or enterprise, and of course, we must prevent from unauthorized access by malicious entities the data in the profiles and the smartphones themselves. So, we are considering a certificates-based solution for authentication in the interactions.

More detailed considerations for authentication and privacy issues have been deliberately ignored in this initial step, where smartphones simply download and run external scripts, but certainly they must be taken into account. This would be future work.

Acknowledgments. This work has been partially financed by the Spanish Government through projects TIN2015-67083-R and TIN2015-69957-R (MINECO/FEDER, UE), by the 4 IE project 0045-4 IE-4-P funded by the Interreg V-A España-Portugal (POCTEP) 2014-2020 program, and by the Regional Government of Extremadura (project GR15098).

References

1. Rodriguez, A.B., Tena, A.R., Garcia-Alonso, J., Berrocal, J., Rosco, R.F., Murillo, J.M.: Using beacons for creating comprehensive virtual profiles. In: García, C.R., Caballero-Gil, P., Burmester, M., Quesada-Arencibia, A. (eds.) UCAmI/IWAAL/AmIHEALTH -2016. LNCS, vol. 10070, pp. 295–306. Springer, Cham (2016). https://doi.org/10.1007/978-3-319-48799-1_34
2. Berrocal, J., Garcia-Alonso, J., Canal, C., Murillo, J.M.: Situational-context: a unified view of everything involved at a particular situation. In: Bozzon, A., Cudre-Maroux, P., Pautasso, C. (eds.) ICWE 2016. LNCS, vol. 9671, pp. 476–483. Springer, Cham (2016). https://doi.org/10.1007/978-3-319-38791-8_34
3. Chawathe, S.S.: Beacon placement for indoor localization using Bluetooth. In: Intelligent Transportation Systems, (ITSC 2008), pp. 980–985. IEEE (2008)
4. Chen, G., Li, M., Kotz, D.: Data-centric middleware for context-aware pervasive computing. Pervasive Mob. Comput. **4**(2), 216–253 (2008)
5. Gronli, T.M., Ghinea, G., Younas, M.: Context-aware and automatic configuration of mobile devices in cloud-enabled ubiquitous computing. Pers. Ubiquit. Comput. **18**(4), 883–894 (2014)
6. Gubbi, J., Buyya, R., Marusic, S., Palaniswami, M.: Internet of things (IoT): a vision, architectural elements, and future directions. Future Gener. Comput. Syst. **29**(7), 1645–1660 (2013)
7. Guillen, J., Miranda, J., Berrocal, J., Garcia-Alonso, J., Murillo, J.M., Canal, C.: People as a service: a mobile-centric model for providing collective sociological profiles. IEEE Softw. **31**(2), 48–59 (2014)
8. Guinard, D., Trifa, V., Mattern, F., Wilde, E.: From the internet of things to the web of things: resource-oriented architecture and best practices. In: Uckelmann, D., Harrison, M., Michahelles, F. (eds.) Architecting the Internet of Things, pp. 97–129. Springer, Berlin, Heidelberg (2011). https://doi.org/10.1007/978-3-642-19157-2_5
9. Hirschfeld, R., Costanza, P., Nierstrasz, O.: Context-oriented programming. J. Object Technol. **7**(3), 125–151 (2008)

10. Hong, J.Y., Suh, E.H., Kim, S.J.: Context-aware systems: a literature review and classification. Expert Syst. Appl. **36**(4), 8509–8522 (2009)
11. Hossain, A.M., Soh, W.S.: A survey of calibration-free indoor positioning systems. Comput. Commun. **66**, 1–13 (2015)
12. International Telecommunication Union (ITU), Telecommunication Development Bureau.: ICT Facts and Figures 2005, 2010, 2014. http://www.itu.int
13. Kovatsch, M.: CoAP for the web of things: from tiny resource-constrained devices to the web browser. In: ACM Conference on Pervasive and Ubiquitous Computing Adjunct Publication, pp. 1495–1504. ACM (2013)
14. Mackensen, E., Lai, M., Wendt, T.: Bluetooth Low Energy (BLE) Based Wireless Sensors. Sensors, IEEE, pp. 1–4 (2012)
15. Marzano, S.: The New Everyday: Views on Ambient Intelligence. 010 Publishers, Rotterdam (2003)
16. Miranda, J., et al.: From the internet of things to the internet of people. IEEE Internet Comput. **19**(2), 40–47 (2015)
17. Perera, C., Liu, C.H., Jayawardena, S., Chen, M.: Context-aware computing in the internet of things: a survey on internet of things from industrial market perspective. CoRR (2015)
18. Sheth, A.: Computing for human experience: Semantics-empowered sensors, services, and social computing on the ubiquitous web. IEEE Internet Comput. **14**(1), 88–91 (2010)
19. Taivalsaari, A., Mikkonen, T.: A roadmap to the programmable world: software challenges in the IoT era. IEEE Softw. **34**(1), 72–80 (2017)
20. Wang, F.Y., Carley, K.M., Zeng, D., Mao, W.: Social computing: from social informatics to social intelligence. IEEE Intell. Syst. **22**(2), 79–83 (2007)

Architecting Self-adaptive Software Systems

Anni Huuhtanen, Niko Mäkitalo(✉), and Tommi Mikkonen

Department of Computer Science, University of Helsinki, Helsinki, Finland
{anni.huuhtanen,niko.makitalo,tommi.mikkonen}@helsinki.fi

Abstract. A growing number of software systems operate in uncertain environments. They benefit from an ability to autonomously adapt to changes during runtime without suffering from a lowered quality of service. Several different architectural approaches to self-adaptive software exist with their sources of inspiration varying from psychology to mathematics. In this literature survey, we study and evaluate four types of approaches: architecture-based, control-based, learning-based and awareness-based approaches. Our aim is to clarify whether a unified, general approach to computational self-adaptivity is possible and what it could look like. We conclude that a general solution should combine aspects of all of the studied approaches.

Keywords: Self-adaptivity · Software architectures
Autonomous systems · Internet of Things · IoT · Web of Things · WoT

1 Introduction

Software systems are becoming increasingly complex as the trend for distributed, heterogeneous and large-scale architectures grows. This is especially visible in the Internet of Things (IoT), and the Web of Things (WoT) systems, which may consist of thousands of parts or subsystems, each processing information locally and exchanging it without any centralized controller. Each subsystem can even be owned by a different agent or organization. Despite possibly having diverse properties and behaviors, they must be able to interact with each other.

In addition, requirements of various stakeholders such as cost, performance and safety can be at odds, meaning that a system must make certain trade-offs. Traditionally, these trade-offs have been analyzed during the design period of software and addressed as various requirements. However, in more and more cases, the runtime operation of the system results from complex interactions between several moving parts and therefore tends to be uncertain at any given time. This uncertainty means that the same behavior does not always lead to the same outcome or that, for example, sometimes a particular subsystem may be accessible to others and sometimes not. The operation of such an uncertain system after deployment is difficult to predict and infeasible to manually control, leading to a need for self-adaptivity.

© Springer Nature Switzerland AG 2018
C. Pautasso et al. (Eds.): ICWE 2018, LNCS 11153, pp. 59–70, 2018.
https://doi.org/10.1007/978-3-030-03056-8_6

Self-adaptivity in software systems means the ability of a system to adapt to changes in its environment during runtime in an independent manner without downtime or penalties [1]. A self-adaptive system is equipped with capabilities to observe itself and its environment in order to make autonomous decisions on how to behave. It can configure, optimize, repair, and protect itself based on what it observes. An observation could be, for example, input from a user or another system, or an anomaly in its own internal state. Self-adaptive mechanisms range from simple conditional expressions where the outcome changes program behavior to more complicated machine learning techniques where behavioral change occurs as a result of learning new knowledge.

A need for computational self-adaptivity arose in the early 2000s when the maintenance and operation of computing systems was still done manually by human administrators [2]. Typical maintenance tasks included installing, configuring and optimizing software and hardware. As the amount of computers and interconnections in computing systems started to grow, manual management proved to be cumbersome and methods to deal with this increasing complexity were needed. The trend for distributed, diverse and large computing systems has continued to this day. Many modern software systems, for example the areas of IoT and WoT, benefit from or even require self-adaptivity in many ways. An example is a cloud-based software service that dynamically allocates resources to a number of applications. In the case of a single application, the service must optimize both quality of service (QoS) and a cost objective [3]. Since the same infrastructure is shared by several applications, it must additionally offer good QoS to all applications. Uncertainty of the runtime environment and possibly conflicting objectives require the service to have self-adaptive properties.

Different architectural approaches to computational self-adaptivity have been developed over time. It can be seen that the approaches build on each other in a wave-like manner [2]. At the moment, the focus has started to move from traditional architecture-based approaches to more mathematical, control-based approaches. Recent attempts to incorporate self-adaptivity into software have also utilized machine learning techniques as well as taken inspiration from psychological theories and concepts such as self-awareness.

Since multiple approaches to computational self-adaptivity exist, it can be difficult to get a holistic understanding of the field. There has also been little comparison between the approaches. A comprehensive theoretical foundation of computational self-adaptivity is still missing and the path to achieve it seems unclear.

In this paper, we examine and evaluate different architectural approaches to developing self-adaptive software based on existing literature. The main purpose of the study is to clarify what is required for a more unified approach to computational self-adaptivity. Using the Goal-Question-Metric approach [4], our goal is formulated as follows:

- **Purpose**: Characterize and evaluate ...
- **Issue**: ... different architectural approaches to self-adaptive software ...
- **Objective**: ... in order to move towards a unified theory ...
- **Viewpoint**: ... from the standpoint of a researcher.

The precise research questions are the following:

- **RQ1**: What kind of architectural approaches to self-adaptive software exist?
- **RQ2**: What are the benefits and problems of different approaches?

The rest of this paper is structured as follows. In Sect. 2, we explain how we searched for articles for our survey and justify their selection. In Sect. 3, we examine different self-adaptive approaches and provide answers to our research questions. In Sect. 4, we discuss another recent literature survey. Finally, in Sect. 5 we draw some final conclusions.

2 Methods

First, we defined the search string to be used for automatic search. While doing initial research on the problem and formulating the research questions, we made a few searches using the single keywords self-adaptive and software. However, it became evident that multiple synonyms for these words existed in literature. For example, self-adaptivity and autonomy were often used interchangeably. Therefore, we defined the final search string as follows.

(self-adaptive OR self-adaptivity OR self-managing OR autonomic OR autonomous OR autonomy) AND (software OR framework OR architecture)

Then, we performed searches using the search string on IEEE Xplore Digital Library (https://ieeexplore.ieee.org/), ACM Digital Library (https://dl.acm.org/), and Google Scholar (https://scholar.google.fi/). We applied all keywords to the title field only, and searched only for articles that were published between 2016 and 2018. The searches resulted in 184 articles on IEEE Xplore, 277 articles on ACM Digital Library, and 653 articles on Google Scholar.

From the results, we chose the most recent literature survey on computational self-adaptivity as a starting point for snowballing. Using the snowballing method, we checked sources used by the survey and then looked at other articles where those sources had been cited. From these, we decided to select articles that present not only general theoretical approaches but also specific models so that we could better evaluate them. Finally, this lead to 10 articles for our survey, from which five articles present a distinct architectural model for computational self-adaptivity, and the rest are about general categories or approaches which these models can be classified into.

3 Results

The approaches we studied can roughly be classified into architecture-based, control-based, awareness-based and learning-based approaches, some having aspects of more than one class. Table 1 summarizes the findings.

Table 1. Identified self-adaptive approaches.

Approach	Examples	Inspiration	Emphasis	Idea
Architecture-based	MAPE-K, 3LA	Software engineering	Basic building blocks of self-adaptive systems	The system is equipped with a self-adaptive architecture following known principles of software engineering
Control-based	SimCA*	Mathematics	Formal guarantees for self-adaptivity	The self-adaptive process is guaranteed to adhere to the requirements of the system with the use of control theory
Learning-based	FUSION	Machine learning, software engineering	Learning self-adaptive logic through experience	The system learns the optimal self-adaptive behavior at runtime using incremental learning algorithms
Awareness-based	SAA	Psychology, machine learning, software engineering	Enhanced building blocks of self-adaptivity, enhanced learning	The system is equipped with an architecture that allows self-awareness, learning occurs on multiple levels, predicting future possible

3.1   Architecture-Based Approaches

Architecture-based approaches emphasize the role of architecture in designing self-adaptive software systems [1]. Instead of focusing on how to encode self-adaptivity into source code, the emphasis is on the structure and interaction of higher level software components and how they could implement self-adaptive behavior. Basic principles of software architecture design such as separation of concern and abstraction are applied. For example, components implementing self-adaptivity are separated from components implementing normal functionality, and each self-adaptive component has its own responsibility. In addition, the details of each component are hidden behind an interface. Components and their connectors can be modified, added and removed at runtime as well as organized in different ways.

MAPE-K is one of the first self-adaptive models that have been developed [5]. In the model, a software system is coupled with a separate managing component that implements four functions: Monitor, Analyze, Plan, and Execute. All functions have access to a shared Knowledge base that includes high-level goals given by the system administrator as well as knowledge gathered during runtime. The Monitor component gathers information about the system and its environment, updating the Knowledge component accordingly. The Analyze component determines whether adaptation actions are required based on the knowledge. If they are, the Plan component creates a plan of action and gives it to the Execution component that implements it. The MAPE-K model is shown in Fig. 1.

The problem with the MAPE-K model is that it specifies the different functions of a self-adaptive system on a very high level [5]. It is also quite simple and unprincipled as a software architecture. However, it gives a general overview of the basic functions needed in almost every self-adaptive system and works as an inspiration for more low-level architectures.

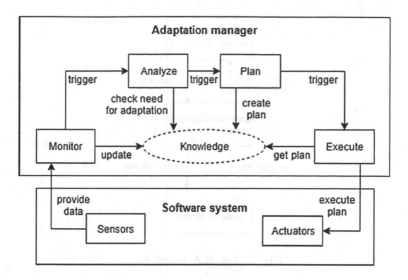

Fig. 1. The MAPE-K model [5].

3LA (Three-Layer Architecture) consists of three layers: Component Control, Change Management and Goal Management [6]. The bottom layer, Component Control, represents the software system itself and is monitored and reacted to by the middle layer, Change Management. The middle layer implements predefined self-adaptation models or plans and can, for example, remove and add components as well as modify their parameters. If no suitable plan exist, the middle layer triggers the top layer, Goal Management. This layer handles the high-level goals of the system and generates new plans for the middle layer. The 3LA model is shown in Fig. 2.

3LA is slightly more precisely defined than MAPE-K because of its layered structure, but it has the same problem of being simple and high-level [6]. It is unclear what the different layers exactly contain, for example.

3.2 Control-Based Approaches

In some software systems, self-adaptivity must occur according to precise requirements and despite restrictions such as time or memory. However, it can be difficult to guarantee these self-adaptation goals are met in architecture-based approaches where traditional verification techniques, for example tests and model checking, are used [7]. The idea with control-theoretical approaches is that formal guarantees for self-adaptation can be provided. Whereas architecture-based approaches are inspired by principles of software engineering, the foundation of control-based approaches is control theory from mathematics. Control theory has traditionally been used to implement self-adaptivity at the level of hardware, for example CPU and memory. Lately, it has also been applied to software adaptation.

Fig. 2. The 3LA model [6].

Control theory focuses on modeling software behavior instead of components [7]. This behavior involves two schemes, feedback control and feedforward control. In feedback control, when the system goes from functioning normally (a steady state) to experiencing internal or external changes or disturbances (a transient state), the output of the system is measured and compared to the self-adaptation goal (setpoint) such as response time. The error between the output and the setpoint determines a control signal that adapts the software system in a way that decreases the error. The system then enters back to a steady state. Feedforward control on the other hand calculates a different control signal based on the setpoint and the values of disturbances instead. It can be said that feedback control selects the initial adaptation strategy, and feedforward control refines it and ensures it is followed. Both schemes can implement different control strategies: in optimal control, the control signal that minimizes a certain cost function is selected while in state feedback, the signal is computed based on state information. Feedback and feedforward controllers may also be composed of multiple hierarchically organized sub-controllers.

SimCA* (Simplex Control Adaptation) is a control-theoretical model that supports three types of goals or requirements [8]. Setpoints (S-reqs) are simple values the system should achieve. Optimizable values (O-reqs) are functions the system should optimize. Threshold values (T-reqs) have to stay below or above a threshold. SimCA* works in four phases: Identification, Control Synthesis, Goal Transformation and Operation. In Identification, SimCA* builds a linear model of each goal by measuring the dependency between different goal values (control signals) and the system output in the form of a coefficient value. In Control Synthesis, a controller function is built for each of these models. The function calculates the control signal based on several values such as the previous control signal, coefficient, and error between the previous control signal and system output. The controller also includes mechanisms for adjusting the linear model and re-triggering Identification during sudden runtime changes. In Goal Transformation, all threshold goals are adjusted in a way that allows other goals to be satisfied as well. In Operation, the controllers output control signals and the final combined control signal is calculated based on them and possible optimization goals. The SimCA* model is shown in Fig. 3.

Although SimCA* is a more formal and mathematical model than MAPE-K, for example, its use in practice does not require a mathematical background which might still make it attractive to a regular software engineer [8]. The problem with SimCA* is that several drastic changes during runtime result in frequent re-identification which is costly and may hinder performance. In addition, the model cannot produce a satisfiable outcome in case of conflicting requirements. Unlike previous control-theoretical approaches, SimCA* is argued to be better suitable for multiple domains and problems. However, the framework has only been tested to work in a couple of scenarios and it is not certain if it generalizes well to different types of problems. Another problem with SimCA* and control-theoretical approaches in general is that not all requirements can easily be transformed into numerical form.

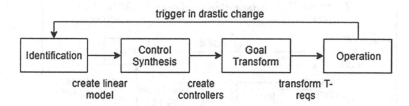

Fig. 3. The SimCA* model [8].

3.3   Learning-Based Approaches

Learning-based approaches utilize statistical and machine learning techniques. They often use a MAPE-K-like architecture, but instead of equipping the software system with an analytical, static model that controls self-adaptation during runtime, learning-based approaches allow the system to learn the optimal adaptation logic through experience.

FUSION (FeatUre-oriented Self-adaptatION) is a learning-based adaptive framework that is based on features [9]. They are abstractions of the system's abilities and the subjects or units of adaptation. Depending on the application, they may correspond to, for example, a set of services, rules or properties. At any given time, the software system has certain features activated and others deactivated. This state is captured in a feature selection string where activated features are set to 1 and deactivated features to 0. The adaptation of the system is modeled as transitions between these feature selection strings.

FUSION involves both an adaptation cycle and a learning cycle as well as an internal model [9]. The adaptation cycle consists of three components, Detect,

Plan and Effect, that are similar to the components in MAPE-K. Detect analyzes metrics gathered from the system and detects if an adaptation goal has been violated. If it has, Plan uses the model to determine which system features should be activated or deactivated, i.e. creates the next feature selection string. Finally, Effect implements the transition from the current feature selection string to the next in a way that ensures system stability. Meanwhile, the learning cycle observes relationships between the system metrics and implemented transitions and looks for unexpected patterns, in which case the model (used by Plan) adjusts to the new pattern, improving future adaptation. The FUSION framework is shown in Fig. 4.

FUSION is argued to be efficient, easy to use and accurate [9]. The abstraction achieved with features improves the generality of the framework. The problem with FUSION is that the incremental learning brings some overhead to the system. In addition, the learning cycle cannot predict abnormal patterns in an opportunistic manner. There has also been little testing of FUSION in real-world scenarios.

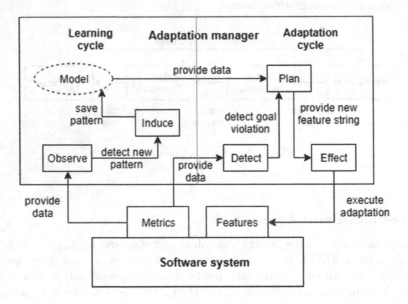

Fig. 4. The FUSION model [9].

3.4   Awareness-Based Approaches

Awareness-based approaches utilize aspects of both architecture- and learning-based approaches. Self-adaptivity is related to the concepts of self-awareness and self-expression that originate from psychology [10]. Lewis et al. have developed five-level model of consciousness (stimulus-awareness, interaction-awareness, time-awareness, goal-awareness, meta-awareness) [10,11] which originate from Neisser's levels of human self-awareness [12].

Computational self-awareness means the ability of a system to know about its own internal state as well as how it is perceived by other systems in its environment. A stimulus-aware system can respond to internal and external stimuli but does not know the difference between different types of stimuli. An interaction-aware system knows that its actions cause effects in the environment because of feedback loops. A time-aware system has knowledge about the past and can predict the future. A goal-aware system is aware of runtime constraints and objectives that are not implicitly present in its design. A meta-self-aware system is aware of being aware and is able to modify all lower layers if necessary. Computational self-expression on the other hand is the behavior resulting from knowledge gained through self-awareness. In the context of self-adaptivity, we can say that self-awareness concerns information processing and that self-expression consists of the resulting adaptive actions. Therefore, an advanced self-adaptive system is both self-aware and self-expressive.

In many modern software systems, the behavior of individual system components is not as important or interesting as the collective behavior emerging from the interaction of multiple components [11]. One observation from biological systems is that self-awareness seems to be an emergent property of distributed information processing, meaning that all components of a system only have access to local knowledge instead of a global, centralized knowledge base. This indicates that a software system could perhaps be more self-adaptive and less fragile with a similar decentralized architecture.

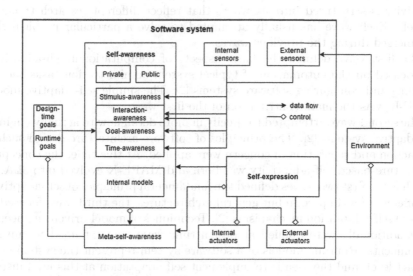

Fig. 5. The SAA model [11].

SAA, an adaptive architecture based on self-awareness, has been introduced [11]. In this architecture, an individual software application includes separate self-awareness and self-expression processes. The self-awareness process has access to internal models and is further divided into sub processes corresponding to the different levels (goal-awareness, stimulus-awareness and so on). Each process analyzes information gathered with internal and external sensors and possibly updates the internal models using its own incremental learning algorithm. The goal-aware sub process also has access to design-time goals, and the meta-self-aware sub process can change the goals as well as the learning algorithms of other sub processes. The models are exposed to the self-expression process that chooses actions based on them. The self-awareness process is also able to monitor what actions are taken. SAA is illustrated in Fig. 5.

As in FUSION, the knowledge in SAA is modified during runtime, meaning the adaptation logic itself can change, and benefits of architecture-based approaches are achieved [11]. Unlike FUSION, the self-aware architecture specifies different types of knowledge representing different levels of self-awareness instead of only one type of knowledge that is used as the basis for adaptation. In addition, the time-aware component allows prediction of future events. The overhead brought by incremental learning and the lack of practical evaluation are problems in SAA as well.

4   Related Work

The work by Weyns et al. provides a perspective on how different self-adaptive approaches have developed over time [2]. The history of research on self-adaptivity is structured into six waves that reflect different research trends in the field. Each wave has usually attempted to solve a particular problem that has emerged during the previous waves.

The first wave defined the basic aspects of computational self-adaptivity and focused on the automation of typical system administration tasks such as installing and configuring software systems [2]. The simple self-adaptive model, MAPE-K, was the main contribution of the first wave.

The second wave attempted to specify in more detail how to actually engineer self-adaptive systems [2]. The principles of software architecture design such as abstraction and separation of concern were applied. At this time, the concept of architecture-based self-adaptivity was born and MAPE-K evolved into 3LA.

While the first two waves defined the fundamental principles of self-adaptivity and offered a few imprecise but general architectures, the third wave focused on concrete self-adaptation mechanisms [2]. Techniques of model-driven engineering that traditionally were applied at design time were now extended to runtime environments. Runtime models of a software system represent the system at an abstract level, and the idea is to implement self-adaptation at this level instead of in the software system itself. Therefore, models work both as information sources that guide adaptation decisions as well as the subjects of adaptation.

The previous waves clarified the requirements of the adaptation manager but the fourth wave stressed the requirements of the software system itself [2]. Examples of these kinds of requirements would be, for example, to keep response time under a specific value or never failing a certain action. The contributions of the fourth wave included different languages for specifying these requirements and communicating them to the adaptation manager.

In the fifth wave, the question was how to guarantee requirements are met in unpredictable runtime environments [2], which is essential in critical self-adaptive systems, with strict requirements. Techniques based on mathematics and statistics such as RQV (Runtime Quantitative Verification) were developed to tackle this problem. Another solution is ActivFORMS (Active FORmal Models for Self-adaptation) that is based on formally guaranteeable models.

The sixth wave also focuses on handling uncertainty but sees control theory as the solution [2]. SimCA* and PBM (Push-Button Methodology) were some of the main contributions of this wave. The study does not discuss learning-based and awareness-based approaches but predicts artificial intelligence, including machine learning, may play a big part in future self-adaptive research for its fundamental ability to handle uncertainty.

5   Conclusion

We studied four general classes of self-adaptive approaches and one specific example from each class. In architecture-based approaches, the focus is on the architectural components of self-adaptive systems and the principles of software engineering that help build them. The more formal control-based approaches apply control theory to software systems in order to formally guarantee self-adaptivity occurs as it should in systems with strict requirements. In learning-based approaches, the traditional MAPE-K architecture is often present but self-adaptivity is improved by allowing the self-adaptive logic itself to change at runtime with incremental learning algorithms. Awareness-based approaches mix aspects of both architecture-based and learning-based approaches while offering improvements such as different types of knowledge and the ability to predict future events.

In the future, it would be important to evaluate and compare self-adaptive approaches more thoroughly, especially in real-world situations. We also left out some approaches, for example those that are architecture-based but still provide formal guarantees for adaptivity. However, based on our results on the benefits and problems of each approach, it seems that an optimal, general self-adaptive solution would combine aspects of all of the studied approaches. In particular, it could be fruitful to base the self-adaptive architecture on the psychological structure of self-awareness and -expression and implement both learning and control processes at the lower levels of this architecture.

References

1. Oreizy, P., et al.: An architecture-based approach to self-adaptive software. IEEE Intell. Syst. **14**(3), 54–62 (1999)
2. Lewis, P.R., et al.: A survey of self-awareness and its application in computing systems. In: 2011 Fifth IEEE Conference on Self-Adaptive and Self-Organizing Systems Workshops, pp. 102–107, October 2011

3. Chen, T., Bahsoon, R.: Self-adaptive and online qos modeling for cloud-based software services. IEEE Trans. Softw. Eng. **43**(5), 453–475 (2017)
4. Van Solingen, R., Basili, V., Caldiera, G., Rombach, H.D.: Goal question metric (gqm) approach. Encyclopedia of Software Engineering (2002)
5. Kephart, J.O., Chess, D.M.: The vision of autonomic computing. Computer **36**(1), 41–50 (2003)
6. Kramer, J., Magee, J.: Self-managed systems: an architectural challenge. In: Future of Software Engineering, pp. 259–268. IEEE Computer Society (2007)
7. Shevtsov, S., Berekmeri, M., Weyns, D., Maggio, M.: Control-theoretical software adaptation: a systematic literature review. IEEE Trans. Soft. Eng.**PP**(99), 1 (2017)
8. Shevtsov, S., Weyns, D., Maggio, M.: Handling new and changing requirements with guarantees in self-adaptive systems using simca. In: 2017 IEEE/ACM 12th International Symposium on Software Engineering for Adaptive and Self-Managing Systems (SEAMS), pp. 12–23, May 2017
9. Elkhodary, A., Esfahani, N., Malek, S.: Fusion: a framework for engineering self-tuning self-adaptive software systems. In: Proceedings of the Eighteenth ACM SIGSOFT International Symposium on Foundations of Software Engineering, pp. 7–16. ACM (2010)
10. Lewis, P.R.: Self-aware computing systems: from psychology to engineering. In: Design, Automation and Test in Europe Conference and Exhibition, pp. 1044–1049, March 2017
11. Faniyi, F., Lewis, P.R., Bahsoon, R., Yao, X.: Architecting self-aware software systems. In: 2014 IEEE/IFIP Conference on Software Architecture, pp. 91–94, April 2014
12. Neisser, U.: The roots of self-knowledge: perceiving self, it, and thou. Ann. N. Y. Acad. Sci. **818**(1), 19–33 (1997)

A Modular Pill Dispenser Supporting Therapies at Home

Paolo Buono, Fabio Cassano(✉), Alessandra Legretto, and Antonio Piccinno

Dipartimento di Informatica, Universitá di Bari Aldo Moro, Bari, Italy
{paolo.buono,fabio.cassano1,alessandra.legretto,
antonio.piccinno}@uniba.it

Abstract. Modern technologies support people's life in multiple contexts like the assistive one. The pervasiveness of the so-called "Smart Objects", related to the Internet of Things technologies, is boosting this in many ways. The support for old people to take the daily tablets through an automatic device is an example. This work presents the prototype of a modular pill dispenser customized by end users according to their specific therapy needs. The prototype is a physical and modular set of pillboxes each containing the pills to be assumed in a therapy. The presented scenario at a specific time, set by the user, one or more pillboxes blink to alert the patient that is pill time. If for a given time interval the patient do not take the pill a sound notification is activated and plays for a given duration. If still nothing happens then a notification is sent to the caregiver's smartphone. The behavior of the pill dispenser is defined by the end user and can be modified any time. One peculiarity of the pill dispenser is that the number of physical boxes are decided by the user and can change any time to best fit the specific therapy. The final goal of this work is to push not professional users, in particular older people, to take advantages of new technologies to improve their life.

Keywords: IoT · Pill dispenser · Elderly therapy

1 Introduction

The Internet of Things (IoT) technology allows devices to connect to the Internet and thus to send information or to be controlled remotely. One of the most explored field of research is how the pervasiveness of those devices can support people in their daily activities. Some solution help people manage and control the home automation [1]. Others use different techniques to push users to create collaborative rules shared solutions for conflicting needs) in the smart home environment [2]. The branch of IoT applied to the health, which is the domain of the work presented in this paper, is also gaining importance. Built-in sensors can be exploited to monitor the health status of a person [3]. Thanks to the continuous reduction of sensor size, the applications and the pervasiveness of the IoT devices is increasing. Indeed, sensors can be implanted into patients to keep track of the health parameters using a smartphone or a tablet [4].

© Springer Nature Switzerland AG 2018
C. Pautasso et al. (Eds.): ICWE 2018, LNCS 11153, pp. 71–82, 2018.
https://doi.org/10.1007/978-3-030-03056-8_7

Such technologies can also be used to support people in their daily activities like taking pills during a therapy. The idea to support people to self-administrate drugs with automatic devices to support pill-based therapies come from the 60's [5]. Nowadays, thanks to the modern communication advances, the availability of Internet connection in such devices, allows physicians to get closer to the user's needs and caregivers, family members and patients are now allowed to remotely monitor the pill therapy [6,7]. Some researchers are addressing the development of systems to control the user/patient health status, while others are investigating on the hardware and electronic to get better and smarter devices in terms of performance when they have to recognize the symptoms of illnesses [8,9].

In this work we have developed a prototype of a modular pill dispenser which can be configured, according to the user's needs, with multiple pill therapies and that belongs to the Web of Things research area [10]. Each pill is associated with a small smart box. The therapy, as well as the alerts are set using a mobile phone app.

The paper is structured as follows: Sect. 2 presents a short overview of some solutions available in the market. Section 3 describes the pill dispenser prototype, while in Sect. 4 a discussion of the results of a pilot test performed with real users is provided. Finally, in Sect. 5, the conclusions of the work is proposed.

2   Existing Proposals

The search for existing solutions was made according to three perspectives: *Integrated Systems*, which allow the users to set therapies using physical devices; *Management Apps*, which support therapies only on mobile devices, and *Consultation Apps* that connect to remote repositories to retrieve information about drugs. In the following we report two representatives for each perspective.

Integrated Systems. *Smart Pill Box*[1] is equipped with six, removable, boxes, having different colors and sizes. The pill box does not contain any electronic inside. It performs the simple function of a pocket box for the patient's pills. The system's logic is managed by the *Pill buddy application* on mobile devices. The application's Graphical User Interface (GUI) recalls the topology of the pill box, using the same colors of the pill box compartments in order to easily identify the different pills. The app is useful as a reminder but lacks the history of the pills taken. *Pillbox by Tricella*[2] is equipped with Bluetooth connectivity and sensors that detect if boxes are opened or closed. Pills are managed on a mobile device. By default, the pill box has seven different boxes, but it is possible to configure an unlimited but fixed number of pill slots per user. The app shows the history of pills taken in a monthly calendar and displays the next pill to take for a specific family member.

---

[1]   http://shop.vitility.com/en/smart-pill-box-zwart, last visited May 2018.
[2]   http://www.tricella.com/, last visited May 2018.

Management apps. *Medisafe*[3] is a medical care management and a pill reminder application that keeps track of blood pressure, glucose and other values, manage physicians and their appointments. Such data must be manually provided by the user. *MyTherapy*[4], is used as the pharmacological and care treatment. It sends the user one or more reminder and keep track of all the medication history.

Consultation apps. *Banca Dati Farmaci*[5], created by the Italian Medicines Agency (AIFA), is the official Italian database that provides summaries characteristics and up-to-date illustrative sheets of drugs sold in Italy. It provides the users the search for a medication, all its variants and package leaflets. An alternative is *Farmaci Lite*[6] that, in addition to the usual data, such as name, active ingredient and manufacturer, provides more detailed information for each drug. On purpose we reduced the scope to Italian databases because we interacted with Italian users. In case of an extension of the user group to other countries further drug databases can be considered.

From the study of the apps we selected the following functionalities that a pill dispenser must have.

- Therapy Management: the possibility to manage the pill therapy (e.g.: adding or removing a pill taking schedule) using the devices or through a mobile app;
- History: lists therapies done and/or the pills taken in the past;
- Caregiver: a person, different from the user, that can have access to the therapy management (including the possibility to edit the schedule and the drug to take);
- Reorder and Refill management: the management of the quantity of pills in the boxes and their refill;
- Drug leaflet: the basic information of pills;
- Drugs details: more details about the implication of drug consequences and uses;
- Drug database: access to publicly available drug databases;
- Report: reports about the pill therapy;
- Freeware: the app is free to use; and
- UI guidelines: standards for the user interface.

Table 1 briefly reports the features available in the selected systems; the tick indicates the presence of the specific functionality. According to the first four rows, the Consultation apps do not have interaction with the user, because such apps are intended just for gathering information and not for managing therapies. All the apps, but *Smart Pill Box* have a drug database. However, only *Farmaci Lite* provides more details; in addition, only the consultation apps provide the drug leaflet. Four out of six apps are freeware and four apps comply with User Interface guidelines. Only *Management apps* show the user a report about therapies.

---

[3] https://medisafe.com/, last visited May 2018.
[4] https://www.mytherapyapp.com/, last visited May 2018.
[5] https://farmaci.agenziafarmaco.gov.it/bancadatifarmaci/, last visited May 2018.
[6] http://www.ilprontuariofarmaceutico.it/, last visited May 2018.

Table 1. Comparison of mobile Apps and IoT solutions to support a user on the pill therapy.

Functionalities	Integrated systems		Management apps		Consultation apps	
	Smart pill box	Pillbox by Tricella	Medisafe	MyTherapy	Banca Dati Farmaci	Farmaci lite
Therapy manager	✓	✓	✓	✓	×	×
History	×	✓	✓	✓	×	×
Caregiver	×	✓	✓	✓	×	×
Reorder & refill management	×	✓	✓	✓	×	×
Drugs leaflet	×	×	×	×	✓	✓
Drugs details	×	×	×	×	×	✓
Drugs database	×	✓	✓	✓	✓	✓
Report	×	×	✓	✓	×	×
Freeware	✓	✓	×	✓	✓	×
UI guidelines	×	✓	✓	✓	×	✓

The study of the existing proposals led to some requirement that the modular pill dispenser should satisfy.

(R1) the need for a modular system. Most of the commercial solution provides a fixed number of *boxes* that are intended to support therapies that do not change over time and are based on the same amount of pills. Since therapies may change over time the modularity must be taken into account, both software and physical modularity.

(R2) feedback about the pills intake. The caregiver must be sure that the patient is taking the pills correctly. A few existing systems address alerts if the pill has not been taken or provides the user with the history of pill taking.

(R3) app customization. Any or very few systems address the dynamic customization of the therapy. If the drugs do not affect the properly patient, the doctor may chose to change it. Often this means deleting the current therapy and set a new one.

The literature proposes many solutions to the problems related to the pill assumption. Morales has performed a study to evaluate how the pillboxes can improve the therapy assumption [11]. In her work Morales demonstrated that it is clear that automatic and electronic pillboxes can improve the therapy assumption. Hayes proposes many solution to constantly monitor whether individuals take the right pill at the right time [12]. It involves constant data collection and elaboration in order to check that the patient has taken the right pill.

Recently, Mira, proposed a pillbox app to monitor elderly patients taking multiple medications [13]. According to their studies, even people with low or no experience are able to use and understand mobile application alerts and respond to them.

Fig. 1. The pill dispenser with two pillboxes (in pink) on top of it (Color figure online)

3   The Proposed Solution

According to the analysis of existing work, we have developed a modular pill dispenser to support people in taking pills therapy. This is an improvement of our previous work, where the user received an alert when the pill had to be taken [14]. The main differences are visible both, in the mobile application and in the modularity of the pill dispenser which also allows multiple therapies at once. The modularity of the device addresses the requirement (R1) by enabling the user to manage any number of needed pill types, according to the specific needs. (R2) requirement is met by adding the *history* to the mobile app and a "notification" feature in case the pill has not been taken at the right time. Also the requirement (R3) is addressed, through the use of the End-User Development approach, which is well known in the Human-Computer Interaction field, and which "encompasses methods, techniques, methodologies, situations, and socio-technical environments that allow end users to act as professionals in those domains in which they are not professionals" [15]. According to such approach the users can tailor the program to the real and current needs, thanks to the efforts of developers that give them more "power". As a matter of facts, more and more projects that allow users to create custom electronic solutions[7] are coming out. The natural evolution of this concept is the "meta-design approach", which empower the users to edit and manipulate the software artifact according to their needs [16].

The proposed solution has the following components: the physical pill dispenser, composed of a microcontroller, sensors, communication modules and a number of boxes that contain the pills. To the user, the pill dispenser appears as

---

[7] http://littlebits.cc/, last visited May 2018.

a set of boxes: the biggest one is the base box that hosts a set of pill boxes, which are the actual pill containers (see Fig. 1); the app allows the user to configure and manage the pill therapy; a server monitors the pill dispenser status and sends all changes performed through the app to the pill dispenser. The server can be connected to external services, such as hospitals, doctors, pharmacies, that can prepare new therapies on behalf of the caregiver. This case, however, is out of the scope of this paper.

One of the problems connecting physical devices to software systems is their initial setup. We introduced a "smart" procedure to allow the communication between the pill dispenser, the pill boxes and the smartphone. By default, the pill dispenser generates a Wi-Fi SSID that the user can use to connect the smartphbone to the pill dispenser. Using the configuration menu of the app, the user can setup the pill dispenser and connect to an existent Wi-Fi network. An alternative for the configuration might be to put such information into an internal SD card, but this means that the user must have some technical skills. After the pill dispenser is connected to the Internet it sends his MAC address and since then this will be the unique identifier for the pill dispenser. Once the connection is set and the device ID is stored into the server the app asks the caregiver to insert the name of the patient and a password. Then the caregiver associates a therapy and a pill dispenser to the user. This is all the needed steps to setup a new pill dispenser.

In order to correctly setup the therapy, each pill type must be associated to a pill box and must be specified the number of pills in the pill box (see Fig. 2).

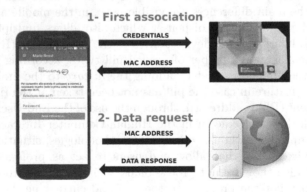

Fig. 2. Identification of a pill dispenser

The app shows a list of "free" boxes, according to the number of pill boxes available on the base box. The user must associate the pill box to the pills and then specify the timing of the LED, the delay before an acoustic sound will be triggered and the duration of the sound, if the default options do not satisfy the user's needs. Through the app, the user can create and review previous therapies and some statistics (see Fig. 3a). One or more drug can be associated

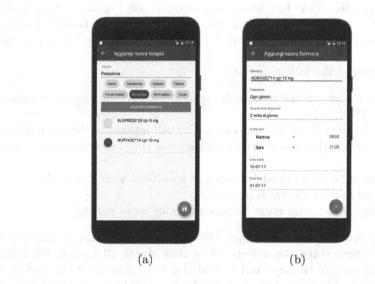

(a)   (b)

Fig. 3. Screenshots of the app representing the creation of a new therapy (a) and the addition of a new drug to the therapy (b)

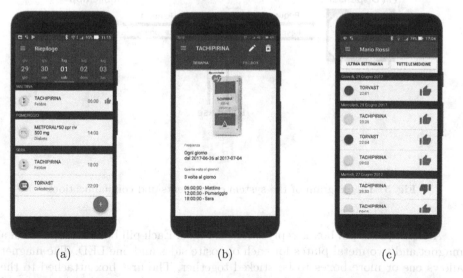

(a)   (b)   (c)

Fig. 4. Screenshots of the app revealing a few features: a calendar-like view to schedule user therapy (a); detailed information about the drug (b); quick view of pill taking (c)

to the therapy (see Fig. 3b). In order to support users to create an event of pill intake, a calendar-like view has been implemented (see Fig. 4a. Details about specific drugs the patient must assume are provided in a specific screen of the app (see Fig. 4b). A summary of "taken" and "lost" pills (see Fig. 4c) is also provided.

Therapies require the following data:

- The drug's name, according to a public agency, we used the "Agenzia Italiana Farmaco" (AIFA);
- Frequency: the time between two consecutive pill intakes of the same drug;
- Interval: for intakes that are alternate with a given time interval (e.g. alternate days);
- Days of week, if the drug must be taken at specific days of the week;
- Start and End date of the therapy; and
- Times per day, if the drug must be taken once or more per day.

In order to get information about the pills, the base box requests and upgrades the system status to a web server that stores all the needed information to setup the pill therapy and user alerts. The diagram of the system is described in Fig. 5. The prototype is made by two hardware parts: the set of pill boxes, which contain the pills, and the base box that contains the micro controller board, a display, a button and a buzzer. By default, each box can contains only one pill type.

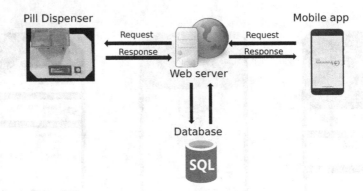

Fig. 5. The diagram of the system components and communications

An example of pill box is represented in Fig. 6. Each pill box is composed of a magnet and two metal plates for each opposite sides and one LED. The magnet allows one or more boxes to be sticked together. The first box attached to the system is connected directly with the base box. The two metal plates, positioned on the same sides of the magnets, power the smart box. The top of the block can be opened to allow the user/patient to put or take one or more pills. A LED, positioned on one side, indicates that an interaction with the box is required.

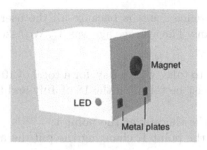

Fig. 6. The 3D model of a pill box

The LED turns "ON" when is pill time; it turns "OFF" when the user takes the pill. In order to tell the pill box that the pill has been taken, the user presses the button. The communication between each pill box and the base is done through an ESP8266-01 programmable module. This component not only allows the box to be wirelessly connected to the pill dispenser, but also to uniquely identify each box. Indeed, every box ID must be recognized by the system in order to "see" that a new pill box exists. The logic of the base box is delegated to an Arduino board. We were comfortable with an Arduino Mega board but with the right optimizations also an Arduino Uno works. Other parts like a buzzer, a button, a display and LEDs are used to interact with the user. The system connects to a wireless network (using the 802.11 b/g/n protocol) with or without encryption. The hardware parts works as a middleware between the software and the pill boxes [17]. When is pill time, the related LED on the base box turns on. If the user does not take the pill, after the amount of time specified by the user, the buzzer starts vibrating, trying to attract the user/patient's attention. The user that takes the pill pushes the button on the base box in order to ask the system to stop other alerts scheduled for the specific pill (see Fig. 1).

4   Discussions

We have proposed a modular pill dispenser to support people that must follow pill-based therapy. The system is composed of three main components: a web server that stores the information about the therapies and send alerts when needed; the mobile application that manages therapies and configure the pill dispenser (including each pillbox); the pill dispenser that is composed of a set of pill boxes and the base box that contains the logic managing sensors and actuators for the interaction with the user. The customization of the pill therapy and the behaviour of the system (through a mobile app) allows the user to tailor the system to the own need and therapy. Moreover, we introduced the possibility to physically change the number of pill boxes that contain the pills of the therapy. This saves space and do not have empty boxes or pills outside the pill dispenser.

In order to check the validity of the approach we performed a formative evaluation with a pilot set of Italian users. The reason why we have decided to use only Italian reference drugs is because all the users who performed the usability test were italians. The average age was 37. We asked 5 people to perform the following 7 tasks:

1. Add the Zimox drug to take twice a day, for a total of 10 days, after the meals;
2. Show which drugs must be taken on the 18 of July and then show the current date;
3. Show the details of the therapy at the point 1;
4. Edit the therapy at the point 1, changing the pill therapy from two times to three times per day;
5. Show the informative sheet of the Zimox drug;
6. Add a family member as caregiver; and
7. Show which drugs have been taken correctly on the 17th of July.

Table 2. The table with the times and the completing rate for each task. S = Success, P = Partial success, F = Failure

	Task 1		Task 2		Task 3		Task 4		Task 5		Task 6		Task 7	
User 1	S	2:30	P	0:50	S	0:50	S	0:32	S	0:26	F	4:30	S	1:32
User 2	S	1:44	P	0:10	S	0:25	S	0:17	S	0:25	F	1:44	S	2:03
User 3	S	2:04	P	0:16	S	0:32	S	0:39	S	0:18	F	2:09	S	2:14
User 4	S	3:20	P	0:21	S	0:16	S	0:35	S	0:10	S	0:57	S	3:35
User 5	S	2:26	P	0:18	S	0:16	S	0:38	S	0:16	S	1:33	S	1:58
Average		2:25		0:23		0:28		0:32		0:19		2:23		2:17

In Table 2 the times taken to complete the tasks are reported. For each user (row), the completing result and the relative time spent to complete it has been shown. The outcome for each task can be "Success" (S) if the user has reached the end of the task; "Partial Success" (P) if the user has partially completed the task; "Failure" (F) if the user has not completed at all the task. The most difficult task was the 6, which required to add a new person in the mobile application in order to set the role of caregiver. Three users out of five failed it due to the difficulty to find the correct menu entry to complete the task. The average success rate of the usability test is about the 84%. Despite this is a really small number and tasks are not reported in detail, the formative evaluation revealed that the most common tasks were easy to reach. The most problematic tasks are those related to the schedule. If they are performed by a trained person this is an acceptable compromise; we are thinking of ways to overcome it.

5   Conclusions

The proposed system contains several strengths but also presents some weaknesses. Currently, the pill dispenser trusts the patient that claim to have taken the pill by pressing a button. A more sophisticated way to be sure the patient actually takes the pill is needed, but this is not easy to achieve, since it would need also more sophisticated equipment at the patient's house. A possible improvement can be to add a sensor that notifies the app when the box has been opened, but it does not completely solve the problem. Currently the pill dispenser is powered by a common phone charger that provides a current of 5 V at 1 A and the base box can easily connect 20 pill boxes. If more pill boxes are needed the pill dispenser could be provided with a specific power supply that would provide more power. Even though the pill dispenser can be easily powered by a portable power bank, it is limited by the wireless connectivity: once the signal is lost, it would not be able to communicate with the server (and the mobile app consequently) anymore. If the user is away from home, and the pill is not taken according to the therapy, the alerting procedure (as described in the Sect. 3) starts. Finally, the current implementation of the system considers just one pill dispenser per user. In the future we plan to address more users per pill dispenser and to improve the entire system to be more fault tolerant in different conditions. Moreover, the mobile app might check the user's position (through the internal GPS sensor) and consequently send an alert if he/she is moving away when the pill therapy time is approaching.

Acknowledgments. This work was partially supported by the EDOC@WORK Project. We are grateful to Nicola Di Stefano and Michele Ruta for developing to the first version of the prototype.

References

1. Kelly, S.D.T., Suryadevara, N.K., Mukhopadhyay, S.C.: Towards the implementation of IoT for environmental condition monitoring in homes. IEEE Sens. J. **13**(10), 3846–3853 (2013)
2. Caivano, D., Cassano, F., Fogli, D., Lanzilotti, R., Piccinno, A.: We@Home: a gamified application for collaboratively managing a smart home. In: De Paz, J.F., Julián, V., Villarrubia, G., Marreiros, G., Novais, P. (eds.) ISAmI 2017. AISC, vol. 615, pp. 79–86. Springer, Cham (2017). https://doi.org/10.1007/978-3-319-61118-1_11
3. Istepanian, R.S.H., Sungoor, A., Faisal, A., Philip, N.: Internet of m-health things'm-iot' (2011)
4. Park, S.W., Ko, H.J., Park, Y.I., Yoo, S.J., Han, Y.C.: Controller, and patch type automated external defibrillator for controlling defibrillation using the same. US Patent 9,757,580, 12 September 2017
5. Moulding, T.: Proposal for a time-recording pill dispenser as a method for studying and supervising the self-administration of drugs. Am. Rev. Respir. Dis. **85**(5), 754–757 (1962)
6. Morak, J., Schwarz, M., Hayn, D., Schreier, G.: Feasibility of mhealth and near field communication technology based medication adherence monitoring. In: 2012 Annual International Conference of the IEEE Engineering in Medicine and Biology Society (EMBC), pp. 272–275. IEEE (2012)

7. Caivano, D., Fogli, D., Lanzilotti, R., Piccinno, A., Cassano, F.: Supporting end users to control their smart home: design implications from a literature review and an empirical investigation. J. Syst. Softw. **144**, 295–313 (2018)
8. Dimauro, G., Caivano, D., Girardi, F., Ciccone, M.M.: The patient centered electronic multimedia health fascicle-EMHF. In: 2014 IEEE Workshop on Biometric Measurements and Systems for Security and Medical Applications (BIOMS) Proceedings, pp. 61–66. IEEE (2014)
9. Yeole, A.S., Kalbande, D.R.: Use of internet of things (IoT) in healthcare: a survey. In: Proceedings of the ACM Symposium on Women in Research 2016, pp. 71–76. ACM (2016)
10. Guinard, D., Trifa, V., Mattern, F., Wilde, E.: From the internet of things to the web of things: resource-oriented architecture and best practices. In: Uckelmann, D., Harrison, M., Michahelles, F. (eds.) Architecting the Internet of Things, pp. 97–129. Springer, Heidelberg (2011). https://doi.org/10.1007/978-3-642-19157-2_5
11. Morales, M.T.S.V.: Study on the use of a smart pillbox to improve treatment compliance. Aten. primaria **41**(4), 185–191 (2009)
12. Hayes, T.L., Hunt, J.M., Adami, A., Kaye, J.A.: An electronic pillbox for continuous monitoring of medication adherence. In: 28th Annual International Conference of the IEEE Engineering in Medicine and Biology Society, EMBS 2006, pp. 6400–6403. IEEE (2006)
13. Mira, J.J., et al.: A spanish pillbox app for elderly patients taking multiple medications randomized controlled trial. J. Med. Internet Res. **16**(4) (2014)
14. Buono, P., Cassano, F., Legretto, A., Piccinno, A.: A homemade pill dispenser prototype supporting elderly. In: Garrigós, I., Wimmer, M. (eds.) ICWE 2017. LNCS, vol. 10544, pp. 120–124. Springer, Cham (2018). https://doi.org/10.1007/978-3-319-74433-9_10
15. Fischer, G., Fogli, D., Piccinno, A.: Revisiting and broadening the meta-design framework for end-user development. In: Paternò, F., Wulf, V. (eds.) New Perspectives in End-User Development, pp. 61–97. Springer, Cham (2017). https://doi.org/10.1007/978-3-319-60291-2_4
16. Costabile, M.F., Fogli, D., Mussio, P., Piccinno, A.: A meta-design approach to end-user development. In: IEEE Symposium on Visual Languages and Human-Centric Computing (VL/HCC), vol. 2005, pp. 308–310. IEEE Computer Society (2005)
17. Bernstein, P.A.: Middleware: a model for distributed system services. Commun. ACM **39**(2), 86–98 (1996)

Towards a Runtime Verification Approach for Internet of Things Systems

Maurizio Leotta(✉), Davide Ancona, Luca Franceschini, Dario Olianas,
Marina Ribaudo, and Filippo Ricca

Dipartimento di Informatica, Bioingegneria, Robotica e Ingegneria dei Sistemi
(DIBRIS), Università di Genova, Genoa, Italy
maurizio.leotta@unige.it

Abstract. Internet of Things systems are evolving at a rapid pace and
their impact on our society grows every day. In this context developing
IoT systems that are reliable and compliant with the requirements is
of paramount importance. Unfortunately, few proposals for assuring the
quality of these complex and often safety-critical systems are present in
the literature. To this aim, runtime verification can be a valuable support
to tackle such a complex task and to complement other software verification techniques based on static analysis and testing. This paper is a first
step towards the application of runtime verification to IoT systems. In
particular, we describe our approach based on a Prolog monitor, the definition of a formal specification (using trace expressions) describing the
expected behaviour of the system, and the definition of appropriate input
scenarios. Furthermore, we describe its application and preliminary evaluation using a simplified mobile health IoT system for the management
of diabetic patients composed by sensors, actuators, Node-RED logic on
the cloud, and smartphones.

1 Introduction

Internet of Things (IoT) systems are composed by interconnected physical
devices that share data and often include a central remote control server on the
cloud. The spread of such systems has had a significant impact on all aspects
of the society and in a few years it has changed the life of billions of people.
Indeed, as the IoT technology continues to mature, more and more novel IoT
systems will emerge in different contexts. For example, to mention a few: smart
city systems allow to intelligently provide the right level of lighting depending on
human activities, time of day, season, and weather conditions hence optimizing
the community energy usage relying on various kinds of interconnected sensors;
mobile health systems are able to determine the optimal patient medicament
doses by analysing data provided by physiological sensors [3].

Ensuring that IoT systems are secure, reliable, and compliant with the
requirements is of paramount importance. Indeed, often such kind of systems

© Springer Nature Switzerland AG 2018
C. Pautasso et al. (Eds.): ICWE 2018, LNCS 11153, pp. 83–96, 2018.
https://doi.org/10.1007/978-3-030-03056-8_8

are safety-critical (e.g., IoT systems used for monitoring patients, infrastructures, traffic, pollution) and given the wide set of disparate hardware and software technologies used to build them and the added complexity that comes with Big Data, this is not an easy task.

In this paper, we propose an approach based on *Runtime Verification* that can be used for assuring the quality of IoT systems. Runtime verification is a software analysis approach in which a running system is observed by monitoring relevant events and their associated information to verify against a given (formal) specification of the expected behaviour. When efficiently implemented, the verification process can be executed (a) before the deployment of the system, for detecting bugs during development and maintenance activities, as well as, (b) after the deployment, in order to provide an additional level of protection against unforeseen events.

We will focus on detecting bugs during the development and maintenance of *Node-RED* based IoT systems. Node-RED[1] is a platform providing a flow-based visual programming language built on Node.js which has been expressly designed for wiring together hardware devices, APIs and online services. Complex behaviours can be included in the flows by using specific JavaScript nodes that can be easily created and combined in a rich browser-based flow editor [7].

This paper is organized as follows: Sect. 2 briefly presents a realistic scenario based on a mobile health IoT system already used in our previous complementary proposal concerning acceptance testing of IoT systems [13,15]. Section 3 describes our proposal for runtime verification of IoT systems. Section 4 reports on the empirical study evaluating our approach and the obtained results. Section 5 discusses the approach and the possible future research directions. Finally, Sect. 6 concludes the paper.

Related Works. To the best of our knowledge, Software Quality Assurance (SQA) of IoT systems has been scarcely investigated. Focusing on runtime verification there are no well-documented approaches except for the recent proposal of Incki et al. [9] that however is very different from ours since it adopts a different formalism for specifying the behaviour and focuses on monitoring network protocols. They used Event Calculus to specify and monitor network message exchanges in the context of Constrained Application Protocol-based IoT systems.

Also IoT software testing has been mostly overlooked so far, both by research and industry [17]. Concerning functional testing of IoT systems, excluded our recent proposal [13,15], we found only very general non-scientific papers[2] and several proposals for testing bioinformatics software (e.g., [5]). Unfortunately, these works cannot be directly used for assuring the quality of IoT systems, since they do not describe a specific testing operational procedure that a tester can follow.

---

[1] https://nodered.org/.

[2] e.g., https://devops.com/functional-testing-iot/.

2   Case Study

We have chosen a diabetes mobile health IoT system as realistic case study for two reasons. First, SQA of mobile health IoT systems is incredibly difficult, second, many IoT systems for patients management including smartphones apps are now available to assist them in making real time decisions [11].

DiaMH is a Diabetes Mobile Health IoT system that: (1) monitors the patient's glucose level, (2) sends alerts to the patient and the doctor when the glucose level trend is out of a pre-specified target range, and (3) regulates insulin dosing. DiaMH consists of the following components: a wearable glucose sensor, a wearable insulin pump, a patient's smartphone, a doctor's smartphone and a cloud-based healthcare system. Glucose sensor and insulin pump are devices (respectively, the sensor and the actuator) connected to the patient's smartphone (using e.g., Bluetooth LE[3]) that is used as a "bridge" between them and the cloud-based healthcare system. Moreover, the smartphone is used by the patient to visualize the glucose tendency and by the doctor to visualize alarms of the patients. Smartphones can access the internet by using high speed connections (e.g., UMTS[4] or LTE[5]). The cloud-based healthcare system is the core of DiaMH and is able to process big data and turn it into valuable information (alerts and novel doses of insulin).

In this scenario a thorough SQA process is required, since DiaMH is a complex, real-time, and safety-critical IoT system.

Specification of the Required Behaviour. The goal of our proposal is to verify an IoT system, thus a precise description of its expected behaviour is required. A possible choice is to formalize it in terms of a UML State Machine (SM) to guide the SQA activities, as suggested in various model-based testing techniques, where state-based models describing systems behaviours are used, for instance, for code generation and test cases derivation [18].

Figure 1 formalizes the expected behaviour of the core part of DiaMH, i.e., the logic that recognizes the status of the patient and decides when providing an insulin dose, manages the glucose sensor and the insulin pump, and allows to show the information on the smartphones. In our simplified case study, we consider the healthcare cloud system as a deterministic system with a precise and repeatable behaviour while real systems could rely on complex algorithms based, for instance, on machine learning. Black transitions lead to DiaMH state updates while the red ones are used for managing the incoming data from the glucose sensor. Notice that each transition in the SM is composed of *trigger [guard]/actions*. The *trigger* is an optional event which activates the transition it is associated with (e.g., startApp()), the *guard* is a boolean expression which must be true to enable the associated transition (e.g., countValues(READ, THRESHOLD) $\geq$ 4), and the *actions* are responses to the trigger activating the associated transition (e.g., READ[i++] = VAL).

---

[3] https://en.wikipedia.org/wiki/Bluetooth_Low_Energy.
[4] https://en.wikipedia.org/wiki/UMTS_(telecommunication).
[5] https://en.wikipedia.org/wiki/LTE_(telecommunication).

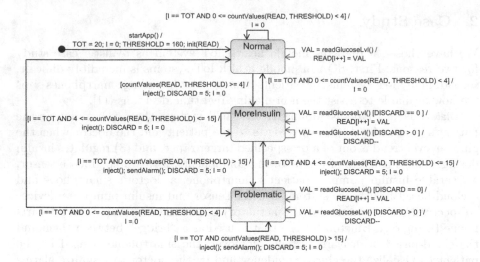

Fig. 1. DiaMH core required behaviour

In the SM of Fig. 1, there are three states representing the possible patient's condition: *Normal*, *MoreInsulin*, and *Problematic*. When the DiaMH is bootstrapped (startApp()), the initial state is set to *Normal* and the glucose threshold (THRESHOLD) discriminating good values from bad ones is set to 160 mg/dl. In the following, we assume to set the DiaMH sampling rate to 1 Hz. Thus, each second, the glucose level is read by the sensor (readGlucoseLvl() in the red transitions) and stored in a 20 elements circular buffer (READ). If there are no more than 3 values in the buffer above the pre-set threshold the patient is considered stable and remains in the *Normal* state. Otherwise, if 4 or more values are above the threshold, a *MoreInsulin* pattern is detected. In this case, a new insulin dose is injected by the pump (inject()) and the system switches to *MoreInsulin* state, while the next 5 readings are discarded, since the injected insulin dose will need time to take effect, which we have hypothetically estimated in 5 time units (i.e., 5 s when the sampling rate is 1 Hz). From this state, if the next 20 readings are between 4 and 15 values above the threshold, the patient is kept in a *MoreInsulin* state, a new insulin dose is injected and the process is repeated. Otherwise, if the dangerous values are no more than 3, the patient is considered stabilized and the system goes back to the *Normal* state. Finally, in case we have more than 15 values above the threshold, a *Problematic* pattern is detected and the system moves accordingly, just after injecting a new insulin dose and notifying the problem by sending an alarm to the patient's and the doctor's smartphones (sendAlarm()). Again, from the *Problematic* state, the next 5 readings are discarded; then, after 20 further readings, the system can stay in the same state, injecting a new dose and sending a new alarm, can move back to *MoreInsulin* after an injection, or can even move to *Normal*.

3   Runtime Verification for IoT Systems: A Proposal

Performing a thorough verification process for an IoT system like DiaMH is a complex task. Indeed, significant challenges have to be faced since IoT systems include several components (applications and devices containing logics) working together and with high risk of individual fail. Moreover, further problems could derive by the integration of the components. Indeed, it is well-known that an "imperfect" integration can introduce a myriad of subtle faults.

In general for an IoT system including software and hardware devices, SQA techniques should be conducted at two different levels:

- *virtualized version of the IoT system*, where real hardware devices are not employed. In their place, virtual devices (e.g., a mock glucose sensor) have to be implemented and used for stimulating the system under test. At this level the goal is verifying only the software developed, i.e., in the case of DiaMH the apps (for patients and doctors) running on the smartphones and the healthcare system running in the cloud. Thus, possible unwanted behaviours of the IoT system due to hardware or network problems cannot be detected in this setting.
- *real IoT system* complete of hardware devices (i.e., in the case of DiaMH glucose sensor and insulin pump). In this case the goal is verifying the system in real conditions, i.e., under real world scenarios like communication of the application with hardware, network, and other applications.

When dealing with safety critical IoT systems, both levels should be considered and the virtualized system could favour earlier implementation problems detection, but also revealing more faults (timings of sensors and actuators can be made shorter and thus a huge quantity of scenarios can be verified in a short time). In this work, we focus on verifying virtualized IoT systems for the following reasons: it is the first step that a SQA team has to face and it can be conducted without employing real sensors and actuators that can be complex to use/set and more expensive.

Note that, beyond Runtime Verification, other two verification techniques could be applied in the case of a IoT system like DiaMH: Software Testing (e.g., acceptance testing for IoT systems [13,15] relying on E2E testing tools [14]) and Formal Verification (e.g., model checking [6]).

Figure 2 reports an overview of the elements involved in our approach: the Prolog Monitor, the Trace Expression (derived from the Behaviour Specification) provided as input to the Monitor, and the Input Scenarios sent to the IoT system. Trace Expression and Input Scenarios change for each monitored IoT system while the Prolog Monitor is general purpose and can be used for monitoring any IoT system. The monitor intercepts the monitored events by means of probes (P) intercepting events (e.g., messages) exchanged between the system components. Moreover, in the case of DiaMH we have: the mocks for glucose sensor and insulin pump, the smartphones, and the healthcare cloud system. Although these components are specific of our case study we claim that any

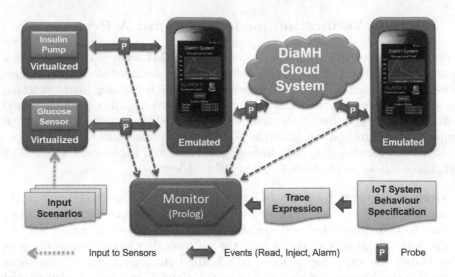

Fig. 2. Components involved in our approach instantiated for the DiaMH case study

IoT system will probably include at least a set of sensors/actuators and some distributed logic.

DiaMH virtualization. Focusing on our case study, the simulation of the glucose sensor and of the insulin pump is performed via *mocks*. In this way, it is possible to provide the DiaMH system with selected input patterns and to evaluate its capability in sending commands to the devices (e.g., perform an insulin injection). We have chosen to implement the mocks simulating the glucose sensor and the insulin pump using Node-RED, a platform providing a flow-based visual programming language built on Node.js which has been expressly designed for wiring together hardware devices, APIs and online services. Complex behaviours can be included in the flows by using specific JavaScript nodes that can be easily created and combined in a rich browser-based flow editor [7]. Also the healthcare cloud system has been implemented in Node-RED according to the UML state machine shown in Fig. 1. Instead, the emulation of the smartphones (and thus of the DiaMH UI) is based on Android Emulator[6]. Then, the logic managing the communication between the various components and the healthcare system running in the cloud has been implemented relying on Node-RED. We wired the mock devices, together with the apps running on the emulated smartphones and with the healthcare cloud system using the TCP protocol.

3.1   Monitor Implementation

Runtime Verification is a software analysis technique that aims at verifying whether a given property holds for a single run of the program under observation, rather than for any possible execution. The program is observed by a

---

[6] https://developer.android.com/studio/run/emulator.html.

monitor, all relevant events are recorded and the resulting trace is matched against the formal specification.

The monitor has been implemented as an HTTP server able to serve the following two kinds of requests: *check-event* and *reset*.

Check-event is a POST request whose associated data must be a JSON object representing the specific event currently perceived and under monitoring; for instance, { "event":"sensor", "value":v} corresponds to a read by the glucose sensor of value v. Upon a *check-event* request, the monitor checks whether the received event is legal in the current state and responds with a corresponding JSON object { "error":b}, where b is a boolean value which is false if and only if the received event is legal; in this case, the monitor performs also a corresponding transition and updates its current state. For simplicity, the server response contains the minimum information required to conduct the experiments reported in Sect. 4, but a more advanced implementation of the monitor should provide a better support for error reporting.

Reset is a GET request that allows the monitor to reset its state into the initial one; this is useful for running automatically the analysis performed in Sect. 4 on different input scenarios.

On the client side, we have implemented a new type of Node-RED node (the Probes in Fig. 2) that takes in input a JavaScript object representing an event, stringifies it in JSON, sends a *check-event* request to the monitor with the corresponding JSON object, and outputs the JavaScript object returned by the server as response.

The implementation of the monitor does not depend on the specification of the behaviour that has to be verified; such a specification must be provided separately, and fully drives the behaviour of the monitor by determining its initial state, and all possible valid state transitions in reaction of the received events. The monitor itself is implemented in SWI-Prolog[7] (around 160 SLOC). Additional details on how we implemented the SWI-Prolog monitor can be found in our previous work [2].

Prolog has been a natural choice as target language to support the implementation of a specification language built on top of the formalism of trace expressions; the rules of the labelled transition system defining the operational semantics of trace expressions can be directly expressed in Prolog; furthermore, the native support for cyclic terms offered by Prolog significantly simplifies the implementation of recursive trace expressions, an essential feature for runtime verification of real systems. Last, but not least, backtracking and integration with constraint logic programming are interesting additional features that can be exploited for using specifications not only for runtime verification, but also for automatically generate test cases able to improve test coverage.

---

[7] http://www.swi-prolog.org.

3.2   Trace Expressions Definition

Trace expressions [1] are a formalism explicitly devised for runtime verification which is strictly more expressive than LTL_3 [1], a temporal logic commonly used in the runtime verification context. The language features a large set of operators, including concatenation ($\tau_1 \cdot \tau_2$), union ($\tau_1 \vee \tau_2$), intersection ($\tau_1 \wedge \tau_2$) and shuffle (a.k.a. interleaving, $\tau_1 | \tau_2$); traces starting with events θ are denoted as $\theta : \tau$, while ϵ corresponds to the empty trace, i.e., no more events are expected. These basic operators can be combined to build higher-level ones, like if-then-else conditionals. Furthermore, (scoped) variables can be introduced in order to make the specification parametric w.r.t. some value that will only be known at runtime ($\{let\ x; \tau\}$). Finally, it is useful to have generic trace expressions that are parameterized: they are denoted as $\tau\langle x\rangle$.

From Behaviour Specifications to Trace Expressions. Starting from the system behaviour properly formalized by means of a SM (see Fig. 1) our approach requires to define an equivalent trace expression. This task can be manually performed by an expert knowing both the SM and the trace expression formalisms. However, we believe that providing a tool for automating this step could favour the adoption of our approach among IoT practitioners (see Sect. 5). Moreover, note that for safety-critical IoT systems we can assume such SM-based behaviour specifications available from the early stages of design and thus even before starting the actual system development phase.

Figure 3 reports the trace expression of the DiaMH case study. The event $read(L, L', n)$ matches an input from the glucose sensor with the following constraints: L is the list of the previous values, L' is L plus the new value (if there were more than 20, the oldest one is removed), and finally there must be at least n values over the threshold. After each insulin injection (*inject*) the following 5 readings are discarded (*Discard$_5$*). Additionally, $read20(L, L', n)$ expects the resulting list L' to have length 20. Finally, [] denotes the empty list.

The target language used for making the specifications executable is Prolog; hence, the formal specification of the DiaMH case study is translated into a sequence of Prolog clauses for a total of 45 SLOC, which is then fed into the monitor.

3.3   Input Scenarios Definition

An Input scenario is a sequence of input values, constrained by the SM and conditions, that allows to reach a specific state following a predetermined path. Input scenarios must be carefully chosen with the goal of maximizing the coverage of the possible behaviours of the IoT system. By analysing the SM describing the required behaviour of the system this corresponds to cover as much as possible paths among states. More specifically, for defining the paths and thus the corresponding input scenarios that lead to execute such paths, several coverage criteria could be considered (e.g., node, transition and path coverage) [4]. However, for the preliminary evaluation of our approach on the DiaMH case study, we believe sufficient to consider a limited set of input scenarios since the approach could be evaluated as even more interesting if it is able to provide good results in this setting. Thus, considering black transitions, we defined at least an input scenario that leads the system in each possible state in SM; if a state can be reached through different transitions, we chose an input scenario that reaches this state for each incoming transition. Moreover, if a state can be reached by a transition but following different combinations of states, then we chose an input scenario for each combination. Finally, for each self-loop in SM, we chose an input scenario that, before ending, follows such loop. To reduce the number of paths, we have chosen to not traverse the same transition in a single path twice (feasible in the DiaMH case study). Having this in mind we have defined ten paths covering all nodes, all transitions and an interesting subset of the possible paths (see Table 1). For instantiating the paths, actual input values are required. Note that several input scenarios can be created for each path. The careful choice of the sequence of values composing an input scenario can drastically change the effectiveness of our approach in detecting problems in the IoT system as we will discuss in Sect. 5. Concerning the DiaMH case study we created only an input scenario for each path by combining values from log files containing realistic glucose patterns (i.e., Normal, MoreInsulin, Problematic).

$$
\begin{aligned}
Main &= Normal\langle[]\rangle \\
Normal\langle L\rangle &= \{let\ L';\ if\ read(L, L', 4)\ then\ inject : Discard_5 \cdot More\langle[]\rangle \\
&\quad else\ read(L, L', 0) : Normal\langle L'\rangle\} \\
More\langle L\rangle &= \{let\ L';\ if\ read20(L, L', 16)\ then\ alarm : inject : Discard_5 \cdot Problem\langle[]\rangle \\
&\quad else\ if\ read20(L, L', 4)\ then\ inject : Discard_5 \cdot More\langle[]\rangle \\
&\quad else\ if\ read20(L, L', 0)\ then\ Normal\langle L'\rangle \\
&\quad else\ read(L, L', 0) : More\langle L'\rangle\} \\
Problem\langle L\rangle &= \{let\ L';\ if\ read20(L, L', 16)\ then\ alarm : inject : Discard_5 \cdot Problem\langle[]\rangle \\
&\quad else\ if\ read20(L, L', 4)\ then\ inject : Discard_5 \cdot More\langle[]\rangle \\
&\quad else\ if\ read20(L, L', 0)\ then\ Normal\langle L'\rangle \\
&\quad else\ read(L, L', 0) : Problem\langle L'\rangle\} \\
Discard_{i>0} &= ignore : Discard_{i-1} \qquad Discard_0 = \epsilon
\end{aligned}
$$

Fig. 3. Trace expression for DiaMH

4 Preliminary Empirical Evaluation

The *goal* of our preliminary empirical evaluation is to investigate the effectiveness of the proposed runtime verification based approach. Therefore we defined the following research question:

What is the effectiveness of our approach in detecting bugs in an IoT system?

To answer the research question we used mutation analysis and the metrics used is the percentage of killed mutants out of the total.

Mutation Analysis. Mutation analysis is a technique traditionally used in the context of testing for evaluating the quality of the produced test scripts [16]. The idea is to exercise them against slight variations of the original code simulating typical errors a developer could introduce during development and maintenance activities. These variations, named mutants, can be used to identify the weaknesses in the verification artefacts by determining the parts of a software that are badly or never checked [12]. In our case the verification artefacts are the runtime monitor and its parameters: the trace expression and the input scenarios. The mutation phase is usually driven by mutation operators which affect small portions of code, exploiting some typical programming mistakes, like a change in a logical operator (e.g., AND instead of OR), a boolean substitution (e.g., from true to false), or a conditional removal (e.g., an IF condition statement is set to true). The idea is the following: monitoring each mutant to verify its correctness. The runtime monitor is effective w.r.t. a mutant if it kills the mutant, i.e., if it can detect the change in the system behaviour introduced by the mutant. Otherwise, if nothing is detected, the mutant survives and a weakness in the verification artefacts (i.e., the monitor, the trace expression, and the input scenarios) is found. The goal is to kill the highest number of generated mutants; *a measure to evaluate the overall verification artefact quality is given by the percentage of mutants killed over the total* (i.e., the higher the better).

Experimental Procedure. Starting from the implementation of DiaMH we proceeded as follows. We selected Stryker (v 0.10.3) as mutation tool, since it is a Javascript mutator, then suited for systems developed using Node-RED (v 0.17.5). Stryker supports various mutant operators, and is largely configurable to properly generate and store the mutated code. It offers mutation operators for unary, binary, logical and update instructions, boolean substitutions, conditional removals, arrays declarations, and block statements removals.

The procedure we adopted for answering the research question is the following:

- *Mutating Javascript functions*: from the original Node-RED flows implementing the core of DiaMH, by using an automated script, we selected all the function nodes embodying Javascript code and we applied Stryker on them using all the supported mutators, resulting in 29 mutants. We implemented a script that automatically and separately injects each mutated Javascript node into the original Node-RED flows, resulting in 29 mutated versions of DiaMH.
- *Mutating switch nodes*: we translated the logic embedded in the switch nodes used in the Node-RED flows in Javascript if then else statements. We mutated them with Stryker resulting in 27 mutants and applied such mutation to the original Node-RED flow, resulting in 27 mutated versions of DiaMH.
- *Evaluation*: finally, each mutated version of DiaMH (56 overall) has been executed with the ten defined input scenarios and monitored by the Prolog monitor (560 monitored executions overall), noting down: (i) whether the mutant was killed, and if so, during the execution of which input scenario and (ii) the results of a detailed analysis to explain why each mutant was killed or not.

Results. Table 1 summarizes the number of mutants killed by each input scenario. As we can see, the number of mutants killed is 44 out of 56 since 12 outlived.

Table 1. Mutants detected by our approach using the ten input scenarios.

Input Scenario	Transitions	Mutants Killed
from_starting_the_app_(S)_to_Normal	1	0
from_S_to_MoreInsulin	2	19
from_S_to_Problematic	3	41
from_S_to_MoreInsulin_and_back_to_Normal	3	39
from_S_to_Problematic_and_directly_to_Normal	4	43
from_S_to_Problematic_and_back_to_MoreInsulin	4	43
from_S_to_Problematic_and_back_to_Normal_(via_MoreInsulin)	5	44
from_S_to_self-loop_to_Normal	2	4
from_S_to_self-loop_to_MoreInsulin	3	38
from_S_to_self-loop_to_Problematic	4	42
Total Mutants killed - (a)		**44**
Total number of Mutants		**56**
Total number of Mutants (excluding equivalent) - (b)		**48**
Mutants detection rate - (a/b)		**92%**

We have analysed each outliving mutant from a code perspective and 8 out of 12 were identified as having an exactly equivalent behaviour with respect to the original system [8,10]. Hence there could not exist a black-box verification approach to detect them (we found them with code inspection). A simplified example is a mutation that changes if (I==20) I=0; to if(I>= 20)I = 0; in a Node-RED function; since the condition is evaluated for each single increment of I, the behaviour of the mutant is equivalent to the original code. Thus, only 4 mutants were considered as real survivors. From our analysis, we discovered that this is due to weaknesses in the provided input, since the input scenarios are not complete enough to cover all possible conditions and properly exercise the boundaries of the original system. Mutations often affect operators used in conditions. If the mutation drastically changes the behaviour (e.g., > in <) the mutant can be easily detected but, if the change is just a little variation of the system behaviour (e.g., > in >= 160), the input scenario must be carefully chosen in order to detect the inconsistency. To test our conjecture, we manually created an ad-hoc input scenario for each of the 4 mutants survived. In this way, all the mutants were identified. As expected, from the results it emerges that longer input scenarios triggering several states changes in the monitored IoT system allow to detect a higher number of bugs. In the next section, we will discuss the obtained results to highlight the strengths and the weakness of the proposed approach and possible future research directions for making it applicable to real complex IoT systems.

5   Strengths/Weakness of the Approach and Future Work

Employing runtime verification for assuring the quality of IoT systems proved to be worth of investigation. Indeed, it was able to detect a relevant portion (i.e., 92%) of the bugs injected in the system implementation. This is a promising result considering that the adopted input scenarios are largely suboptimal. From our preliminary experimentation the main weakness concerns two aspects of the input scenarios: (1) the definition of the paths to follow among the possible system states and (2) the choice of the sequences of input values useful to follow each path. We plan to replace the ad-hoc strategy used for manually defining a set of *interesting* paths by investigating how constraint solvers can be used for the generation of all the paths of bounded length. Once paths are defined we plan to investigate how effective input scenarios can be generated. Indeed, for each path several input scenarios must be created following the boundary value analysis approach extended to input sequences and taking into account the specification provided by the SM. For example, in the case of DiaMH several boundaries are present in the specification: the glucose threshold (160), the number of readings above the glucose threshold (4,15). Another aspect that could limit the adoption of our approach is the manual definition of the trace expression starting from the SM specification. For this reason, we plan to investigate the automatic generation of the trace expressions from the SM; this will allow developers without a specific background in runtime verification to adopt our method.

We plan to compare the effectiveness of runtime verification against testing (we proposed a companion approach using acceptance testing tools in [13,15]). We believe that the two approaches have different strengths and weaknesses and thus can be used together for detecting a higher number of bugs. For example, acceptance tests allow to test also the system GUI (e.g., the smartphone app) and interact with it to send commands (e.g., accepting an insulin dose if required). On the other hand, it is difficult to adopt functional test automation for automating a relevant number of test scenarios since it is by far more complex to generate test scripts involving GUI interactions. Finally, we noticed that it is not easy to pinpoint the root cause of failure when the monitor detects a problem since anything in the entire flow could have contributed. Thus, we plan to improve the monitor in order to provide detailed information concerning the current expected IoT system status when a problem is detected (currently only the corresponding value of the input scenario is reported, e.g., error @ insulin = 175).

6   Conclusions

In this work, we have presented our preliminary approach for the runtime verification of IoT systems. To explain and validate it we employed a realistic mobile health system composed by local sensors and actuators, a remote cloud-based healthcare system for taking decisions and smartphones. It is worth noting that the proposed approach is not limited to the mobile health context, but can be applied to any IoT system, providing that the messages among the devices can be intercepted by the probes of our runtime monitor. Our approach has been proposed for detecting bugs in IoT systems during development and maintenance activities; however, by removing input scenarios and relying on input provided by real sensors it can be adopted also for monitoring deployed IoT systems to provide an additional level of protection against unforeseen events. We have discussed the pro and cons of the approach and some possible interesting future research directions such as: automatically generating the input paths and input sequences to improve coverage and thus bugs detection, automatically generating the trace expressions from the system behaviour specifications, combining runtime verification with acceptance testing to further increase bugs detection capabilities, and including time constraints in trace expressions.

Acknowledgements. This research was partially supported by Actelion Pharmaceuticals Italia and DIBRIS SEED 2016 grants.

References

1. Ancona, D., Ferrando, A., Mascardi, V.: Comparing trace expressions and linear temporal logic for runtime verification. In: Ábrahám, E., Bonsangue, M., Johnsen, E.B. (eds.) Theory and Practice of Formal Methods. LNCS, vol. 9660, pp. 47–64. Springer, Cham (2016). https://doi.org/10.1007/978-3-319-30734-3_6
2. Ancona, D., Franceschini, L., Delzanno, G., Leotta, M., Ribaudo, M., Ricca, F.: Towards runtime monitoring of Node.js and its application to the Internet of Things. In: Pianini, D., Salvaneschi, G. (eds.) Proceedings of 1st Workshop on Architectures, Languages and Paradigms for IoT (ALP4IoT 2017), EPTCS. vol. 264, pp. 27–42. arXiv (2018)
3. Atzori, L., Iera, A., Morabito, G.: The internet of things: a survey. Comput. Netw. **54**(15), 2787–2805 (2010)
4. Beizer, B.: Software Testing Techniques. Wiley, New York (1990)
5. Chen, T.Y., Ho, J.W., Liu, H., Xie, X.: An innovative approach for testing bioinformatics programs using metamorphic testing. BMC Bioinform. **10**(1), 24 (2009)
6. Clarke, E., Grumberg, O., Peled, D.: Model Checking. MIT Press, Cambridge (1999)
7. Desolda, G., Ardito, C., Matera, M.: Empowering end users to customize their smart environments: model, composition paradigms, and domain-specific tools. ACM Trans. Comput. Hum. Interact. **24**(2), 12:1–12:52 (2017)
8. Grün, B.J., Schuler, D., Zeller, A.: The impact of equivalent mutants. In: Proceedings of 2nd International Conference on Software Testing, Verification and Validation Workshops, ICSTW 2009, pp. 192–199. IEEE (2009)
9. Incki, K., Ari, I.: A novel runtime verification solution for IoT systems. IEEE Access **6**, 13501–13512 (2018)
10. Jia, Y., Harman, M.: An analysis and survey of the development of mutation testing. IEEE Trans. Softw. Eng. **37**(5), 649–678 (2011)
11. Klonoff, D.C.: The current status of mHealth for diabetes: will it be the next big thing? J. Diab. Sci. Technol. **7**(3), 749–758 (2013)
12. Kochhar, P.S., Thung, F., Lo, D.: Code coverage and test suite effectiveness: empirical study with real bugs in large systems. In: Proceedings of 22nd International Conference on Software Analysis, Evolution and Reengineering, SANER 2015, pp. 560–564. IEEE (2015)

13. Leotta, M., et al.: An acceptance testing approach for Internet of Things systems. IET Softw. **12**(5), 430–436 (2018). IET Digital Library. https://doi.org/10.1049/iet-sen.2017.0344, https://digital-library.theiet.org/content/journals/10.1049/iet-sen.2017.0344
14. Leotta, M., Clerissi, D., Ricca, F., Tonella, P.: Approaches and tools for automated end-to-end web testing. Adv. Comput. **101**, 193–237 (2016)
15. Leotta, M., et al.: Towards an acceptance testing approach for Internet of Things systems. In: Garrigós, I., Wimmer, M. (eds.) ICWE 2017. LNCS, vol. 10544, pp. 125–138. Springer, Cham (2018). https://doi.org/10.1007/978-3-319-74433-9_11
16. Offutt, A.J., Untch, R.H.: Mutation 2000: uniting the orthogonal. In: Wong, W.E. (ed.) Mutation Testing for the New Century. ADBS, vol. 24, pp. 34–44. Springer, Boston (2001). https://doi.org/10.1007/978-1-4757-5939-6_7
17. Rosenkranz, P., Wählisch, M., Baccelli, E., Ortmann, L.: A distributed test system architecture for open-source IoT software. In: Proceedings of 1st Workshop on IoT Challenges in Mobile and Industrial Systems, IoT-Sys 2015, pp. 43–48. ACM (2015)
18. Utting, M., Legeard, B.: Practical Model-Based Testing: A Tools Approach. Morgan Kaufmann, Burlington (2010)

4th International Workshop
on Knowledge Discovery on the Web
(KDWEB2018)

KDWEB 2018: 4th International Workshop on Knowledge Discovery on the Web

In the current era of digital and social data, the world became more connected, networked, and traceable, with the consequent exponentially growth of data creation, sharing, and storing. In particular, data changed from static, complete, and centralized to dynamic, incomplete, and distributed; furthermore, data rapidly increased its scope and size, with the continuous increase of volumes, varieties, and velocities. All these aspects led to new challenges undertaken by the field of Big Data Analysis. Consequently, there is the need for novel computational techniques and tools able to assist humans in extracting useful information (knowledge) from the huge volumes of data. Knowledge Discovery is an interdisciplinary area focusing upon methodologies for identifying valid, novel, potentially useful and meaningful patterns from such data, and is currently widespread in numerous fields, including science, engineering, healthcare, business, and medicine. A major aspect of Knowledge Discovery is to extract valuable knowledge and information from data. Typical tasks are aimed at gathering only relevant information from digital data (e.g., text documents, multimedia files, or webpages), by searching for information within documents and for metadata about documents, as well as searching relational databases and the Web. Recently, the rapid growth of social networks and online services entailed that Knowledge Discovery approaches focused on the World Wide Web (WWW), whose popular use as global information system led to a huge amount of digital data. Typically, a webpage has unstructured or semi-structured textual content, leading to present to users both relevant and irrelevant information. Hence, there is the need of novel techniques and systems able to easily extract information and knowledge from the huge web data.

KDWEB, the international workshop on Knowledge Discovery on the Web, is focused on the field of Knowledge Discovery from digital data, with particular attention for Data Mining, Machine Learning, and Information Retrieval methods, systems, and applications. KDWEB provides a venue to researchers, scientists, students, and practitioners involved in the fields of Knowledge Discovery on Data Mining, Information Retrieval, and Semantic Web, for presenting and discussing novel and emerging ideas. In particular, the workshop is meant to collect investigations that concern both traditional and novel applications of the World Wide Web, including social, semantic and mobile declinations of the net. The aim is to present, discuss, and compare novel and emerging solutions based on intelligent techniques falling in the area of Web Engineering, with an emphasis and preference for works that are motivated by real-life applications and constructed upon experimental results.

KDWEB 2018, held in Caceres (Spain) on June 5th, 2018, has been the 4th edition of the workshop. All previous editions (2015–2017) have been held in Cagliari (Italy). More info about the workshop is available at the link http://www.iascgroup.it/kdweb2018.html.

KDWEB 2018 Organizers

Workshop Chairs

Giuliano Armano	Department of Electrical and Electronic Engineering - University of Cagliari, Italy
Matteo Cristani	Department of Computer Science - University of Verona, Italy
Alessandro Giuliani	Department of Electrical and Electronic Engineering - University of Cagliari, Italy
Álvaro Rubio-Largo	Universidade NOVA de Lisboa, Portugal

Publication Chair

Alessandro Bozzon	Software and Computer Technology Department - Delft University of Technology, Netherlands

A User Modeling Pipeline for Studying Polarized Political Events in Social Media

Roberto Napoli[1], Ali Mert Ertugrul[2], Alessandro Bozzon[3](✉),
and Marco Brambilla[1]

[1] Politecnico di Milano, Milan, Italy
roberto1.napoli@mail.polimi.it, marco.brambilla@polimi.it
[2] Graduate School of Informatics, Middle East Technical University, Ankara, Turkey
e150236@metu.edu.tr
[3] Web Information Systems, Delft University of Technology, Delft, The Netherlands
a.bozzon@tudelft.nl

Abstract. This paper presents a user modeling pipeline to analyze discussions and opinions shared on social media regarding polarized political events (e.g., public polls). The pipeline follows a four-step methodology. First, social media posts and users metadata are crawled. Second, a filtering mechanism is applied to filter spammers and bot users. As a third step, demographics information is extracted out of the valid users, namely gender, age, ethnicity and location information. Finally, the political polarity of the users with respect to the analyzed event is predicted. In the scope of this work, our proposed pipeline is applied to two referendum scenarios (independence of Catalonia in Spain and autonomy of Lombardy in Italy) in order to assess the performance of the approach with respect to the capability of collecting correct insights on the demographics of social media users and of predicting the poll results based on the opinions shared by the users. Experiments show that the method was effective in predicting the political trends for the Catalonia case, but not for the Lombardy case. Among the various motivations for this, we noticed that in general Twitter was more representative of the users opposing the referendum than the ones in favor.

1 Introduction

Elections are political events in which people are invited to vote on a candidate or political party. Predicting the outcome of elections is a topic that has been extensively studied in political polls, which have generally provided reliable predictions by means of statistical models [12]. On the other hand, the large-scale diffusion of social media has offered fertile soil for researchers to conduct their experiments in the context of the political discussion. The idea that social media may be an alternative to traditional polls is very alluring, since they provide large amounts of post and user data at no expense. In particular, Twitter, a micro-blogging platform in which users post short messages (*tweets*), has established as the favored platform for the following reasons. Most of its content is publicly

© Springer Nature Switzerland AG 2018
C. Pautasso et al. (Eds.): ICWE 2018, LNCS 11153, pp. 101–114, 2018.
https://doi.org/10.1007/978-3-030-03056-8_9

accessible, while in other social networks (e.g. Facebook) plenty of user activity involves private interactions. It provides free APIs for collecting tweets and users metadata. Moreover, Twitter is one of the favored platform for discussing topics and spreading information; according to [10], users use Twitter mostly for informative purposes rather than social networking. They can follow other users and receive their updates on their timeline. The mechanism of *retweet* is instead used for spreading information.

In this paper, we restrict our focus on referendums, i.e. political events which split the electorate into two opposing factions. In particular, we focus on the analysis of two referendums, namely the Catalan Independence Referendum and the Lombardy Autonomy Referendum. These differ substantially in impact on the affected countries, as the Lombardy referendum had almost no impact on the political status quo of the country and was met with lukewarm interest in Italy, while the Catalan referendum was cause of much turmoil and upheavals that shook some parts of the country. In particular, the latter drew international attention in the news and social media due to several protests culminated in violence. The difference of the impact of those events was also reflected in Twitter in terms of number of posts concerning those topics.

To analyze those use cases, we have employed the same methodology: after collecting the data, we made a first screening of spam and bot users. We then extracted demographics information out of the remaining users and predicted their political polarization by means of a learning-based approach. The questions this paper seeks to tackle are the following ones.

- Which methodology can we build in order to systematically study polarized political events in social media?
- How can we extract and analyze the demographics of the users discussing about these political events?
- Are the results produced by this methodology effective in predicting the real-world outcomes?

In this paper we provide detailed results from the application of the proposed pipeline and try to give an answer to these questions.

2   Related Work

In this section we discuss the research related to our work, organizing them in four categories: election prediction, user demographics, spam/bot analysis, and diffusion of social media content in networks.

Social Media for Predicting Elections. Although a substantial literature has thrived since the birth of Twitter, social media analysis cannot yet equal traditional polls [2,8]. This is in part caused by the ineffectiveness of the approaches which have been employed in the past research: tweets volume count and sentiment analysis. The bad performance of sentiment analysis is attributable to the fact that most researches have employed simplistic approaches, usually limited to lexicon-based techniques [8]. [2] also claimed that professional polling cannot be emulated by social media because it is impossible to collect a random sample of users in Twitter via its APIs; in fact, correct predictions require the ability of sampling likely voters randomly and without any bias.

Users Demographics in Twitter. Studies have demonstrated that users in Twitter are predominantly male, younger and better educated [3,13,15]; the white race is also the most predominant, although racial minorities are present as well [3]. In geographic terms, the most populated locations (e.g. metropolitan areas) are over-represented [15]. With respect to the political activity, users are more politically attentive and more liberal [13]. [3] also added that users tend to exhibit strong partisanship to a political party, suggesting that Twitter is being employed as an alternative medium for political activists to spread their opinion.

Impact of Spam and Bot Accounts. Another factor which should be kept into account when analyzing the political discussion is the presence of spam bots spreading disinformation and false rumors, usually in order to support one political party or candidate over the other. [16] described the use of fake accounts in Twitter to spread disinformation by spamming targeted users who, in turn, would retweet the message achieving viral diffusion. [7] instead studied the disinformation campaign against Macron during the French Presidential Election in 2017. A thorough analysis led to the discovery of why it was not successful for that event; it was also effective in hinting that there exists a black market of reusable political disinformation bots.

Diffusion of Social Media Content in Networks. Of interest to this analysis is how the social media content is spread in social networks, as this can affect the opinion of the online community. The retweet mechanism is considered by many studies as an important metric to study the spread of user influence across the network [5], while the follow-up relationship is not [18]. Indeed, retweets cause a tweet to reach a certain number of audience no matter how many followers a user possesses [10]. Information cascade models are usually considered when analyzing information spread. According to [9], most cascades have small depth and occur in a short period of time; the majority of information diffusion processes are shallow and do not reach many users. Besides, any user on the network has potential to start widely scattered cascades. Finally, several studies have examined the political polarization within communities. [10] claimed networks exhibit some level of homophily; as such, users tend to have contacts who have common shares with themselves. [20] claimed that there exists topic polarization among communities where each community acts as a sort of echo-chamber within itself.

Our proposed pipeline addresses all the previously discussed categories. We first remove spam and bot accounts which have been shown to negatively affect the analysis of elections. We then extract users' demographics to account for the demographics bias. Finally, we predict the election results by analyzing social media content trying to address the limitations previously exposed.

3   Pipeline Architecture

Our proposed social media pipeline for modeling users in the context of political elections consists of four main steps, namely data collection, filtering mechanism, demographics analysis and political polarization prediction, as shown in Fig. 1. The function of each step is described as follows:

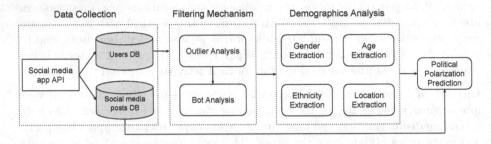

Fig. 1. Social media pipeline architecture.

1. **Data Collection**: This step includes activities related to collecting social media posts and profile information from social media users. Posts are gathered based on the predefined topical keywords and hashtags.
2. **Filtering Mechanism**: The purpose of this step is to eliminate the social media users that are less likely to belong to humans, in particular bots and organizational accounts. There is a significant increase of such users in social media in order to create the illusion of artificial grassroots for supporting a determined political faction [17].
3. **Demographics Analysis**: This step extracts the demographic information from the profiles of those social media users percolated by the filtering mechanism. Extracted demographics include the information related to age, gender, ethnicity and location.
4. **Political Polarization Prediction**: This step aims to predict the political alignment of users by analyzing their posts relevant to the topic of interest. A number of approaches can be applied to predict the users' political alignments, including a keyword-based approach or a learning-based approach.

4   Implementation and Experiments

This section presents the application of our proposed pipeline on two real-world referendum scenarios, namely Catalonia and Lombardy referendums, which were held on Oct 1st, 2017 and Oct 22nd, 2017, respectively. For both cases, we used Twitter as a source of social content.

4.1 Data Collection

For both referendum cases, the collection of the data started from three months before the corresponding events (Jul 1st, 2017 for Catalonia and Jul 22nd, 2017 for Lombardy). Twitter Streaming API was used for the data collection process. To collect the relevant data, a set of predefined referendum specific topical keywords and hashtags were used. Since we wanted to maximize the number of topic-related tweets to be collected, we also utilized more generic keywords, yet still relevant to the topic of interest. Furthermore, we collected the tweets of several important figures of these referendums to increase the recall. As a result, we collected 6.61M tweets from 1.55M users and 74 K tweets from 26 K users for the Catalonia and Lombardy referendums, respectively. The hashtags are accessible at the following url: https://bit.ly/2Jd5r9E.

4.2 Filtering Mechanism

This step aims at filtering non-human accounts out of all the collected users to obtain more accurate results for analyzing elections in social media. It consists of two consecutive processes, namely **outlier analysis** and **bot analysis**.

First, the outlier users were identified based on the volume of posts they had shared using inter-quartile range. We took the lifetimes of users into account, since older accounts are likely to have more online activities than younger ones. Therefore, the social media post volume of the users was normalized on the basis of their account age (in months). Hence, the outliers were detected based on the normalized values. As a result, the users whose normalized volume of social media posts was greater than the upper bound were filtered out.

Secondly, bot analysis was applied on non-outlier users using the Botometer API proposed by Davis et al. [6] and enhanced by Varol et al. [21]. This API assigns a score (between 0 and 100) to a given Twitter user, based on some types of features. The higher the score, the more likely the user has been evaluated as being a bot. Since a few features are English-dependent, the tool provides also a score calculated by considering only language-independent features of the user. We preferred the latter score since both considered scenarios are characterized by a prevalence of Italian and Spanish language tweets. The threshold score was set to 40 in both scenarios to distinguish bot users from non-bot ones.

4.3 Demographics Analysis

This step includes the tasks related to the extraction of demographics out of those users considered as human accounts. Several off-the-shelf third party API services were employed.

Gender Extraction. The gender information of the users was identified by applying two approaches. First, we used Face++[1], which identifies the gender of people in a given photo. We thus fed this service the profile pictures of the

---

[1] https://www.faceplusplus.com/.

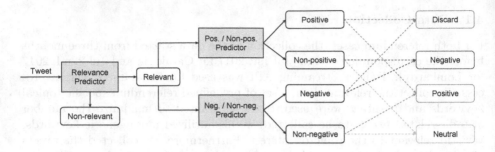

Fig. 2. Two-staged political polarity prediction approach.

users to analyze. However, it successfully extracted gender information for only a small amount of the users due to reasons such as missing profile pictures, pictures including more than one person and non-human portraits. Accordingly, we utilized an additional service, called Genderize[2], which returns the gender of the user based on the user's first name.

Age Extraction. The age information of the users was extracted using Face++ as well. Therefore, the number of users whose age was identified was expected to be low due to the same reasons discussed in gender extraction.

Ethnicity Extraction. The ethnicity of users was analyzed by employing the 'Name Ethnicity Classifier' model proposed by [1]. This classifier takes the names of the users as input and predicts their ethnicity at different levels of a decision tree. In particular, the ethnicity values correspond to the leaf nodes of this tree.

Location Extraction. To identify the home location of users, two approaches were employed. First, for those who had posted any geo-located tweet, their home location was extracted by majority voting over the locations of their tweets. This approach provides a reliable and up-to-date indication of the user's location. However, it is well-known that only a small amount of tweets provide geo-location information (0.85% according to [19] and 2.02% according to [11]). For this reason, we looked up the 'location' field in the user profile for those users who had not posted any geo-located tweet. This information was fed to the Geonames[3] service, which returns detailed information at different levels of granularity (e.g. country, region, city level) based on the given free text of the location.

4.4 Political Alignment Prediction

To predict the political alignment of a user, we employed a predictive approach for classifying polarities of tweets based on their text representation. The overall workflow of the proposed approach is given in Fig. 2.

We employed a two-step classification process. We first built a binary classifier, called relevance predictor, to label tweets into *relevant* (i.e. related to the

---

[2] https://genderize.io/.
[3] http://www.geonames.org/.

referendum) and *non-relevant* classes. Then, for those tweets labeled as relevant, we applied another classification step, using two independent binary classifiers to further label them as *positive/non-positive* and *negative/non-negative*. With *positive* and *negative*, here we mean "in favour of the referendum" and "against the referendum" respectively.

Such a nested classification approach has been shown to work successfully in the case of imbalanced classes [4]. Furthermore, the labels assigned by the two predictors at the second step were compared to assign a final polarity label to the corresponding tweet. For instance, if the positive predictor had assigned non-positive label and the negative predictor had assigned negative label to a given tweet, this was finally assigned the negative label. In case both predictors had labelled the tweet as negative (non-positive and non-negative), the tweet was considered as neutral. On the other hand, if both predictors had labelled it as positive (positive and negative), the tweet was discarded. Finally, the overall polarity of the user was decided by majority voting over the classified tweets.

For the classification, each tweet was represented as a vector using Word2Vec [14] model, which allows to capture the syntactic and semantic word relationships within the tweet corpus. Separate Word2Vec models were trained for Catalonia and Lombardy cases using 2M and 30 K tweets of the human-like users, respectively. Each tweet representation was obtained by averaging the representation of words that the corresponding tweet included. Before training the models, a pre-processing step was performed in which URLs, punctuation marks, special characters and stop-words were stripped.

After the tweet representations were obtained, the predictors (relevance, positive and negative) were trained. The ground truth was composed of manually annotated tweets for the Lombardy scenario, since a keyword-based approach based on polarized keywords to label the tweets had produced scarce results. On the other hand, the keyword-based approach was successful in labelling a sufficient number of tweets for the Catalonia scenario. In total, there were 500 positive, 500 negative, 400 neutral and 1000 non-relevant labelled tweets for both cases. For training and testing the relevance predictor, a set of 1000 non-relevant and 1000 relevant tweets was employed. For training and testing the positive predictor, 500 positive and 500 non-positive tweets were used where the non-positive samples contained a balanced mix of negative and neutral tweets. The same approach was followed for training and testing the negative predictor. Furthermore, for both cases, the datasets were split into training and test sets (80% and 20%) and 10-fold cross-validation was applied for the training. Predictors were based on the SVM classifier with linear kernel. The datasets employed to test the performance of the predictors are accessible at the following url: https://bit.ly/2Jd5r9E.

5   Results

This section presents the results of the application of the proposed pipeline on the two referendum cases. First, we provide descriptive results concerning the demographics of the filtered users. Then, we evaluate the performance of the polarity predictors. Finally, we present additional descriptive statistics concerning the trends of the polarity of users enriched with the demographics information and compare some results of our predictions with the actual referendums results.

Table 1. Number of users after each step in filtering mechanism.

	# total users collected	# users after outlier analysis	# users after bot analysis
Catalonia	1,548,745	1,376,375	582,039
Lombardy	25,487	22,375	10,801

5.1 Descriptive Results

Concerning the filtering mechanism, Table 1 indicates the number of users after outlier analysis and bot analysis. Nearly 12% of all collected users exhibited a greater post activity than the other users for both cases and those users were eliminated by outlier analysis. Next, the remaining users were exposed to bot analysis with 42% and 48% of them identified as non-bots for the Catalonia and Lombardy cases, respectively. After discarding the bots, the following demographics analyses were applied on the remaining users.

We can observe that **gender** information of 80% and 71% of the users was identified for the Catalonia and Lombardy cases. Among them, only 36% and 33% were classified as female for Catalonia and Lombardy, respectively. Furthermore, the **age** information of 40% and 45% of the users could be extracted for the Catalonia and Lombardy cases, respectively. For the Catalonia case, 4.9% were below 18, 22.1% were in range [18–30], 41.0% were in range [31–45], 29.4% were in range of [46–65], and 2.6% were above 65. For the Lombardy case, 5.5% were below 18, 24.3% were in range [18–30], 37.6% were in range [31–45], 30.0% were in range of [46–65], and 2.6% were above 65. We can thus conclude that for both gender and age the two use cases display similar patterns about social media participation. Furthermore, **ethnicity** of 90.7% and 76.2% of the users was identified for Catalonia and Lombardy, respectively. Considering the users classified by ethnicity, we observed that for the Catalonia scenario the Hispanics made up the majority of the users at 24.27%, British at 18.35% and Italians at 11.45%. For the Lombardy scenario, the Italians made up the majority of the users at 41.44%, followed by British at 12.12% and Hispanics at 9.4%. These results clearly demonstrate that the Spanish and Italian users composed the majority of the user base; the high British percentage may be due instead to the presence of tweets in English language. Finally, we report the information about home **location** of the users detected by the pipeline. In the Catalonia referendum, home locations of 34.4% of the users were identified in country-level. 40% of these identified users were from Spain, where the highest social media participation occurred. On the other hand, home locations of the 54.8% of the users were detected in country-level for the Lombardy referendum. Among them, 80%

of participants were from Italy. This confirms that the Lombardy referendum was a local referendum compared to the Catalonia case. We finally list the top five regions in Spain where the social media participation occurred, in order: Catalonia, Andalusia, Community of Madrid, Valencian Community, Galicia. On the other hand, Lombardy, Veneto, Latium, Emilia-Romagna and Tuscany are the top five regions where the social media participation was highest in Italy.

5.2   Polarity Prediction Performance

Table 2 reveals the performance of the individual predictors used for political polarity assignment on the test set in terms of precision, recall, f-score and accuracy. Among them, relevance predictor is the most successful predictor on both cases. The higher results of relevance predictor compared to polarity predictors may be caused by the fact that identification of relevance is an easier task compared to detection of polarity of the tweets having the same topic of interest. Moreover, Neg./Non-neg. predictor and Pos./Non-pos. predictors achieved similar performances on Catalonia case whereas the latter performs better than the former in Lombardy case.

Table 2. Performance of the individual predictors.

	Relevance predictor				Neg./Non-neg. predictor				Pos./Non-pos. predictor			
	Pre.	Rec.	F-sc.	Acc.	Pre.	Rec.	F-sc.	Acc.	Pre.	Rec,	F-sc.	Acc.
Catalonia	0.874	0.863	0.868	0.869	0.755	0.799	0.775	0.773	0.774	0.759	0.765	0.770
Lombardy	0.876	0.946	0.910	0.905	0.715	0.712	0.713	0.706	0.738	0.789	0.761	0.756

Table 3. Distribution of polarity among users for both referendums.

	Positive	Negative	Neutral	Total (polarized)	Total (analyzed)
Catalonia	4,043	6,683	4,238	14,964	40,000
Lombardy	1,767	2,368	2,042	6,177	10,801

5.3   Descriptive Results Aggregated with Political View

In this section, we analyze the (non-bot) users who were assigned a political polarity by our proposed polarity prediction approach. First, we provide the statistics about the polarity of the users for both cases in Table 3. Note that for the Catalonia case we did not make our analyses on the whole set of users, rather we randomly sampled 40 K users for a total of 139.79 K tweets. The proposed pipeline assigned a polarity label to 37.4% and 57.2% of the users for the Catalonia and Lombardy referendums, respectively. Note that the remaining ones were not assigned any polarity label since all of their tweets were either irrelevant or discarded by the pipeline. For the Catalonia case, 27%, 44.7% and 28.3% of the users were assigned positive, negative and neutral polarity. On the other hand, 28.6%, 38.3% and 33.1% of the users in the Lombardy referendum were assigned positive, negative and neutral polarity. Analyses show that the general opinion of social media users in Twitter is negative for both referendums.

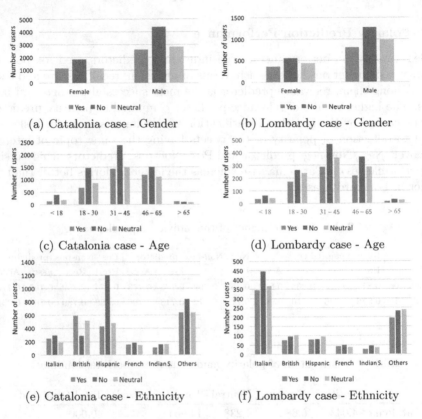

Fig. 3. Predicted polarity distribution of users by gender, age and ethnicity for the Catalonia and Lombardy cases.

We further analyzed the relationship between demographics and predicted the political polarity of users. The pipeline identified the gender of 93.2% and 71.3% of the users and age of 87.1% and 46.4% of the users for the Catalonia and Lombardy cases, respectively. We explored the political polarity with respect to gender (see Fig. 3a and b) and age (see Fig. 3c and d). In both cases, the majority of males, females and each of the age groups have negative opinion. We also examined the relationship between political polarity and ethnicity (see Fig. 3e and f). Note that the pipeline identified the ethnicity of 14.2% and 14.3% of the users for Catalonia and Lombardy cases, respectively. We visualize the top-5 ethnicity classes in terms of social media participation and collect the rest under

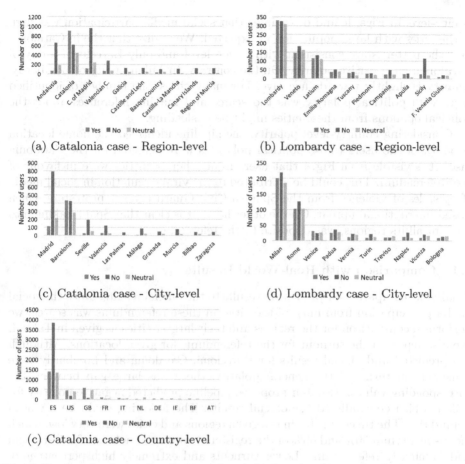

(a) Catalonia case - Region-level

(b) Lombardy case - Region-level

(c) Catalonia case - City-level

(d) Lombardy case - City-level

(c) Catalonia case - Country-level

Fig. 4. Predicted polarity distribution of users by location (region-level, city-level and country-level) for the Catalonia and Lombardy cases.

'Others' category. In Catalonia, we observe a significant difference in negative opinion for Hispanic users with respect to the other ethnicities. On the other hand, in the Lombardy case, although the general opinion of Italians is negative, the difference is not so significant.

We then analyzed the relationship between the political polarity of users and their identified locations in region-level and city-level. For region-level, location of 37.5% and 12.7% was identified for the users for the Catalonia and Lombardy scenarios, respectively. On the other hand, the corresponding values for city-level were 21.3% and 8.0%. The following figures display the top 10 locations with highest social media participation from politically polarized users. We observe in Fig. 4a and b that Catalonia was the only region with positive polarity with respect to the independence of Catalonia, while the other regions exhibited significantly negative polarity. Similarly, in the Lombardy case, the only region with positive polarity was Lombardy. When we analyze the results in city-level in Figs. 4c and d, we infer that social media participation was high in the cities with large population as expected. We realize that the in Catalonia case the patterns are consistent with region level and only Barcelona, a city of Catalonia, has positive polarity. On the contrary, in Milan, a city of Lombardy, polarity is slightly towards negative. For many cities, the number of identified users with political polarity was too scarce and making inferences about the political opinions from these cities might be misleading.

Considering country-level polarity, the pipeline identified the home location of 65.6% of the users whose political polarities were detected for the Catalonia case. It is visible from Fig. 4 that users from other countries were in favour of the Referendum. This could be attributed to the viral circulation in social media of episodes of violence from the Spanish Civil Guard against protesters which raised international uproar. On the other hand, it is clear that Spain, taking into account all its regions, was opposite to the referendum.

5.4   Comparison with Real-World Results

Finally, we compared our prediction results to the official results. Since the social media participation from most of the cities in these referendums was scarce, we performed comparison for the regions and their largest cities as given in Table 4. We also reported the turnout for the referendums for given locations. Although the predicted and official results for Barcelona, Catalonia and Lombardy were consistent in terms of the general polarity, there was large gap between the corresponding values. Also, our proposed pipeline predicted negative polarity for Milan, which contradicted the official results. The following could be a reason behind this. The turnout rates in the given regions and cities were very low, which means more than 50% and 60% of the registered voters did not vote for Catalonia and Lombardy referendums. Lower turnouts and extremely high percentage of official positive polarity results may indicate that those with negative polarity may have protested the referendum and refused to vote.

Table 4. Percentages for the predicted results, the official results and the turnout.

	Barcelona	Catalonia	Milan	Lombardy
Predicted (% of yes)	51.53	59.53	48.82	50.38
Official (% of yes)	89.93	92.01	93.67	96.02
Turnout (%)	43.03	42.01	31.23	38.21

6   Conclusion

In this work, we have proposed a social media pipeline for modeling users in the context of political elections and have applied it on two real-world election scenarios. This pipeline enabled us to perform a detailed analysis on user modeling and understand the reflection on political polarization of the people in social media. The analysis of the Catalonia scenario revealed that the predicted results were effective in predicting the trend of the real results. On the other hand, for the Lombardy scenario, the analysis showed that what users had expressed in Twitter was not aligned with the actual results, as in the real-world the pro-referendum result had absolute dominance, while in Twitter the alignment was considerably more mixed, with arguably a prevalence of opponents and skeptics. This demonstrates that analyzing social media may reveal more about the discussion preceding a political event, although it may not produce accurate predictions on the outcomes.

Limitations and Future Work. The third party APIs employed for the user modeling did not always produce reliable results. This was especially the case of the ethnicity analysis. Demographics bias was neglected even when it is well known that social media is not a random sample of the population while predicting the referendum results. Another limitation regards the predictive approach employed for the polarization assignment. As a future work, we plan to consider demographics bias during polarity prediction. We consider to replace ground-truth preparation process with more sophisticated approaches such as distant supervision learning. Finally, we will compare our prediction approach with different machine learning models such as logistic regression and random forest.

References

1. Ambekar, A., et al.: Name-ethnicity classification from open sources. In: ACM SIGKDD (2009)
2. Avello, G., et al.: Limits of electoral predictions using Twitter. In: ICSWM (2011)
3. Bekafigo, M.A., McBride, A.: Who tweets about politics? Political participation of Twitter users during the 2011 gubernatorial elections. Soc. Sci. Comput. Rev. **31**(5), 625–643 (2013)
4. Budak, C., et al.: Fair and balanced? Quantifying media bias through crowdsourced content analysis. Publ. Opin. Q. **80**(S1), 250–271 (2016)
5. Cha, M., Haddadi, H., Benevenuto, F., Gummadi, K.P.: Measuring user influence in Twitter: the million follower fallacy. In: ICWSM (2010)
6. Davis, C.A., et al.: BotOrNot: a system to evaluate social bots. In: WWW (2016)
7. Ferrara, E.: Disinformation and social Bot operations in the run up to the 2017 French presidential election. First Monday **22**(8) (2017)
8. Gayo-Avello, D.: A meta-analysis of state-of-the-art electoral prediction from twitter data. Soc. Sci. Comput. Rev. **31**(6), 649–679 (2013)
9. Kurka, D.B., Godoy, A., Zuben, F.J.V.: Online social network analysis: a survey of research applications in computer science. CoRR abs/1504.05655 (2015). http://arxiv.org/abs/1504.05655
10. Kwak, H., et al.: What is Twitter, a social network or a news media? (2010)
11. Leetaru, K., et al.: Mapping the global twitter heartbeat: the geography of twitter. First Monday **18**(5) (2013)
12. Lewis-Beck, M.: Election forecasting: principles and practice. Br. J. Politics Int. Relat. **7**(2) (2005)

13. Mellon, J., Prosser, C.: Twitter and Facebook are not representative of the general population: political attitudes and demographics of British social media users. Res. Polit. **4**(3) (2017)
14. Mikolov, T., et al.: Distributed representations of words and phrases and their compositionality. In: Advances in Neural Information Processing Systems, pp. 3111–3119 (2013)
15. Mislove, A., et al.: Understanding the demographics of Twitter users. In: ICWSM (2011)
16. Mustafaraj, E., Metaxas, P.T.: From obscurity to prominence in minutes: political speech and real-time search (2010)
17. Ratkiewicz, J., et al.: Truthy: mapping the spread of astroturf in microblog streams. In: WWW (2011)
18. Romero, D.M., Galuba, W., Asur, S., Huberman, B.A.: Influence and passivity in social media. CoRR abs/1008.1253 (2010). http://arxiv.org/abs/1008.1253
19. Sloan, L., Morgan, J.: Who tweets with their location? Understanding the relationship between demographic characteristics and the use of geoservices and geotagging on Twitter. PloS one **10**(11), e0142209 (2015)
20. Takikawa, H., Nagayoshi, K.: Political polarization in social media: analysis of the "Twitter political field" in Japan. CoRR abs/1711.06752 (2017). http://arxiv.org/abs/1711.06752
21. Varol, O., et al.: Online human-Bot interactions: detection, estimation, and characterization. arXiv preprint arXiv:1703.03107 (2017)

The Problem of Data Cleaning for Knowledge Extraction from Social Media

Emre Calisir(ID) and Marco Brambilla(✉)(ID)

Dipartimento di Elettronica, Politecnico di Milano, Informazione e Bioingegneria
Piazza Leonardo da Vinci, 32, 20133 Milano, Italy
{emre.calisir,marco.brambilla}@polimi.it

Abstract. Social media platforms let users share their opinions through textual or multimedia content. In many settings, this becomes a valuable source of knowledge that can be exploited for specific business objectives. In this work, we report on an implementation aiming at cleaning the data collected from social content, within specific domains or related to given topics of interest. Indeed, topic-based collection of social media content is performed through keyword-based search, which typically entails very noisy results. Therefore we propose a method for data cleaning and removal of off-topic content based on supervised machine learning techniques, i.e. classification, over data collected from social media platforms based on keywords regarding a specific topic. We define a general method for this and then we validate it through an experiment of data extraction from Twitter, with respect to a set of famous cultural institutions in Italy, including theaters, museums, and other venues. For this case, we collaborated with domain experts to label the dataset, and then we evaluated and compared the performance of classifiers that are trained with different feature extraction strategies.

Keywords: Social media · Knowledge discovery · Data cleaning
Data wrangling · Text classification

1 Introduction

Social media has become one of the most powerful information channels in the digital age. Today, more than 1.6 billion social network users actively create content on these platforms for more than two hours each day.[1] For instance, in Twitter, the well-known social media platform where the users are writing short texts called "tweets", the creation of new content is so fast that 100 million Twitter users post 500 million tweets every day.[2] Consequently, the immense

---

[1] Statista, on social media usage. https://www.statista.com/statistics/433871/daily-social-media-usage-worldwide/, Last accessed 4 Apr 2018.
[2] Omnicore Agency, https://www.omnicoreagency.com/twitter-statistics/, Last accessed 4 Apr 2018.

© Springer Nature Switzerland AG 2018
C. Pautasso et al. (Eds.): ICWE 2018, LNCS 11153, pp. 115–125, 2018.
https://doi.org/10.1007/978-3-030-03056-8_10

amount of user generated data provides a good opportunity for every field of study.

On the other hand, the human-generated content brings many challenges for extracting knowledge for specific topics. The traditional rule-based content extraction features provided by social network platforms (e.g., through API) are based on keyword or metadata search queries. In principle, these systems are designed to retrieve topic-specific data. However, in practice they are not able to address the problem properly, especially for what concerns the relevance of the collected content: indeed, the risk is that they return related and unrelated content altogether, due to various issues, including synonyms, shared keywords across topics, and so on. This is also due to the noise in the data, specifically caused by grammar and spelling errors, or multiple meanings of words [1]. Consequently, it is strongly needed to build new systems that are capable of obtaining clean and trusted topic-specific datasets from social media, after a first data collection phase (typically built on keyword-based search) is performed.

In this study, we propose to use supervised learning, with its ability to learn significant features of topic-relevant posts from a trusted labeled dataset, by devising an approach that is applicable to all kinds of social media platforms. We define our problem setting and research questions as follows:

Input: Human-generated textual content shared on social media platforms; and definition of a specific topic, named entity or context of interest.

Collected data: Set of human-generated textual content collected by querying the social media platform APIs based on the topic, entity or context of interest. Content collected in such way may include irrelevant data, due to synonyms, common keywords, excessively broad context, and so on.

Research Question: Given a set of social media content items collected as above, extract a sub-selection of content items if and only if they are actually relevant to the topic or context of interest.

In the paper we propose a general approach to this issue and then we test the approach over a real use case on Twitter data.

The paper is organized as follows. In Sect. 2, we provide prominent studies in knowledge extraction from social media data. Then in Sect. 3, we explain our methodology by presenting our applied machine learning algorithm and the different feature extraction strategies including n-grams, word2vec, the combination of additional features with word2vec and the dimensionality reduction. In Sect. 4, we explain our experiment on a real-world use case, which is the exploration of tweets about cultural institutions of Italy. In Sect. 5, we show how the different classifiers having different feature extraction strategies impact the accuracy of Machine learning classifier. And finally, in Sect. 6, we conclude our study and give information about our future work.

2   Related Work

Researchers have shown great interest to obtain a clean dataset from social media data for several years. In one of the earliest studies [2], the authors created an early earthquake alarm system based on tweets in order to deliver the announcements much faster than Japan Meteorological Agency. In that study, the researchers trained a Support Vector Machine (SVM) classifier by extracting a variety of features such as keywords, the number of words, and the context of target-event words. In another study [3], the purpose is to detect influenza-like illnesses (ILI) from tweets. It is indicated that Bag-of-Words (BoW) based Logistic regression model could achieve a correlation of .78 with statistics of Centers for Control and Prevention. In another health-related study [4], the authors filtered out the non-relevant content for a health topic related study, and they implemented a binary logistic regression model with unigram, bigram and trigram word features. In a recent health-related study [5], the authors investigated the prevalence and patterns of abuse of specific medications based on an automatic supervised classifier trained by annotated tweets. In [6], the authors tracked baseball and fashion topics over streaming tweets by implementing unigram language models that are smoothed using a normalized extension of stupid back-off. In [7], the authors argue that BoW classifiers fail to achieve good accuracy in short texts. They propose to use Multinomial Naive-Bayes and a collocation feature selection algorithm to increase the performance of BoW. In [8], the authors built a classifier to filter out noisy events for an event detection system from the Twitter stream. In another study [9], the authors did not filter out the non-relevant tweets from a chosen topic, but they performed a more general analysis on all tweets containing trend topic hash-tags to assess whether they are credible in terms of relevancy. They evaluated the performance of different algorithms such as SVM, decision trees, decision rules, and Bayes networks, and they achieved the best performance with a J48 decision tree method.

On the other hand, in some studies, the researchers have needed to enrich the tweet information with external data sources such as search engines [10], page content of linked embedded URLs in tweets [11], and other data sources such as Wikipedia [12]. These approaches are targeting to increase the amount of text data for tweets, but they don't enable to build real-time information filtering systems [13].

In addition to supervised learning based studies, in a recent research [14], the researchers focused on an unsupervised learning method, which is based on a pooling method combining both Information retrieval (IR) and Latent Dirichlet Allocation (LDA) in order to prune the irrelevant tweets.

As it can be understood from all of the studies explained in this section, there is a continuous interest in topic-based information filtering on Twitter. With the approach of comparing n-grams and word embedding techniques and having a real-world use case, we believe that our research could contribute to the existing studies.

3   Methodology

The most basic solution to knowledge extraction about a topic using social media data is to build a rule-based system. In this approach, there are explicitly defined rules, such as storing all of the records containing specific keywords, hash-tags or account names. However, the disadvantage of this approach is that it produces very noisy data. To prevent this issue, we propose to implement a machine learning system, with a classifier trained on the specific context. Consequently, the system could recognize the relevant and non-relevant tweets; and it becomes possible to obtain a clean dataset in given context. Figure 1 represents the high-level flow diagram of the proposed method.

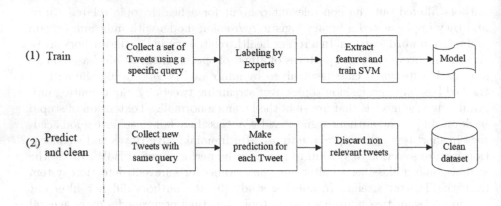

Fig. 1. Proposed data cleaning method for knowledge extraction

3.1   Machine Learning Classifier

In our study, we used Support Vector Machine (SVM) [15] with Linear Kernel which is the recommended algorithm for text classification on high dimensional sparse data [16].

3.2   Feature Extraction Strategies

In terms of building the classifier, there are several approaches such as using only the text content [17], or combining the text content with additional specific features [18]. In this study, we built four different models to observe how the different feature sets impact the accuracy of the SVM-based classifier.

Model 1 (only n-grams): N-grams is one of most widely used text representation techniques. This method combines information derived from n-grams (consecutive sequences of n characters or n words) with a simple vector-space technique [19].

Model 2 (only word2vec): Basically, word2vec creates semantic connections between words. It produces word vectors with deep learning via word2vec's skip-gram and CBOW models, using either hierarchical softmax or negative sampling [20]. This technique enables positioning word vectors in the vector space such that words that share common contexts in the corpus are located in close proximity to one another in the space.

Model 3 (word2vec + additional features): In the previous feature extraction strategies, we were considering only the text data. However, there are useful attributes that could be added into the same machine learning pipeline. In this model, we used all attributes shown in Table 1 as input features.

Table 1. Attributes of Tweet: each attribute points out the relevancy of tweet.

Attribute	Data type	Context
Text	Text value	Tweet
Count of favorites	Numerical value	Tweet
Count of retweets	Numerical value	Tweet
Count of lists	Numerical value	Author
Count of tweets	Numerical value	Author
Count of accounts followed by	Numerical value	Author
Count of accounts followed	Numerical value	Author
Is geographic enabled	Categorical value	Author
Is verified account	Categorical value	Author
Is default profile	Categorical value	Author
Source of posts	Categorical value	Author

Model 4 (PCA applied on word2vec+additional features): In this model, we apply Principal Component Analysis (PCA) over the features of Model 3 in order to reduce the number of features. PCA transforms existing features to new features, which better represent the data, with fewer features having higher variance. Another advantage of using PCA is that it is one of the methods to prevent overfitting of the model.

4   Experiments

In our real-world scenario, the purpose is to obtain a clean dataset from Twitter about cultural institutions in Italy, including theaters, museums, and other venues. We extract possibly relevant tweets by querying the social network using the most typical keywords and ashtags referring to those venues, and then we aim at cleaning the collected data by removing all the non-pertinent contents.

In our experiment, we focused specifically on tweets related with Pompei, Colosseum and Teatro Alla Scala. Pompei is a city in southern Italy's Campania region overlooked by the active volcano at Vesuvius. The Colosseum is the oval amphitheater in the center of the city of Rome. Built of travertine, tuff, and brick-faced concrete, it is the largest amphitheater ever built. And finally, Teatro alla Scala is a famous opera house in Milan.

We applied our method in this use case in the following way: (1) We collected tweets using Twitter Search API. (2) We provided the tweets to the experts for labeling process. (3) We received a set of 726 tweets from the experts, in which the non-relevant and relevant tweets are equally distributed. (363 non-relevant and 363 relevant tweets) (4) We built four different Machine Learning models having the different type of features as described in Sect. 4.2. (5) We evaluated the prediction performance of the models using cross-validation.

4.1 Data Collection Phase

Twitter enables accessing to the publicly shared posts with Search and Stream API. The standard version of these services gives random 1% of tweets in a given criteria. For our real-world experiment, we used Search API to collect tweets posted in a specific time period. In order to determine the scope of the use case, we worked with subject matter of experts of famous cultural institutions of Italy, and we finally prepared the following search query:

"@teatroallascala or #TeatroallaScala or Colosseo or #colosseo or Pompei or #Pompei"

Also, we specified the date period of tweets as:

"since:2017-12-01 until:2018-01-31" .

Tweets contain a variety of fields that could be useful for a classification task. For our use case, we have decided to use the attributes described in Table 1.

4.2 Annotating the Relevant and Non Relevant Tweets

In terms of giving correct decisions in labeling process, we collaborated with the experts. By looking at the textual content of the tweets, the experts manually labeled a set of tweets as relevant and non-relevant, depending on whether they are in context. In this process, they did not eliminate the tweets regarding its written language due to the limited size of our dataset.

Below, there is an example of a relevant and a non-relevant tweet. It is clear that the non-relevant tweet should be eliminated from dataset since it is a commercial advertisement for an hotel in Pompei. In contrast, the relevant tweet contains valuable information about the historical background of Pompei, and it should remain in the dataset.

Non-relevant Tweet: Best #Hotel Deals in #Pompei #HotelDegliAmiciPompei starting at EUR99.60 https://t.co/5DxkKn4o69 https://t.co/akyJoBLwq3.

Relevant Tweet: Pompei Hero Pliny the Elder May Have Been Found 2000 Years Later https://t.co/PyR2rP1Xpe #2017Rewind #archaeology #archeology #history #Pompei #rome #RomanEmpire #history.

4.3   Feature Transformations

For this use-case, by using the feature extraction strategies explained in Sect. 4.2., we transformed the tweets into a convenient structure for the classifier in the following ways.

Model 1 (only n-grams): As an input of this model, we initially transformed the text of tweet to the word sets of unigrams, bigrams, and trigrams as a similar approach to [4]. In addition, we applied Term Frequency - Inverse Document Frequency (TF-IDF) technique over the n-grams.

Model 2 (only word2vec): For the word2vec based models (Model 2, 3, and 4), we built the vocabulary using the full-text content of 2558 tweets. The word2vec vocabulary size is equal to 34029. We determined to use 25-dimensional vectors due to the fact that we have a limited word2vec vocabulary. Indeed, after doing several experiments on different vector dimensions, we observed that the performance of word2vec models having higher vector dimensions are less successful in constructing semantic connections when the vocabulary size is low.

The word similarities of our word2vec model is shown with a small example in Table 2. It is not very surprising that most similar words of *scala* are *aux*, *camelias* and *milano*, because Teatro Alla Scala is the opera house located in Milan, where the famous ballet *La Dame aux camélias* is staged. In contrast, we observe that the limited vocabulary size caused some unexpected similarities as well, as in the case of *pompei* and *retweeted*.

Table 2. Word Similarities in trained word2vec Model: for each sample word, the list of the top-3 most similar words are shown, with the respective similarity score.

Word	First similar word	Second similar word	Third similar word
Colosseum	Rome (0.994)	Roma (0.994)	Coliseum (0.994)
Colosseo	Anfiteatro (0.995)	Travel (0.994)	Italia (0.994)
Scala	Aux (0.993)	Camelias (0.992)	Milano (0.992)
Pompei	Retweeted (0.988)	Nuovi (0.979)	Settembre (0.978)
Roma	Rome (0.995)	Metro (0.994)	Colosseum (0.994)
Italia	Anfiteatro (0.995)	Rome (0.995)	Colosseo (0.994)
Italy	Travel (0.998)	Davanti (0.997)	Photography (0.997)

Model 3 (word2vec + additional features): In Table 1, we present the additional features that describe different aspects of tweets. In this model, we are combining word2vec representation of text content with the categorical and numerical features. In order to use them efficiently in a classifier, we apply Min-Max scaling to numerical variables and One-hot encoding to categorical variables. Consequently, we obtained more than 125 features.

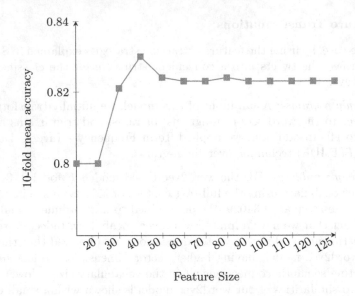

Fig. 2. Principal component analysis: the change in the accuracy based on the target feature size

Model 4 (PCA applied on word2vec + additional features): In this model, we applied PCA over the feature set of Model 3 due to the fact that one-hot encoding increased the feature dimensions in a significant manner. Here, we determined the size of PCA applied feature set by measuring the accuracy of classifier for each possible dimension. The model reaches to the best accuracy when the dimension size is 40 (see Fig. 2).

5   Results

By using the equally distributed dataset described in Sect. 5, a rule-based system which filters tweets regarding the existence of specific hash-tags or keywords could make a prediction with an accuracy of 0.5. However, even though we have a very limited dataset and word2vec is unable to perform perfectly with a small amount of data, all of the classifiers achieved similar and high prediction scores as shown in Table 3. Here we determined to use 10-fold cross validation due to the fact that our dataset is not very large, and cross-validation could give more trusted results.

In addition to the performance indicators shown in Table 3, it is also important to interpret a classifier with its structure of Receiver Operating Characteristic (ROC) curve and Area Under Curve (AUC) scores. The ROC curves clearly illustrate the prediction success of the models (see Fig. 3).

When we compare the models between each other, it is easy to see that the n-grams based model (Model 1) had the best performance among all models. One possible explanation could be the limited word2vec vocabulary. Actually,

Table 3. 10-fold mean average values of models for each feature extraction strategy

Machine learning model	Accuracy	Precision	Recall	F1-Score
Model 1	0.84	0.844	0.832	0.838
Model 2	0.816	0.785	0.869	0.824
Model 3	0.823	0.834	0.807	0.819
Model 4	0.83	0.844	0.81	0.826

word2vec requires very large amounts of training data to provide better results. On the other hand, we observe that combining multiple features had a positive impact on classifier performance. Also, the dimensionality reduction technique increased the accuracy as expected.

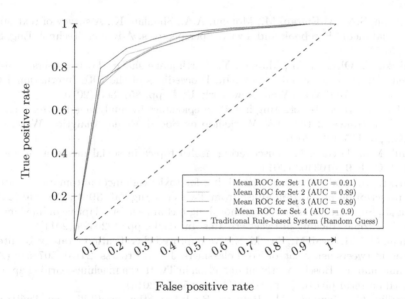

Fig. 3. Comparison of ROC graphs: for each model, the ROC curve and AUC values are shown.

6   Conclusions and Future Work

In this study, we proposed Machine learning based methods to obtain a clean and trusted topic-specific dataset from Twitter. In a real-world use case, we proved that our approach achieves high accuracy even though the training dataset is very limited. In the future studies, we will collect more tweets to build a larger corpus for word2vec models, and also increase the size of annotated training dataset.

Also, we will explore the impact of adding additional tweet-specific features that could improve the performance of our models, such as number/presence of hashtags, hyperlinks, user mentions, and length of the tweet. Moreover, we will analyze the performance of classifiers by using separate tweet data sets for each language, and we will observe how n-grams and word2vec perform on the uni-language corpus.

Acknowledgements. We gratefully acknowledge Fluxedo S.r.l. (http://www.fluxedo. com/) for sharing the data used for our experiments and the Osservatorio MIP Innovazione Digitale nei Beni e Attività Culturali (https://www.osservatori.net/it_ it/osservatori/innovazione-digitale-nei-beni-e-attivita-culturali.) for the useful insights and discussion on the matter.

References

1. Salloum, S.A., Al-Emran, M., Monem, A.A., Shaalan, K.: A survey of text mining in social media Facebook and Twitter perspectives. Adv. Sci. Technol. Eng. Syst. J. (2017)
2. Sakaki, T., Okazaki, M., Matsuo, Y.: Earthquake shakes Twitter users: real-time event detection by social sensors. In: Proceedings of the 19th International Conference on World Wide Web, New York, USA, pp. 851–860 (2010)
3. Culotta A: Towards detecting influenza epidemics by analyzing Twitter messages. In: Proceedings of the First Workshop on Social Media Analytics, Washington, D.C., pp. 115–122 (2010)
4. Paul, M.J., Dredze, M.: Discovering health topics in social media using models. PLoS ONE **9**, e103408 (2014)
5. Sarker, A., et al.: Social media mining for toxicovigilance: automatic monitoring of prescription medication abuse from Twitter. Drug Saf. **39**(3), 231–240 (2016)
6. Lin, J., Snow, R., Morgan, W.: Smoothing techniques for adaptive online language models: topic tracking in tweet streams. In: KDD, pp. 422–429 (2011)
7. Khan, M.A.H., Iwai, M., Sezaki, K.: An improved classification strategy for filtering relevant tweets using bag-of-word classifiers. J. Inf. Process. **21**(3), 507–516 (2013)
8. Kunneman, F., Bosch, A.: Event detection in Twitter: a machine-learning approach based on term pivoting. In: BNAIC, pp. 65–72 (2014)
9. Castillo, C., Mendoza, M., Poblete, B.: Information credibility on Twitter. In: Proceedings of the 20th International Conference on World Wide Web, Hyderabad, pp. 675–684. ACM (2011)
10. Bollegala, D., Matsuo, Y., Ishizuka, M.: Measuring semantic similarity between words using web search engines. In: Proceedings of the 16th International Conference on World Wide Web (WWW2007), pp. 757–766. ACM Press, New York (2007)
11. Yang, S., Kolcz, A., Schlaikjer, A., Gupta, P.: Large-scale high-precision topic modeling on Twitter. In: Proceedings of the 20th ACM SIGKDD International Conference on Knowledge Discovery and Data Mining (KDD 2014), pp. 1907–1916. ACM, New York (2014)
12. Banerjee, S., Ramanathan, K., Gupta, A.: Clustering short texts using Wikipedia. In: SIGIR, pp. 787–788 (2007)

13. Li, Q., Liu, X., Shah, S., Nourbakhsh, A.: Tweet topic classification using distributed language representations. In: Proceedings of the 2016 IEEE/WIC/ACM International Conference on Web Intelligence, Nebraska, USA (2016)
14. Hajjem, M., Latiri, C.: Combining IR and LDA topic modeling for filtering microblogs. Procedia Comput. Sci. **112**, 761–770 (2017)
15. Joachims, T.: Text categorization with support vector machines: learning with many relevant features. In: Nédellec, C., Rouveirol, C. (eds.) ECML 1998. LNCS, vol. 1398, pp. 137–142. Springer, Heidelberg (1998). https://doi.org/10.1007/BFb0026683
16. Lewis, J.P.: Tutorial on SVM. In: CGIT Lab, USC (2004)
17. Sun, A.: Short text classification using very few words. In: SIGIR, pp. 1145–1146. ACM (2012)
18. Sriram, B., Fuhry, D., Demir, E., Ferhatosmanoglu, H., Demirbas, M.: Short text classification in Twitter to improve information filtering. In: Proceedings of the 33rd International ACM SIGIR Conference on Research and Development in Information Retrieval (2010)
19. Damashek, M.: Gauging similarity with n-grams: language independent categorization of text. Science **267**(5199), 843–848 (1995)
20. Mikolov, T., Chen, K., Corrado, G., Dean, J.: Efficient estimation of word representations in vector space. In: Proceedings of Workshop at ICLR (2013)

From Web to Physical and Back:
WP User Profiling with Deep Learning

Christian Joppi[✉], Pietro Lovato, Marco Cristani, and Gloria Menegaz

Department of Computer Science, University of Verona,
Strada Le Grazie 15, Verona, Italy
christian.joppi@studenti.univr.it, pietro.lovato@humatics.it,
{marco.cristani,gloria.menegaz}@univr.it

Abstract. This position paper discusses the definition and implementation of *Web-Physical (WP) user profiles*, which allow the creation of personalized recommendations and innovative behavioral predictions in particular scenarios, i.e., fairs. The nature of a WP profile builds upon two different worlds: the Web (social networks and web applications) and the Physical one, each one of them being explored through (big) data collection platforms. These two platforms collect radically different information: on the one hand, information of appreciation towards a particular product or service (web domain) together with other metadata; on the other, the leases (x, y) of users in the exhibition space (physical domain). In this scenario, our research idea consists in identifying how the information in the two domains can be merged in a whole entity under a theoretical point of view: this will unleash tangible repercussions in terms of personalized recommendations and effective behavioral predictions, where with personalized recommendation we mean a suggestion to a user in physical terms (eg a pavilion to visit) and / or in web terms (eg a site to visit) and with behavioral prediction a prediction of where a user can go in the future, even in a multimedia perspective (physical + web).

Keywords: Recommendation systems · Multimedia · Fairs

1   Introduction

International trade fairs and exhibitions represent an essential part of the marketing strategy for many products and services, and accounts for the second most important promotional factor influencing buying decisions of industrial purchases (after personal selling) [15,28]. For this reason, fairs are a multibillion-dollar business: in the 2010 CEIR report[1] it is stated that – in the north of USA alone – exhibition events attracted in 2009 more than 60 million visitors and 1.5 millions of exhibitors, generating a revenue of 11.2 billion of dollars.

---

[1] http://www.ceir.org.

© Springer Nature Switzerland AG 2018
C. Pautasso et al. (Eds.): ICWE 2018, LNCS 11153, pp. 126–135, 2018.
https://doi.org/10.1007/978-3-030-03056-8_11

Other than being a rich and productive sector, the exhibitions industry is extremely dynamic, and is constantly striving to improve the experience of both visitors and exhibitors: a fair is no longer a mere seller of physical booths, but also a provider of high-end services ranging from catering or organization of congresses and parallel events, to online information and apps provided to assist every actor participating to the fair.

In particular, in recent years fair organizers started a process of digital transformation, taking newly available technologies, adapting them to deliver value to their existing or new customers, and developing new business models and work processes. Thus, a vast amount of heterogeneous data is rapidly becoming available and is being collected by the fair organizations. On one hand, data is gathered in the physical spaces of an exhibition, mainly by using indoor sensors that provide location data for each device connected to the Internet[2], based on Bluetooth Beacon, GPS tracking, or WiFi network cells [5].

On the other hand, a huge amount of input is available on the web domain, mainly in the form of users feedback on social media that can be expressive of a particular sentiment experienced before, during, or after the event. In others words, the fair ecosystem employs a variety of platforms that collect different types of information, related to two very distinct but complementary modalities: in the physical modality, users' trajectories are tracked in the exhibition spaces; in the web modality, social network activities and interactions are monitored to understand their sentiment.

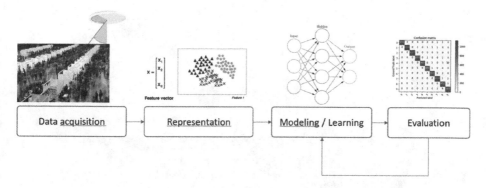

Fig. 1. Common steps of a machine learning pipeline.

Integrating and distilling such knowledge allows for a rich user profiling, which can profitably be exploited by many different actors. By profiling visitors online, and identifying their needs/wants, it is possible for exhibitors to better target the marketing efforts, and increase sales by offering recommendation of relevant products and services. By understanding how visitors physically interact

---

[2] http://www.iaee.com/wp-content/uploads/2016/04/2016-IAEE-Future-Trends-Impacting-the-Exhibitions-and-Events-Industry-White-Paper.pdf.

with the environment, and how they behave as individuals and groups, the fair organizers may decide to make improvements to the exhibition layouts and make better use of spaces. Finally, the visitor can make use of its profile to have a more personalized experience of the exhibition, thanks to the personalized recommendation made on her/his sentiments and locations previously visited.

In this position paper, we sketch the steps of a systematic study towards the creation of a pipeline to build the profile of a user in the trade fair context. Our proposed framework is within the scope of machine learning and deep learning, where the profile of a user is posited to be a numeric vector which is learned on the available data (a possible pipeline is depicted in Fig. 1, and should account for both modalities jointly, if possible), and represents a suitable signature that can be successfully employed to perform a variety of tasks:

- multimodal visitors recommendation, i.e. a suggestion to a user both in physical terms (ex: a pavilion to visit) and/or in web terms (ex: a site to visit, see Fig. 2);
- multimodal exhibitors analytics, i.e. tailored statistics to exhibitors about target customers, general impressions;
- behavioral prediction, i.e. where a user can go in the future, again from a multimodal perspective (physical and web);
- Fair space planning and layout optimization, i.e. suggest to the organizers how to spatially arrange the different booths to minimize crowded bottlenecks.

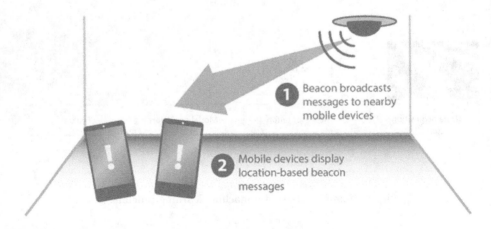

Fig. 2. Use of Bluetooth Beacons to give personalized recommendations.

The analysis of geo-located patterns to give personalized recommendations is a rather novel research field. According to Google Scholar, in 2012 the works containing as keywords "geolocation + big-data + recommendation + prediction" were about 356; last year (2017), the same research produced 1350 new sources. Studies on combining this geo-located modality with the web are very scarce, and the few references available are mostly related to surveillance scenarios and information fusion [3,23]. This context also lacks a formal framework and rigorous definitions that describe how the two modalities are related, from simple correlations to causal relationships. From the web/multimedia perspective, the prediction of a physical behavior from online social dynamics is completely new, and this may be attributed to the lack of a platform able to collect a sufficiently large and informative dataset.

The remainder of the paper is organized as follows: in Sect. 2 the literature on user profiling is reviewed, considering physical location, online, and also from a multimodal perspective; in Sect. 3, we analyze some proposed approaches within the scope of deep learning to solve our proposed task; in Sect. 4, challenges and open questions are discussed, and research directions envisioned. Finally, some conclusive remarks are given in Sect. 5.

2   State of the Art

In this section we discuss the related works linked to our proposal task. We start to explore the web domain, then the physical one and finally the two domains combined together.

2.1   Web Domain

Recommender systems [2] represent one of the most important research domain where user profiles are strongly exploited, the majority of them focusing on the web domain. In particular, recommender systems aim to suggest products which should be highly preferable by the user, matching his personal profile. These profiles exploit visual data [11], text [1,25] or combination of them [13], especially when it comes to social networks [7–9,16,18]. These approaches can be named as *content-based* approaches since they infer on the genuine content expressed by a media. Other approaches use metadata such as web log-data, indicating the websites visited by a user, the objects bought in an e-commerce platform etc. [12,17,19–21,25], to build a profile. In this case, such profiles are used more in terms of *collaborative filtering*, that is, the recommender systems provide suggestions considering similarities among users' behavior (the user is recommended items that people with similar log data liked in the past).

The approaches which consider log data are more interesting for our research project, since they model a sort of dynamics which can be considered also in the physical domain.

Deep learning comes into play in the recommender systems realm (considering web data) since they are capable of managing huge quantities of data. Actually, they need to be fed with a large amount of training information for adequately tune the weight of the neurons. In addition, they are particularly suited to fuse different data modalities. A recent deep learning approach [14] uses multimodal data (texts, images, social relations), by combining the decision of separate networks to infer age, gender and personality traits of social media users.

2.2   Physical Domain

Besides this, other studies exploit static location information of users and items to capture the local preference and the geographical clustering phenomenon. With the increasing deployment and use of GPS-enabled devices, massive amounts of GPS data are becoming available. In [4], they propose a general framework for the mining of semantically meaningful, significant locations from such data. They present techniques capable of extracting semantic locations from GPS data. They capture the relationships between locations and users with a graph.

The advances in location-acquisition and mobile computing techniques have generated massive spatial trajectory data, which represent the mobility of a diversity of moving objects, such as people, vehicles, and animals. Many techniques have been proposed for processing, managing, and mining trajectory data. In [29], an overview is reported on the trajectory data mining challenge.

Other papers exploit various features of users and points of interest (POIs) for accurate POI recommendation. In [10] a novel POI recommendation framework named RecNet is proposed, which is developed on top of a deep neural network to incorporate various features in LBSNs (location-based social networks) and learn their joint influence on user behavior. More specifically, co-visiting geographical and categorical influences in LBSNs are exploited to alleviate the data sparsity issue in POI recommendation and are converted to feature vector representations of POIs and users via feature embedding.

In [6], the focus is on cross-scene crowd counting. To address this problem, the authors propose a deep convolutional neural network for crowd counting, and it is trained alternatively with two related learning objectives, crowd density and crowd count.

Recently, a huge line of research tries to solve the recommendation problem using generative models. In [24] an overview of the main Data Mining techniques used in the context of the recommender systems is given. First, they describe common preprocessing methods such as sampling or dimensionality reduction. Next, they review the most important classification techniques, including Bayesian Networks, etc. Finally, they survey these techniques uses in recommender systems and present cases where they have been successfully applied.

Even in this case, the studies can help us, but they does not describe exactly the problem that we have considered.

2.3   Multimodal Domain

Few approaches in the recent literature try to unify web and physical information to increase the quality of recommendations.

One of the few works proposes LA-LDA [26], a location-aware probabilistic generative model that exploits location-based ratings to model user profiles and produce web recommendations. While most of the existing recommendation models do not consider the spatial information of users or items, LA-LDA supports three classes of location-based ratings: spatial user ratings for non-spatial items, non-spatial user ratings for spatial items, and spatial user ratings for spatial items.

However, in the overlying articles, they use fixed location coordinates of the user or item derived from social platforms information (Foursquare, Meetup, etc.). In our work we want to keep in consideration also the movement of the user inside the fair, a completely different type of information that may be important to improve the recommendation quality.

3   The WP User Profile

Our research proposal wants to integrate data coming from the web domain and the physical one in a different way than what has appeared so far in the literature. The idea is motivated by the fair environment, which is a sufficiently large but still measurable scenario, where exhibitors are densely located and where crowds of people are moving. The physical domain in this case is highly informative, more than what happens in an generic urban area. In addition, exhibitors have always a web counterpart which can be accessed by the users, and this create the territory to build a genuinely hybrid framework of user profiling. The WP user profile is designed as a data structure made by attributes which come from the web and physical domain. For example, web attributes could be content based (which type of product the user like the most) or log-based (which website have been visited). Physical attributes are the locations visited during the event, composed are spatio-temporal trajectories which in turn can be described by attributes themselves (is the user moving quickly in the fair environment? Is the user preferring to stay in few locations?). Privacy concerns, obviously present here, can be managed easily: in fact, it is a common habit in the big fairs to have a set of "buyers", that is, people that usually has an important role in the fairs since they do business at a certain level. Buyers want to have particular services in terms of recommendations, and they agree to give permission to access personal data, from the web behavior to the physical one when they are in the fair area. On these type of users, we want to do research for creating WP profiles.

Many research questions arise, which are listed in the following together with the intended directions we want to follow.

4   Research Questions and Proposed Directions

In this section we will individuate some research questions (letter Q). Then, we will try to provide our intuitions about possible answers (letter A), exploiting some literature of the human sciences and/or our speculations.

Q1 - How we model the WP profiles? We need to have a common space where the different attributes coming from the web and physical domain can co-exist.

A1 - Our idea is to exploit latent embedding techniques and in particular multi-modal deep learning [22]. With this family of techniques, cross modality feature learning is exploited, with the rationale that better features for one modality (e.g., web) can be learned if multiple modalities (e.g., web and physical) are present at feature learning time. Deep learning is particularly suited for this type of analysis since, other than being capable of managing huge amounts of data, it can be understood by *visualization approaches* [27] which open the box of a deep network, highlighting the features which have been more responsible to explain the data.

Q2 - Is there any statistical relation between the two different modalities? We want to understand if it exists a relation between the Web modality and the Physical modality.

A2 - In the case the previous challenge is solved, the two modalities W and P are coexisting in a latent subspace, that is, in the same numerical space (features space). At this point, statistical relations can be considered and evaluated, and this will represent one of the most intriguing aspect of the research. In fact, it will be possible to check standard connections (a user is interested in web sites of dogs, and in the fair is expected spend time near exhibitors of dogs) but truly novel characteristics, as

- The dynamics in the web space when exploring web site (in a single day a big number of websites has been visited) could be associated to a physical behavior in the fair (a fast exploration of many exhibitors)?
- Is the sociability in the web domain correlated to a tendency of engaging social exchanges in the physical world?
- is there any relation of causality between the web and the physical world exploration? If yes, which sense regulates the relation? Is the web domain the triggers the curiosity of the user towards some exhibitors or does the viceversa rules the joint domain?
- the time spent on a particular website does correlate with the time spent in a physical exposition?

Q3 - How we understand if the two modalities are "asymmetric"? It is possible to understand if one of the two modalities is more informative than the other?

A3 - A way to find the information amount of the two different modalities is to separate these and making an evaluation for each of them. Thus, the most powerful modality is the one that provide the best recommendation fidelity.

Q4 - Can we employ the user profiling in order to identify the behaviour of a particular visitor? By this question we want to understand if it is possible to gather more data about a user, such as sociability, passions, hobbies. Through these information the quality of recommendations could considerably increasing.

A4 - There are many works addressing the challenges of social network and social media analysis in terms of prediction and inference the life-style. These include generating realistic social network topologies, awareness of user activities, topic and trend generation, estimation of user attributes from their social content, and behavior detection. The answer to this question could be new analysis framework based on examining mining methods for the vast amount of social content produced by the visitors during the fair.

Q5 - How can we measure the goodness of recommendation? With this question we want to understand how to get a benchmark over the recommendation results.

A5 - To obtain a benchmark of accuracy, the standard Pattern Recognition procedures can be employed. More in detail, we can divide the data in a training partition (for the creation of the recommendation) and a test set, where the ground truth labels do exist in both the web domain, capturing whether the user buys the item, and in the physical domain in the form of particular itineraries inside the exhibitions (correct if the user follows that particular trajectory, entirely or partially).

Q6 - Which other scenarios could exploit user profiling in terms of recommendation and behaviour prediction? The question is aimed at finding other possible application fields other than the Fair Industry.

A6 - Nowadays, there exists a lot of events that have mobile application and social network pages. These tools are well suited to generate digital information. Moreover, these events that have web registration systems that can be employed to gather data from participants or visitors. These scenarios can be theme-parks, cinemas, museums, etc. In all of these places it is also possible to install sensors that provide location data for each device connected. Thus, both web and physical modalities are present and can be exploited to create personalized services and recommendations.

5   Conclusion

This proposal paper presents our direction about the user profiling for the recommendation and behavioral prediction inside the fair industry. The insertion of these system may have important relapsed for the tourism economy. It could improve the visitors experience (ex: decrease the waste time) within the fair and thus the exhibitors revenues. Indeed, the huge amounts of data are useful feedback to improve the exhibitions structure from year to year.

References

1. Adeniyi, D., Wei, Z., Yongquan, Y.: Automated web usage data mining and recommendation system using k-nearest neighbor (KNN) classification method. Appl. Comput. Inf. **12**(1), 90–108 (2016)
2. Adomavicius, G., Tuzhilin, A.: Toward the next generation of recommender systems: a survey of the state-of-the-art and possible extensions. IEEE Trans. Knowl. Data Eng. **17**(6), 734–749 (2005). https://doi.org/10.1109/TKDE.2005.99

3. Bello-Orgaz, G., Jung, J.J., Camacho, D.: Social big data: recent achievements and new challenges. Inf. Fusion **28**, 45–59 (2016)
4. Cao, X., Cong, G., Jensen, C.S.: Mining significant semantic locations from GPS data. Proc. VLDB Endow. **3**(1–2), 1009–1020 (2010). https://doi.org/10.14778/1920841.1920968
5. Chen, L.H., Wu, E.H.K., Jin, M.H., Chen, G.H.: Intelligent fusion of wi-fi and inertial sensor-based positioning systems for indoor pedestrian navigation. IEEE Sens. J. **14**(11), 4034–4042 (2014). https://doi.org/10.1109/JSEN.2014.2330573
6. Zhang, C., Li, H., Wang, X., Yang, X.: Cross-scene crowd counting via deep convolutional neural networks. In: Proceedings of IEEE Conference on Computer Vision and Pattern Recognition 2015 (2015)
7. Cristani, M., Burato, E., Santacá, K., Tomazzoli, C.: The spider-man behavior protocol: exploring both public and dark social networks for fake identity detection in terrorism informatics. In: CEUR Workshop Proceedings, vol. 1489, pp. 77–88 (2015)
8. Cristani, M., Fogoroasi, D., Tomazzoli, C.: Measuring homophily. In: CEUR Workshop Proceedings, vol. 1748 (2016)
9. Cristani, M., Olivieri, F., Tomazzoli, C.: Viral experiments. In: CEUR Workshop Proceedings, vol. 1959 (2017)
10. Ding, R., Chen, Z.: RecNet: a deep neural network for personalized poi recommendation in location-based social networks. Int. J. Geograph. Inf. Sci. **0**(0), 1–18 (2018). https://doi.org/10.1080/13658816.2018.1447671
11. Dominguez, V., Messina, P., Parra, D., Mery, D., Trattner, C., Soto, A.: Comparing neural and attractiveness-based visual features for artwork recommendation. In: Proceedings of the 2nd Workshop on Deep Learning for Recommender Systems, DLRS 2017, pp. 55–59. ACM, New York (2017). https://doi.org/10.1145/3125486.3125495
12. Dumais, S., Jeffries, R., Russell, D.M., Tang, D., Teevan, J.: Understanding user behavior through log data and analysis. In: Olson, J.S., Kellogg, W.A. (eds.) Ways of Knowing in HCI, pp. 349–372. Springer, New York (2014). https://doi.org/10.1007/978-1-4939-0378-8_14
13. Elkahky, A.M., Song, Y., He, X.: A multi-view deep learning approach for cross domain user modeling in recommendation systems. In: Proceedings of the 24th International Conference on World Wide Web, pp. 278–288. International World Wide Web Conferences Steering Committee (2015)
14. Farnadi, G., Tang, J., De Cock, M., Moens, M.F.: User profiling through deep multimodal fusion. In: Proceedings of the 11th ACM International Conference on Web Search and Data Mining. ACM (2018)
15. Herbig, P., O'Hara, B., Palumbo, F.: Differences between trade show exhibitors and non-exhibitors. J. Bus. Ind. Market. **12**(6), 368–382 (1997)
16. Ikeda, K., Hattori, G., Ono, C., Asoh, H., Higashino, T.: Twitter user profiling based on text and community mining for market analysis. Knowl.-Based Syst. **51**, 35–47 (2013)
17. Dhana Lakshmi, P., Ramani, K., Eswara Reddy, B.: Efficient techniques for clustering of users on web log data. In: Behera, H.S., Mohapatra, D.P. (eds.) Computational Intelligence in Data Mining. AISC, vol. 556, pp. 381–395. Springer, Singapore (2017). https://doi.org/10.1007/978-981-10-3874-7_35
18. Li, R., Wang, S., Deng, H., Wang, R., Chang, K.C.C.: Towards social user profiling: unified and discriminative influence model for inferring home locations. In: Proceedings of the 18th ACM SIGKDD International Conference on Knowledge Discovery and Data Mining, pp. 1023–1031. ACM (2012)

19. Maheswari, B.U., Sumathi, P.: A new clustering and preprocessing for web log mining. In: 2014 World Congress on Computing and Communication Technologies (WCCCT), pp. 25–29. IEEE (2014)
20. Munk, M., Kapusta, J., Švec, P.: Data preprocessing evaluation for web log mining: reconstruction of activities of a web visitor. Procedia Comput. Sci. **1**(1), 2273–2280 (2010)
21. Nasraoui, O., Soliman, M., Saka, E., Badia, A., Germain, R.: A web usage mining framework for mining evolving user profiles in dynamic web sites. IEEE Trans. Knowl. Data Eng. **20**(2), 202–215 (2008)
22. Ngiam, J., Khosla, A., Kim, M., Nam, J., Lee, H., Ng, A.Y.: Multimodal deep learning. In: Proceedings of the 28th International Conference on Machine Learning (ICML-11), pp. 689–696 (2011)
23. Williams, M.L., Burnap, P., Sloan, L.: Crime sensing with big data: the affordances and limitations of using open-source communications to estimate crime patterns. Br. J. Criminol. **57**(2), 320–340 (2017)
24. Amatriain, X., Jaimes*, A., Oliver, N., Pujol, J.M.: Data mining methods for recommender systems. In: Ricci, F., Rokach, L., Shapira, B., Kantor, P.B. (eds.) Recommender Systems Handbook, pp. 39–71. Springer, Boston, MA (2011). https://doi.org/10.1007/978-0-387-85820-3_2
25. Yang, Y.C.: Web user behavioral profiling for user identification. Decis. Support Syst. **49**(3), 261–271 (2010)
26. Yin, H., Cui, B., Chen, L., Hu, Z., Zhang, C.: Modeling location-based user rating profiles for personalized recommendation. ACM Trans. Knowl. Discov. Data **9**(3), 19:1–19:41 (2015). https://doi.org/10.1145/2663356
27. Yosinski, J., Clune, J., Nguyen, A., Fuchs, T., Lipson, H.: Understanding neural networks through deep visualization. arXiv preprint arXiv:1506.06579 (2015)
28. Yuksel, U., Voola, R.: Travel trade shows: exploratory study of exhibitors' perceptions. J. Bus. Ind. Market. **25**(4), 293–300 (2010). https://doi.org/10.1108/08858621011038252
29. Zheng, Y.: Trajectory data mining: an overview. ACM Trans. Intell. Syst. Technol. **6**(3), 29:1–29:41 (2015). https://doi.org/10.1145/2743025

Making Sentiment Analysis Algorithms Scalable

Marco Cristani[✉], Matteo Cristani, Anna Pesarin, Claudio Tomazzoli,
and Margherita Zorzi

University of Verona, Verona, Italy
{marco.cristani,matteo.cristani,anna.pesarin,claudio.tomazzoli,
margherita.zorzi}@univr.it

Abstract. In this paper we introduce a simplified approach to sentiment analysis: a lexicon-driven method based upon only adjectives and adverbs. This method is compared in cross-validation with other known techniques and then compared directly to the gold standard, a sample of human subjects asked to deliver the same class of judgments computed by the method. We prove that the method is similar in accuracy and precision with the other methods. We finally argue that the approach we employ is more valid than others for it is scalable, and exportable to languages other than English.

1 Introduction

Sentiment Analysis (SA) concerns the use of natural language processing and text mining for the automatic tagging of a text as *positive, negative* or *neutral*, on the basis of its content. Natural language, however, is inherently vague and often unstructured. As a consequence, the automatic understanding of the "polarity" of a text is a challenging problem, that can be expressed in term of questions we should answer as follows: "What is an opinion?" and "How can we summarize a set of opinions?"

An *opinion* is a judgment expressed by someone over an object, individual, animal, or fact. In [16] authors draw special attention to the fact that there are several kind of sentences, each of which can express "sentiment" in different ways. Therefore, we ought to consider several kinds of opinions, formally summarised in the following classification:

Direct Opinions: the opinion is clearly expressed in the words of the sentence so that it can be extracted using only the words themselves: i.e. "image quality is perfect").

Indirect Opinions: the opinion is *not* clearly expressed in the words of the sentence, which contains also some implicit knowledge so that it cannot be extracted without the additional use of this knowledge: i.e. "I bought this mattress two months ago and now there is a sinking in the middle". To understand the underlying opinion we need to know what to expect from a mattress.

© Springer Nature Switzerland AG 2018
C. Pautasso et al. (Eds.): ICWE 2018, LNCS 11153, pp. 136–147, 2018.
https://doi.org/10.1007/978-3-030-03056-8_12

Comparative Opinions: they express a comparison: i.e. "Image quality is better in Iphone than in Blackberry".

Subjective Opinions: they express a personal judgment: i.e. "I like the new smartphone"

Objective Opinions: they express a fact: i.e. "My new smartphone doesn't work any longer"

Several algorithms for *opinion mining*, also called *sentiment analysis* based on a statical approach over single words in sentences have been proposed as *specific procedures*: they can extract sentiment of a particular kind, e.g. direct opinions rather than indirect ones. In other words, algorithms for Sentiment Analysis are hardly *scalable*, i.e. enough general to address the detection of a general opinion.

This is principally due to the fact that sentiment analysis algorithm are often based on very strong assumption about the language, specifically oriented to the detection of a single form: for example, comparative opinions are recognized thanks to some regular constructs such as "but, nevertheless, even if, etc.": Unfortunately, since written natural language is generally unstructured, these constructs might or might not be present. This clearly provides an irremediable failure in the opinion mining. A simple example is the sentences "I do prefer Iphone to Blackberry thanks to image quality": it contain a comparative form, but it can not be detected by regular constructs mentioned above.

It is evident that efficiency and scalability are two strongly related goals in Sentiment Analysis algorithm design.

The recognition of subjective and objective opinions is a subtask in Sentiment Analysis: in some work [13] authors state that subjective sentences are more likely to contain opinions than objective ones and thanks to this they use subjectivity detection techniques as pre-computation steps in sentiment analysis.

Consider the sentence below, where more than one opinion is summarised

Example 1. I bought an iPhone a few days ago. It is such a nice phone. The touch screen is really cool. The voice quality is clear too. It is much better than my old Blackberry, which was a terrible phone and so difficult to type with its tiny keys. However, my mother was mad with me as I did not tell her before I bought the phone. She also thought the phone was too expensive.

We can have several analysis aspects:

- document level: is the review a "+" or a "–" ?
- sentence level: each sentence is a "+" or a "–" ?
- entity and feature/aspect level: bind any subject (entity) in the sentence to adjectives which can describe one or more aspect of these subjects and then evaluate the sentiment of these adjectives, who expressed it (opinion holder) and the time frame in which it has been stated.

To better model all these analysis aspects, in [12] Liu formally defines an opinion as a tuple:

$$(entityaspect(i,j), sentiment(i,j,k,l), opinionholder(k), date(l)) \qquad (1)$$

given that, an *opinion document* can be defined a collection of opinions.

Sentiment Analysis goal is therefore to find all the tuples in an opinion document.

This can be a quite complicated task, due to the complexity and the lack of fixed structure in natural language, so that using current algorithms entity-aspects detection and opinion holder detection are complex task, linking them is a challenging task while sentiment determination is somehow simpler.

Distinguishing between direct and indirect opinions and identification of sarcasm and irony are still open problems.

Therefore a simpler goal, but more likely to be achieved, is a reduced version of the original goal such as determining the sentiment only, without entity-aspects detection.

2   Basics

In Sentiment analysis there are several features that can be taken into account, either combined or by themselves, to try and understand the polarity of a text.

Most important sentiment indicators are words called *sentiment words* also called *opinion words*. These words are commonly used to express appositive or negative sentiment, such as "good, bad, amazing, etc." In addition to single words there are also small sentences or *part of speech* (PoS) like "cost someone an arm and a leg".

A *sentiment lexicon* is a list of such words and PoS each coupled with a polarity value typically ranging between -1 and 1. It might be generated either manually or automatically: in this latter case from each *seed word* in a given list is considered along with its lexical relationships such as hyponym or hyperonym. In [21] the authors choose synonyms and antonyms using the dictionary Wordnet [14]. The most widely used sentiment lexicon for english language is named "Sentiwordnet" [10]. For other languages there isn't any renown efficient public available sentiment lexicon; for instance for italian language there is a tool named "Sentix", built in a completely automatic way, which presents some drawbacks such as errors in polarity and low coverage (ca. 60.000 word and PoS compared to the 117.000 in Sentiwordnet).

Frequency Term. A classical feature in Sentiment analysis is a vector in which every component corresponds to a word or word sequence (n-gram), meaning that the value on the ith axes is the relative frequency within the document (or document collection) of the corresponding word. Often used are sophisticated measures like Term Frequency Inverse Document Frequency (TFIDF) in which the ratio between word occurrences and number of documents is taken into account. These features are typical of the discipline of text retrieval and text classification.

Part of Speech (PoS tag). Natural Language Processing (NLP) techniques allow the coupling of words to their Part of Speech (POS tag) so that a label can be applied to a word to determine whether it is a verb, noun, adjective or adverb. Current Part of Speech tagger are known to achieve an accuracy close to 95%. This is quite relevant in sentiment analysis because of the importance of the knowledge of the kind of a word: it has been shown that adjective and adverbs are relevant indicators when dealing with the polarity of a text, as stated originally in Pang and Lee [15].

Sentiment Shifters. Sentiment shifters are words used to change the orientation such as negation words, (e.g. not, don't) or intensifier (very, absolutely, rarely).

Dependency Parser. A dependency parser is a method to analyse the grammatical structure of a sentence so that relationships between subsets of words can be inferred. These subsets represent periods in a sentence, verbal predicates, nominal predicates and relationships can be organised in a tree to better represent internal hierarchies. Root node identifies the whole text, its descendants represents sentences, incidental phrases, verbal predicates, nominal predicates conjunctions down to the leafs which stands for PoS tag and single words.

3   Related Work

Sentiment analysis main approaches can be divided in two macroclasses: (1) Lexicon-based, and (2) Machine learning-based. There are also some hybrid approaches that combine these above mentioned.

Sentiment lexicon based methods makes extensive use of the polarity of single words as a mean to create a measure of the overall sentence sentiment. Turney [19] proposes the use of the mean of adjective and adverb polarities to help predict the sentiment orientation, while Taboada et al. [18] lexicon-based approaches made also use of negation and intensifiers (i.e. very, really, extremely etc.) Lexicon-based methods can be considered accurate in classification task but they suffer a few drawbacks:

- A single word can have both a legitimate positive or negative orientation, depending on the context. A simple example is the word *cheap* can be generally considered positive, such as in *This hotel is cheap*, nevertheless can be use in negative meaning, such as in *as cheap as it's worth*.
- a sentence may include sentiment word even though it does non express any opinion, i.e. *Can you tell me which Sony camera is good?* or *If I can find a good camera in the shop, I will buy it.*
- a sentence without sentiment words may legitimately express a sentiment, and almost all indirect opinions are in this form.

These methods are based on machine learning and more specifically supervised classification techniques. Given that some kind of words are relevant indicators of the polarity of the sentence in which these words appear, the probability of a text to belong to a certain polarity class (positive, negative, neutral) can be devised from the presence and the number of these kind of words in the text. This is similar to a traditional classification problem, when a text has to be classified based on topic (i.e. sport, politics or science), so that a common approach is using words as features (bag of words) and then apply supervised classification methods such as naïve Bayes classifier or support vector machine (SVM) [11]. Among the advantages these technique allows, we can count the possibility to adapt the training set to fit the context of the application, whereas with lexicon based approaches we cannot easily adapt the lexicon to the specific problem at hand.

These techniques have been used to classify movie reviews as *positive or negative* [15]; using single words (unigrams) as features and combining bag of word and SVM the results outperformed the ones obtained using other classical classifiers. Moreover, PartOfSpeech tags, bigram, adjectives and their combinations have been tested.

A well known approach involves the combination of Natural Language Processing (NLP), machine learning and lexicon-based techniques. In [8] a dependency parser is used as preprocessing step of an algorithm named "sentiment propagation". A dependency parser identifies relationships between words set of words so that a tree structure representation can be created. The authors makes the assumption that every linguistic element such as nouns, verbs, etc. has a latent sentiment value, which is propagated throughout the tree structure identified by the dependency parser. Propagation rules var according to construct: adverbial modifiers (i.e. very, weaken) may strengthen or weaken the sentiment of a specific word. Prepositions such as *to, with, in* are considered as channels through which sentiment flows across words. In another paper [17] has been shown that the majority of sentiment analysis techniques are based on semantic of single words, which suffer the drawback of missing to understand the relationship between words and therefore phrasal semantics. The authors therefore propose a method based on recursive neural network in which words are represented with a matrix and a vector. The latter catches the meaning of the item (word, sentence, PoS) while the matrix identifies the meaning of elements related to the item itself.

Some investigations have also been performed about multi language sentiment analysis algorithms. These need at least sentiment lexicon for each language and a wide ground truth for each language (hopefully context aware).

It has been shown that performance of sentiment analysis applied to an automatically traduced text are comparable with the ones given by english language [2].

4 A Simple Method for Scalable Sentiment Extraction

In this section we introduce the methodology we developed to make easier and more efficient multi language sentiment analysis. Our goal can be summarised in the following main objectives:

- to reduce lexical resources needed to mine the polarity of a word (this aims to make easier the multi language approach)
- to efficiently identify discriminant lexical pattern for sentiment analysis.

It is known from literature [3] that different POS methods have different effect on the results of SA extraction, and that a simple POS tagging is not enough to obtain efficient performances [15]; moreover we need to keep trace of *shifters* such as negations. We therefore try to design an efficient word labeling based on finite sequence of POS tagging to be later coupled with an efficient use of the sentiment lexicon and we named it SiSeSa, acronym for "*Simple Sentiment Scalable Algorithm*". The result has been a vectorial description of information related of a word (POS tag plus polarity prevision), that we will called *information vector*. In the following sections we describe the main phases of the method: *text preprocessing* and *creation of the information vector*.

4.1 Lexicon Based Polarity Analysis

Each document we process (a customer review, as exploited in the following) is preprocessed in order to simplify further computation. In particular, we extract, for each word, a part of speech tag, a polarity and a probability. Given a text, it is possible to classify each word into a lexical category (with a related probability) by a Part of Speech algorithm. We use very standard subroutines such as tokenisation, lemmization and we retrieve POS information with the OpenNLP package[1].

Since word polarity is strongly influenced by the presence of negation in phrases, we exploit a dependency parser to detect negations and their scopes [8]. The presence of a negation influences the polarity of a word with a negative multiplicative factor (-1).

Once POS-tagging and negation information have been detected, the polarity of a word can is finally extracted. We use the sentiment lexicon Sentiwordnet[2] [1] which associates to each group of word with equivalent or similar meaning (named *synset*) in its knowledge base a triple of values ps_s, ns_s and os_s, where ps_s denotes the positivity degree, ns_s denotes the negativity degree, os_s denotes the objectivity of the words so that neutral polarized words can be easily detected; we have $ps_s + ns_s = 1$. The overall polarity of the synset is computed as $p_s = ps_s - ns_s$. To each synset can be associated more than a single lemma (a word p_w in the text), and to each POS-tagged lemma can be associated more than a single synset.

To relate a single score to each word p_w, a weighted average of the valued of all synset p_w is associated to is computed. The weights come from the ranking of the synsets, and is a function of the probabilities that link p_w to each synset. Therefore we have $p_w = \frac{1}{r_s} \sum_{s \in S} p_s$, where S is the set of the synsets related to w and r_s is the rank of the synset s.

In our classification, after the labeling of each word by one of the three possible polarity classes (positive, negative and neutral), we further classify as neutral those words showing very small positive or negative polarity. In particular we empirically choose $\pm 0, 1$ as a threshold for the classification of neutrals.

---

[1] OpenNLP package (http://opennlp.sourceforge.net).
[2] http://sentiwordnet.isti.cnr.it/.

4.2   Information Vector Creation Using Markov Model

Following [9], a sequence of n POS-tags can be viewed as a Markov chain of order n. In the rest of the paper, we will denote a Markov Model (MM). Each state k of the chain represents a triple $\langle l, s, p \rangle$, where: l is a POS-tag; s is an information about the polarity of the word; p is a probability associated to the state, depending on the $k - 1$ predecessor states; As previously stated, in the context of SA the component s is crucial, in particular when the word is classified as an adjective. This information ranges over a set of polarity value, i.e. negative, positive and neutral.

We define an eight state MM, claiming that each state assumes one of the following possible overall values: (i) negative adjective, (ii) neutral adjective, (iii) positive adjective, (iv) adverb, (v) noun, (vi) negative verb, (vii) neutral verb, (viii) positive verb.

Overall state values are determined by the component l and s. When l tag the word as an adverb or a noun, we assume to have the "neutral element" polarity ϵ in s.

Once a text has been converted into a sequence of states, we can calculate the transition matrix. Let us denote state variables as S_t, with $t \in \{1, \ldots, N\}$. Expressions of the form $P(S_t | S_{t-1}, S_{t-2} \ldots, S_{t-k})$ denote transition probabilities for a k-order MM. Throughout the analysis of transition matrices, an algorithm can detect sequences of states which may identify relevant sentiment information.

We recall that weights of a Markov chain can be estimated by counting state frequencies. The associated transition matrix has dimension $N \times N \times k$, where N is the number of states and k is the order of the chain.

The transition matrix can be successively converted into a vector and, following a discriminative approach, can be viewed as a point in a l-dimension space, for a suitable dimension l.

We therefore apply a supervised discriminative classification technique, such as the well known support vector machine (SVM) [20].

5   Experiment

The initial data set we consider for our experiment is built upon 380 costumer reviews from the web sites Amazon.com and TripAdvisor.com. Reviews from Amazon concern books and technological devices, whereas reviews form Trip Advisor are about evaluation of restaurants. Each review is written in English language and contains at least 40 characters. To create a gold standard we performed a manual revision: all reviews in the dataset have been manual annotated by 38 students in Foreign Language. The reviewer's task has been to express a positive, negative or neutral judgment about the review, in a blind setting. In order to make the annotation more sharp, each review has been evaluated twice (by different reviewers) and, following a standard praxis in reference standard creation, a third opinion has been provided. The third opinion is directly represented by the numeric overall judgment (the "star" evaluation), ranging in the interval 1 to 5. Following [15], numerical judgments have been converted into the corresponding qualitative classes: negative judgement (values 1 and 2), positive judgment (values 4 and 5) and neutral judgment (value 3).

One of the most important aspect of the gold standard is of course the quality: in other word, we aim to compare experimental results against a robust reference truth. To this end, is central to evaluate it, or, at least, to know and predict possible errors can occur.

In our setting, errors can be related to the following aspects: (i) subjective judgement, occurring when the user and the reviewers evaluate the product or the service in a different way; (ii) wrong description, when word in the text are not enough to correctly express the judgement, and (iii) textual description and overall evaluation ("stars") disagree; inaccuracy, when the user is not able to express a fair and consistent opinion.

Looking for manual reviews, a percentage of $78,6\%$ received coincident judgements (no review has been evaluated as both negative and positive). Reviews that obtained the agree between the user and only one reviewer reach the 89%. Only the 0.15% of the total received three discordant opinion.

In the experiment described below, we will use the two following datasets, built upon the initial data set of 380 Amazon and Trip Advisor reviews:

– Dataset MA (Manual Annotation): includes all reviews that received equal judgment by reviewer and the gold standard is represented by reviewers' evaluations.
– Dataset CSR (Costumer Satisfaction Rating): includes all the reviews in the main dataset and the gold standard is represented by users' evaluations.

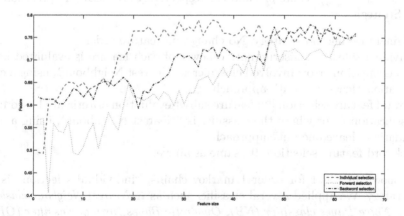

Fig. 1. Feature selection curves for 1-order MM using SVM classifiers on MA dataset

For each review, an eight state MM has been trained, with states representing, as in Sect. 4.2: (i) negative adjective, (ii) neutral adjective, (iii) positive adjective, (iv) adverb, (v) noun, (vi) negative verb, (vii) neutral verb, (viii) positive verb.

Table 1. Accuracy values for order 1, 2, 3 markov chains on MA and CSR dataset.

Dataset	1st order	2nd order	3rd order
MA	0.79	0.80	0.77
CSR	0.70	0.69	0.64

The order in Markov chain has been varied between 1 and 3 given 64, 512 and 4096 transition probabilities which we will call *feature*.

The goal being to understand which features were relevant in determine whether a sentiment was neutral, positive or negative, we made extensive use of support vector machine technique. Having a limited set of valid samples, we used a cross validation "leave one out" approach, iteratively considering each review as test element while all the others were the training set.

We tested our framework against two scenario each including the three classes of *positive (PosR), neutre (NeuR) and negative (NegR)* reviews:

- (A) PosR versus NegR;
- (B) PosR versus NeuR versus NegR.

Due to feature vector dimension, we applied some feature strategies in order to better understand the most significant transition probability subset: individual selection, forward selection, backword selection [9].

Each strategy leads to a particular feature ordering. Classification performances have been evaluated using single class F-score, the classifier being a Support Vector Machine with a 10 fold cross validation to avoid overfitting. $Fscore_A = 2 \cdot \frac{pre \cdot rec}{pre+rec}$ where *pre* and *rec* respectively are class "A" precision and recall. Strategies:

1. Original ranking: no strategy. No changes in feature order.
2. Individual selection: discriminative power of each feature is evaluated based on classification error: involved classifier is "Nearest Neighbour", using a cross validation "leave one out" approach.
3. Forward feature selection [9]: feature subset evaluation criteria are based upon classification error where the classifier is "Nearest Neighbour", using a cross validation "leave one out" approach.
4. Backword feature selection [9]: same as above.

As shown in Fig. 1 for order 1 markov chains, "individual selection" is the best strategy. We applied several classifier such as *K-Nearest Neigbour classifier (KNN), Naive Bayes classifier (NB), Quadratic Bayes Normal classifier (QBN), Support Vector Machine (SVM)* and we observed their behavior when varying feature number. As can be seen in Fig. 2 individual behavior are similar up to almost 30 features, whereas SVM and NB maintain their performances even with larger number of features.

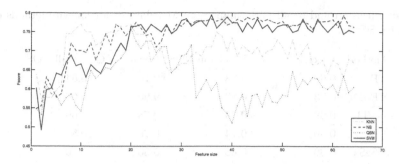

Fig. 2. Individual feature selection curves for 1-order MM using 4 different classifiers on MA dataset.

Classification results shown in Table 1 highlights performances of the method, while in Table 2 precision and recall are detailed with respect to both positive and negative polarity classes.

Table 2. Precision and recall performances detailed with respect to both positive and negative polarity classes.

Dataset	Markov order	Precision NEG	Precision POS	Recall NEG	Recall POS
MA	1	0.79	0.80	0.80	0.78
MA	2	0.80	0.80	0.80	0.80
MA	3	0.75	0.79	0.80	0.73
CSR	1	0.72	0.72	0.73	0.71
CSR	2	0.71	0.69	0.67	0.72
CSR	3	0.63	0.67	0.60	0.67

Table 3. Accuracy values on MA dataset for known methods compared with SiSeSa

TF	TFIDF	posTF	SL	SiSeSa
0.70	0.78	0.72	0.78	0.80

We tested the method SiSeSa against other well known from the literature, such as Term Frequency (TF), Term Frequency Inverse Document Frequency(TFIDF), POStag and sentiment lexicon. We performed the comparison on dataset MA, using SVM classifier following [15] with a "leave one out" cross validation technique; results are summarised in Tables 2, 3 and 4.

As can be seen in these tables SiSeSa outperforms current techniques.

Table 4. Precision and recall performances on MA dataset for known methods compared with SiSeSa.

Method	Precision NEG	Precision POS	Recall NEG	Recall POS
TF	0.68	0.73	0.76	0.64
TF-IDF	0.73	0.87	0.90	0.66
posTF	0.69	0.75	0.78	0.66
LB	0.80	0.74	0.76	0.81
SiSeSa	0.80	0.80	0.80	0.80

6   Conclusions

In this paper we dealt with the problem of building a method for sentiment analysis that results scalable. The core idea of the method consists in using only adjectives and adverbs as indicators of orientation of a document. In particular we settle an experiment for comparing the results of the method with the gold standard of human subjects expressing the same judgments. The method is proven to be effective and shows the potential of being applied to languages other than English, both properties that are not general for sentiment analysis methods.

Further investigations will be performed towards specific lexicon-driven methods, similarly to what has been done with other methods in various context, in particular in pharmacology [4–6, 22–24]. One application that is consequent to a study performed by some of the authors regards viral experiments on-line [7].

References

1. Baccianella, S., Esuli, A., Sebastiani, F.: Sentiwordnet 3.0: an enhanced lexical resource for sentiment analysis and opinion mining. In: Proceedings of the Seventh International Conference on Language Resources and Evaluation (LREC 2010). European Language Resources Association (ELRA) (2010)
2. Balahur, A., Turchi, M.: Multilingual sentiment analysis using machine translation? In: Proceedings of the 3rd Workshop in Computational Approaches to Subjectivity and Sentiment Analysis, WASSA 2012, pp. 52–60 (2012)
3. Benamara, F., Cesarano, C., Picariello, A., Reforgiato, D., Subrahmanian, V.S.: Sentiment analysis: adjectives and adverbs are better than adjectives alone. In: Proceedings of the International Conference on Weblogs and Social Media (ICWSM) (2007)
4. Combi, C., Zorzi, M., Pozzani, G., Arzenton, E., Moretti, U.: Normalizing spontaneous reports into MedDRA: some experiments with MagiCoder. IEEE J. Biomed. Health Inform. 1–8 (2018). https://doi.org/10.1109/JBHI.2018.2861213
5. Combi, C., Zorzi, M., Pozzani, G., Moretti, U., Arzenton, E.: From narrative descriptions to MedDRA: automagically encoding adverse drug reactions. J. Biomed. Inform. **84**, 184–199 (2018)
6. Cristani, M., Bertolaso, A., Scannapieco, S., Tomazzoli, C.: Future paradigms of automated processing of business documents. Int. J. Inf. Manag. **40**, 67–75 (2018)

7. Cristani, M., Olivieri, F., Tomazzoli, C.: Viral experiments. In: 3rd International Workshop on Knowledge Discovery on the WEB, KDWeb 2017, vol. 1959. CEUR Workshop Proceedings, pp. 27–35 (2017)
8. Di Caro, L., Grella, M.: Sentiment analysis via dependency parsing. Comput. Stand. Interfaces **35**(5), 442–453 (2013)
9. Duda, R.O., Hart, P.E., Stork, D.G.: Pattern Classification. Wiley, New York (2001)
10. Esuli, A., Sebastiani, F.: Sentiwordnet: a publicly available lexical resource for opinion mining. In: Proceedings of the 5th Conference on Language Resources and Evaluation, LREC 2006, pp. 417–422 (2006)
11. Joachims, T.: Making large-scale SVM learning practical. In: Advances in Kernel Methods - Support Vector Learning. MIT Press (1999)
12. Liu, B.: Sentiment analysis and opinion mining (2012)
13. Lyu, K., Kim, H.: Sentiment analysis using word polarity of social media. Wirel. Pers. Commun. **89**(3), 941–958 (2016)
14. Miller, G.A.: Wordnet: a lexical database for English. Commun. ACM **38**(11), 39–41 (1995)
15. Pang, B., Lee, L., Vaithyanathan, S.: Thumbs up? Sentiment classification using machine learning techniques. In: Proceedings of the ACL02 Conference on Empirical Methods in Natural Language Processing, EMNLP 2002, vol. 10, pp. 79–86. Association for Computational Linguistics (2002)
16. Ramanathan, N., Bing, L., Alok, C.: Sentiment analysis of conditional sentences. In: Proceedings of the 2009 Conference on Empirical Methods in Natural Language Processing: Volume 1, EMNLP 2009, vol. 1, pp. 180–189 (2009)
17. Socher, R., Huval, B., Manning, C.D., Ng, A.Y.: Semantic compositionality through recursive matrix-vector spaces. In: Proceedings of the 2012 Joint Conference on Empirical Methods in Natural Language Processing and Computational Natural Language Learning, EMNLP-CoNLL 2012, pp. 1201–1211 (2012)
18. Taboada, M., Brooke, J., Tofiloski, M., Voll, K., Stede, M.: Lexicon-basedmethods for sentiment analysis. Comput. Linguist. **37**(2), 267–307 (2011)
19. Turney, P.D., Littman, M.L.: Measuring praise and criticism: inference of semantic orientation from association. ACM Trans. Inf. Syst. **21**(4), 315–346 (2003)
20. Vapnik, V.: The Nature of Statistical Learning Theory. Springer, New York (1995). https://doi.org/10.1007/978-1-4757-3264-1
21. Williams, G.K., Anand, S.S.: Predicting the polarity strength of adjectives using wordnet. In: ICWSM. The AAAI Press (2009)
22. Zorzi, M., Combi, C., Lora, R., Pagliarini, M., Moretti, U.: Automagically encoding adverse drug reactions in MedDRA. In: Proceedings of the 2015 IEEE International Conference on Healthcare Informatics, ICHI 2015, pp. 90–99 (2015)
23. Zorzi, M., Combi, C., Pozzani, G., Arzenton, E., Moretti, U.: A co-occurrence based MedDRA terminology generation: some preliminary results. In: ten Teije, A., Popow, C., Holmes, J.H., Sacchi, L. (eds.) AIME 2017. LNCS (LNAI), vol. 10259, pp. 215–220. Springer, Cham (2017). https://doi.org/10.1007/978-3-319-59758-4_24
24. Zorzi, M., Combi, C., Pozzani, G., Moretti, U.: Mapping free text into MedDRA by natural language processing: a modular approach in designing and evaluating software extensions. In: Proceedings of the 8th ACM International Conference on Bioinformatics, Computational Biology, and Health Informatics, ACM-BCB 2017, pp. 27–35 (2017)

Using $\varphi - \delta$ Diagrams on Web Data

Giuliano Armano$^{(\boxtimes)}$ and Alessandro Giuliani

Department of Electrical and Electronic Engineering,
University of Cagliari, Cagliari, Italy
{armano,alessandro.giuliani}@diee.unica.it

Abstract. As the Web is still expanding, also the demand for fast and accurate tools aimed at analyzing digital documents (e.g., webpages) is constantly growing. In this scenario, the main strategies for producing accurate predictive models are mostly focused on the assessment of classifiers performances and features. In this work, a graphical tool, called $\varphi - \delta$ diagrams, is applied to some use cases aimed at highlighting its potential in supporting development and implementation of Web systems and services. In particular, $\varphi - \delta$ diagrams permit to visualize (i) classifier performance, in terms of accuracy and bias, and (ii) variable importance, useful to define feature ranking, selection or reduction algorithms. The proposed use cases emphasize the usefulness of the tool when dealing with Web data.

Keywords: Classifier performances · Feature selection · Web data

1 Introduction

In the current era of digital and social data, categorizing Web documents is an essential activity to improve user experience [14]. To this end, each document is typically labeled with one category. The categorization may be performed for different purposes. For example, the goal may be to identify topics discussed in documents [18,19], the language of a webpage, or the nature of a website (e.g., blog, forum, or news). When the amount of data is huge, as typically occurs when dealing with Web data, greater care must be taken in adopting reliable classifiers. To this end, the assessment of their performance plays an essential role. On the other hand, before performing classification, data preprocessing is typically used to analyze features with the aim of identifying similarities, relationships, and correlations. The goal of this preliminary step is to discover which features (or which combinations of them) are relevant for building effective prediction models. With the continuous growth of social and digital tools, services, and platforms, webpage classification rapidly attracted the scientific attention, particularly when classes are topics [15,20] and when the page at hand must be labeled as relevant or not [16]. In this work, we adopt a graphical tool able to clearly visualize, in a binary classification scenario, both classifier performance and feature importance. The former kind of analysis permits to support

© Springer Nature Switzerland AG 2018
C. Pautasso et al. (Eds.): ICWE 2018, LNCS 11153, pp. 148–158, 2018.
https://doi.org/10.1007/978-3-030-03056-8_13

researchers and scientists in evaluating and selecting the most suitable and reliable classifiers, whereas the latter is useful to perform feature ranking and/or selection, with the goal of reducing data dimensionality (thus, optimizing the use of computational resources). The rest of the paper is organized as follows: Sect. 2 introduces the background on Web document classification; in Sect. 3 the adopted tool is described; Sect. 4 illustrates some uses cases that show how to apply $\varphi - \delta$ tool to Web data; Sect. 5 ends the paper with conclusions.

2 Background

The Web is constantly expanding, and the demand for quick and accurate webpage categorization and filtering is becoming even more an essential issue in building systems and services able to improve user experience. For example, search engines are highly useful for retrieving only relevant documents. These systems are able to categorize, filter, and rank webpages, according to user queries. The capability of retrieving relevant pages only is a continuous challenge in this research field, as the amount of false positives may downgrade the performance of the search engine. Indeed, also the most acknowledged systems, like Google, struggle in this task. The consequent issue is that users must make the effort to recognize which documents are really relevant in the list of search results. Let us point out that classification is an activity on which, beyond search engines, also web services and systems may rely on. For example, anti-spam, web security, anti-phishing, online recommender systems, and social networks are based on classifiers that support networks services to make the right decision or to suggest relevant items to users. One of the current main challenges, in this scenario, is to access and propose the most valuable information, as fast and accurate as possible. Therefore, researchers and scientists are more focused on investigating novel methods for improving Web document classification and for optimizing time and computational resources. How to assess classifier performance is a key issue in the task of selecting and setting classifiers. The most acknowledged performance measures are *accuracy, precision, sensitivity* (also called *recall*) and *specificity*. These measures shares a common source, as they are derived from confusion matrices. Other classical measures are Mean Square Error [4] and cross-entropy [10]. Moreover, there are also several graphical representations and tools for model evaluation. In particular, receiver operating characteristic (ROC) curves [8] are generated by plotting the true positive rate (i.e., the *sensitivity*) against the false positive rate (i.e., *1-specificity*) in a 2D space. The integral of a ROC curve, the so-called area under the curve (AUC), is typically used for estimating the predictive ability of learning algorithms [3,12]. ROC curves give information about the "intrinsic" performance of a classifier, as they do not take into account the imbalance between negatives and positives samples [7,11]. Coverage plots [9] may be used instead of ROC curves to perform classifier assessments in presence of imbalance. ROC curves and coverage plots appear to be the best option when the focus is on specificity and sensitivity. However, a typical main goal for researchers involved in building and testing classifiers is to assess performances in terms of *accuracy* and *bias*. In particular, webpage classification is usually evaluated measuring the accuracy [18].

As already pointed out, the amount of data can be huge, as often occurs for Web data. Therefore, classifiers may require heavy computational resources, which is reflected in the need of optimizing execution time, particularly in real-time applications. To this end, one of the most popular ways adopted for time optimization is to reduce the feature space. Indeed, a Web document is nowadays described by many attributes. For example, beyond its content, a webpage embeds further information, such as social annotations, tags, or anchor text. Across many training documents, features are typically sparse and numerous, leading to the so-called curse of dimensionality [2]. To overcome this problem, feature ranking and/or selection is typically performed, being a key issue in Web document classification, under real time constraints. The largest family of the cited techniques aims at ranking features according to their usefulness for classification. In particular, most of the corresponding algorithms require the evaluation of correlation coefficients between target class and independent features. However, which correlation coefficients should be adopted mainly depends on the type of features used. For example, Pearson's correlation coefficient [17] should be applied to continuous parameters, while Cramer's V [6] should be applied for nominal parameters. As Web data are becoming more and more heterogeneous, feature handling should also take into account the variety of types of involved parameters (e.g., binary, nominal, range, and continuous).

Recent works proposed methodologies that try to take into account the balance between classifiers performances and time reduction [5,13]. According to these findings, a tool able to take into account and analyze both aspects is described in the next section.

3   The $\varphi - \delta$ Tool

$\varphi - \delta$ diagrams have been proposed by Armano in 2015 [1] –with the twofold aim of assessing (i) classifier performance and (ii) feature importance. These diagrams, deployed in a 2D space, are based on two measures, namely φ (in the x-axis) and δ (in the y-axis), whose semantics depend on the task diagrams are used for. The space, enclosed in a rhomboidal area, is depicted in Fig. 1.

Classifier Assessment. At a first glance, $\varphi - \delta$ diagrams may be considered as variations of ROC curves. In fact, ROC curves are focused on sensitivity and specificity, whereas $\varphi - \delta$ diagrams on accuracy and bias (in particular, φ and δ reports the values of bias and accuracy, respectively, both mapped in the range $[-1, +1]$). $\varphi - \delta$ diagrams should be the primary choice when one is interested in assessing a classifier in terms of accuracy and bias, as these measure are immediately highlighted therein. As depicted in Fig. 1, the top corner of a $\varphi - \delta$ diagram coincides with the behavior of an "oracle" (i.e., a classifier with this behavior is expected to never fail), whereas the bottom corner represents an "anti-oracle" (i.e., a classifier with this behavior is expected to always fail). As

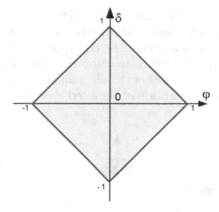

Fig. 1. The $\varphi - \delta$ 2D space.

for the left- and right-hand corners, they represent "dummy" classifiers, which classify *any* instance as negative and positive, respectively. See also Fig. 2 for a graphical representation of the cited aspects.

It is worth pointing out that $\varphi - \delta$ diagrams are also useful to inspect the variance of a classifier when trained on a given dataset. Typically, this scenario requires a k-fold cross validation strategy. In particular, assuming that performance is measured on each fold, its variance can be highlighted by looking how the $\varphi - \delta$ values evaluated on the k folds are scattered along the $\varphi - \delta$ space.

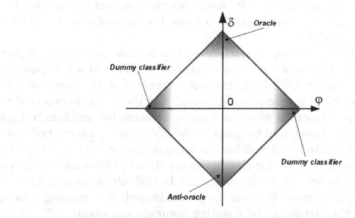

Fig. 2. Classifier semantics and $\varphi - \delta$ diagrams.

Feature Assessment. $\varphi - \delta$ diagrams can also be used to analyze feature importance, looking at features as "single feature classifiers". When framed in this setting, δ highlights to what extent the feature is covariant or contravariant (upper and lower corner of the rhombus, respectively) with the main category, whereas φ highlights to what extent the feature is characteristic for the dataset at hand. In particular, features close to the upper/lower corner are in strict agreement/disagreement with the main category, whereas features located close to the right-hand/left-hand corner of the diagram are mostly true/false. See also Fig. 3 for a graphical representation of the cited aspects.

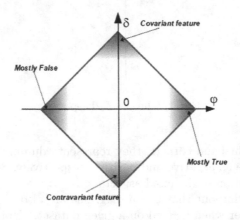

Fig. 3. Feature semantics and $\varphi - \delta$ diagrams.

In feature ranking or selection tasks, a relevant feature is expected to have a high discriminant value, regardless of its sign, whereas irrelevant features tend to be located along the φ axis. Our insight is to adopt the value of δ as an indicator of feature importance of data.

A further utility of $\varphi - \delta$ diagrams, when used for feature assessments, is that the overall scattering represents the "class signature", from which it is possible to make hypotheses on the difficulty of training a classifier on the given data. In particular, a dataset having a signature flattened over the φ axis is expected to be difficult, whereas datasets in which at least one feature has medium-to-high absolute value of δ are expected to be easier to classify. Figure 4 reports two cases of class signature, generated with well-known datasets downloaded from the UCI machine learning repository. As for the *mushroom* dataset (left-hand side), one may argue that the classification task should not be difficult, as several features are spread along the $\varphi - \delta$ space far from the φ axis. Indeed, after running a naive Bayes classifier on this datasets, the resulting accuracy was about 0.98. As for the *dota2* dataset (right-hand side), one may argue that the classification task is expected to be difficult, as all features lay along the φ axis. Indeed, after running a naive Bayes classifier on this dataset, the resulting accuracy was about 0.61.

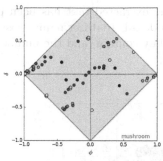
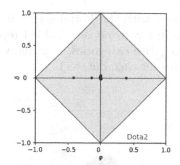

(a) Example of "good" signature   (b) Example of "bad" signature

Fig. 4. Examples of "good" and "bad" signatures obtained with two historical UCI datasets: (a) *mushroom*, on mushroom edibility, and (b) *dota2*, an online game.

4   Use Cases: Webpage Classification

This section reports some relevant use cases aimed at explaining the usefulness of the tool. Several experiments have been performed on real Web datasets, in a binary classification scenario.

Table 1. Details of adopted datasets.

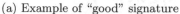

	Dataset name	Positive class	Negative class	#Positive samples	#Negative samples	#Features
(a)	Math vs Biology	Math	Biology	1002	2468	3486
(b)	Mission vs NASA	Missions	NASA	146	174	2884
(c)	Dogs vs Cats	Dogs	Cats	497	430	2400
(d)	Hiking vs Fishing	Hiking	Fishing	225	292	2647
(e)	Music vs Movies	Music	Movies	996	1025	3538
(f)	Software vs Hardware	Software	Hardware	2606	564	3708

Datasets Description. We generated several datasets from the Open Directory Project[1] (ODP), which has been for two decades the largest publicly available Web directory. ODP catalogs a huge number of webpages by means of a suitable taxonomy, where each node contains webpages related to a specific topic. Each dataset consists of a pair of categories (i.e., nodes of the ODP taxonomy), in which webpages have been preprocessed to extract textual content only. In particular, all unwanted elements (e.g., HTML tags, scripts, punctuation, and hyperlinks) have been removed from each webpage, and all terms have been

---

[1] http://opendirectoryproject.org/.

stemmed with the Porter's algorithms. Then the extracted text has been projected in a vector space. Table 1 reports datasets details (dataset name, positive and negative categories, how many documents they contain, and the number of features for each dataset).

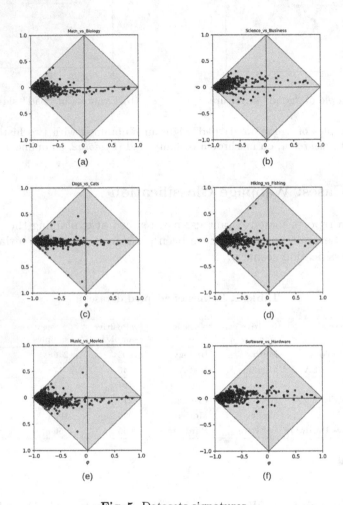

Fig. 5. Datasets signatures.

Using $\varphi - \delta$ Diagrams on Real-World Datasets. Experiments have been performed in a text categorization scenario, using binary features to account for the absence or presence of a word in a document. Figure 5 reports all signatures for datasets described in Table 1, each point corresponding to a single feature.

Let us remark that, for text data, rare terms (i.e., features being mostly false in the corpus) are located close to the left-hand corner of the $\varphi - \delta$ space, whereas features occurring in the majority of documents (common terms) lay close to the right-hand corner of the diagram. However, either rare or common, these terms are not discriminant for the category at hand. Conversely, a feature occurring very often in the positive category and rarely in the alternate category falls in the upper corner, where the δ value is highly positive, whereas terms that occur often in the negative category and rarely in the positive one are located in the lower corner. In both cases, the corresponding term is in fact a discriminant feature.

In each diagram of Fig. 5 the majority of features are located close to left-hand corner, meaning that most terms are rare and uncommon. This behavior, typical of text categorization, is in accordance with the Zip's law [21]. This law states that the majority of terms occur rarely in a given corpus, and that the most frequent terms are stopwords. According to the latter aspect, $\varphi - \delta$ diagrams are also able to identify *stopwords*. Indeed, they appear to lay along the positive φ axis, as they occur very often in both categories. To better clarify this behavior, let us report, for example, that the 5 highly values of φ in the diagram depicted in Fig. 5a correspond to the words "the", "end", "to", "in", and "for".

Let us now recall that the identification of relevant features consists of checking whether one or more features have a δ value significantly high (as absolute value). To this end, Table 2 reports the five best features for each dataset. The reported terms indirectly confirm the usefulness of $\varphi - \delta$ diagrams in the task of identifying relevant terms, as they are strictly related to the associated category.

Table 2. Best feature subsets of each class.

	Dataset name	Best features (Positive class)	Best features (Negative class)
(a)	Math vs Biology	mathematics, theory, compute, algebra statistics	species, plant, biology habitat, animal
(b)	Missions vs NASA	spacecraft, orbit launch, mission, surface	nasa, research, center update, curator
(c)	Dogs vs Cats	dog, puppy, kennel club, obedience	cat, kitten, cattery feline, pet
(d)	Hiking vs Fishing	hiking, trail, walk mountain, park	fish, angler, fly boat, catch
(e)	Music vs Movies	music, song, composer sing, instrument	film, movie, story screen, director
(f)	Software vs Hardware	user, software, windows IT, version	product, us, printer fax, call

Furthermore, Fig. 5 highlights that datasets *Math_vs_Biology* (diagram *a*), *Dogs_vs_Cats* (*c*), *Hiking_vs_Fishing* (*d*), and *Music_vs_Movies* (*e*) have one or more terms with significant values of δ, whereas the datasets *Missions_vs_NASA* (*b*) and *Software_vs_Hardware* (*f*) have flatter signatures. According to these findings, one should expect the performance of classifiers trained in the latter

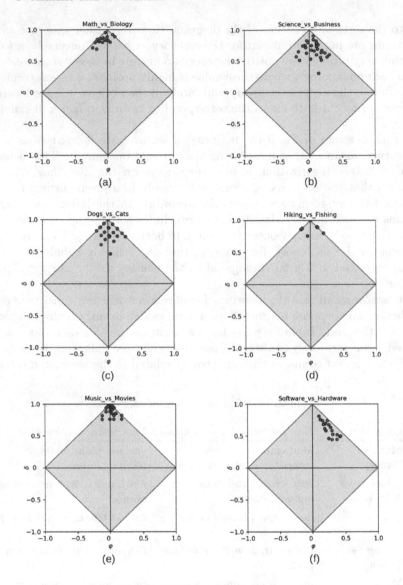

Fig. 6. Classifiers performance.

datasets be lower than the one shown on the former ones. To verify this assumption, 30-fold cross-validation, using a linear SVM, has been performed on each dataset. We used $\varphi - \delta$ diagrams to visualize the performance of each classifier, as reported in Fig. 6. In the reported diagrams each point corresponds to $\varphi - \delta$ values evaluated on a distinct fold.

Figure 6 confirms the expectations, as, on average, the corresponding δ values are close to the upper corner for datasets a, c, d, and e, whereas the the ones of datasets b and f are significantly closer to the φ axis. This aspect is summarized in Table 3, which reports the average classification accuracies. Note that the accuracies measured on datasets a, c, d, and e are greater than 0.90, whereas those measured on b and e are significantly lower.

Table 3. Average accuracies.

	Math vs Biology (a)	Missions vs NASA (b)	Dogs vs Cats (c)	Hiking vs Fishing (d)	Music vs Movies (e)	Software vs Hardware (f)
Accuracy (average)	0.93	0.78	0.90	0.96	0.94	0.86

5 Conclusions

In this paper we proposed some uses cases able to show the potential of $\varphi - \delta$ diagrams. These diagrams have been applied to Web data analysis, showing how they can give support to researchers and scientists in the development and implementation of Web systems and services. In particular, this paper give an insight on how the proposed tool is able to provide a reliable support in feature and classifier assessment, in a Web-oriented scenario. The reported use cases have shown that $\varphi - \delta$ diagrams could be a useful starting point for developing (i) novel feature selection algorithms, as they are able to clearly highlight variable importance, and (ii) novel classifier assessment methodologies, as they are able to highlight performances in terms of accuracy and bias.

References

1. Armano, G.: A direct measure of discriminant and characteristic capability for classifier building and assessment. Inf. Sci. **325**, 466–483 (2015)
2. Bellman, R.: Adaptive Control Processes. Princeton University Press, Princeton (1961)
3. Bradley, A.: The use of the area under the ROC curve in the evaluation of machine learning algorithms. Pattern Recognit. **30**, 1145–1159 (1997)
4. Brier, G.W.: Verification of forecasts expressed in terms of probability. Mon. Weather Rev. **78**(1), 1–3 (1950)
5. Cano, A., Zafra, A., Ventura, S.: Speeding up multiple instance learning classification rules on GPUs. Knowl. Inf. Syst. **44**(1), 127–145 (2015). https://doi.org/10.1007/s10115-014-0752-0
6. Cramer, H.: Mathematical Methods of Statistics/by Harald Cramer. Princeton University Press, Princeton (1946)
7. Elazmeh, W., Japkowicz, N., Matwin, S.: A framework for comparative evaluation of classifiers in the presence of class imbalance, p. 25 (2006)
8. Fawcett, T.: An introduction to ROC analysis. Pattern Recognit. Lett. (Special issue: ROC analysis in pattern recognition) **27**(8), 861–874 (2006)

9. Fürnkranz, J., Flach, P.A.: Roc 'n' rule learning - towards a better understanding of covering algorithms. Mach. Learn. **58**(1), 39–77 (2005)
10. Good, I.J.: Rational decisions. J. R. Stat. Soc. (Series B) **14**, 107–114 (1952)
11. Guo, X., Yin, Y., Dong, C., Yang, G., Zhou, G.: On the class imbalance problem. In: Proceedings of the 4th International Conference on Natural Computation, ICNC 2008. IEEE (2008)
12. Huang, J., Ling, C.X.: Using auc and accuracy in evaluating learning algorithms. IEEE Trans. Knowl. Data Eng. **17**, 299–310 (2005)
13. Jaderberg, M., Vedaldi, A., Zisserman, A.: Speeding up convolutional neural networks with low rank expansions. In: Proceedings of the British Machine Vision Conference. BMVA Press (2014)
14. Kalinov, P., Stantic, B., Sattar, A.: Building a dynamic classifier for large text data collections. In: Proceedings of the Twenty-First Australasian Database Conference on Database Technologies, (ADC 2010), Brisbane, 18–22 January 2010, pp. 113–122 (2010)
15. Kenekayoro, P., Buckley, K., Thelwall, M.: Automatic classification of academic web page types. Scientometrics **101**(2), 1015–1026 (2014). https://doi.org/10.1007/s11192-014-1292-9
16. Mohammad, R.M., Thabtah, F.A., McCluskey, L.: Predicting phishing websites based on self-structuring neural network. Neural Comput. Appl. **25**(2), 443–458 (2014)
17. Pearson, K.: VII. Mathematical contributions to the theory of evolution.—III. Regression, heredity, and panmixia. Philos. Trans. R. Soc. Lond. A Math. Phys. Eng. Sci. **187**, 253–318 (1896). http://rsta.royalsocietypublishing.org/content/187/253
18. Qi, X., Davison, B.D.: Web page classification: features and algorithms. ACM Comput. Surv. **41**(2), 12:1–12:31 (2009). https://doi.org/10.1145/1459352.1459357
19. Schonhofen, P.: Identifying document topics using the Wikipedia category network. In: Proceedings of the 2006 IEEE/WIC/ACM International Conference on Web Intelligence, WI 2006, pp. 456–462. IEEE Computer Society, Washington, DC (2006)
20. Zhu, J., Xie, Q., Yu, S.I., Wong, W.H.: Exploiting link structure for web page genre identification. Data Min. Knowl. Discov. http://hdl.handle.net/10754/566107
21. Zipf, G.K.: Human Behaviour and the Principle of Least Effort. Addison-Wesley, Cambridge (1949)

1st International Workshop on
Engineering Open Data (WEOD)

1st International Workshop on Engineering Open Data (WEOD)

Cáceres, Spain, June 5th, 2018, held in conjunction with the
18th International Conference on Web Engineering (ICWE)

Preface

More and more data is becoming available online every day coming from both the public sector and private sources. Indeed, the open data movement promises to bring to the fingertips of every citizen all the data they need, whether it is for planning their next trip or for government oversight. Most of this data is available via some kind of (semi) structured format (e.g., XML, RDF, JSON,…) which, in theory, facilitates its consumption and combination. Unfortunately, this is still far from reality. Our society is gradually opening its data but not building the technology required to enable citizens to access and manipulate it. Only technical people have the skills to consume the heterogeneous data sources while the rest is forced to depend on third-party applications or companies.

The 1st International Workshop on Engineering Open Data (WEOD) was arranged to bring together researchers, practitioners, stakeholders and users of Open Data. The focus of the workshop is to present latest research on practical engineering approaches (a) to design and develop means for promoting the consumption of Open Data and, by leveraging on well-known existing techniques (e.g., conceptual modeling, data mining, data intelligence, etc.), (b) to design and develop composition mechanism that help combining Open Data sources. The workshop was held on June 5th, 2018 in conjunction with the 18th International Conference on Web Engineering (ICWE) in Cáceres, Spain.

The workshop included a *hands-on* session based on a case study to illustrate the discovery, composition and consumption of Open Data on practice, as well as promoting the practical engineering nature of the event. The call for papers therefore included an additional track for papers developed in the context of this case study. Additionally, the workshop closed with a discussion session were different topics were treated.

After the peer-review process, 3 papers were selected to be presented at the workshop, where 1 of them was developed in the context of the case study. The papers covered different aspects of engineering Open Data, as we briefly describe below. Also, the workshop also invited the rest of the authors who submitted a paper to briefly present their work in the venue.

The 1st paper was "SemQuire - Assessing the Data Quality of Linked Open Data Sources" by André Langer, Valentin Siegert, Christoph Göpfert and Martin Gaedke from Technische Universität Chemnitz, Germany. The paper presented SemQuire, a quality assessment tool for analyzing quality aspects of particular Linked Data sources both in the Open Data context as well as in the Enterprise Data Service context.

The 2nd paper was "Model-Driven Analytics for Open Data APIs" by Elena Planas and David Bañeres from Universitat Oberta de Catalunya, Spain. The paper presented a Model-Driven Analytical tool for Open Data APIs. The tool allows visualizing how end-users interact with Open Data sources relying on two kind of metrics: (1) performance metrics (e.g., response time) and (2) semantic metrics (e.g., concepts queried). This paper was developed in the context of the case study presented in the workshop.

The 3rd paper was "Geo-Time Broker: a Web Agent of Dynamic flows of Geo-Temporal Activity for Smart Cities" by Alvaro Prieto, Juan Carlos Preciado, José María Conejero, Fernando Sánchez-Figueroa and Álvaro Rubio-Largo from Escuela Politécnica. Universidad de Extremadura, Spain. The paper presented a tool, called Geo-Time broker, that uses Dynamic Activity Flows of a Smart City to design and visualize complex behaviours in the city based on maps.

The discussion and wrapping up session was very fruitful and allowed the participants to debate on latest research and trends in the field, namely: (1) what is required by the stakeholders when publishing data versus what is actually published, and how to facilitate government to release data (e.g., by providing guidelines); (2) the need of efficient means to deal with massive amount of data usually available in Open Data as well as their composition; (3) the relevance of licensing and privacy issues.

We are grateful to the Program Committee members for their work on the paper review and selection process. We would also like to thank all the authors and workshop participants for the interesting discussions.

Javier Luis Cánovas Izquierdo
Roberto Rodriguez-Echeverria

Organization

Program Committee

Óscar Corcho	Polytechnic University of Madrid, Spain
Luis-Daniel Ibáñez	University of Southampton, UK
Marijn Janssen	TUDelft, The Netherlands
Francesco Leotta	Sapienza Università di Roma, Italy
Andrea Mauri	TUDelft, The Netherlands
José Norberto Mazón	University of Alicante, Spain
Massimo Mecella	Sapienza Università di Roma, Italy
Gustavo Rossi	University of La Plata, Argentina
Adolfo Lozano	University of Extremadura, Spain
Álvaro E. Prieto	University of Extremadura, Spain
Adrian Rutle	Bergen University College, Norway

SemQuire - Assessing the Data Quality of Linked Open Data Sources Based on DQV

André Langer$^{(\boxtimes)}$ (iD), Valentin Siegert (iD), Christoph Göpfert,
and Martin Gaedke (iD)

Technische Universität Chemnitz, Chemnitz, Germany
{andre.langer,valentin.siegert,christoph.goepfert,martin.gaedke}
@informatik.tu-chemnitz.de

Abstract. The World Wide Web represents a tremendous source of knowledge, whose amount constantly increases. Open Data initiatives and the Semantic Web community have emphasized the need to publish data in a structured format based on open standards and ideally linked to other data sources. But that does not necessarily lead to error-free information and data of good quality. It would be of high relevance to have a software component that is capable of measuring the most relevant quality metrics in a generic fashion as well as rating these results.

We therefore present SemQuire, a quality assessment tool for analyzing quality aspects of particular Linked Data sources both in the Open Data context as well as in the Enterprise Data Service context. It is based on open standards such as W3C's RDF, SPARQL and DQV, and implements as a proof-of-concept a basic set of 55 recommended intrinsic, representational, contextual and accessibility quality metrics. We provide a use case for evaluating SemQuire's feasibility and effectiveness.

Keywords: Linked data · Open data · Semantic web · Data quality
Quality assessment

1 Introduction

The hurdle-free publication of correct information enables consumers from the public and business sector to solve particular tasks based on available data. However, it is not sufficient to make a bunch of data available through the World Wide Web. Several other requirements have to be fulfilled so that information from a certain knowledge domain becomes valuable and useful for a particular usage scenario. This involves both accessibility aspects in the data retrieval step as well as intrinsic demands on the data itself.

Data Quality (DQ) is a concept describing the appropriateness of a data set based on concrete use case requirements. The examined data set is of excellent quality if it conforms to all needs and is free if defects [10] ("fitness for use" [12]).

© Springer Nature Switzerland AG 2018
C. Pautasso et al. (Eds.): ICWE 2018, LNCS 11153, pp. 163–175, 2018.
https://doi.org/10.1007/978-3-030-03056-8_14

Otherwise, the quality of a data source is described as poor, if it does not meet the expectations. Quality aspects are usage dependent in general. Information from a data source can be of good quality for one intended use, and totally inappropriate for another purpose (e.g., by lacking required information). This involves requirements both on data instance level, schema level as well as on service level [7].

The analysis of data quality issues is not new and originates already in the 1970s. In Information Science, it involves the formulation of required aspects in terms of quality metrics as indicators and the test of data sets against these quality requirements. Commonly, quantitative measurements with a concrete numeric output are run in (semi-)automated processes, but qualitative analysis steps are possible as well. However, it is still controversial, which quality metrics are of major interest and if a basic set of general-purpose metrics makes sense in general. An excellent overview on this topic was recently provided in publications by Zaveri [13], Hogan [6] or Flemming [3].

Furthermore, the comparison of quality metric measurements and the overall quality assessment among multiple data sources, a series of points in time, or different quality checker tools is not trivial. Several propositions have already been made for exchanging quality measurement results. Mainly, they originate in the Semantic Web community [2] [4], resulting in a recommendation for a Data Quality Vocabulary (D3V)[1] by W3Cs Data Quality Working Group.

We have adopted these previous contributions from other authors and used it in the context of an industrial Linked Enterprise Data Services (LEDS) growth-core project for a proof-of-concept in practise. As a result, we want to present the following contributions:

- The realization of an up-to-date implementation of a DQ Assessment Component (SemQuire) for the general analysis of structured RDF data sources that returns a machine-readable DQV export of measurement results
- A rating approach that maps each measurement value to a numeric quality assessment score for better interpretability
- The brief discussion of implementation aspects for well-accepted quality metrics

The rest of the paper is structured in the following way. Section 2 contains a more detailed description on DQ metrics and provides an overview on functional requirements for a Data Quality Assessment component. Sect. 3 presents the prototypical implementation of our SemQuire software component and a list of experiences during the implementation process. Sect. 4 analyses the correctness of our implementation based on a concrete Use Case with measurement results. In Sect. 5, we mention recent publications of other authors in the quality assessment domain and contrast our work from existent alternative quality checkers from the past. Finally, Sect. 6 sums up our results and contains a plan for future work.

---

[1] https://www.w3.org/TR/vocab-dqv/.

2   Challenges in Measuring Quality Metrics

Our driving research question is whether the quality state in online published data sources can be monitored in an automated fashion and compared among different data sources, assessment tools or points in time by the mean of using a set of standard quality metrics and the mapping to a rating score.

The term quality in the context of data source analysis is diffuse and encompasses aspects that go beyond a simple syntactic validation or a correctness check for the absence of contradictions and errors in local data sets. Research in the past has already focused on this challenge and multiple times investigated the different dimensions of quality. Publications like ISO/IEC 25012[2] provide a comprehensive overview and definitions for common and generally accepted metrics and try to classify and cluster the metrics in a more general scheme. We base our research on the data quality dimensions and their categorization identified in a systematic literature review by [13]. They suggest a classification of these metrics and corresponding indicators into four primary groups entitled with Accessibility, Representational, Contextual and Intrinsic Quality aspects. The implementation of such a quality metric should be possible straight-forward according to their unambigious conceptual description in the corresponding literature.

Stakeholders with potential interest on quality measurement results can be found both on data publication as well as on data consumption side. A data curator or service provider of a data portal is interested to publish correct data in a useful way. Data consumers on the contrary are interested to find data sources that fit test to their current needs. As a consequence, measurements can be run from all stakeholder groups on all available resources and data service endpoints. These measurement results can then be published as meta data in a machine-readable format for further processing and comparison activities.

In order to do that, analyzed data quality metrics should be stated in an unambiguous and referenceable fashion. The data quality vocabulary (DQV) therefore introduces a set of properties to announce quality measurement results. To identify particular quality aspects, URIs are used as a reference. It is intentionally not the objective of the W3C working group "to define a normative list of dimensions and metrics"[3], thus they only state some basic examples. However, it is also mentioned that "relying on existing classifications and metrics increases interoperability" which symbolizes a valuable intension for Open Data exchange. (A similar approach is followed in the Linked Data community to reference particular existing entities with URIs e.g., in the DBpedia project[4], though it does not contain entries for abstract concepts such as data metrics yet). We therefore put in front in the following a list of potential quality metrics together with a recommended URI in Table 1. Be aware, that we currently do not focus on metrics of a limited application domain, metrics with already profound tool support or metrics involving sophisticated data mining or AI methodologies.

---

[2] http://iso25000.com/index.php/en/iso-25000-standards/iso-25012.
[3] https://www.w3.org/TR/vocab-dqv/#DimentsionsMetricsHints.
[4] https://dbpedia.org.

Table 1. In SemQuire implemented DQ metrics with recommended Concept URI

Accessibility metrics	
(01)	http://dataconcepts.net/metrics/quality/**AuthenticityMetric**
(02)	http://dataconcepts.net/metrics/quality/**DereferencedBacklinksMetric**
(03)	http://dataconcepts.net/metrics/quality/**DereferencedForwardLinksMetric**
(04)	http://dataconcepts.net/metrics/quality/**DigitalSignatureMetric**
(05)	http://dataconcepts.net/metrics/quality/**DumpDownloadAvailableMetric**
(06)	http://dataconcepts.net/metrics/quality/**ExternalLinksMetric**
(07)	http://dataconcepts.net/metrics/quality/**HighThroughputMetric**
(08)	http://dataconcepts.net/metrics/quality/**HumanReadableLicenseMetric**
(09)	http://dataconcepts.net/metrics/quality/**LowLatencyMetric**
(10)	http://dataconcepts.net/metrics/quality/**MachineReadableLicenseMetric**
(11)	http://dataconcepts.net/metrics/quality/**NoMisreportedContentTypeMetric**
(12)	http://dataconcepts.net/metrics/quality/**SPARQLAccessibilityMetric**
(13)	http://dataconcepts.net/metrics/quality/**URIDereferenceabilityMetric**
(14)	http://dataconcepts.net/metrics/quality/**ScalabilityMetric**
(15)	http://dataconcepts.net/metrics/quality/**SlashURIMetric**
Contextual metrics	
(16)	http://dataconcepts.net/metrics/quality/**CommunicationChannelMetric**
(17)	http://dataconcepts.net/metrics/quality/**ContentTrustMetric**
(18)	http://dataconcepts.net/metrics/quality/**CurrencyFreshnessMetric**
(19)	http://dataconcepts.net/metrics/quality/**DatasetFreshnessMetric**
(20)	http://dataconcepts.net/metrics/quality/**ExampleSPARQLQueryMetric**
(21)	http://dataconcepts.net/metrics/quality/**HumanReadableLabelsMetric**
(22)	http://dataconcepts.net/metrics/quality/**ProviderTrustworthinessMetric**
(23)	http://dataconcepts.net/metrics/quality/**ReasoningTrustworthinessMetric**
(24)	http://dataconcepts.net/metrics/quality/**ReputationMetric**
(25)	http://dataconcepts.net/metrics/quality/**ResourceTrustworthinessMetric**
(26)	http://dataconcepts.net/metrics/quality/**StatementDatasetRuleTrustworthinessMetric**
(27)	http://dataconcepts.net/metrics/quality/**StatementTrustworthinessMetric**
(28)	http://dataconcepts.net/metrics/quality/**URIExamplePatternMetric**
(29)	http://dataconcepts.net/metrics/quality/**URIRegExPatternMetric**
(30)	http://dataconcepts.net/metrics/quality/**VocabularyIndicationMetric**
Intrinsic metrics	
(31)	http://dataconcepts.net/metrics/quality/**CorrectDomainRangeDefinitionMetric**
(32)	http://dataconcepts.net/metrics/quality/**DatatypeOrObjectPropertyMisuseMetric**
(33)	http://dataconcepts.net/metrics/quality/**DeprecatedMisuseMetric**
(34)	http://dataconcepts.net/metrics/quality/**EntityAsDisjointClassMembersMetric**
(35)	http://dataconcepts.net/metrics/quality/**HighExtensionalConcisenessMetric**
(36)	http://dataconcepts.net/metrics/quality/**HighIntensionalMetric**
(37)	http://dataconcepts.net/metrics/quality/**InterlinkingCompletenessMetric**
(38)	http://dataconcepts.net/metrics/quality/**InverseFunctionalPropertyUseMetric**
(39)	http://dataconcepts.net/metrics/quality/**MisplacedClassesOrPropertiesMetric**
(40)	http://dataconcepts.net/metrics/quality/**NoMalformedDatatypeLiteralsMetric**
(41)	http://dataconcepts.net/metrics/quality/**NoRDFSyntaxErrorMetric**
(42)	http://dataconcepts.net/metrics/quality/**OntologyHijackingMetric**
(43)	http://dataconcepts.net/metrics/quality/**PopulationCompletenessMetric**
(44)	http://dataconcepts.net/metrics/quality/**PropertyCompletenessMetric**
(45)	http://dataconcepts.net/metrics/quality/**SchemaCompletenessMetric**
(46)	http://dataconcepts.net/metrics/quality/**SyntacticAccurateValuesMetric**
Representational metrics	
(47)	http://dataconcepts.net/metrics/quality/**BlankNodesMetric**
(48)	http://dataconcepts.net/metrics/quality/**DataInterpretabilityMetric**
(49)	http://dataconcepts.net/metrics/quality/**ProlixRDFFeaturesMetric**
(50)	http://dataconcepts.net/metrics/quality/**ReusedVocabularyMetric**
(51)	http://dataconcepts.net/metrics/quality/**SelfDescriptiveFormatMetric**
(52)	http://dataconcepts.net/metrics/quality/**SerializationFormatMetric**
(53)	http://dataconcepts.net/metrics/quality/**ShortURIMetric**
(54)	http://dataconcepts.net/metrics/quality/**UndefinedClassPropertyUsageMetric**
(55)	http://dataconcepts.net/metrics/quality/**VariousLanguageMetric**

We pose the following requirements on a software tool that should be capable of measuring the mentioned quality metrics:

RQ1 It can be applied on data sets containing structured data in an RDF serialization format (unstructured or semi-structured data sources can be processed to some extend using document converters in advance[5])

RQ2 Input data can be specified in a push (direct input,upload) and/or pull (fetch from url, fetch from SPARQL endpoint) manner

RQ3 Relevant metrics that should be measured can be selected in advance from a list of available implemented metrics

RQ4 If metrics depend or relate to each other, any dependencies should be resolved during calculation without remeasuring duplicate aspects

RQ5 The measurement assignment as well as the metrics should be reference-able by using a persistent URI

RQ6 A measurement report should be generated after finishing all measurements containing concrete measurement values

RQ7 The measurement report should be exportable in a machine-readable format, preferably using DQV

RQ8 Optionally, an overall quality assessment score should be calculated with ratings for each measurement result

RQ9 Optionally, the current measurement should be comparable with other quality measurements

RQ10 The software tool should provide a Web UI for human interaction and presentation as well as a service backend for automation purposes and bulk processing

A conceptual program flow for fulfilling these requirements is briefly depicted in Fig. 1.

3   The SemQuire Approach

In the following, we present SemQuire, a practical engineering approach for the data quality assessment of structured data sources. SemQuire is a result of the German Linked Enterprise Data Services (LEDS) growth-core project. The primary objective of the LEDS project is to build a novel, future-proof technology platform that is capable of combining, extending and enriching corporate data stores with external, open-available data. One of the most critical aspects in this concept is the (automated) assurance of certain quality requirements in the process of knowledge combination. Open Data Services often provide hereby an inhomogeneous variety of data structures ranging from very detailed, conscientiously curated data collections with a very high number of corresponding properties down to data providers with only little information value.

---

[5] https://www.w3.org/wiki/ConverterToRdf#Frameworks.

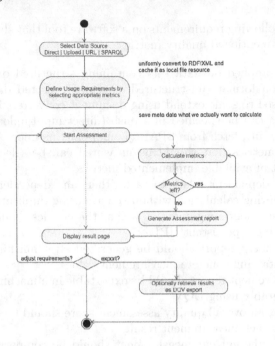

Fig. 1. Activity diagram for a data quality assessment tool

The SemQuire application consists out of four main components:

- A WebGUI for enabling human users to manually check particular data sets for quality issues, relying on Googles MDL front-end template library
- A RESTful web service API for machine-to-machine interaction, currently implemented in NodeJS with TypeScript Transpiling
- A set of implemented metrics that is easily extensible, mainly based on rdflib and other Python libraries
- A graph database, currently using Stardog, accessed via an industrial data middleware (eccenca DataPlatform)

The entire system architecture is depicted in Fig. 2 and deployed in a Docker container. In contrast to other previously existing quality checker tools, SemQuire is to the best of our knowledge the first that allows the machine-readable export of all measurement results in DQV, follows a rating concept for all quality measurements and calculates a comparable overall assessment score. The SemQuire component can be publicly accessed via https://goo.gl/nYv9sX for demonstration purposes. Figure 3 depicts screenshots of the SemQuire prototype.

We implemented a set of common quality metrics from multiple quality groups (see Table 1) dealing with different views on a data source.

Metrics from the Accessibility group deal with technical data access aspects. Some of them are not applicable to data sets that are provided in a push manner to the system by the user (e.g., a file upload of a data dump or directly by

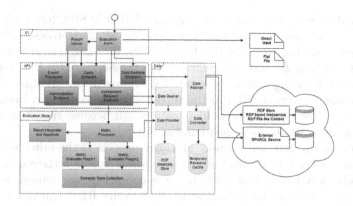

Fig. 2. Components of the SemQuire quality assessment tool

(a) Start dialog

(b) Data Source selection

(c) A simple SPARQL query on DBpedia

(d) Metric selection

(e) Assessment result

(f) DQV export

Fig. 3. SemQuire WebUI screenshots

pasting the data content), and refer to remote URLs or SPARQL endpoint concerns such as *Latency, Scalability, Throughput* or *SPARQLAccessibility*. Others evaluate meta data contained in the document itself or in retrievable well-known access paths such as *License information*, the *Availability of a Dump download, Digital Signiture* or *appropriate ContentType information*. Another dimension checks contained external URIs in the retrieved data set for dereferenceability. Especially the execution of the ladder metrics can become time-consuming for large documents with an increased number of URIs.

A second group dealt with representational aspects of the provided data. We implemented metrics, that check if the same data can be retrieved in different RDF serialization formats, if well-known vocabularies are reused, and if the usage of constructs like BlankNodes or other prolix RDF features is avoided. The usage of ShortURIs might also be seen as an intrinsic aspect and are subject for discussion regarding the char length of a concept representation. From our experience during implementation, this can be use case and domain dependent. As other publications did not state a recommended explicit maximum length for a short URI, we used 80 chars as a general threshold.

In the following, we were interested in analyzing general intrinsic quality aspects of open accessible structured data. After checking the general validity with a respective validator, SemQuire converts them internally uniformly into RDF/XML. Next, either traditional RDF validators can be applied or more sophisticated third-party tools such as RDFAlerts [5]. In order to check other intrinsic dimensions such as consistency, completeness and conciseness metrics, it is first of all necessary to retrieve schema information on the used ontologies in the document. Dereferencing all used namespaces within one document is one possible, flexible automated approach. However, still not all ontology description sites offer a machine-readable version of the vocabulary. Completeness checks provide another challenge for a quality checker by requiring additional background knowledge ("gold standard"). Obviously, this is hard to achieve for certain application domains under an Open World Assumption for distributed data. Additionally, a comparison based on literal values is not practical useful for different languages or spellings. Instead, a completeness check based on entity URIs is more valuable. However, it also has to consider owl:sameAs relationships for similar concepts identified under different URI domain names. SemQuire checks all intrinsic metrics based on available document from the current and linked documents.

In contrast, contextual metrics require an additional usage context for the concrete application scenario by the user. For some contextual dimensions such as timeliness or understandability, simple parameter inputs can be requested by the system or even meaningful standard values can be applied statically. Checking relevancy needs a complex contextual input to satisfy the metric on a high level. Assessing trust either needs kinds of black- or whitelists, an authority or also a complex contextual input. Provenance data can hereby also be an input regarding some trust metrics. To circumvent a complex input, the PageRank approach can be used to return a initialization regarding the relevance and the more detailed trust metric about content trust. Such an initialization will still not behalf as a high-end trust network or description of relevance, but gives the contextual metrics a kick-off in the right direction. Solving a contextual metric with crowd-sourcing seems not to fit for us, as each human brings in his own bias.

For all metrics of interest, each measurement result value is then mapped to a rating score, representing the fulfillment of the investigated aspect. It is a numeric value between 0.0 (not fulfilled at all) and 1.0 (perfect). All individual ratings are then linearly combined to an overall quality assessment score. Details can be found in [8].

4   Evaluation

To show the effectiveness of SemQuire, we conducted a case study and used a small example of real-world open data resources to solve a common task for evaluation purposes. In our example case, a user is interested in getting information on all existing movies in the film series of *James Bond*. We chose three different linked open data source candidates, which we queried with SemQuire, and compared later on the results. Namely, the three selected providers were *DBpedia*[6], *Wikidata*[7] and *LinkedMDB*[8].

Therefore, we designed three different SPARQL CONSTRUCT queries manually to obtain with SemQuire all information about movies of the *James Bond* film series. The queries differ mainly in the used vocabularies for each data provider, but the semantic is always the same as we search for all *James Bond* films and their outgoing relations or properties.

Not all offered metrics by SemQuire are relevant for the test case, so we carefully selected only metrics that help in the assessment process of finding the most appropriate data source for solving the task. The metrics were chosen by either importance for the test case or based on interesting differences in the results and ratings of SemQuire. Hence, we will show in the following differences between the data provider candidates according to the scenario with respect to six metrics and the underlying data. The corresponding measurement' ratings are shown in Table 2. Additionally, we provide the numbers of returned triples (T#) as a statistical meta info for better understanding. Two metrics' results are further shown in Fig. 4 for contrasting purposes of results and ratings in SemQuire.

Population Completeness (PopulComp). Regarding the test case of gathering all *James Bond* films, it is important if the endpoints really return all relevant movies, thus have a population completeness of *100%*. Surprisingly, metric (43) shows that *LinkedMDB* is not referencing all *James Bond* films, but only *48%*. It could be the case that *LinkedMDB* is not referencing all *James Bond* films to the category about *James Bond* films, which would explain this low percentage.

---

[6] http://dbpedia.org/.
[7] http://wikidata.org/.
[8] http://linkedmdb.org/.

Serialization Format (SeriForm). As the test case does not explicitly specify how the data will be used, it can be very interesting for further processing to have the possibility of retrieving different serialization formats. Metric (52) measures in how many formats the data can be provided. SemQuire indicates that only *DBpedia* is able to provide more than one, so more than the standard RDF/XML format with content negotiation.

Various Languages (VarLang). Beyond the processing of the data, the data might also be shown to humans and thus it can be important that various languages are included in the data set. As our queries are not filtering on any language, metric (55) is able to check if there are various languages or not in the underlying data. *LinkedMDB* is again beyond the two others, as it is only providing the information in one language.

URI Dereferenceability (URIDeref). The metric (13) about dereferenceability of the URIs is relevant for the evaluation, as the importance of SemQuire's mapping approach from absolute values to normalized ratings can be seen. The results of this metric depict the count of all dereferenceable URIs within the data. All endpoints provide a different amount of triples, and thus there are also differences in the results. On the contrary, the ratings of this metric show that the difference between the three endpoints is not even relevant, as they are for all pretty good and close. The rating is hereby created with respect to the overall triple numbers of the data, and is thus more significant than the results.

External Links (ExternL). With regard to an open world model, one endpoint is often not able to provide all information within its domain. The metric (06) is checking whether the provided data includes a link to external data outside the data endpoint domain. Interestingly, only DBpedia provides external links to other domains.

Low Latency (LowLat). The advantages of a low latency for one request to the endpoint can be important at tasks with a time factor that often live-update their data. The test case is not necessarily referring to a need of low latency, but the metric (09) is still interesting for a general QoS rating of the endpoint and a possible extension of the test scenario. The results are quite different, but the rating again gives an idea on how good these results are.

Based on the results and ratings of the six metrics, a decision upon which endpoint should be used, is required (which involved human interaction in the past). We use SemQuire's possibility to combine the discussed measurements to an overall quality assessment value (Score). The resulting order is depicted in Table 2, the recommended endpoint to choose is consequently in our test case *DBpedia*.

5   Related Work

Examples for vocabularies to describe data and service quality from the Semantic Web community are the daQ [2], DQM vocabulary [4] or the current W3C

Table 2. SemQuire's ratings, score and T# for each endpoint

Endpoints	Score	T#	URIDeref	ExternL	LowLat	PopulComp	SeriForm	VarLang
DBpedia	0.97	10001	0.9802	1	0.8653	1	1	1
Wikidata	0.65	9626	0.9996	0	0.9176	1	1	0
LinkedMDB	0.38	724	0.9795	0	0.8216	0.48	0	0

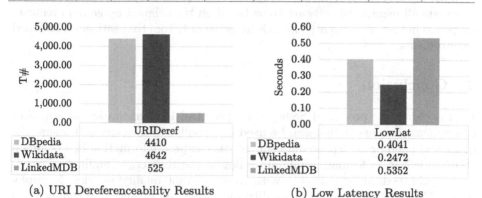

(a) URI Dereferenceability Results   (b) Low Latency Results

Fig. 4. URIDeeref & LowLat Results

draft for a data quality vocabulary (DQV)[9]. Furthermore, several data quality checker implementations already existed in the past. They differ on various characteristics such as functionality, processable data format, implementation language, user interface or result output manner. Examples are Diachron [13], KBMetrics [11], LDSrcAss [3], Luzzu [2], RDFAlerts [5], Roomba OpenData Checker [1], Sieve [9] or SWIQA [4]. Some of them only focused on a limited use case or are not publicly available any longer. Moreover, assessment results were often provided in different output formats and not comparable to each other. For

Table 3. Comparison of quality assessment tools wrt. requirements from section 2

Criterion	Diachron	KBMetrics	LDSrcAss	Luzzu	RDFAlerts	Roomba	SemQuire	LDIF/Sieve	SWIQA
Available	y	n	n	y	y	y	y	y	n
Language	Java	?	?	Java	Java	NodeJS	NodeJS	Java	?
RQ1	y	y	y	y	y	(y)	y	y	y
RQ2	n	n	n	n	n	n	y	y	n
RQ3	y	y	(y)	y	n	(y)	y	y	y
RQ4	n	n	n	y	?	n	y	n	n
RQ5	y	n	n	(y)	(y)	n	y	n	n
RQ6	y	y	y	y	y	y	y	y	y
RQ7	n	n	n	y	n	(y)	y	n	?
RQ8	n	y	y	y	n	n	y	n	y
RQ9	n	y	n	y	n	n	y	n	n
RQ10	y	y	y	y	y	n	y	n	?

---

[9] https://www.w3.org/TR/vocab-dqv/.

instance, the OpenData Checker calculated metrics from data quality indicators specifically for CKAN data stores and simply outputed them in percent. KBMetrics used a scoring system to make different data sources comparable. SWIQA calculated a quality score based on the percentage how many instances violate given data quality rules. Emphasis has therefore been placed on the requirement to make quality measurements comparable by using semantic means. Table 3 contrasts all mentioned software tools based on the original usage requirements we posed in Sect. 2. Currently, SemQuire is the only tool that satisfies all defined requirements.

6   Conclusion

In this paper, we presented SemQuire a practical implementation of a quality assessment component that can be used as a toolkit to measure and assure the quality of open or enterprise data sources that expose information in a common RDF serialization format. SemQuire relies on the theoretical findings of previously published surveys dealing with most relevant quality metrics. It implements 55 of the most common quality indicators. In advance, we conducted a brief market overview and compared other existing tools with our component with the result, that there is currently, to the best of our knowledge, no other software component available that fulfills all requirements of interest.

Acknowledgment. This work was supported by the grant from the German Federal Ministry of Education and Research (BMBF) for the LEDS Project under grant agreement No 03WKCG11D.

References

1. Assaf, A., Troncy, R., Senart, A.: Roomba: an extensible framework to validate and build dataset profiles. In: Gandon, F., Guéret, C., Villata, S., Breslin, J., Faron-Zucker, C., Zimmermann, A. (eds.) ESWC 2015. LNCS, vol. 9341, pp. 325–339. Springer, Cham (2015). https://doi.org/10.1007/978-3-319-25639-9_46
2. Debattista, J., Lange, C., Auer, S.: daQ, an ontology for dataset quality information. In: CEUR Workshop Proceedings, vol. 1184 (2014)
3. Flemming, A.: Qualitätsmerkmale von Linked Data-veröffentlichenden Datenquellen, pp. 1–174 (2011). http://www.dbis.informatik.hu-berlin.de/fileadmin/research/papers/diploma_seminar_thesis/Diplomarbeit_Annika_Flemming.pdf
4. Fürber, C., Hepp, M.: Towards a vocabulary for data quality management in semantic web architectures. Proceedings of the 1st International Workshop on Linked Web Data Management - LWDM 2011, p. 1 (2011)
5. Hogan, A., Harth, A., Passant, A., Decker, S., Polleres, A.: Weaving the pedantic web. In: CEUR Workshop Proceedings, vol. 628 (2010)
6. Hogan, A., Umbrich, J., Harth, A., et al.: An empirical survey of linked data conformance. Web Semant. **14**, 14–44 (2012)
7. Langer, A., Gaedke, M.: Fame.q -a formal approach to master quality in enterprise linked data. In: Proceedings of the 15th International Conference WWW/Internet (ICWI2016), pp. 51–58. IADIS, October 2016

8. Langer, A., Gaedke, M.: DaQAR - an ontology for the uniform exchange of comparable linked data quality assessment requirements. In: Mikkonen, T., Klamma, R., Hernández, J. (eds.) ICWE 2018. LNCS, vol. 10845, pp. 234–242. Springer, Cham (2018). https://doi.org/10.1007/978-3-319-91662-0_18

9. Mendes, P.N., Mühleisen, H., Bizer, C.: Sieve: linked data quality assessment and fusion. In: Proceedings of the 2012 Joint EDBT/ICDT Workshops, EDBT-ICDT 2012, pp. 116–123. ACM, New York (2012)

10. Redman, T.C.: Data Quality: The Field Guide. Digital Press, Newton (2001)

11. Ruan, T., Dong, X., Li, Y., Wang, H.: KBMetrics A Multi-purpose Tool for Measuring the Quality of Linked Open Data Sets (2015)

12. Wang, R.Y., Strong, D.M.: Beyond accuracy: what data quality means to data consumers. J. Manage. Inf. Syst. **12**(4), 5–33 (1996)

13. Zaveri, A., Rula, A., Maurino, A., et al.: Quality assessment for linked open data: a survey. Semant. Web J. **1**, 1–31 (2014)

Model-Driven Analytics for Open Data APIs

Elena Planas[✉] and David Baneres[✉]

Universitat Oberta de Catalunya (UOC), Barcelona, Spain
{eplanash,dbaneres}@uoc.edu

Abstract. Nowadays, the amount of open data sources is increasing exponentially from both the public and private sectors. These data are commonly available from different end-point services that can be queried following the standards of the technology used to create the service. Despite the great potential of open data, and the valuable information that its usage can report to improve the data itself, currently most of the data providers are unaware of how their data is used by end-users. This paper focuses on the design of a Model-Driven Analytical tool for Open Data APIs. Our tool is able to visualize how end-users interact with open data sources regarding two types of metrics: (1) *performance metrics*, focused on general usage parameters like response time; and (2) *semantic metrics*, focused to analyze contextualized data. The tool is described and a case study is presented based on a model manually composed from two Open Data APIs. The monitoring of the open data consumption reports highly valuable information to data owners, guaranteeing the return-on-investment.

Keywords: Open data · Analytics · Visualization · Heatmap · Splunk

1 Introduction

More and more data is becoming available online every day coming from both the public sector and private sources. Government, cities, and private industry are producing a massive amount of data that can be publicly accessed. As an example, the European data portal[1] registers more than 800,000 public datasets online until April 2018. Web APIs (Application Programming Interface), which wrap the data sources and expose a set of methods to access them, are becoming the most popular way to access open data sources. For example, in April 2018, Programmable-Web[2] lists more than 19,415 public APIs. REST is the predominant architectural style for building Web APIs. REST is growing especially in the private sector since APIs offer, among other benefits, a fine-grained control on the access requests over the data. Also, REST Web APIs are a specific kind

This work has been supported by the Spanish government (TIN2016-75944-R project).

[1] https://www.europeandataportal.eu.
[2] https://www.programmableweb.com.

of web services that adhere to the Representational State Transfer architectural style and rely on the HTTP protocol for communication.

The open data movement, through the use of open data sources, aims to empower end-users to exploit and benefit from these data. However, despite the great potential of open data sources, and the valuable information that its consumption can report to improve the data itself, nowadays most of the data providers are unaware about how their data is used by end-users. An example is the open government data [5] which, without data usage analysis, a government will be unable to prioritize which data is relevant for citizens or even curate the available one. In other words, only when data providers get feedback regarding how their data is consumed, the use of open data can provide a guaranteed return-on-investment. Therefore, there is an increasing demand to analyze how and which data are consumed. As reported in [6], collected usage statistics are considered to be valued feedback to data owners, since they give notion of the relevance and enable segmentation. Servers are capable to generate and analyze logs based on traffic but they lack the capacity to diagnose the data based on a known model that is commonly accessed.

This paper focuses on the design of a Model-Driven Analytical tool for Open Data APIs. Our tool is able to visualize how end-users interact with open data sources regarding several metrics. Similarly to [1], our approach follows the Model-Driven Analytics paradigm, which pursues the idea of Model-Driven Engineering [2] to the domain of data analytics. Model-Driven Analytics defines a transparent and continuous process of decomposing knowledge into various analytic elements which can help to decompose the complexity of understanding as a composition of various analytical tools [4].

The monitoring of the open data consumption using tools similar to the one we propose can report highly valuable information to data providers. For instance, to improve data (e.g. updating outdated data, improving data precision, avoiding overlapping, removing non-accessed data,...) and to infer new useful knowledge (e.g. detect new content they should publish, identify potential partnerships based on data typically queried,...), among many others.

The remainder of this paper is structured as follows. Section 2 introduces the running example used along the paper. Section 3 describes the metrics used in our tool and Sect. 4 presents the overall approach we propose to visualize the results. Finally, Sect. 5 concludes the paper.

2   Case Study: Battuta and RestCountries Web APIs

In this paper we use a case study based on two RESTful Web APIs: (1) **Battuta**[3], which provides worldvwide location (country/region/city) service; and **RestCountries**[4], which provides information about countries and languages.

Figure 1 provides the global UML model representing the data managed by Battuta and RestCountries Web APIs. This model has been obtained from a

---

[3] https://battuta.medunes.net.
[4] https://restcountries.eu.

previous semi-automatic process. First, the individual model of each API has been automatically generated based on a discovery process that generates model-based OpenAPI specifications for REST Web APIs by using API call examples [3]. Then, both individual models have been manually merged.

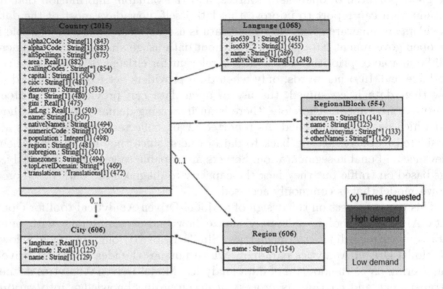

Fig. 1. Global UML model from Battuta and RestCountris Web APIs annotated with two semantic metrics (heat UML model and entity/field consumption).

A custom intermediate service has been implemented to perform general requests to the global model and automatically generate sub-requests to the different API end-points to resolve the general request. This custom service will help to gather log data to show the potential of the developed Model-Driven Analytical tool.

3   Usage Metrics

In order to monitor the consumption of open data sources, we have defined two types of metrics: *performance metrics* and *semantic metrics*.

Performance metrics measure and report mostly performance and volumes of manipulated APIs. These types of metrics are similar to the metrics used for web server analytical tools. Currently, we have defined and implemented the following performance metrics:

1. **Average response time by API:** The tool analyses individually the response time by API end-point.
2. **Average response time by request/sub-requests:** Similarly, the tool is capable to offer more fine-grained information for each individual request and their generated sub-requests.

3. **Average number of accessed APIs and generated sub-requests for each request:** These first three metrics may help to evaluate the complexity of the general request.
4. **API reliability:** This metric stands for knowing the reliability of the APIs by collecting the response codes of each sub-request.
5. **Query history** (with date-range): All previous information could be analyzed by any date range (specific date, relative to a date, real-time, among others). Filtering data may help to evaluate data consumption over time.

On the other hand, the aim of the semantic metrics is to show the ratio of consumed data within the global model. Based on the model that represents the relationship among data stored in one API or several APIs, semantic metrics help to analyze which entities (UML classes) and fields (UML attributes) are mostly demanded. We have defined and implemented the following metrics:

1. **Heat UML Model:** This metric transforms the model to a heat map where entities consumption is highlighted using different colors. This metric will be useful to evaluate which data is mostly accessed.
2. **Entity/field consumption:** Additionally, the number of requests to an specific entity or field is quantitatively shown in the model by general requests and sub-requests. This metric is a fine-grained view of previous metric by showing which fields are mainly used.
3. **Query diagram:** The Open Data protocol allows to merge in a single request information of different entities. This metric focuses on showing the navigability to resolve the performed query. For instance, in our model, the query from Spanish-talking countries get all the cities in OData protocol is "/Countries("ES")/Cities". Thus the query diagram will show a navigability from the entity *Countries* to *Cities* in this specific query.

Fig. 2. Overview of the Model-Driven Analytics process.

4   Model-Driven Analytics

In this section, the Model-Driven Analytics process and the corresponding tool are described (see Fig. 2).

The global process is performed in three steps:

Step 1: Log gathering process

The goal of the log gathering process is to record all requests to the different API end-points. Every time a request is performed, a new entry is added to the log. Note that, the gathering process can be done automatically within the web server by using any logger package. In this paper, the logger package `log4j`[5] has been used into the intermediate service described in Sect. 2.

We have defined an specific log format to be able to record requests and sub-requests. Each log entry is composed by: (1) the initial line, which contains the initial timestamp and the URL of the request; (2) as many lines as the number of sub-queries the request needs to be resolved, with specific information of each sub-query; and (3) the final line, which contains the final timestamp, the URL request again and information about the reliability of the query.

Step 2: Transformation process

A subset of the metrics described in Sect. 3 cannot be computed directly from the log information. Thus, a preprocessing is needed. The gathered log file generated in the previous step is transformed using an ETL (Extract, Transform, Load) process and stored in another log file.

Step 3: Computing metrics and visualization process

The last step of the process is to compute the presented usage metrics and visualize them. This step takes as input: (1) the transformed log file, with information about all the requests performed; and (2) the global UML model that represents the structure of the information contained in the queried APIs.

In order to compute and visualize the assembled information, we use the tool Splunk[6]. Splunk is a software for analyzing and visualizing machine-generated data via a web-style interface. Splunk has a friendly user interface to create queries from log files. Additionally, custom dashboards can be created in web format. Using Splunk capabilities, we have designed a custom and interactive web dashboard to show the metrics described in Sect. 3. The dashboard has been implemented with HTML, JavaScript, formatted with Bootstrap (HTML5) and JointJS[7] to visualize the UML model.

Figure 1 shows a screenshot of part of the implemented Dashboard visualizing the *heat UML model* and the *entity/field consumption* metrics. Figure 3 shows other metrics based on random requests performed to the model on the entity *Countries*. Here, the metrics *average response time*, *APIs reliability* and *query diagram* from performed requests are shown.

5   Conclusions and Future Work

In this paper, we have presented a Model-Driven Analytics process, and the corresponding tool, to monitor and visualize the consumption of open data sources through the use of Web APIs. Our tool allows visualizing the consumption of

---

[5] https://logging.apache.org/log4j/2.x/manual/customloglevels.html.

[6] https://www.splunk.com.

[7] https://www.jointjs.com/.

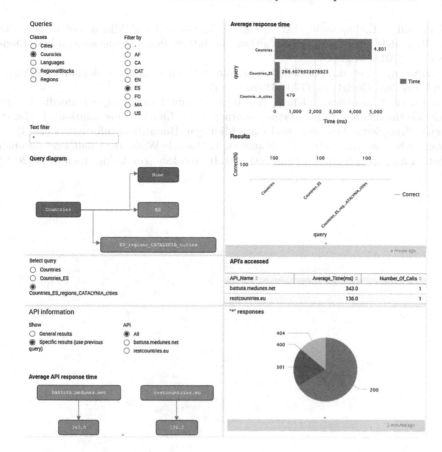

Fig. 3. Screenshot of the Dashboard visualizing a subset of metrics.

several Web APIs in a unified view regarding several performance and semantic metrics defined in the context of this paper.

As a further work we are interested to facilitate the definition of metrics and the creation of customized dashboards by the end-users through the use of DSLs. Additionally, we will continue studying how Model-Driven Analytics can be adapted based on user preferences and satisfiability and how this information can be used to improve and curate the current data accessible from Web APIs.

References

1. Bernaschina, C., Brambilla, M., Mauri, A., Umuhoza, E.: A Big Data analysis framework for model-based web user behavior analytics. In: International Conference on Web Engineering, pp. 98–114 (2017)
2. Brambilla, M., Cabot, J., Wimmer, M.: Model-Driven Software Engineering in Practice. Synthesis Lectures on Software Engineering. Morgan & Claypool (2017)

3. Ed-Douibi, H., Izquierdo, J.L.C., Cabot, J.: OpenAPItoUML: a tool to generate UML models from OpenAPI definitions. In: International Conference on Web Engineering (2018, in press)
4. Hartmann, T., et al.: Model-driven analytics: Connecting data, domain knowledge, and learning. CoRR, abs/1704.01320 (2017)
5. Holzinger, A., Jurisica, I.: Knowledge discovery and data mining in biomedical informatics: the future is in integrative, interactive machine learning solutions. In: Interactive Knowledge Discovery and Data Mining in Biomedical Informatics (2014)
6. Vander Sande, M., Portier, M., Mannens, E., Van de Walle, R.: Challenges for open data usage: open derivatives and licensing. In: Workshop on Using Open Data (2012)

Geo-Time Broker: A Web Agent of Dynamic Flows of Geo-Temporal Activity for Smart Cities

Álvaro E. Prieto[✉] [ID], Juan Carlos Preciado [ID],
José María Conejero [ID], and Álvaro Rubio-Largo

Grupo QUERCUS de Ingeniería del Software, Escuela Politécnica,
Universidad de Extremadura, 10003 Cáceres, Spain
{aeprieto, jcpreciado, chemacm, arl}@unex.es

Abstract. In the last years, the Smart City term has appeared in roadmaps and digital agendas for many public administrations in both regional and national contexts. Following this trend, many cities have made important efforts to deploy a network of sensors with the aim of gathering a huge amount of networking related data. Most of these cities are publishing their data through Open Data portals in order to facilitate access and re-use of these data by third parties. Unfortunately, just 5% of the gathered data are currently processed; therefore, the actual contributions extracted from the usage of these data are far from the potential benefits that they may offer. This work presents a first prototype based on the Geo-Temporal Dynamic Activity Flows concept that ease processing and consuming these data. These Dynamic Activity Flows are based on the usage of a resource commonly used to represent cities, their maps.

Keywords: Smart Cities · Intelligent data flows · Open data

1 Introduction

The Smart City concept [1] has been developed over recent years with a sharp focus on the introduction of sensor systems, measuring and control infrastructures, and closely connected to energy efficiency and optimisation [2]. Recently, the model has been reconceived in accordance with the demands of the different actors who intervene in a city on the improvement and everyday usage of the new technologies [3], until reaching the well-known present-day smart city concepts such as government, mobility, energy and environment, etc.

So far, any city that has decided to set in motion the advantages that technology lavishes on us solves its problems by using the aforementioned technologies and has made significant investments in physical devices and infrastructures [4]. Over these last few years the introduction of data acquisition systems has increased exponentially. This new infrastructure is generating a huge volume of city activity data [5] that are originated from multiple sources and coming in extremely diverse formats, normally conceived with different ends, methods, profiles, production rates and consumption rate. In this sense, it is acknowledged that the availability of an open data portal

© Springer Nature Switzerland AG 2018
C. Pautasso et al. (Eds.): ICWE 2018, LNCS 11153, pp. 183–188, 2018.
https://doi.org/10.1007/978-3-030-03056-8_16

providing accurate public data is one of the foundations of Smart Cities [6]. So, many Smart Cities are releasing great part of their data through these portals trying to encourage the reuse and combination of such data by third parties. Even though, we are faced with a situation where, in some cases, we are only capable of processing 5% of the whole mass of data [7].

These are highly relevant data, that should be considered when designing and developing the cities of the future (re-designing the cities of the present). The proper evolution of cities is of utmost importance, since they have a huge impact on the economic and social development of the regions they belong to. They are authentic platforms where people work and live, where companies perform their activity, where the public authorities must work for the wellbeing of their citizens.

To date, the solutions proposed have been disjointed, actions put into practice because of fashions or through the deployment of a certain known technology, but without a perspective of the specific necessities of the city. The challenge is no longer the evolution and development of the technology, the problem is no longer the generation and acquisition of data – now we are faced with new challenges and new problems concerning the treatment of these data. At present, these affairs have little to do with the technological infrastructures of the city and data gathering, but they are closely related to the treatment and transformation of these data into information.

Therefore, it is important to design a system that aids the transformation of this data diversity into information according to the user profiles of citizens who are consumers within the city system environment. In this sense, Business Intelligence (BI) and Business Analytics (BA) techniques could be applied. This is due to the fact that the objective of BI and BA is to transform data into useful and relevant information (in time and format) for the consumer.

Bearing these ideas in mind, this paper presents a prototype called Geotime Broker, a Web Agent of Dynamic flows of Geo-Temporal Activity for Smart Cities for the design and visualization of the behaviours of Smart Cities. This prototype tackles the complexity generated by the increasing volumes of data generated by the city based on their encapsulation into the concept called Dynamic Activity Flows (DAFs) for the Smart City.

The rest of the paper is organized as follows: Sect. 2 introduces the concept of Dynamic Activity Flows (DAFs), Sect. 3 presents Geo-Time Broker and Sect. 4 describes the first case where it has been applied to, the school allocation of freshman primary students.

2   Dynamic Activity Flows

The DAFs concept is inspired by the traditional representation that has been used over the history for representing cities, the map. The maps have been always used as a geo-referencing frame for the different facts that occur in a city. So, based on this assumption, it is natural to use this tool for representing the knowledge that is generated from the Smart City data considering three different dimensions: (i) *what*, i.e. the data that are being analysed and represented; (ii) *where*, i.e. their geolocation based on the coordinates and the influence areas; (iii) *when*, i.e. the temporal range when this information has been generated.

The combination of the aforementioned dimensions conforms the concept of DAFs, being an entity at a higher abstraction level than just the data. In other words, this concept comprises the result of selecting, processing and combining Smart City data that are related to particular locations and specific temporal ranges. In summary, they allow showing different behaviours of Smart Cities.

3   Geo-Time Broker

Geo-Time Broker is a web agent with the next characteristics:

- It is a framework for the design of behavioural patterns by identifying, orchestrating and processing data sets that a city generates
- It is an interface for the definition of intelligence rules, processing capabilities and scaling analytics for the DAFs generated so that they may be:
  - visualized and interacted allowing users to build behaviours over a particular temporal range in a flexible way
  - dynamically transformed into useful and relevant information according to the consumer profile

In short, the main goal of Geo-Time Broker is allowing users to apply different algorithms to one or more DAFs in order to visualize complex behaviours in the city based on maps. Figure 1 depicts the conceptual architecture of Geo-Time Broker.

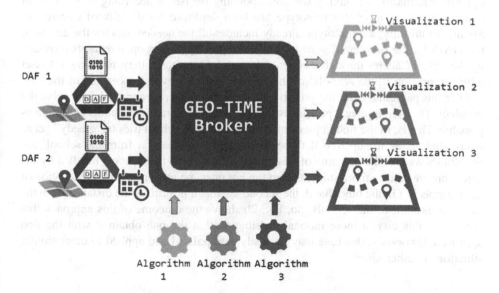

Fig. 1. Geo-time broker conceptual architecture

4   Application Scenario: School Allocation of Freshman Primary Students

This section describes an application scenario that has been used to illustrate the first version of the prototype that has been built for Geo-Time Broker. This scenario tries to solve the problem of allocating new students at the primary schools of a city. This is a recurrent problem that most cities in Spain (and other countries) must face at the beginning of every academic year. To tackle the problem, not only the existing schools in the city must be considered but also the population around each school. However, there is a challenge that has not been solved yet: would it be feasible to dynamically and automatically adapt the influence area of each school according to the actual population (at any time) and necessities around each school?

Currently, solving this problem is complex since performing any change at real time becomes highly expensive (in both, time and effort). However, based on the usage of DAFs we may combine and orchestrate the locations of the schools over the city map and define, for each one, the optimum capacity of the classrooms or the estimated surrounding area according to the actual population, the families with children in scholar age, the distance to the homes by walking, the combination of public transports for reaching the school and the number of private vehicles existing within the context of the school. This may be automatically and optimally provided in a system that covers the whole city. Moreover, considering the time dimension, this information may be also compared with rush-hour traffic according to the entrance and exit times for schools so that graphical simulations with different DAFs configurations may be executed at real time. So, a visualization dashboard may be created that offers the optimal information for taking the corresponding decisions according to the current data. A first version of this prototype has been deployed for the city of Cáceres, in Spain. For this city, the prototype already includes all the needed data for the design of the DAFs for the problem described. Thus, the prototype uses open datasets provided by the city of Cáceres through its open data portal. Concretely, they are using a dataset with information of the schools[1] of the city and a dataset with the census[2] of the city.

For this particular case, the prototype is using two different approaches to solve the problem. The first approach prioritizes that the occupation ratio of schools is as high as possible. That is, in the first implemented algorithm each school tries to "greedy" get as many students as it can even if those students live in areas far from the school. So, Fig. 2a shows that the outcome of this approach is that the first schools handled by the algorithm are getting more students than the last ones, no matter how far the location of the students is. On the other hand, the second approach prioritizes the distance from the students location to the schools. So, Fig. 2b shows the outcome of this approach that seems, for this city, a more rational distribution that the one obtained with the first approach. Obviously, this case may be easily extrapolated and applied to other similar situations in other cities.

---

[1] http://opendata.caceres.es/dataset/centros-docentes-caceres.

[2] http://opendata.caceres.es/dataset/informacion-del-padron-de-caceres-2017.

Fig. 2. a. Allocation prioritizing occupation ratio b. Allocation prioritizing students distance

5 Conclusions

This work has presented the first version of the Geo-Time Broker prototype that uses DAFs of a Smart City to design and visualize complex behaviours in the city based on maps. Moreover, an application scenario has been introduced that allows illustrating the potential benefits of the approach. Other application scenarios that the approach may be used for and that provide contributions are the next:

1. Create graphical market analyses at real time about the DAFs based on the combination of contextual data, geo-population, concrete facts georeferenced and other data sources. Notice that the term of market analysis is used here in the most wide sense and going beyond just buying and sell opportunities.
2. Perform analyses based on visual patterns about DAFs in the cities to evaluate different actions such as economic or social investments. Similarly, an adequate roadmap for cities may be identified with concrete actions that are prioritized according to the data.
3. End-user development of DAFs based on auto-design or auto-consumption as a Self-Service Smart City Service.
4. Creation of visual projections and predictions by means of machine learning algorithms applied to DAFs designed by consumers in order to support decision making.
5. Implement a high level dashboard for intra and inter city DAFS. This dashboard will allow managing, displaying and comparing the behaviour of DAFs from different geographical locations.

Acknowledgment. Authors would like to thank (i) TIN2015-69957-R (MINECO/ERDF, EU) (ii) POCTEP 4IE (0045-4 IE-4-P) and (iii) Consejería de Economía e Infraestructuras/Junta de Extremadura - European Regional Development Fund (ERDF)- IB16055 project and GR15098 project for their support in the development of this work.

References

1. Budde, P.: Smart cities of tomorrow. In: Rassia, S.Th., Pardalos, S.Th. (eds.) Cities for Smart Environmental and Energy Futures. ENERGY. pp. 9–20. Springer, Heidelberg (2014). https://doi.org/10.1007/978-3-642-37661-0_2
2. Nam, T., Pardo, T.A.: Conceptualizing smart city with dimensions of technology, people, and institutions. In: Proceedings of the 12th Annual International Digital Government Research Conference: Digital Government Innovation in Challenging Times, pp. 282–291. ACM, New York (2011)
3. Nam, T., Pardo, T.A.: Smart city as urban innovation: focusing on management, policy, and context. In: Proceedings of the 5th International Conference on Theory and Practice of Electronic Governance, New York, NY, USA, pp. 185–194 (2011)
4. da Silva, W.M., Alvaro, A., Tomas, G.H., Afonso, R.A., Dias, K.L., Garcia, V.C.: Smart cities software architectures: a survey. In: Proceedings of the 28th Annual ACM Symposium on Applied Computing, pp. 1722–1727. ACM, Coimbra (2013)
5. Hernández-Muñoz, J.M., et al.: Smart cities at the forefront of the future internet. In: Domingue, J., et al. (eds.) FIA 2011. LNCS, vol. 6656, pp. 447–462. Springer, Heidelberg (2011). https://doi.org/10.1007/978-3-642-20898-0_32
6. Mulligan, C.E., Olsson, M.: Architectural implications of smart city business models: an evolutionary perspective. IEEE Commun. Mag. **51**(6), 80–85 (2013)
7. David, B., et al.: SMART-CITY: problematics, techniques and case studies. In: Proceedings of the 8th International Conference on Computing Technology and Information Management (ICCM), vol. 1, pp. 168–174. IEEE, Seoul (2012)

1st International Workshop on Knowledge Graphs on Travel and Tourism (TourismKG 2018)

1st International Workshop on Knowledge Graphs on Travel and Tourism (TourismKG 2018)

Mariano Rico, Nandana Mihindukulasooriya, and
Freddy Priyatna

Ontology Engineering Group,
Universidad Politécnica de Madrid, Madrid, Spain
http://tourismkg.github.io/2018/

Preface

The 1st International Workshop on Knowledge Graphs on Travel and Tourism (TourismKG 2018) has been a **full-day** workshop at the 18th International Conference on Web Engineering (ICWE 2018).

Travel and Tourism is a multibillion-dollar industry having a major impact on the global economy. An increasing number of people use applications on the Web to plan their trips. Although current applications are focused on humans, in the era of Big Data and Artificial Intelligence, there is a need for machine-readable data.

Semantic Web techniques such as ontologies or vocabularies allow domain experts to represent knowledge with explicit semantics in a machine-readable way. Besides, datasets can be transformed and integrated with this knowledge in order to create the so-called Knowledge Graphs. Such Knowledge Graphs, together with Machine Learning techniques, are used by popular applications such as Siri, Google Now, or Alexa. The success of these applications depends on the existence of high-quality knowledge graphs.

While Knowledge Graphs have been successfully used in other domains such as finance, medical or e-commerce, little attention has been paid to apply these technologies in the Tourism and Travel industry. Thus, the goal of this workshop is to raise the awareness of the importance of Knowledge Graphs on the travel industry and discuss their usage, challenges, enhancement, and ways of commercial exploitation.

We have used easychair to organize the workshop, with 18 reviewers from 9 countries. The selected papers come from five countries. Each paper had a minimum of two reviewers. We want to thank everyone for their excellent work despite the tight agenda.

Organization

Organizing Committee

Mariano Rico	Ontology Engineering Group, Universidad Politécnica de Madrid, Spain
Miriam Scaglione	School of Management & Tourism of the University of Applied Sciences Valais (HES-SO Valais), Switzerland
Filip Radulovic	Sépage, Paris, France
Rodolfo Baggio	Bocconi University, Milano, Italy
Freddy Priyatna	Ontology Engineering Group, Universidad Politécnica de Madrid, Spain
Nandana Mihindukulasooriya	Ontology Engineering Group, Universidad Politécnica de Madrid, Spain

Program Committee

Alicia Orea Giner	Universidad Rey Juan Carlos, Spain
Andrés García Silva	Expert System, Spain
Boris Villazón-Terrazas	Fujitsu Laboratories of Europe, Madrid, Spain
Carlos Buil Aranda	Universidad Técnica Federico Santa María, Chile
Chun Lu	Sorbonne University, France
Daniel Garijo	University of Southern California, USA
Dimitris Kontokostas	AKSW Group, Leipzig University, Germany
Ghislain Atemezing	Mondeca, France
Giuseppe Rizzo	Istituto Superiore Mario Boella (ISMB), Italy
Ioan Toma	Onlim GmbH, Austria
Jean-Paul Calbimonte	Institute of Information Systems (IIG), HES-SO, Switzerland
Jeremy Debattista	ADAPT Centre, Trinity College Dublin, Ireland
Jose Luis Redondo García	Amazon, Cambridge, UK
Jorge Gracia	Universidad de Zaragoza, Spain
Lucas Carvalho	Instituto de Computação, Universidade Estadual de Campinas
Oshani Seneviratne	Rensselaer Polytechnic Institute (RPI), Troy, NY, USA
Udana Wickramasinghe	Director - ICT, Sri Lanka. Tourism Promotion Bureau, Sri Lanka
Roland Schegg	Institut Tourisme, University of Applied Sciences and Arts, Switzerland

Sponsors

We want to thank TAIGER (http://www.taiger.com/), OEG and ODI Madrid. Without their support all this would have been impossible.

Publishing Tourism Statistics as Linked Data a Case Study of Sri Lanka

Nandana Mihindukulasooriya[✉], Freddy Priyatna, and Mariano Rico

Ontology Engineering Group, Universidad Politécnica de Madrid, Madrid, Spain
{nmihindu,fpriyatna,mariano.rico}@fi.upm.es

Abstract. Tourism is a crucial component of Sri Lanka's economy. Intelligent business decisions by means of thorough analysis of relevant data can help the Sri Lankan tourism industry to be competitive. To this end, Sri Lanka Tourism Development Authority makes tourism statistics publicly available. However, they are published as PDF files limiting their reuse. In this paper, we present how to transform such data into 5-star Linked Open Data by extracting the statistics as structured data; modelling them using the W3C RDF Data Cube vocabulary and transforming them to RDF using W3C R2RML mappings. Furthermore, we demonstrate the benefits of such transformation using two real-world use cases.

Keywords: Tourism · Open data · Linked Data · RDF
RDF Data Cube · R2RML

1 Introduction

The tourism industry in Sri Lanka is a crucial component of the island's economy. In 2016, it was ranked as the third highest foreign exchange earner in the country (14.20%) [1]. The Sri Lankan government is taking many initiatives to foster tourism industry in the country. One of these initiatives is to make tourism data available as open data so that stakeholders of the tourism industry can make intelligent business decisions backed by thorough analysis of data. Tourism statistics are in the center of such open data because statistical data play a key role in policy prediction, planning and formulating growth strategies. Furthermore, as most of these decision making processes are increasingly backed by data-driven approaches and artificial intelligence algorithms, it is important to make these data easily accessible, web-friendly, and provided with explicit semantics, in a machine understandable manner with enough contextual information.

The *Linked Data* principles[1] help creating a global data space with typed links between data from different sources. Publishing data as *Linked Data* bring several advantages including (a) global identifiers for data that can be accessed

---

[1] https://www.w3.org/DesignIssues/LinkedData.html.

© Springer Nature Switzerland AG 2018
C. Pautasso et al. (Eds.): ICWE 2018, LNCS 11153, pp. 193–201, 2018.
https://doi.org/10.1007/978-3-030-03056-8_17

using the Web infrastructure and typed links between data from different sources; (b) the graph-based RDF data model allows consuming and merging data from different sources without having to do complex structural transformations; and (c) explicit semantics of data expressed in RDF Schema or OWL ontologies which can be aligned and mapped to data models of other applied using techniques such as ontology matching. Thanks to the typed links to external sources, data can be enriched and more context about the data can be discovered by traversing the links.

RDF Data Cube [2] is a standard vocabulary published by W3C based on Statistical Data and Metadata Exchange (SDMX) to publish statistical data in a standard manner. In addition to all benefits of Linked Data, RDF Data Cube enables reuse of standardized tools and components such as visualization tools. Thanks to the semantics defined in RDF Data Cube, the structure of the data can be defined in a manner that can be automatically discovered and be used for generating common visualizations such as line graphs, bar chats, pie charts, etc. R2RML [3] is a W3C recommendation for a mapping language from tabular data to RDF. R2RML can be used to define the mapping between the tabular data in the tourism statistics to RDF in a standard reusable manner.

The objective of the work presented in this paper is to transform the tourism statistics currently published as PDF files into *5 star open data* by semantically annotating them as Linked Data using the W3C RDF Data Cube vocabulary. For the sake of reproducibility all the datasets and results are publicly available at Datahub.io[2] and at the website[3].

2   Sri Lankan Tourism Statistics

2.1   Overview

Sri Lanka Tourism Development Authority (SLTDA) performs data collection and market research about tourism in Sri Lanka and publishes a comprehensive statistics both as monthly statistical bulletins and annual statistical reports. Such reports include information about (a) trends and structural characteristics of tourist traffic, (b) scheduled airline operators & passenger movements, (c) accommodation industry - capacity and its utilisation, (d) income and employment, (e) tourist prices, (f) foreign travel by Sri Lankans, (g) growth of travel and tourism, and (h) revenue from tourism. These reports are currently available as PDF files[4]. Even though a lot of valuable information are made public in these reports, we argue that their exploitation is limited by the fact that they are published as PDF files.

---

[2]   https://datahub.io/nandana/sri-lanka-tourism-statistics.
[3]   http://tourismkg.linkeddata.es.
[4]   http://www.sltda.lk/statistics.

2.2 5 Star Open Data

In his original note about Linked Data, Tim Berners-Lee, introduced the concept of 5 star open data[5]. Under this scheme, the first star is given if the data is available on the Web with an open license. The second star is given if the data is published using as structured data format such as Excel instead of an image or a PDF file. The third star is given if the selected structured data format is open and non-proprietary, for instance, as CSV or JSON instead of Microsoft Excel. The forth star is given when the data uses URIs to denote things so that items in data have global identifiers and can be dereferenced. The fifth star is given when the data has linked to other knowledge graphs so that data is put in context and additional information can be obtained by traversing the links. In its current form, Sri Lankan tourism statistics can be attributed only the first star of the 5 star open data.

2.3 W3C RDF Data Cube Vocabulary

The W3C RDF Data Cube vocabulary [2] enables statistical data, which is typically modelled as multi-dimensional data, to be represented in RDF, and published as Linked Data. Tourism statistics is a good example of such data. Tourism statistics generally contain numerical values associated with different geographical regions (e.g., countries, provinces, cities), time periods (e.g., a given year or a month), and other classifications (e.g., purpose of visit, airline).

In RDF Data Cube, data that follows a certain structure is modelled as a *dataset*. The data in a dataset includes (a) *observations*, *i.e.* the actual data in the statistics; (b) *organisational structure*, *i.e.* information about how the data is organised such as dimensions and slices; (c) *structural metadata*, *i.e.* additional information that helps to interpret the observations such as the unit of measurements and whether a value is measured or calculated; (d) reference metadata, *i.e.* metadata about the dataset such as its publisher or the SPARQL endpoint for querying the data.

3 Methodology

Figure 1 illustrates the transformation process followed to publish the tourism statistics as 5 star open data.

As the first step, tables containing statistics are extracted as CSV files[6] using the tabula-java[7] library. By doing so, we can move the tourism statistics from *1-star open data* to *3-star* directly as CSV is an open and non-proprietary format.

---

[5] https://www.w3.org/DesignIssues/LinkedData.html.

[6] https://github.com/tourism-data/tourism-data.github.io/tree/master/sri-lanka/ csv/arrivals-country-month.

[7] https://github.com/tabulapdf/tabula-java.

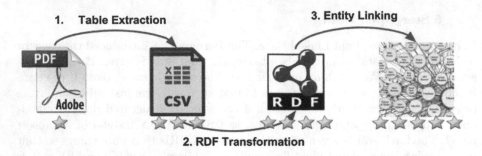

Fig. 1. Transformation process and number of stars achieved.

Then, the extracted CSVs are converted to RDF using R2RML mappings[8]. Finally, entities in the statistics such as countries are linked to DBpedia and Wikidata using the DBpedia Spotlight[9] entity annotator. We have minted IRIs using the *w3id* service[10]. Each observation is available on the web with its global permanent identifier, for example, (http://w3id.org/sri-lanka/tourism/values/ arrivals-country-year-month/spain-2016-jan). These resources are dereference-able and support content negotiation common RDF formats such as Turtle, RDF/XML, and JSON-LD. The complete dataset is available for download at Datahub[11].

To illustrate the transformation process using a running example, Table 1 presents an example table from Sri Lankan Tourist Statistics annual reports. It contains the number of tourists from each country arrived to Sri Lanka in each month of the year 2016. Each numerical cell in Table 1 refers to an observation measured by SLTDA using the official data from the immigration records. Such observations are multi-dimensional and concretely associated with three dimensions, *i.e.*, (i) the country of residence, (ii) the year of arrival, and (iii) the month of arrival. This organisational structure can be defined using the RDF

Table 1. An example - tourist arrivals by country of residence

Country of Residence	Year - 2016					
	January	February	March	April	May	...
France	9,878	14,602	11,175	7,518	3,281	...
Italy	4,131	3,607	2,683	1,455	1,010	...
Russia	8,358	6,958	5,916	4,081	1,756	...
Spain	984	1,054	1,587	856	719	...

---

8   https://github.com/tourism-data/tourism-data.github.io/tree/master/sri-lanka/ mappings/arrivals-country-month.
9   http://www.dbpedia-spotlight.org.
10 https://w3id.org.
11 https://datahub.io/nandana/sri-lanka-tourism-statistics.

Data Cube vocabulary as shown in the Listing 1.1. Using the defined structure, each cell value can be transformed to an observation as shown in Listing 1.2. During this process, the values for dimensions country of residence is linked to DBpedia countries and months are linked to Time Intervals Ontology[12].

```
1  @prefix qb: <http://purl.org/linked-data/cube#> .
2  @prefix sltsv: <http://w3id.org/sri-lanka/tourism/vocab/> .
3  @prefix rdfs: <http://www.w3.org/2000/01/rdf-schema#> .
4
5  _:structure-arrivals-month-by-residence a qb:DataStructureDefinition;
6      qb:component [ qb:dimension sltsv:countryOfResidence;
7              rdfs:label "The country of residence of the tourist"@en;
8              rdfs:label "El pas de residencia del turista"@es ];
9      qb:component [ qb:dimension sltsv:month;
10             rdfs:label "The calendar month of arrival"@en;
11             rdfs:label "El mes calendario de llegada"@es ];
12     qb:component [ qb:dimension sltsv:year;
13             rdfs:label "The calendar year of arrival"@en;
14             rdfs:label "El ao calendario de llegada"@es ];
15     qb:component [ qb:measure sltsv:numberOfArrivals;
16             rdfs:label "The number of tourists arrived"@en;
17             rdfs:label "La cantidad de turistas"@es ] .
```

Listing 1.1. An example data structure definition

```
1  @prefix qb: <http://purl.org/linked-data/cube#> .
2  @prefix interval: <http://reference.data.gov.uk/def/intervals/> .
3  @prefix sltsv: <http://w3id.org/sri-lanka/tourism/vocab/> .
4  @prefix xsd: <http://www.w3.org/2001/XMLSchema#> .
5
6  _:obs1  a qb:Observation;
7  qb:dataSet _:dataset-arrivals-month-by-residence;
8  sltsv:countryOfResidence <http://dbpedia.org/resource/Spain>;
9  sltsv:year "2016"^^xsd:gYear;
10 sltsv:month interval:January;
11 sltsv:numberOfArrivals "984"^^xsd:int .
```

Listing 1.2. An example observation

4 Exploitation

In this section, we analyze two use cases before and after the conversion of data into Linked Data.

Analysis of Spanish Speaking Tourists. In this use case, a travel agent wants to filter the statistics for tourists who are from Spanish speaking countries in order to take a business decision on whether to spend more money on advertising in

---

[12] http://reference.data.gov.uk.

Spanish. Before transforming into Linked Data, an analysis had to manually extract information about all countries, to find out if the mother tongue of citizens of each country is Spanish, and prepare a subset of data based on that.

If the PDF file (or even its equivalent CSV) is the only information the travel agent, it will need to check manually which countries speak Spanish. But with Linked Data, contextual information such as the language spoken by a specific country can be obtained other datasets by traversing the links. In this concrete example, the countries in the dataset are linked to DBpedia, and DBpedia contains information about the official language of each country.

```
1  PREFIX qb: <http://purl.org/linked-data/cube#>
2  PREFIX sltsv: <http://w3id.org/sri-lanka/tourism/cube-vocab/>
3  PREFIX dbo: <http://dbpedia.org/ontology/>
4
5  select ?country ?year ?month ?arrivals where {
6
7    ?obs a qb:Observation;
8    sltsv:countryOfResidence ?country;
9    sltsv:year ?year; sltsv:month ?month; sltsv:numberOfArrivals ?
         arrivals .
10
11   ?country a dbo:Country .
12   ?country dbo:officialLanguage | dbo:language  ?language  .
13   ?language dbo:iso6391Code "es"
14 }
```

Listing 1.3. A query for Spanish speaking tourists

Custom Visualisations of Data. In this use case, a tourism investor wants to visualise some specific information of a subset of the tourism data that is relevant to her investment. More concretely, she is interested in monthly arrival patterns of some countries. As the PDF files can not possibly cover all different scenarios, this specific visualization is not present in the reports published by SLTDA. Before transformation of the data, an analyst has to extract the data, understand the structure of data, and create visualisations manually.

Thanks the standard W3C RDF Data Cube vocabulary, most common graphs for a specific selection of data (using RDF cube dimensions) can be drawn with few clicks resuing the existing RDF Cube visualization tools such as Cube Viz[13], LinkedPipes[14], and OpenCube[15]. The structure, ordering, labels, multilingual content are automatically detected by the tools using the RDF Data Cube semantics (Fig. 2).

---

[13] http://cubeviz.aksw.org.
[14] https://visualization.linkedpipes.com.
[15] http://opencube-toolkit.eu.

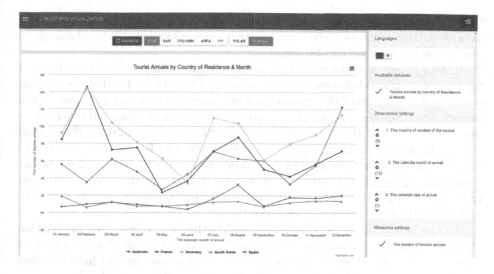

Fig. 2. A custom visualisation of tourist statistics

5   Related Work

EuroStat publishes tourism statistics[16] about European countries but mainly as tabular data. Similarly, SLTDA produces early reports about tourism statistics as PDF files. Sabou *et al.* [4] has transformed tourism data from TourMI, an online database that consists of tourism market research data from several European countries. In contrast to their approach of building an specific ontology by scratch, we focus on reusing existing standard vocabularies such as W3C RDF Data Cube.

RDF Data Cube has been used to transform statistical data from other domains such as census data [5], Open Government Data [6], clinical trial data [7], and meteorological sensor data [8].

There are several visualisation tools that support data described using the RDF Data Cube vocabulary including Cube Viz [9], OpenCube [10], LinkedPipes [11]. Furthermore, there are tools for validating data represented using the RDF Data Cube vocabulary such as RDF Data Cube Validation tool [12]. Any of these tools can be used to validate and to visualise the Tourism Statistics Linked Data generated by the work presented in this paper.

6   Conclusion

Sri Lanka Tourism Development Authority makes tourism statistics publicly available through annual statistics reports, however, as they are released as PDF files their reuse needs a lot manual effort. Nevertheless, to get the real value of

---

16 http://ec.europa.eu/eurostat/web/tourism/overview.

this data and foster their reuse, this data needs to be provided as structured data with their semantics and links to other external knowledge graphs so more contextual information can be found.

In this paper, we presented how we have transformed 1-star Open Data of Sri Lankan tourism statistics into 5-star Linked Open Data. Further, we demonstrated some benefits of the transformation using two common use cases. Even though the proposed approach depends on extracting tabular information, it can be improved if the data publisher, *i.e.* SLTDA, incorporates the Linked Data generation into their pipeline. For example, the PDF reports aggregate values for many countries as "Others" in order to make the tables short and fit them into a page. If such information were provided directly as data, all those values can be provided and the consumers can filter the data relevant for them, and create their own tables or visualise them.

To the best of authors' knowledge, this is the first linked data publication of the Sri Lankan government open data. We believe that publishing data in a more accessible web-friendly manner with explicit semantics and links to other knowledge graphs will help to foster the use of open data in Sri Lanka.

Acknowledgments. This work was funded by the Spanish Ministry of Economy and Competitiveness (MINECO) with the BES-2014-068449 FPI grant, DATOS 4.0: Retos y soluciones (TIN2016-78011-C4-4-R) and esTextAnalytics (RTC-2016-4952-7) projects.

References

1. Sri Lanka Tourism Development Authority: Annual statistical report 2016. Technical report, Sri Lanka Tourism Development Authority (2016)
2. Cyganiak, R., Reynolds, D., Tennison, J.: The RDF data cube vocabulary, W3C recommendation 16 January 2014. World Wide Web Consortium (2014)
3. Das, S., Sundara, S., Cyganiak, R.: R2RML: RDB to RDF Mapping Language. Technical report, W3C RDB2RDF Working Group (2012)
4. Sabou, M., Braşoveanu, A.M., Arsal, I.: Supporting tourism decision making with linked data. In: Proceedings of the 8th International Conference on Semantic Systems, pp. 201–204. ACM (2012)
5. Petrou, I., Papastefanatos, G., Dalamagas, T.: Publishing census as linked open data: a case study. In: Proceedings of the 2nd International Workshop on Open Data, p. 4. ACM (2013)
6. Hoxha, J., Brahaj, A.: Open government data on the web: a semantic approach. In: 2011 International Conference on Emerging Intelligent Data and Web Technologies (EIDWT), pp. 107–113. IEEE (2011)
7. Leroux, H., Lefort, L.: Using CDISC ODM and the RDF data cube for the semantic enrichment of longitudinal clinical trial data. In: SWAT4LS. Citeseer (2012)
8. Lefort, L., Bobruk, J., Haller, A., Taylor, K., Woolf, A.: A linked sensor data cube for a 100 year homogenised daily temperature dataset. In: Proceedings of the 5th International Conference on Semantic Sensor Networks-Volume 904, pp. 1–16. CEUR-WS. org (2012)

9. Abicht, K., Alkhouri, G., Arndt, N., Meissner, R., Martin, M.: CubeViz. js: a lightweight framework for discovering and visualizing RDF data cubes. In: INFOR-MATIK 2017 (2017)
10. Kalampokis, E., et al.: Exploiting linked data cubes with opencube toolkit. In: International Semantic Web Conference (Posters & Demos), vol. 1272, pp. 137–140 (2014)
11. Klímek, J., Helmich, J., Nečaský, M.: LinkedPipes visualization: simple useful linked data visualization use cases. In: Sack, H., Rizzo, G., Steinmetz, N., Mladenić, D., Auer, S., Lange, C. (eds.) ESWC 2016. LNCS, vol. 9989, pp. 112–117. Springer, Cham (2016). https://doi.org/10.1007/978-3-319-47602-5_23
12. Janev, V., Mijović, V., Vraneš, S.: LOD2 tool for validating RDF data cube models. In: Web Proceedings of the 5th ICT Innovations Conference, pp. 12–15 (2013)

Linked-Fiestas: A Knowledge Graph to Promote Cultural Tourism in Spain

Andrea Cimmino(✉), Nandana Mihindukulasooriya(✉), Freddy Priyatna(✉), and Mariano Rico(✉)

Ontology Engineering Group, Universidad Politécnica de Madrid, Madrid, Spain
{cimino,nmihindu,fpriyatna,mariano.rico}@fi.upm.es

Abstract. Spain is a hot-spot for the European tourism that conforms an important part of its economy. Large cities tend to monopolize this sector unbalancing the outcome of the tourism in Spain. Promoting festivals from less-known regions that belong to the Spanish cultural heritage has been proposed as a solution to balance the economy of this sector. Unfortunately there is a lack of visibility of such festivals that hinders the feasibility of such approach. In this paper we introduce the Linked-Fiestas dataset that aims at providing data of festivals and events from not so well-known regions, so spreading their cultural heritage, bringing visibility to them, and thus, increasing tourists interest. Linked-Fiestas gathers data from well-known datasets, such as DBpedia and Wikidata, and from other datasets outside the Web of Data community.

Keywords: Festivals · Linked-data · Cultural-heritage

1 Introduction

Tourism is an emerging industry in Europe that has witness a significant growth during the last decade [1]. Southern countries as Spain are specially suitable to be visited namely due to their weather, their rich cultural heritage of national and international interest, and other bespoke country characteristics [2]. However the economy related to this sector is not balanced at all, less known regions have to compete with big well-known cities in order to attract tourists [3].

Promoting festivals that are part of the Spanish cultural heritage is one strategy to increase the tourists interest on those less-known Spanish regions [3]. Unfortunately, although many of these festivals have been designated as national and international interests, their lack of visibility keeps them unknown even for the locals.

In this paper we aim at publishing a dataset containing namely not so well-known Spanish festivals according to the linked data principles, so producing 5-star quality data[1]. In addition, we aim at showing that there is a lack of this kind of data in the Web of Data. To accomplish our former goal we have explored

---

[1] https://www.w3.org/DesignIssues/LinkedData.html.

© Springer Nature Switzerland AG 2018
C. Pautasso et al. (Eds.): ICWE 2018, LNCS 11153, pp. 202–205, 2018.
https://doi.org/10.1007/978-3-030-03056-8_18

different available datasets of both structure and semi-structured nature, then we transformed all the data into RDF format using *Schema* [4] vocabulary. Following, we linked by means of *owl:sameAs* all instances of the datasets, the links were later validated by a domain expert ensuring their quality. As a result we have produced one dataset containing festivals. Finally, we show that datasets that have been included from the Web of Data do not contain relevant data for this scenario.

This paper is organized as follows: in Sect. 2 we present the relevant existing datasets containing festivals in Spain. In Sect. 3 we describe the followed methodology to generate Linked-Fiestas. In Sect. 4 we report the existing datasets' coverage regarding the festivals categorized by the size of the cities where they are held. Finally in Sect. 5 we present our conclusions and our future work. For sake of reproductibility, all the datasets and/or source code is available at http:// tourismkg.linkeddata.es.

2 Datasets

To generate Linked-Fiestas we linked two datasets from two tourism-oriented webpages (`fiestas.net` and `spain.info`) with two datasets from the Web of Data.

DBpedia and Wikidata are two examples of cross-domain knowledge graphs available on the Web of Data. While the contents of both system are generated by crowd-sourced community, there is one fundamental difference regarding the generation process. The content of DBpedia is structured data extracted from Wikipedia while the content of Wikidata is a platform that enables a collaboration of structured data without the need of extraction from wikipedia. As for the number of festivals in Spain, we have found that there are 721 Spanish festivals in DBpedia and 873 in Wikidata.

`fiestas.net` is a website that focuses on providing a list of festivals in Spain while `spain.info` is the official tourist information portal that contains not only festivals, but also many types of useful information for tourist. `fiestas.net` contained 532 Spanish festivals and 268 in `spain.info`.

3 Methodology

The generation of Linked-Fiestas comprised the following steps:

Data Transformation: The webpages `fiestas.net` and `Spain.info` provide data embedded in HTML tables. To generate RDF we relayed on `import.io` to extract and convert such tables in *CSV* files. Following, we transformed the *CSVs* into RDF: first we annotated the *CSVs* with semantic types from the *Schema* vocabulary [4]; then we generated R2RML [5] mappings to represent those annotations; finally we relayed on morph-RDB[2] to execute the R2RML mappings and transform the tabular data into RDF.

---

[2] https://github.com/oeg-upm/morph-rdb.

Instances Filtering: DBpedia and Wikidata are huge cross-domain datasets that contain data outside the scope of this paper which hinders the Linkset Generation. We filtered the DBpedia and Wikidata instances keeping only those that refer to Spanish holidays.

Linkset Generation: Once the four datasets were in RDF we linked their instances by means of *owl:sameAs* relaying on Teide [6]. To link the instances we relied on their locations and names, with some slight differences that we will explain below:

- **Wikidata with Fiestas.net and Spain.info:** In these two scenarios we linked those instances that where held exactly in the same location by means of a *Levenshtein* similarity (Teide similarities return 0.00 when two strings are different and 1.00 when are the same). Then, we pruned the linked instances which festivals or events had a *QGrams* similarity score under a 0.70 threshold.
- **DBpedia with Fiestas.net and Spain.info:** In this two scenarios we followed a different approach because a large number of DBpedia festivals and events were lack of their location. We generate a first linkset taking advantage of the instances that have the location, so we linked those which location had a *JaroWinklerTFIDF* similarity score above 0.80 and their festivals or event names above 0.60. Then we generate a second linkset with those instances which names had a *JaroWinklerTFIDF* similarity score above 0.80. Finally we produced our final linkset by including the links from both.

Data Validation: Finally a domain expert validated our dataset. On the one hand the quality of the data produced from the *CSV* files was checked, on the other hand, all the generated *owl:sameAs* links were verified and corrected if required.

Linked Fiestas is available at http://tourismkg.linkeddata.es[3].

4   Results

We analyzed where the festivals from the existing datasets were hold. Table 1 shows the percentage of festivals hold in cities grouped depending on their population, i.e., +100K, +50K, +20K +10K, −10K. Table 1 proves that Linked-Fiestas namely integrates not so well-known festivals. DBpedia is the only exception since 40% of its instances belong to large cities (+100K).

Table 2 shows the number of *owl:sameAs* links generated between datasets and the number of instances linked from DBpedia and Wikidata with the other datasets. Notice that less than 25% is covered by the other datasets and thus Linked-Fiestas really gathers sparse festivals that are not so well-known.

---

[3] Its DCAT description at https://github.com/fpriyatna/linked-fiestas/blob/master/linked-fiestas-dcat.ttl.

Table 1. Festivals allocated in cities and their population size

	+100K	+50K	+20K	+10K	−10K
DBpedia	40%	16%	13%	14%	17%
Wikidata	6%	6%	13%	15%	61%
Fiestas.net	14%	11%	21%	14%	40%
Spain.info	17%	11%	18%	16%	38%

Table 2. Festivals allocated in cities and their population size

	Fiestas.net	Spain.info
DBpedia	162 (23%)	137 (19%)
Wikidata	180 (20%)	179 (21%)

5   Conclusion

We have presented 5-stars quality Linked-Fiestas dataset that aims at providing visibility to the Spanish cultural heritage. Most of them are held in small cities and are unknown even for Spaniards. Our goal is promote the tourism in such cities that have been eclipsed from by large cities.

During the generation of Linked-Fiestas, we analyzed the location where the festivals were hold, concluding that most of the festivals integrated are hold in medium-small cities. In addition DBpedia lacks of a large number of locations. In conclusion, Linked-Fiestas fills the gap of the missing data.

As future work we aim at exploring vocabularies for this domain: DBpedia contains many too generic types that lead to misleading instances, and on the opposite end Wikidata has too specific types that make hard to find instances. Furthermore both datasets lack of special properties for this kind of data.

Acknowledgements. This work was partially funded by the Spanish MINECO Ministry (project RTC-2016-4952-7).

References

1. Ibarra, J.G.: European Tourism trends & prospects. Quarterly report (2017)
2. Cortés-Jiménez, I.: Which type of tourism matters to the regional economic growth? The cases of Spain and Italy. Int. J. Tour. Res. **10**, 127–139 (2008)
3. Ibarra, J.G.: Análisis de la oferta de turismo cultural en españa. Estudios turísticos (2001)
4. Guha, R.V., Brickley, D., Macbeth, S.: Schema.org: evolution of structured data on the web. Commun. ACM **59**, 44–51 (2016)
5. Das, S., Sundara, S., Cyganiak, R.: R2RML: RDB to RDF mapping language, W3C recommendation. W3C, Cambridge, MA, 27 September 2012 (2012)
6. Cimmino, A., Corchuelo, R.: A hybrid genetic-bootstrapping approach to link resources in the web of data. In: de Cos Juez, F., et al. (eds.) HAIS 2018, vol. 10870, pp. 145–157. Springer, Cham (2018). https://doi.org/10.1007/978-3-319-92639-1_13

DBtravel: A Tourism-Oriented Semantic Graph

Pablo Calleja[(✉)], Freddy Priyatna[(✉)], Nandana Mihindukulasooriya[(✉)],
and Mariano Rico[(✉)]

Ontology Engineering Group, Universidad Politécnica de Madrid, Madrid, Spain
{pcalleja,fpriyatna,nmihindu,mariano.rico}@fi.upm.es,
http://www.oeg-upm.net/

Abstract. We present DBtravel, a tourism-oriented knowledge graph generated from the collaborative travel site Wikitravel. Our approach takes advantage of the recommended guideline for contributors provided by Wikitravel and extracts the named entities available in Wikitravel Spanish entries by using a NLP pipeline. Compared to a manually annotated gold standard, results show that our approach reaches values for precision and recall around 80% for some sections of Wikitravel for the Spanish language.

Keywords: DBpedia · Name entity recognition · Wikitravel

1 Introduction

Wikitravel is a web site, inspired by Wikipedia, in which users can contribute content in a collaborative way in different languages, aimed at providing travel guides. In 21 languages and with 116 thousand entries for English, Wikitravel contains high valuable and useful information for tourists in natural language that currently is only exploited by humans reading its entries. In order to help user to create entries, Wikitravel provides a guideline[1] to recommend the entry sections and how to structure the information in each section. For example, a Wikitravel entry of a city should have these sections: **See**, **Eat and Drink** (restaurants and bars), **Sleep** and **Get Out** with a specific format of the information in each section such as lists or relevant concepts in bold. This guideline can be considered as a template from which we can extract information, as DBpedia does with Wikipedia infoboxes [3]. Figure 1 shows the sections **See** and **Get Out** of a Wikitravel entry in Spanish, specifically Valladolid, a medium size city located in Spain.

The main purpose of this work is to create a knowledge graph of tourism-oriented information by means of exploiting the information stored in Wikitravel entries. Compared to DBpedia [1], the generated graph (DBtravel) is focused on tourism-specific information. The information extraction process is driven by a

---

[1] https://wikitravel.org/en/Wikitravel:Manual_of_style.

© Springer Nature Switzerland AG 2018
C. Pautasso et al. (Eds.): ICWE 2018, LNCS 11153, pp. 206–212, 2018.
https://doi.org/10.1007/978-3-030-03056-8_19

named entity recognition process over different sections of each Wikitravel entry, exploiting the structure information provided by the guideline. In this work we focus on the Spanish version of Wikitravel, specifically on **See** and **Get Out** sections. Section **See** provides points of interest (POIs) to see in a city such as monuments, buildings or locations. Section **Get Out** provides near cities or towns near the city of the entry. Both sections can be used for holiday planning: POIs can be used to compute how many days a tourist should stay in a particular city and near cities could help to recommend day-trip destinations a tourist could follow when they have extra days. The result of the experiments described in this paper show that we can identify around 80% of the named entities in Wikitravel.

The paper is structured as follows. Section 2 describes related work and Sect. 3 proposes the method to exploit Wikitravel entries to extract structured information. Section 4 discusses the obtained results and Sect. 5 presents some conclusions and highlights future work. For sake of reproductibility, all the datasets and/or source code is available at http://tourismkg.linkeddata.es.

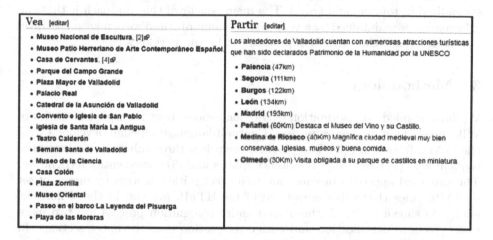

Fig. 1. Snapshot of the Wikitravel entry for Valladolid (a city located in Spain) in Spanish. On the left side, the section See (in Spanish *Vea*). Right side shows the section Get Out (in Spanish *Partir*).

2   Related Work

The semantic web platform 3cixty [5] enables building real-world and comprehensive knowledge bases in the domain of culture and tourism for cities. The entire approach has been tested first for the occasion of the Expo Milano 2015 [4], where a specific knowledge base for the city of Milan was developed, and is now refined with the development of knowledge bases for the cities of Nice and London. They contain descriptions of events, places (sights and businesses), transportation facilities and social activities, collected from numerous static, near- and real-time local and global data providers, including Expo Milano 2015 official services in the case of Milan, and numerous social media platforms.

In its current state, the SPARQL endpoint[2] provides detailed information about a few cities (e.g. London, Amsterdam) and regions (e.g. Côte d'Azur, Canary Islands, which comprise a few hundreds of small and medium size cities). Three types of data sources were used for populating 3cixty: global web sources (e.g. Foursquare, Yelp, Google, Facebook, Eventful, Evensi, Eventbrite, OpenAgenda), hyper local sources (e.g. E015 data services in Milan, Tourism Office in Nice or Cannes) and specialized sources (e.g. EXPO feeds, Cannes Palais des Festivals feeds, or data curated by an editorial team). This information is consumed by a mobile application in order to assist users travelling to these cities or regions.

Our approach is by far much more modest. DBtravel can provide information about more cities but less detailed (fewer information) because we exploit only two sections of Wikitravel. However, concerning data sources, to our best knowledge, this work is the first one that exploits a wiki (contributors based site) specialized in tourism and travel. The main benefit of this approach is that the information is maintained by a very active community and we can keep DBtravel updated because the extraction process can be run periodically.

3   Methodology

We have applied an information extraction process over the Spanish entries of Wikitravel. This process comprises a natural language pipeline developed with the GATE framework [2]. The pipeline comprises three sub-processes executed sequentially: (1) tokenizer, (2) sentence splitter and (3) named entity recognition. The proposed approach provides an entity recognition process by means of set of JAPE rules that takes advantage of the HTML markup in the Wikitravel entry. As shown in Fig. 2, the named entity recognition process has two main tasks: section identification and entity recognition over the entry sections. In Fig. 2, only sections **See** and **Get Out** are show, but the process can consider additional sections.

The tokenizer and the sentence splitter are default modules in GATE, for which we have no provided enhancements. However, the named entity recognition process is an ad hoc development that comprises two main tasks that are described below.

The first task in the named entity recognition process, the section identification, aims at detecting the target section from which entities are going to be extracted. The proposed method is focused on sections **See** and **Get Out**. The identification of the section is based on rules that match the starting point of the HTML section and the ending point.

The second task aims at identifying the named entities over the recognised section. For each section there is a specific process because the information is

---

[2] See http://kb.3cixty.com/sparql.

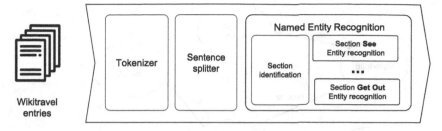

Fig. 2. GATE pipeline. The processes are a tokenizer, a sentence splitter and a named entity recognition. The named entity recognition process is divided in two steps: section identification and section entity recognition (specific for each section).

presented with a different format and the entity types are different. Section **See**, according to the guideline, should present POIs as a list in bold format. Normally, each list item is a POI finished with a dot but, sometimes, contributors add more information after the dot. This extra information can contain additional POIs.The process for this section is focused on the recognition of the list elements that are in bold. Section **Get Out** present near locations as a list of elements. The process for this section uses a gazetteer of Spanish towns extracted from the Spanish Statistics National Institute (INE)[3] to detect near locations.

With the entities extracted from these two section we create a knowledge graph of cities and towns connected between them (extracted from section **Get Out**) and linked to their most important POIs (extracted from section **See**), as shown in Fig. 3 with the information provided by the Wikitravel entry shown in Fig. 1. This can be a valuable information for tourism applications, for instance to create holiday tours.

4   Evaluation

The evaluation of our named entity recognition process has been carried out by comparing to a reference gold standard corpus. To our best knowledge there is no similar gold standard so, we have created our own gold standard. It was created manually by two domain experts annotating entities from Wikitravel entries. The evaluation measures the precision (p) and recall (r) of our method to detect entities under two matching criteria: strict or partial [6]. In the one hand,under the strict matching criteria, the entity detected by the method and the entity annotated in the gold standard corpus must have the same structural position and contain identical entity text. In the other hand, under the partial matching criteria, the annotated entities retrieved by the system can take more or less tokens than the tokens the gold standard has (e.g. retrieve only 'Cervantes' from the entity 'Casa Cervantes'). The partial criteria takes as correctly retrieved, entities that only differ in one side of the span text.

---

[3] Available at http://www.ine.es/daco/daco42/codmun/codmunmapa.htm.

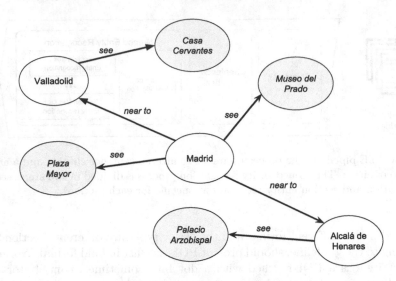

Fig. 3. Tourism-oriented graph. White nodes represent cities connected by the 'near to' relation extracted from Get Out section. Grey nodes represent POIs connected by the 'see' relation extracted from See section.

In the next sections we describe the gold standard used in the evaluation and the results achieved.

4.1   Gold Standard

The gold standard corpus has been created collecting 20 Wikitravel entries in Spanish for cities in Spain: 18 cities are province capitals including Madrid and Barcelona and 2 cities are small cities. The gold standard corpus comprises 78,058 tokens (NLP basic units). Two domain experts annotated manually sections **See** and **Get Out** for all these entries. They found 431 entities in the **See** section and 104 entities in the **Get Out** section.

4.2   Results

The evaluation results of the named entity recognition process are shown in Table 1. This table shows precision (P), recall (p) and F-measure (F) for sections **See** and **Get Out** under the aforementioned matching criteria (*strict* and *partial*). Results show that the proposed method has a precision and recall higher than 80% for the **See** section. Results also show that the entities extracted in this section are barely sensible to the *partial* criteria (only increases around 0.4% precision and recall).

Analyzing the gold standard corpus we have found that 5 Wikitravel entries do not follow the recommended guideline: 4 entries present their POIs as a list without the bold markup and one entry presents its named entities as free text without list format. Also, there are Wikitravel entries that follow the guideline but have additional markup to classify POIs (e.g., 'Museums' or 'Churches') formatted in bold. Therefore, our named entity recognition process identifies them but, in the evaluation process, are considered as false positives.

The evaluation results of the **Get Out** section are quite different. The recall and precision values are lower than the ones for the **See** section, although it is remarkable that the effect of the matching criteria is similar. Analysing the corpus we have found that 10 out of 20 documents provided in the corpus do not contain any information in **Get Out** section. Most of these low-coverage documents belong to small cities/towns because they lack of nearby cities relevant as POIs. Despite this general rule, one big city, Barcelona, does not provide any information in this section. Also, one of the entries presents this section in natural language without any list information. As our process catches any city or town described in any list entry, the retrieved results tend to include other cities or towns that are not representative (false positives). This effect explains the relatively low values achieved for precision and recall for section **Get Out**.

Table 1. Precision (p), recall (p) and F-measure (F) for the proposed named entity recognition process for Wikitravel sections **See** and **Get Out** under two different matching criteria (strict and partial).

	Strict			Partial		
	p	r	F	p	r	F
See	0.91	0.80	0.85	0.95	0.83	0.89
Get Out	0.59	0.74	0.66	0.64	0.79	0.71

5   Conclusion and Future Work

In this paper we have introduced DBtravel, a tourism-oriented knowledge graph that is generated by extracting **See** and **Get Out** sections from the Spanish entries of the Wikitravel site, exploiting the entry-structure guideline provided by Wikitravel. Our evaluation shows that big cities/towns have better Wikitravel entries than small cities/towns in the sense that they contain more information that follows the edition guideline.

We would like to emphasise the usage of the guideline. Collaborative platforms are exposed to have very unstructured data and it is sensitive to each editor speech. However, guidelines can alleviate this, provided that the community is aware of its presence. This factor is reflected in Wikitravel entries: bigger cities, which normally have more tourist attractions, have more collaborators and follow the guideline better than the smaller cities.

Other sections such as **Eat** and **Drink** have more noisy data because collaborators tend to explain the information in natural language with fewer markup information. Future work will tackle these sections in order to generate a more comprehensive knowledge graph. As DBtravel contains entities that could be represented in the DBpedia graph, our immediate next step is to enrich the named entity recognition process with an entity linking to DBpedia.

Acknowledgments. This work has been supported by a research assistant grant by the Consejo de Educación, Juventud y Deporte de la Comunidad de Madrid partially founded by the European Social Fund (PEJ16/TIC/AI-1984) and by the Spanish MINECO Ministry (project RTC-2016-4952-7).

References

1. Auer, S., Bizer, C., Kobilarov, G., Lehmann, J., Cyganiak, R., Ives, Z.: DBpedia: a nucleus for a web of open data. In: Aberer, K., et al. (eds.) ASWC/ISWC -2007. LNCS, vol. 4825, pp. 722–735. Springer, Heidelberg (2007). https://doi.org/10.1007/978-3-540-76298-0_52
2. Cunningham, H.: GATE, a general architecture for text engineering. Comput. Humanit. **36**(2), 223–254 (2002)
3. Mihindukulasooriya, N., Rico, M., García-Castro, R., Gómez-Pérez, A.: An analysis of the quality issues of the properties available in the Spanish DBpedia. In: Puerta, J., et al. (eds.) CAEPIA 2015. LNCS (LNAI), vol. 9422, pp. 198–209. Springer, Cham (2015). https://doi.org/10.1007/978-3-319-24598-0_18
4. Rizzo, G., Troncy, R., et al.: 3cixty@ Expo Milano 2015: Enabling Visitors to Explore a Smart City. In 14th International Semantic Web Conference (ISWC), Semantic Web Challenge (2015)
5. Troncy, R., Rizzo, G., et al.: 3cixty: building comprehensive knowledge bases for city exploration. Web Semant. Sci. Serv. Agents World Wide Web **46–47**, 2–13 (2017)
6. Tsai, R.T., et al.: Various criteria in the evaluation of biomedical named entity recognition. BMC Bioinform. **7**(1), 92 (2006)

La Rioja Turismo: The Construction and Exploitation of a Queryable Tourism Knowledge Graph

Ricardo Alonso-Maturana(✉), Elena Alvarado-Cortes,
Susana López-Sola, María Ortega Martínez-Losa,
and Pablo Hermoso-González

GNOSS: RIAM I+L LAB. S.L,
C/Piqueras nº 31 4ª planta, 26007 Logroño, La Rioja, Spain
{riam, elenaalvarado, susanalopez,
mariaortega}@gnoss.com, pablohermoso@gmail.com

Abstract. The institutional website for La Rioja tourism (https://lariojaturismo.com) is a working example of the construction and exploitation of a tourism Knowledge Graph where all digital contents referring to attractions, accommodation, tourism routes, activities, events, restaurants, wineries, etc., are semantically represented in RDF/OWL. The construction of the Knowledge Graph was carried out through the conceptualization of a Digital Semantic Model that hybridized and extended several existing ontologies and vocabularies (mainly Harmonise, OnTour, Geonames, Rout, FRBR and rNews). The overarching objective was to generate a digital space where information retrieval was simpler, more useful and more practical, offering a much more friendly and satisfactory website experience. At present, the Knowledge Graph is made up of more than 7,000 digital contents; 67,284 entities; 472,361 relations; and 675,368 triples. The digital space receives more than 40.000 visits per month. The most important Knowledge Graph exploitations are associated with the existence of a metasearch engine, faceted search engines for each knowledge object, contextual information systems, and Graph visualization systems through combination of map and semantic geo-positioning.

Keywords: La Rioja · Knowledge Graph · GNOSS · Semantic technologies Cognitive platform · Smart tourist destination · Digital Semantic Model

1 Introduction: The La Rioja Turismo Portal as a Queryable Knowledge Graph for Building a Smart Tourist Destination

In 2014, La Rioja, the smallest autonomous community in Spain, decided to represent its tourism content semantically. The main reason they built a tourism Knowledge Graph was to contribute to the configuration of La Rioja as a smart tourism destination. A technological strategy was utilized that offered tourists a simple, useful, practical and user-friendly experience with the information, while facilitating the more efficient management of tourism information by various stakeholders (tour operators, journalists,

© Springer Nature Switzerland AG 2018
C. Pautasso et al. (Eds.): ICWE 2018, LNCS 11153, pp. 213–220, 2018.
https://doi.org/10.1007/978-3-030-03056-8_20

the regional tourism sector). Configuring the Knowledge Graph allowed foundations to be laid in a simpler and more agile way so as to be able to later extend and expand the model, as well as to integrate and link (linked data) [1] other digital contents whose primary purpose is not tourism, as opposed to cultural or journalistic contents, yet could in fact exercise this function and enrich the first graph created. The possibility of configuring a website with tourism data that could be related to other semantically-expressed data did not exist with other technological approaches.

The project integrated and linked the region's tourism contents through the construction and exploitation of La Rioja's tourism Knowledge Graph[1], implementing a modification from the traditional operational mode that is still common in most digital projects for public and private institutions. In this model, contents are labeled and managed in traditional content management systems (CMS) such a Drupal, Workpress, Liferay, etc. The approach used for La Rioja was based on the creation of a Digital Semantic Model[2], which identified existing entities, their properties and relations. Existing ontologies were hybridized and extended with the interests of the end user in mind and an integrated Semantic Content Manager allowed data to be published natively in RDF/OWL. This creates advantageous exploitation possibilities together with a much more useful and efficient web experience.

This project contributed to the development of a smart tourist destination, as could be read in September 2015 in "Smart Tourism Destinations: constructing the future" [2], a report prepared by *Sociedad Estatal para la Gestión de la Innovación y las Tecnologías Turísticas, S.A.* (SEGITTUR), within the framework of the *Plan Nacional de Ciudades Inteligentes* [Spanish National Smart Cities Plan] by Spain's Digital Agenda institution.

The creation of the Knowledge Graph and its exploitation needed to increase the value of its contents, that is, to make them more known, more accessible, better positioned on the internet for search engine retrieval. They had to be able to be linked so as to offer tourists a website user experience wherein a search transforms into a path to learning and discovery.

This enriched user experience stimulates the desire not just to spend more time on the travel destination website, but above all, to physically visit the place. In other words, increasing the value of digital content means increasing the conversion rate, transforming the mere search and inquiry for information into the visit of and consumption and purchase at the specific destination.

This objective has been met; portal usage data shows that the portal's usage ratio increased by 42.66% from 350,589 users in 2014 to 503,017 users in 2017. These users visit 2.5 million web pages and spend an average of 2.5 min on the website.

---

[1] "Web Semántica y Turismo" (2014), https://es.slideshare.net/gnoss/web-semntica-y-turismo-caso-la-rioja-turismo-gnoss-2014. Accessed 2018/04/03.

[2] Museo del Prado. Digital Semantic Model https://www.museodelprado.es/en/modelo-semantico-digital/el-prado-en-la-web.

2   The Knowledge Graph and Its Main Applications

2.1   Definition: The La Rioja Turismo Knowledge Graph

The La Rioja Turismo Knowledge Graph is the semantically-represented (RDF/OWL) system comprising the region's more than 7,000 tourist resources (accommodation, restaurants, wineries, tourist services, events, tourism routes, attractions, and villages and urban centers) using entities and entity attributes. The Graph understands facts about them, as well as any object potentially linked to them (news, brochures, activities, schedules, bids, multimedia resources). In particular, it understands the way that this set of entities is interconnected.

The La Rioja Turismo Knowledge Graph now integrates 7,045 digital resources with 67,284 entities and 472,361 relations. Entities are used to understand the meaning of the term that the user searches for and offers a system by which to explore all of its resources. This tool is based on a faceted search engine, among other utilities, and avails the user of all possible navigation modes concerning that set of entities. The number of triples in the Knowledge Graph is 675,368.

2.2   Properties of the La Rioja Turismo Knowledge Graph

The La Rioja Turismo Knowledge Graph has four main properties that make it uniquely efficient at meeting specific objectives. The Knowledge Graph is:

- **Unified** because it enables data that are hosted in scattered, heterogeneous and diverse management systems to be integrated. These data may exist in a variety of formats and be structured to several different degrees. For example, content originating from distinct data sources such as CRM, ERP, Document Managers and Content Managers could be integrated using this "semantic layer", similarly to the Prado Museum[3]. In the case of La Rioja Turismo, this step was simplified since only one data source was used, from which all resources were obtained. The contents of the old portal content manager were migrated. From that point on, the new contents were created directly using semantic CMS. A metadata layer represented semantically in RDF/OWL has been generated for all contents. The contents are connected within a Digital Semantic Model that represents the entities, their attributes and their relations, linking all contents into a single graph, independently of their sources of departure.

- **Queryable, by both people and machines.** With the former, humans are able to generate information retrieval systems that enable reasoning. We demonstrate this using faceted searches [3], whose purpose is to provide a means by which to retrieve information for anyone who visits the website, and to do so according to their interests and intentions. Faceted search enables iterated interrogations, and therefore the ability to refine searches as much as desired. In turn, it becomes possible to provide users with well-organized, enriched and contextualized faceted

---

[3] The Museo del Prado's Knowledge Graph. https://www.museodelprado.es/en/modelo-semantico-digital/el-grafo-de-conocimiento-del-museo-del-prado.

results [4] that correctly correspond to their search. The specific aim is to provide access to the portal to the public with an intuitive, personalized, semantically meaningful and effective smart browsing and search experience, thus encouraging them to continue exploring the graph. These exploitations may be carried out in all case studies completed by GNOSS.

- **Expressive:** the semantic representation of contents in RDF/OWL can be as rich and expressive as its semantic model; a machine will be able to "understand", interpret, and therefore make use of the entities, attributes and relations that define a given digital resource. For example, in the case of an event, his includes where it takes place, on which dates, what restaurants are nearby, etc. Thus, machines are able to understand what each digital resource means and thereby help users to connect data with data. In addition, this enables interoperability with other systems.
- **Extensible,** because new entities, the properties of existing or new entities, and new relationships between them can be agilely and flexibly incorporated. This makes it possible to integrate and link data with new data from the same source or with other data banks and contents in an appropriate way. The Digital Semantic Model's level of abstraction facilitates extension to new data, other data sources and other sets of content much simpler way than the traditional data model.

2.3   La Rioja Turismo's Ontological Model

The configuration of the Digital Semantic Model for the La Rioja Turismo web portal was the first step in constructing the La Rioja Knowledge Graph and its advantageous exploitation for the end user. An exhaustive study of state-of-the-art semantic standards, ontologies and existing ontological models was carried out as part of model creation. The goal was to take advantage of all existing developments that were useful for mixing, hybridizing, extending and combining them in the best manner possible, focusing on the construction of a useful, practical, simple web experience that stimulates visitors when questioning, inquiring and discovering information.

The ontological project carried out with La Rioja Turismo for the construction of its Knowledge Graph hybridized a wide range of domain ontologies, integrating them into a common ontological framework that represented the contents and activities in the tourism field. These range from content related to accommodation, dining and activities to tourism routes, towns and attractions, as well as tourism services, news and related articles. Below we present the set of hybridized vocabularies in the La Rioja Turismo project.

Semantic Digital Model

The hybrid ontology discussed here has been consolidated into what could be called the Rioja Turismo Digital Semantic Model. It is composed of a set of vocabularies developed to represent a large portion of the contents and tourist activities. The following diagram represents the first La Rioja Turismo Digital Semantic Model, which displays the set of ontologies that were combined in the ontological story.

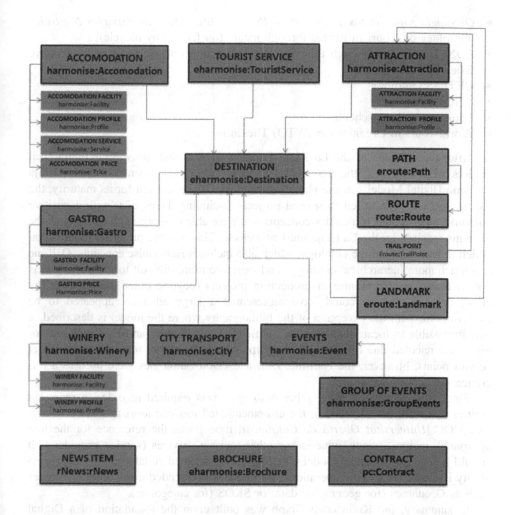

The following ontological models were analyzed [5] in order to construct the Digital Semantic Model. The original bibliography consulted included:

- Harmonise Ontology
- Mondeca Tourism Ontology
- Hi-Touch Ontology
- QALL-ME Ontology[4]
- DERI e-Tourism Ontology
- cDott Ontology
- Cross Ontology
- Contur Ontology

---

[4] https://hlt-nlp.fbk.eu/technologies/qall-me-ontology.

- *Ontología sobre Rutas Turísticas (a Pie o en Bicicleta) por Espacios Naturales* [Ontology on Tourism Routes through nature (on foot or by bicycle)]
- EON Traveling. Although this was one of the first ontologies, it seems to have fallen into disuse
- GETESS Ontology
- ANOTA ontology
- Tourism ontology schema
- World Tourism Organization (WTO) Thesaurus

After the contents of the La Rioja Turismo website and the various ontological models were analyzed, the main basis used for the development of the La Rioja Turismo Digital Model was the Harmony ontology. It was chosen for its maturity, the fact that it had been tested in several projects (including Turespaña) with a positive outcome, and because it includes concepts that were able to represent a majority of the contents required by the La Rioja tourism website. This was the preferred model upon which to base the Qall-me ontology, which also includes Harmonise concepts. Qall-me is a much more hierarchical ontology (and therefore more difficult to maintain) and is not as mature as Harmonise in production projects (beyond other prototypes). The cDott ontology, which could have represented a large advance, appeared to be experimental; with the exception of the bibliography where the model is described, it was impossible to locate the complete ontology. The Mondeca and Hi-Touch ontologies were rejected due to private ownership. Where the model required extension at certain points, however, the Qall-me, Deri and cDott ontologies were used as a reference (destination/location).

Finally, an expansion using other ontologies was required in order to represent entities that were not included in the aforementioned models: tourism tours or routes (the UOC [*Universitat Oberta de Catalunya*] model was the reference for the first approach), recipes, wines, wineries or other tourism services (service providers). It should be noted that where model enrichment was deemed suitable due to interoperability issues or for specific operations, the model was extended using other ontologies such as Geonames (for geographic data) or SKOS (for categories).

In summary, the Knowledge Graph was built upon the foundation of a Digital Semantic Model designed for the La Rioja tourism web portal in addition to hybridized and extended several ontologies and existing vocabularies:

- Harmonise ontology[5], to represent tourist destinations, attractions, events, services, accommodation, restaurants and wineries.
- OnTour ontology, to express certain properties not encompassed by Harmonise.
- Rout, to model routes[6].
- Geonames[7] for locations and WGS84 to express latitude and longitude.

---

[5] http://www.harmosearch.com/.

[6] http://openaccess.uoc.edu/webapps/o2/bitstream/10609/2284/1/igutierrezl_articulo.pdf.

[7] Geonames: http://www.geonames.org/.

- Functional Requirements for Bibliographic Records (FRBR)[8] to represent document data
- rNews[9], for news.

2.4 Main Exploitations of the Knowledge Graph: Advantages

For the end user, the main advantages of browsing www.lariojaturismo.com are:

- A graph querying system where information can be found in a much more precise, useful, and practical way, which saves time and finds what the user wants to find. This can be observed through the metasearch engine (a search engine that performs global searches of all website content) and the specific faceted search engines for each case, together with specific facets according to the type of element selected (for example, search engines specific to wineries and restaurants, locations and attractions, routes, activities, or accommodation, among others) [6].
- Its system for generating informative contexts. When information on a winery, restaurant, hotel or activity is presented, the graph displays the most pertinent related resources based on shared attributes. La Rioja Turismo contexts are configured so that once the tourist views information about a resource, they are able to see what they can do, where to eat and where to sleep in relation to the content visited.
- Graphic visualization and enriched information on a map thanks to semantic geolocation. Visualizing the Knowledge Graph allows the user to combine the map view and locate information of interest to them. Faceted search both permits filtering in order to refine searches. It also displays information about other attributes related to the object sought. For example, as the user zooms in on the map to view wineries in Haro, other winery-specific attributes appear on the screen, such as their portfolio of services, hours, the languages in which they offer their services, types of facilities, and more. Latitude/longitude is one of many attributes of the entity 'winery' and one can "reason" using these attributes. By zooming in on the map, the data corresponding to the defined area are reconfigured and adapted to the selected space. Corresponding valuable information is made available as the search progresses. Likewise, summarized information may be displayed for each element located on the map without having to leave the map.

3 Conclusion

The www.lariojaturismo.com website has served as a case study in the efficient and practical exploitation of a built Knowledge Graph. The conceptual and technological difficulties, as well as the corresponding opportunity that arose from them, arose from the lack of a complete ontological model for the expression of an institutional tourism

---

[8] http://www.sparontologies.net/ontologies/frbr.

[9] http://dev.iptc.org/rNews.

website. This created the need for a Digital Semantic Model where several existing ontologies hybridized and mixed.

The main challenge of this project was convincing of the need to dispense with the limits and obligations linked to transactional logic and filing documents. SQL logic prevented expressing the content and its meaning in an expressive way, and therefore limited the ability to discover information, query as a human would, and make inferences of interest.

Through the linking of semantically-represented data, the extensibility of the Knowledge Graph enables the advancement and incorporation of new information relevant to the next stages, such as cultural data that have value in tourism.

It also enables the enrichment of information through connection with other datasets such as those in the DBPedia. The next steps concern the extension and deepening of the Knowledge Graph "inward": generating a semantic marketplace for tourism resources, improving the information access system via a system accompanying the tourist on a "here and now" visit that provides them with more useful information when planning their visits, and generating a digital backpack where interesting tourism resources can be shared with other users through the increasingly intense exploitation of the social graph.

La Rioja Turismo shows how the creation and exploitation of Knowledge Graphs in the tourism sector is a winning strategy when it comes to addressing the future of smart organization search and query systems. A queryable Knowledge Graph enables the implementation of personalized search strategies based on reasoning and the capacity to contextualize systems.

References

1. Serna, A., Murua, I., Gerrikagoitia, J.K., Alzua, A., Lizarralde, O., Larrinaga, F.: Economía de Datos en Turismo proceso para la publicación de LOD en turismo. tourGUNE J. Tour. Hum. Mobil. (2013)
2. Alonso Maturana, R.: El valor de los contenidos digitales en los destinos turísticos inteligentes. Informe Destinos Turísticos Inteligentes: construyendo el futuro, Segittur, pp. 126–129 (2015)
3. Suominen, O., Viljanen, K., HyvÄnen, E.: User-centric faceted search for semantic portals. In: Franconi, E., Kifer, M., May, W. (eds.) ESWC 2007. LNCS, vol. 4519, pp. 356–370. Springer, Heidelberg (2007). https://doi.org/10.1007/978-3-540-72667-8_26
4. Ferré, S., Hermann, A., Ducassé, M.: Semantic faceted search: safe and expressive navigation in RDF graphs. Research report (2011). ISSN 2102-6327
5. Kathrin Prantner, Y., Michael Luger, Z.: Austria. "Tourism ontology and semantic management system: state-of-the-arts analysis". In: IADIS International Conference WWW/Internet 2007 (2007)
6. Dal Mas, M.: Faceted semantic search for personalized social search. In: Computing Research Repository, abs-1202-6685 (2012). http://arxiv.org/abs/1202.6685

Linked Data Graphs for Semantic Data Integration in the CART System

Marwa Boulakbech, Nasredine Cheniki, Nizar Messai, Yacine Sam[✉],
and Thomas Devogele

University of Tours, Tours, France
{marwa.boulakbech,nasredine.cheniki,nizar.messai,yacine.sam,
thomas.devogele}@univ-tours.fr

Abstract. Tourists often face the problem of planning itineraries that cover the most interesting attractions and best match their preferences and constraints. We have proposed a configuration-theory-based tool, called CART, that takes as input data from touristic APIs and produces as output personalized touristic itineraries. In this paper, we extend our proposal using semantic technologies to enable better content management, knowledge discovery and semantic search. Through semantic annotations, we perform data integration of heterogeneous and evolving touristic APIs. This makes content more accessible and enhances information retrieval by providing semantic querying capabilities to the CART system.

Keywords: Graph database · Trip recommendation · Semantic Web
API

1 The CART Trip-Planning System

In order to select touristic attractions that best match their preferences and constraints, tourists usually consult different information sources such as Yahoo Travel[1], TripAdvisor[2] or Lonely Planet[3], etc. However, being overwhelmed by the huge amount of data available on these Web sites, users often find difficulties to identify interesting attractions. Point of Interest (PoI) recommender systems [1] can help users to find their favorite PoIs, i.e., museums, restaurants, hotels, etc. They recommend lists of individual PoIs deemed to be popular but they do not take into account users preferences and/or their trip constraints [2]. We proposed CART[4] (Configured mAshup Recommender application for personalized Trip planning), a context-aware touristic planning tool that allows finding a suitable set of touristic activities considering user constraints [3]. The system,

---

[1] www.yahoo.com/lifestyle/tagged/travel.
[2] www.tripadvisor.com.
[3] www.lonelyplanet.com.
[4] https://smartloire.firebaseapp.com/cart.html.

© Springer Nature Switzerland AG 2018
C. Pautasso et al. (Eds.): ICWE 2018, LNCS 11153, pp. 221–226, 2018.
https://doi.org/10.1007/978-3-030-03056-8_21

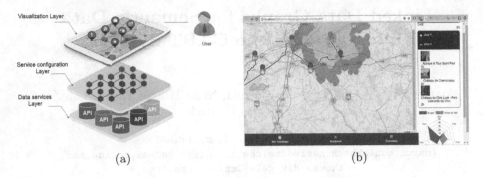

Fig. 1. CART's general architecture (a) and user interface (b)

based on configuration theory takes as input (syntactic) data from touristic APIs and user-profile information to produce personalized touristic itineraries. CART adopts an interactive and incremental process; the user provides her/his constraints on a specific category of PoIs then the system leverages the constraints to suggest the first batch of PoIs from which the user selects preferred ones. The next batch of PoIs is then proposed and the process repeats until the user is satisfied. In other words, instead of asking the user to examine all the PoIs before deciding on the itinerary, our goal is to ask the user to examine only a subset of those PoIs in multiple steps, each with a small number of increasingly relevant PoIs, thereby reducing the overall efforts required on the user to construct the itinerary.

As shown in Fig. 1a, the main CART layers are Data Services, Service Configuration, and Visualization. Travel-related data is collected from various RESTful-APIs and pre-processed in the Data Services layer then migrated to the Service Configuration layer. Mashups processes are applied on data dumped from Data Services to define composite services according to certain logical rules implemented based on the configuration theory that respond to user's request and recommend personalized touristic plans. Visualization layer constitutes the interface that allows users to interact with the system (Fig. 1b).

2   Extending CART with Semantic Technologies

In CART, besides weather forecasting and transportation APIs, we have mainly exploited travel related-data about places to visit, e.g., castles, museums, parks, events, restaurants and hotels, from Tourinsoft[5] system in the context of Loire Valley region (France). Many other large data sets are however unexploited because they are sitting in isolated data silos. Finding links between data from different sources can constitute a non-trivial task. We are convinced that Semantic Web Technologies (including ontologies) and Linked Open Data (LOD), can

---

[5] www.tourinsoft.com.

help to create semantically-rich links between data from multiple various touristic APIs. They can disambiguate data retrieval by helping machines to "understand" words meaning using ontologies. Moreover, they allow bridging complementary information from different LOD sources to bring, hence, an interesting added-value for tourism data. Semantic technologies and graph databases will be used to integrate and better exploit as much as possible the isolated data and extract insight from it by discovering relationships between names, concepts, and entities. In other words, LOD and ontologies can turn heterogeneous data from multiple APIs into semantically-rich interlinked knowledge graph.

We propose extending our CART system by introducing a new semantic layer, called Semantic Integration Layer, between the Service Configuration Layer and Data Services Layer. The extension constitutes an integrated platform bringing together tourists data, locally events data, weather data, etc., from heterogeneous, probably inter-organizational, APIs. This will give rise to process big amounts of data with the objective to help tourists benefiting from our LOD-based application and find data and services (destinations, activities, etc.) that conform to their constraints and preferences. The interest of using Semantic Web technologies (ontologies) here is to ensure a unified representation model for all the data sources. This allows a seamless integration process of heterogeneous tourism data gleaned from various APIs. The resulted integrated data can be then enriched and interconnected to LOD. A LOD-based similarity measures is then applied to the resulted final data in order to estimate similarity degree between services. The similarity measure is exploited here to provide alternative plans in a reconfiguration process.

Using Semantic Web technologies, our system can moreover exploit continuously increasing tourists data thanks to the rising use of IoT, social media and different smart devices in order to better handle tourists profiles, improve the user experience and predict future travel trends. This will help further touristic actors (travel operators, hotels, etc.) and local governments to promote their tourist sector.

The architecture of our extended system is depicted in Fig. 2. The new semantic data integration layer implements a lightweight integration process allowing to enrich the DATAtourisme[6] dataset that aims to centralize, within a national French shared platform, travel information produced by different Tourism Committees. Such information is published as LOD to facilitate the creation of innovative travel applications. As DATAtourisme dataset remains limited, we propose to enrich it by collecting data from travel APIs such as Foursquare[7], Google Places[8], Sygic Travel[9], Tourinsoft[10], etc. and map the different pieces of data using the DATAtourisme ontology. This ensures a unified data representation model and helps then to transform non-rdf data into semantic ones in order

---

[6] www.datatourisme.fr/ontologie.

[7] https://foursquare.com.

[8] https://developers.google.com/places.

[9] https://www.sygic.com/developers.

[10] http://www.tourinsoft.com/.

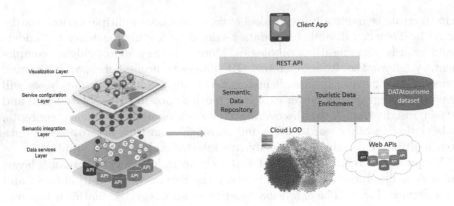

Fig. 2. CART extended architecture

to complete the missing information in DATAtourisme dataset. Moreover, to model information that is not covered by this ontology, we can use Schema.org (already partially reused by DataTourisme ontology), tourism-domain ontologies or parts from Mio! ontology network [4]. Furthermore, mapping the resulted unified semantic data to existing LOD datasets such as DBpedia[11] allows, in some cases, completing missing information that is not provided by API data sources. The mapping could then be exploited by LOD-based similarity measures such as LODS [5] to propose similar touristic data. The final rich and semantically generated data is stored in a local RDF store (Jena TDB store[12]). Stored data will then be available to the CART's Service Configuration Layer to query a unified semantic rich data source during the travel plan composition process, through CRUD (Create, Read, Update and Delete) operations. The configuration process generates a context-aware travel plan by selecting and composing travel data with context information like weather data based on configuration knowledge [3]. Generated plans can be reconfigured by providing users the possibility to personalize their initial plan through adding or removing travel activities as well as adapting properties of a travel activity such as time activity for example. The reconfiguration process exploits LODS [5], a LOD-based similarity measures, to produce similar travel activities as alternatives to the initial ones.

We illustrate in the Fig. 3 a simplified example of data integration process. As we can see, the tourism service information retrieved from two APIs (Google Places and Sygic Travel) are transformed (from XML and JSON respectively) into a semantic representation (rdf) before being integrated with DATAtourisme. New properties (rating and visit duration) have then been added to enrich the same service in DATAtourisme dataset.

---

[11] http://dbpedia.org/.
[12] https://jena.apache.org/documentation/tdb/.

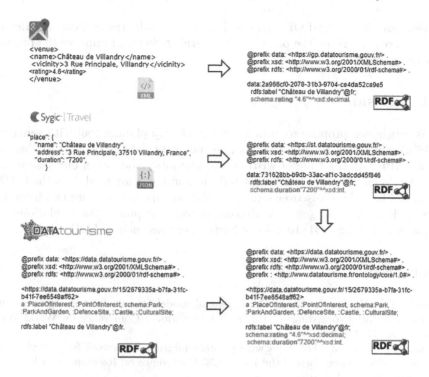

Fig. 3. Example of tourism data integration

3   Related Work

Some existing PoIs recommendation studies [6,7] have made use of location based services to provide the user with PoIs lists tailored to her needs and preferences. Our approach organizes moreover the returned PoIs as itineraries adhering to user constraints/preferences. Other approaches have tried to take advantage from metadata available on social networks, such as Flickr[13] or Panoramio[14], to recommend PoIs. For instance geotagged photos have represented a valuable and reliable source of metadata to track millions of tourists and propose trip patterns [8] labeled using tags under themes, i.e., landmarks, nature or food tasting. The proposed patterns are however generic and lack of personalization. Our CART system is a personalized system that takes more advantage from semantic Web technologies, i.e., semantic meta-data and inference techniques, in order to explore larger amounts of semantically linked data from heterogeneous and evolving touristic APIs. The work in [9] tackles the same data integration problem, however the proposed approach is based only on ontologies.

---

[13] www.flickr.com/.

[14] https://www.panoramio.com/.

Our proposal, involving LOD and ontologies, will make the content of different sources more accessible, the proposed itineraries richer and improve the personalization process.

4 Conclusion

In this article, we propose to enrich our CART trip planing tool with semantic capabilities in order to easily access and integrate data from multiple heterogeneous APIs. At the time of writing, the semantic modules of our system are under development. Once this completed, the configuration module of the CART system will be able to discover semantic relationships between entities from different APIs in order to generate alternative touristic plans. These relationships are discovered using LOD-based similarity measures such as LODS [5].

References

1. Pham, T.-A.N., Li, X., Cong, G.: A general model for out-of-town region recommendation. In: Proceedings of the 26th International Conference on World Wide Web, pp. 401–410 (2017)
2. Benouaret, I., Lenne, D.: A package recommendation framework for trip planning activities. In: Proceedings of the 10th ACM Conference on Recommender Systems, pp. 203–206. ACM (2016)
3. Boulakbech, M., Messai, N., Sam, Y., Devogele, T.: Visual configuration for restful mobile web mashups. In: 2017 IEEE International Conference on Web Services (ICWS), pp. 870–873. IEEE (2017)
4. Villalon, M.P., Suárez-Figueroa, M.C., García-Castro, R., Gómez-Pérez, A.: A context ontology for mobile environments. In: Proceedings of Workshop on Context, Information and Ontologies - CIAO 2010 Co-located with EKAW 2010, vol. 626. Alemania: CEUR-WS, Octubre 2010, ontology Engineering Group? OEG. http://oa.upm.es/5414/
5. Cheniki, N., Belkhir, A., Sam, Y., Messai, N.: LODS: a linked open data based similarity measure. In: 25th IEEE International Conference on Enabling Technologies: Infrastructure for Collaborative Enterprises, WETICE 2016, Paris, France, pp. 229–234. IEEE (2016)
6. Hawalah, A., Fasli, M.: Utilizing contextual ontological user profiles for personalized recommendations. Expert Syst. Appl. 41(10), 4777–4797 (2014)
7. Viktoratos, I., Tsadiras, A., Bassiliades, N.: A context-aware web-mapping system for group-targeted offers using semantic technologies. Expert Syst. Appl. 42(9), 4443–4459 (2015)
8. Arase, Y., Xie, X., Hara, T., Nishio, S.: Mining people's trips from large scale geo-tagged photos. In: International Conference on Multimedia, pp. 133–142 (2010)
9. Soualah-Alila, F., Faucher, C., Bertrand, F., Coustaty, M., Doucet, A.: Applying semantic web technologies for improving the visibility of tourism data. In: Proceedings of the Eighth Workshop on Exploiting Semantic Annotations in Information Retrieval, ESAIR 2015, Melbourne, Australia, pp. 5–10 (2015)

Destination Attractions System and Strategic Visitor Flows

An Exploratory Study

Rodolfo Baggio[1,2] and Miriam Scaglione[3(✉)]

[1] Master in Economics and Tourism, Bocconi University, Milan, Italy
rodolfo.baggio@unibocconi.it
[2] National Research Tomsk Polytechnic University, Tomsk, Russia
[3] Institute of Tourism, University of Applied Sciences and Arts Western
Switzerland Valais, Sierre, Switzerland
miriam.scaglione@hevs.ch

Abstract. Spatial based tourism behavior shows the relationship between visitors with the land and services environments. In the 1990s a *tourism attraction systems* model was proposed as a theoretical framework to answer this research question; this concept has been then enriched and updated by employing *travel network* concepts after the eruption of users of mobile IT (Information Technology). The description of general or aggregate patterns of tourism movements in a given area and their underlying network structures are central for these characterizations, they are referred to as *Strategic Visitor Flows* (SVF). This research uses data recorded during a test carried out in collaboration with Swisscom-the major Swiss mobile company and consists of an anonymized and highly aggregated mobile phone data set. The aim of this exploratory study is to show there is link between the relative importance level of attractions within a tourism system network and the length of stay of the visitors.

Keywords: Spatial movement patterns of travelers · Network models · Travel networks · Tourism attraction systems

1 Introduction

Tourism behavior has been considered as one of the most important aspects of tourism research in the XXI century. There is a general agreement that network structure is an appropriate tool to describe such behaviour [1, 2]. In the 1990's Tourism attraction systems [3, 4] focused on attractions as touch points or nodes mostly identified by their special locations.

During this century, the generalized use of smart phones and the spread of free access to wi-fi facilities enriched tourism experiences [5]. The visitor interacts not only with service infrastructures in the destination but retrieves and shares information before, during and after the vacation experience [6, 7]. As a result, the Travel networks concept [8, 9] added a new characterization level to Tourism attraction systems' touch points: they could be either physical or virtual and, therefore, experiences and

© Springer Nature Switzerland AG 2018
C. Pautasso et al. (Eds.): ICWE 2018, LNCS 11153, pp. 227–237, 2018.
https://doi.org/10.1007/978-3-030-03056-8_22

informational elements are included. The use of smartphones not only shapes the tourism experience [10] but has facilitated in visitors more opportunistic behaviours: they are increasing willing to change the planned itinerary on the spot, due, for example to such things as bad weather forecast conditions [11].

Nevertheless, describing general spatial patterns of travellers' movements or visitor flows (VF) is an important part of the story and it is the main part of this research project [12].

The aim of this research is to show a link of relative importance of attractions (such as being a nucleus, central or marginal) within a tourism attraction system network and the length of stay using VF network analysis on highly aggregated mobile data.

The paper is organized in the following way: the literature review discusses different theories about tourism system elements and relevance of the planning vacation process (PVP) timing. The second section contains the description of the data and network methodology analysis. The third section presents the results. The fourth section analyses the results. The final section discusses the results in terms of scientific and management dimensions and implications for future research.

2   Literature Review

The aim of describing the spatial tourism behavior is central not only for land-planners and policy makers but also for destination management organizations [13–16].

Such descriptions of spatial behaviour's paradigms can be either focused on nodes or flows when they are based on the Network structure theory.

Tourism attraction systems [3, 4] focused on attractions as touch points or nodes may be mostly identified by their spatial locations. As it was pointed out above, the attraction systems approach has been modelled as networks in both theoretical [i.e. 17, 18] and empirical [19 ch. 5, 20] researches. Leiper defined the tourist attraction system as "an empirical connection of tourist, nucleus and markers" [17, p. 367]. The nucleus is the central element of a tourism attraction system, and it could be any feature or characteristic of a place that travellers visit. A marker is the link, namely an item of information that links the human and the nuclear element of an attraction system and allows one to distinguish the nucleus from other similar phenomena [op. cit. p. 8]. The centrality of the nucleus in the attraction system does not mean that such attractions are isolated elements; the expression nuclear mix was coined by Leiper [17] as a combination of nuclei which are significant in the experiences during the trip. Nevertheless, there is a hierarchical classification of nuclei: primary, secondary and tertiary. This classification mainly relies on the traveller's knowledge of their existence before they arrive at the site or destination. Tourists could suspect the existence of the secondary attraction but probably not of the tertiary ones. Figure 1(a) and (b) illustrate these theoretical concepts.

The maps in Fig. 1 has been obtained after the analysis of 803 valid observations gathered by survey carried out on the field, during the summer season: 2016 for La Gruyère district and 2017 for all the others [21]. Each district is a regional tourism destination. In the survey the following questions were raised: "Please name the attractions you've already visited", "Please name the attraction you are planning to

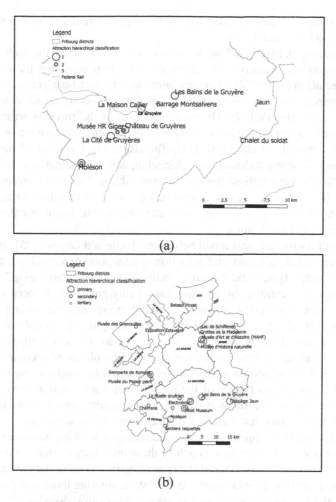

Fig. 1. Examples of system attractions maps in Fribourg canton in Switzerland. Panel (a) an example of a cluster of attraction obtained for tourists, (b) a cluster obtained for day trippers.

visit", and the name of the attraction where the survey was taken place was also gathered as data. The observations have been classified as tourists, people spending at least one night in the canton or day-trippers.

Each obtained cluster shows the set of the attractions to be visited, regardless of the trajectory followed. Panel (a) shows one of the clusters belonging to tourists whereas Panel (b) concerned only day-trippers. Both clusters have attractions of three distinct levels: primary, secondary and tertiary. Panel (a) shows a whole attraction system contained within one destination (*La Gruyère*). Panel (b) includes 3 attraction systems located in three different destinations (*La Gruyère*, *La Sarine* and *La Glâne*). The three sets deserve the definition of attraction system because each of them contains primary attractions. Other districts such as *La Veveyse* and *La Broye* have not any primary attractions but some places are included in day-tripper circuits thanks to the relevant primary attraction situated nearby.

Another paradigm, based on flows instead of nodes, consists on the study of the most generalized itineraries, namely SVF. Some researchers pointed out its importance in market segmentation [4, 19, 22] others are interested in describing general or aggregate patterns of movements in a given area [23] and their underlying structure has been characterized as a network [17]. The basic structure of the travel itinerary pattern is origin-destination-origin where lines are routes in between, but there are other kinds of tourist itinerary models as shown in [24]. Therefore, itineraries could have different patterns among destinations/attractions, including single destinations, hub and tour patterns with their representations having a network shape. Two new concepts have been added to this flow approach: gateway (the first destination/attractions) reached before beginning a multiple destination itinerary) and egress (the last destination/attraction visited before going back home).

In a study of Swiss residents travel behaviour, Hyde and Laesser [25] combined the two approaches namely itinerary and attraction system point of view. Hyde and Laesser individualized three typical behaviour patterns: "stay-put", "arranging", and "free-wheeling" touring vacations. In the first case, "stay-put", this is very close to the traditional concept of a single destination vacation; the second, the "arranging" touring consists of a visit of several destinations with overnights in multiple locations that could be self-arranged by the traveller themselves prior to the departure; finally, the "freewheeling" vacationer has pre-arranged only a few places of accommodation and has a high flexibility and spontaneous choice of vacation elements. These three patterns show different choices and timing of the macro-level frame such as travel routes and accommodation. Moreover, the increasing flexibility during travel allows the selection of secondary destinations that were not planned prior to the departure.

Scholars inspired by Leiper [17], classified attractions taking into account the time that the visitor decides to expend on each of them once they decide the destination in the PVP. Therefore, this classification states as primary and secondary attractions those whose length of visit can be evaluated. Tertiary attractions are those that the visitors are not aware of their existence when they made the destination decision [26].

The aim of this research is to show that within a geographical area, namely Fribourg canton in Switzerland, the importance of attractions (nucleus, gateway and egress) varies depending on the length of stay of the visitor trajectories. In order to fulfil this objective, mobile data are used to demonstrate generalized patterns of tourist movements in the canton.

2.1 Passive Mobile Positioning Data

The use of smartphones has increased in the everyday life of consumers such as when using social networks on mobiles phones [27] and the same during vacation periods [5]. The capabilities of mobile phone positioning data have therefore become an interesting and pertinent tool for monitoring VF. Advantages include the following: "data can be collected for larger spatial units and in less visited areas; spatial and temporal preciseness is higher than for regular tourism statistics" [28, p. 469].

The term passive mobile positioning data refers to automatically stored information that are kept in log files by mobile operators. The mobile geo-localisation information relies on the position of the cell network. A cellular network is physically placed at base stations which are usually towers supporting one or more directional antennae. The localisation of the cell network is determined by the base station (in the case of only one antenna) or several antennae. The size of the cell network is not fixed, therefore, and depends on the average load or number of phones connected. When the network is crowded, phones cannot switch to the nearest base station but connect to another one in the neighbourhood. The optimal distance from handset to antenna is less than 60 km [28]. There have been two major projects running contemporaneously in Europe focusing on passive mobile data use and tourism. The first one was a Eurostat project named "Feasibility Study" on the use of mobile positioning data for Tourism Statistics [29]. The second was a feasibility project named Monitour [30], which was financed by Swiss research funds. Both projects used the coordinates of the base station as proxy of the location of the mobile, thus geo-localising anonymised visitor data [cf. 29, p. 18]. The studies showed that the method is quite beneficial and able to provide many useful insights.

Reliability evaluation of passive mobile positioning data was one of the aims of the European project. In the estimation of tourism frequentation, the results show that the quality and exhaustivity of those data is not inferior to other alternative methods such as surveys, moreover, their estimations are in coherence and well fitted with the official data gathered by Eurostat [29]. One of the main difficulties that passive mobile positioning data faces is the identification of "natural environment" or "residence place" for the anonymised visitor and this concept is central in tourist identification. The European project solved this issue by the analysis of extended anonymous user's data in order to follow the anonymous subscribers over "a longer period than the one under study in order to establish their residency and/or usual environment" [29, p. 18]. In the same manner, anonymised visitors can be categorized as day-trippers or overnight tourists, the first category is difficult to grasp with traditional frequentation data gathering techniques [31], even though bias in the classification between these two categories cannot be excluded.

3 Data and Methods

3.1 Data Description

Swisscom, which is the major Swiss mobile provider having 60% of the market is a partner of this research and provided a set of test data.

The data consists of 18,138 anonymized mobile users belonging to one of the top European incoming countries in Fribourg canton tourism. The period under study is 11 days, from 17 and 28 August 2014. For confidentiality purposes, Swisscom has anonymized the users using Hashing-Algorithm techniques and shifting of the date; no characteristics of the users are given. From hereafter we will refer to the anonymized mobile users as AMU. It is worth noting that this anonymization process does not affect the results of this research, whose aim is to show the inference of SVF using mobile data.

The data is comprised of 2G A Interface data, 2G IuPS Interface data, 3G IuCS data and 3G IuPS data, technology which does not allow accurate geo-localization of the mobile position, i.e. it was not possible to associate the data to specific tourist attractions. Thus, the authors used the position of the cells (namely antennas) as proxy for the geo-localization of AMU, and it is acknowledged that this is a limitation of this research. There are approximately 1,500 cells.

In order to identify SVF, the authors programmed a customized routine in Java which was run by the computer centre of Swisscom in order to yield a file consisting of trajectories. The structure of that file has the following fields: AMU, trajectory identification, time stamp, duration and cell identification. The time stamp field indicates the moment when AMU was captured by the cell identified in the observation. The duration indicates the period of time that the AMU remained captured by the latter cell, but this data was not used in this first analysis.

The data includes 18,138 trajectories having a mean duration of 3 days and 15 h and a standard deviation of 2 days 14 h. The median number of trajectories per AMU is 13.

The dataset was then split into three segments containing the trajectories with overall duration of one hour, less than one day, and more than one day. From these three networks were built using the same procedure. Tracks were extracted that contain the different points (antennas) that recorded a single AMU.

3.2   Methodology: Network Analysis

The literature review gives some evidences about the relevance of network analysis as a toolbox for the analysis of spatial patterns of movements (VF). This approach provides several metrics useful for describing different aspects of the structural and dynamic characteristics of the object of study [32, 33]. Some of the main measurements that allow the characterisation of topology and behaviour of actors, such as VF, are used in our analysis: the distribution of each node connection (degree distribution), the length of the paths connecting any two nodes (in number of links), and the mesoscopic structure of the network (number and type of clusters of nodes).

The 18,138 trajectories were then combined into a network $G(V, E)$ in which the set of vertices (nodes) V is composed of the antennas, and the set of links E is made of the directed paths connecting the nodes. The paths are directed (from node x to node y) and are the cumulated tracks followed by AMUs moving from one antenna location to another. The links have also a weight value representing the number of AMUs that followed that particular segment from one antenna to another. The networks were then analysed using standard methods (the interested reader can find all methodological details for this analysis in [2, 33, 34]). In particular we use the degree distribution $N(k)$ (the statistical distribution of the number of links each node has) as an indicator of the overall structural characteristics of a network (see e.g. [35]). All measurements were calculated by using the Python Networkx library [36]. Network visualizations were obtained in Pajek [37].

4   Results and Discussion

The results will be focus on the metric first of nodes and of paths.

Among the different metrics, the degree distribution (the statistical distribution of the links between nodes) is commonly used as an indicator of the overall structural characteristics of a network. They are shown in Fig. 2.

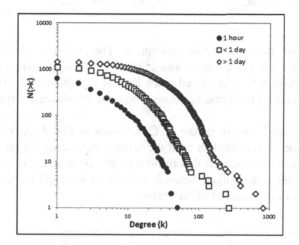

Fig. 2. The cumulative degree distributions of the networks

Apart from a scale factor (the three networks have different sizes), the distributions show a substantial similarity that translates into a similarity in the visitors' mobility behaviours. The power-law shape of these distributions signals a great heterogeneity in the choices of the places to visit.

In a directed network, it is possible to identify a so-called bow-tie structure. The network can be considered as composed of a large strongly connected component (SCC), and an IN and OUT component with a unidirectional connection to SCC; the network can also exhibit a TUBE connecting IN and OUT directly, and a disconnected (DSC) component [38]. The results for the three networks are shown in Fig. 3 and Table 1.

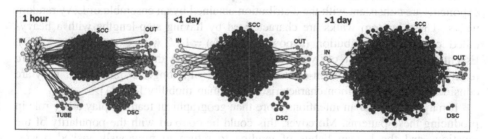

Fig. 3. The bow-tie schematic structure of the three networks

Table 1. The bow-tie components (fraction of nodes in the different components)

Bow-tie component	1 h	<1 day	>1 day
SCC	59.0%	95.2%	98.7%
IN	16.6%	1.8%	0.7%
OUT	8.9%	2.1%	0.4%
TUBE	3.0%		
DSC	12.5%	0.8%	0.1%

With this view interesting differences appear. The bow-tie analysis shows a high concentration of the paths in a certain area and the very high proportion of nodes in the SCC of longest stays networks, signal some kind of repetition in the tracks. Tourists seem to visit repeatedly the same locations, while for the shortest stays the walks are more dispersed.

The geographical locations of the SCC is shown in Fig. 4. As can be seen, the differences are much less clear than what the network representation provides, which is a further evidence of how multiple descriptions greatly increase the comprehension of a system and how network analytic methods are able to highlight characteristics otherwise difficult (if not impossible) to recognize.

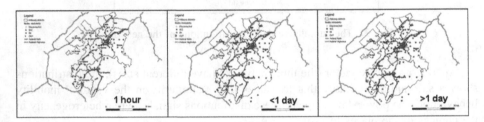

Fig. 4. The geographic rendering of SCC component yield by the bow-tie analysis by length of stay.

Another interesting result comes from the analysis of the lengths of the paths travelled by the visitors. The cumulative distributions are shown in Fig. 5.

They are all consistent with a power-law with exponents (calculated according to [39]): 2.95 ± 0.22 (1 h), 2.70 ± 0.13 (<1 day), and 2.62 ± 0.07 (>1 day). Shape and exponents are consistent with the distribution obtained by an ensemble of Lévy random walks. These random walks are characterized by having step-lengths with a heavy-tailed probability distribution (a power-law $p(L) = L^{-k}$ with exponent $1 < k < 3$). Essentially, they consist of 'walk clusters' in which within-cluster movements are relatively short, while between-cluster transfers are of a longer displacement. They are considered to be a common characteristic of human mobility [40, 41].

It may be that human intentions more than geographical features play a key role in producing these patterns. Moreover, this could be coupled with the popularity of the locations and the human habits of tending to return to previously visited places.

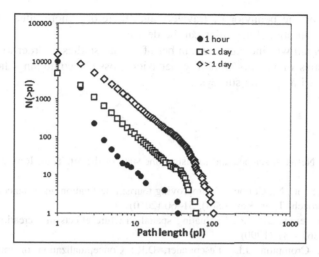

Fig. 5. The path lengths cumulative distributions

Obviously, the accessibility, or the ease of movement, especially for the longer displacements, strongly affects the patterns of visit. Therefore, a logical conclusion for an attraction, would be to use promotional activities for increasing its popularity but also keeping in mind the possibilities of physical reachability.

5 Conclusion, Limitations and Future Research

The limitations of the work presented here are basically due to the lack of richer information that was not made available about the tourists (due to the anonymization procedure). Little to no information is available about the qualitative aspects such as socio-demographic characteristics (excluding country of the company mobile provider), expenditure, purpose of the trip, etc. This does not permit a more in-depth analysis and verification of the interpretations that were supported by recent literature. Moreover, this research is restricted to AMUs of only one European country and limited in time.

Some other limitations are more difficult to overcome such as related to coverage issues, or with the telecommunications market itself, such as the cost of calls or texting or roaming fees that could affect the use of mobiles especially in the case of international tourists [29]. Another limit is the nature of this research which is exploratory.

However, there are two important outcomes from the study: firstly, from a methodological point of view, network analytic methods have provided some interesting and not easily predictable results on the visitors' behaviours. Secondly: the relative ease in obtaining these results (once data are available) results in destination and attraction managers having a powerful set of tools for the evaluation of tourists' actual movements. If these are combined with some more traditional surveys this can complement and better frame the results obtained, thereby giving a deeper understanding of the behavior of travelers and, therefore, more effective and better planning and promotional activities can be devised.

Future research will increase the number of similar studies in order to better assess the characteristics of visitors' mobility behavior, possibly combining the techniques discussed here with specific surveys.

References

1. Baggio, R.: Network science and tourism – the state of the art. Tour. Rev. **72**(1), 120–131 (2017)
2. Baggio, R., Scott, N., Cooper, C.: Improving tourism destination governance: a complexity science approach. Tour. Rev. **65**(4), 51–60 (2010)
3. Kim, S.I., Fesenmaier, D.R.: Evaluating spatial structure effects in recreation travel. Leis. Sci. **12**(4), 367–381 (1990)
4. Lue, C.-C., Crompton, J.L., Fesenmaier, D.R.: Conceptualization of multi-destination pleasure trips. Ann. Tour. Res. **20**(2), 289–301 (1993)
5. Wang, D., Xiang, Z., Fesenmaier, D.R.: Smartphone use in everyday life and travel. J. Travel Res. **55**(1), 52–63 (2016)
6. Zach, F., Gretzel, U.: Tourist-activated networks: implications for dynamic bundling and EN route recommendations. Inf. Technol. Tour. **13**(3), 229–238 (2011)
7. Xiang, Z., Wöber, K., Fesenmaier, D.R.: Representation of the online tourism domain in search engines. J. Travel Res. **47**(2), 137–150 (2008)
8. Stienmetz, J.L., Fesenmaier, D.R.: Traveling the network: a proposal for destination performance metrics. Int. J. Tour. Sci. **13**(2), 57–75 (2013)
9. Stienmetz, J.L., Fesenmaier, D.R.: Validating volunteered geographic information: can we reliably trace visitors' digital footprints? In: Proceedings of the 2016 TTRA International Conference, Vail, CO, USA (2016)
10. Wang, X., Li, X., Zhen, F., Zhang, J.: How smart is your tourist attraction?: Measuring tourist preferences of smart tourism attractions via a FCEM-AHP and IPA approach. Tour. Manag. **54**, 309–320 (2016)
11. Marchiori, E., Scaglione, M., Schegg, R., Cantoni, L.: Research agenda for analysing online climate and weather information in the process of vacation planning. e-Review Tour. Res. **9**, (2018). (ENTER 2018 Conference on Information and Communication Technologies in Tourism Research Notes, January 2018). https://journals.tdl.org/ertr/index.php/ertr/article/view/122
12. Baggio, R., Scaglione, M.: Strategic visitor flows and destination management organization. Inf. Technol. Tour. **18**(1), 29–42 (2018)
13. Gunn, C.A., Var, T.: Tourism Planning Basics, Concepts, Cases, 4th edn. Routledge, London (2002)
14. Beritelli, P., Bieger, T., Laesser, C.: The new frontiers of destination management: applying variable geometry as a function-based approach. J. Travel Res. **53**(4), 403–417 (2014)
15. Beritelli, P., Reinhold, S., Laesser, C., Bieger, T.: The St. Gallen Model for Destination Management (IMP-HSG 2015) (2015)
16. Reinhold, S., Laesser, C., Beritelli, P.: 2014 St. Gallen consensus on destination management. J. Destin. Mark. Manag. **4**(2), 137–142 (2015)
17. Leiper, N.: Tourist attraction systems. Ann. Tour. Res. **17**(3), 367–384 (1990)
18. Lew, A.: A framework of tourist attraction research. Ann. Tour. Res. **14**(4), 553–575 (1987)

19. Gunn, C.A.: Tourism Planning Basics, Concepts, Cases, 3rd edn. Taylor & Francis, London (1994)
20. Richards, G.: Tourism attraction systems: exploring Cultural Behavior. Ann. Tour. Res. **29**(4), 1048–1064 (2002)
21. Scaglione, M., Baggio, R.: Etude complémentaire au projet des impacts économiques du tourisme dans le canton de Fribourg. Institute Tourism- HES-SO Valais (2018)
22. Dredge, D.: Destination place planning and design. Ann. Tour. Res. **26**(4), 772–791 (1999)
23. Orellana, D., Bregt, A.K., Ligtenberg, A., Wachowicz, M.: Exploring visitor movement patterns in natural recreational areas. Tour. Manag. **33**(3), 672–682 (2012)
24. Lew, A., McKercher, B.: Trip destinations, gateways and itineraries: the example of Hong Kong. Tour. Manag. **23**(6), 609–621 (2002)
25. Hyde, K.F., Laesser, C.: A structural theory of the vacation. Tour. Manag. **30**(2), 240–248 (2009)
26. Botti, L., Peypoch, N., Solonandrasana, B.: Time and tourism attraction. Tour. Manag. **29**(3), 594–596 (2008)
27. Scaglione, M., Giovannetti, E., Hamoudia, M.: The diffusion of mobile social networking: exploring adoption externalities in four G7 countries. Int. J. Forecast. **31**, 1159–1170 (2015)
28. Ahas, R., Aasa, A., Roose, A., Mark, Ü., Silm, S.: Evaluating passive mobile positioning data for tourism surveys: an Estonian case study. Tour. Manag. **29**(3), 469–486 (2008)
29. Eurostat: Feasibility study on the use of mobile positioning data for tourism statistics (2013)
30. Scaglione, M., Favre, P., Trabichet, J.-P.: Using mobile data and strategic tourism flows. pilot study monitour in Switzerland, pp. 69–72 (2016)
31. Scaglione, M., Perruchoud-Massy, M.-F.: The use of indirect indicators to estimate a destination's visitor counts. Transfert **1**, 40–65 (2013)
32. Baggio, R., Del Chiappa, G.: Complex tourism systems: a quantitative approach. In: Management Science in Hospitality and Tourism: Theory, Practice, and Applications, p. 21 (2016)
33. Baggio, R., Scott, N., Cooper, C.: Network science: a review focused on tourism. Ann. Tour. Res. **37**(3), 802–827 (2010)
34. Baggio, R., Scaglione, M.: Strategic visitor flows (SVF) analysis using mobile data. In: Schegg, R., Stangl, B. (eds.) Information and Communication Technologies in Tourism 2017, pp. 145–157. Springer, Cham (2017). https://doi.org/10.1007/978-3-319-51168-9_11
35. Newman, M.E.J.: Networks an Introduction. Oxford University Press, Oxford (2010)
36. Hagberg, A.A., Schult, D.A., Swart, P.: Exploring network structure, dynamics, and function using NetworkX, pp. 11–16 (2008)
37. Batagelj, V., Mrvar, A.: Pajek-program for large network analysis. Connections **21**(2), 47–57 (1998)
38. Broder, A., et al.: Graph structure in the web. Comput. Netw. **33**(1), 309–320 (2000)
39. Clauset, A., Shalizi, C.R., Newman, M.E.: Power-law distributions in empirical data. SIAM Rev. **51**(4), 661–703 (2009)
40. Gonzalez, M.C., Hidalgo, C.A., Barabasi, A.-L.: Understanding individual human mobility patterns (2008). arXiv preprint: arXiv:0806.1256
41. Rhee, I., Shin, M., Hong, S., Lee, K., Kim, S.J., Chong, S.: On the Levy-walk nature of human mobility. IEEE/ACM Trans. Netw. **19**(3), 630–643 (2011)

SanTour: Towards Personalized Recommendation of Hiking Trails to Health Profiles

Jean-Paul Calbimonte[1]([✉]), Nancy Zappellaz[1], Emeline Hébert[2], Maya Simon[2], Nicolas Délétroz[2], Roger Hilfiker[3], and Alexandre Cotting[1]

[1] Institute of Information Systems, University of Applied Sciences and Arts Western Switzerland HES-SO Valais-Wallis, Sierre, Switzerland
[2] Institute of Tourism, University of Applied Sciences and Arts Western Switzerland HES-SO Valais-Wallis, Sierre, Switzerland
[3] Institute of Health, University of Applied Sciences and Arts Western Switzerland HES-SO Valais-Wallis, Sierre, Switzerland
{jean-paul.calbimonte,nancy.zappellaz,emeline.hebert,
maya.simon,nicolas.deletroz,roger.hilfiker,alexandre.cotting}@hevs.ch

Abstract. Health tourism represents a promising niche still insufficiently exploited in Europe and Switzerland. Hiking has been a popular tourist activity for years and staying healthy is an important motivation for hiking. However, physical and psychological limitations in potential hikers often represent an unsurmountable barrier to complete a particular path. This mismatch between trail and user results in a poor visitor experience, affecting negatively both the user and the touristic destination. This paper presents SanTour, a novel concept in health tourism centered on the needs of visitors by considering their physical capacities and limits, as well as their expectations. SanTour exploits two main knowledge bases: one centered on the user, including a health profile, and another centered on the hiking trails. In a pilot phase, the concept has been prototyped and tested on a limited scale, with support from a tourist office in Switzerland. We plan to further develop this application that will provide an innovative service to hikers by cross-referencing their physical abilities and the characteristics of the hiking trails.

Keywords: Health tourism · Health recommendation
Tourism knowledge base

1 Introduction

Outdoor activities are a key part of the touristic offer in Switzerland. Hiking trails, with a varying degree of difficulty, and accessible under different conditions depending on the season and weather, attract both local and foreign visitors alike. Their popularity among the population is due in part to their accessibility, the direct contact with nature, relatively low price, and perceived benefits to

C. Pautasso et al. (Eds.): ICWE 2018, LNCS 11153, pp. 238–250, 2018.
https://doi.org/10.1007/978-3-030-03056-8_23

health and wellbeing. Even if these benefits are generally acknowledged, there are still important barriers for segments of the population, especially those who have physical or psychological limitations. These limitations refer not only to highly vulnerable segments (e.g. people suffering chronic diseases, arrhythmia, and/or disabilities), but also to visitors having varying degrees of endurance, fear of heights, lack of balance, difficulties walking through rough trails, vertigo, etc. In fact, features of a hiking trail that may seem attractive to some visitors, such as a suspended bridge, or a cliff-facing path, can be unsurmountable obstacles for others. The limited amount of detailed information about these difficulty points, and the lack of appropriate means to match them with the personal conditions of the visitors, leads to poor user experience and even the abandon of hiking trails as preferred choice for leisure and health-related activities.

This paper introduces SanTour, a novel concept for health tourism that relies on knowledge bases centered on two main aspects: the visitor's health profile, and the hiking trail profiles (Fig. 1). The main idea is that a system can be built in order to match the health profile with the available trails, so that a set of recommendations can be provided. The concretion of this idea is not straightforward. It lies in the intersection of disciplines that include tourism, health and wellbeing, and knowledge acquisition and management. Therefore, it requires a careful analysis of needs, requirements, and perception from the different stakeholders involved in the topic, including: regional tourist offices, local development authorities, health professionals, mountain guides, and potential hikers.

In this work we present the general concept of SanTour (Sect. 2), and an analysis of needs performed through focus groups and questionnaires with relevant stakeholders (Sect. 3). We then describe the knowledge base for SanTour, which includes the characterization of hiking trails, and user health profiling (Sect. 4). Section 5 describes the prototype Web and mobile application[1]. We describe related work on this area (Sect. 6), and discuss future challenges and open points in Sect. 7.

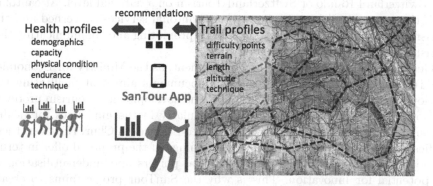

Fig. 1. The SanTour concept: recommendations based on health profile and the characterization of hiking trails.

---

[1] SanTour proof of concept: http://santour.ch.

2   SanTour: A Novel Concept in Health Tourism

Health tourism is a promising trend that could boost the attractiveness of mountain destinations during all seasons. The vast variety, both in terms of the offers and the targeted visitors, makes it a suitable choice for different types of scenarios. These offers can be developed, for instance, as part of a tourist office strategy, or as a health-care-oriented offering complementary to patient treatment, or as a wellness program sponsored by insurance companies, etc.

SanTour positions itself as a health tourism solution for hiking trails targeting the general population, with a special focus on those users who may require tailored advice for their choices. SanTour adopts the goals of adapting the hiking offer to the physical condition and limiting factors (e.g. vertigo, lack of balance, etc.) of the users, and is positioned as an instrument of prevention –not of care– intended for both healthy people and those with reduced mobility and affected by chronic diseases. The project takes into account that in Switzerland, individuals are increasingly aware of the relationship between a healthy lifestyle and the prevention of certain pathologies. Also, the regular practice of sports activities tends to increase strongly and explains the current boom in outdoor tourism and the initiatives taken by tourist destinations that seek to expand, diversify and segment their offer. In this context, hiking is an interesting and popular tourist product that has enjoyed great success for several years. This is confirmed by current statistics: 44% of the Swiss population is engaged in this type of activity and the number of hikers has increased by 7% compared to 2008, in addition to 300,000 foreign tourists[2]. The use of hiking trails comes in many forms ranging from short easy walks to running in the mountains, in tours over one or more days.

In Switzerland, there is a wide range of hiking trails, covering more than $65,000\,km^2$. Many actors, at several levels, are concerned. The task of the municipalities is to maintain the roads, to guarantee their quality and to approve them. The paths are then listed or promoted by various organisations such as SuisseMobile, Switzerland Rando or Switzerland Tourism on a national level. At cantonal level, the cantonal hiking associations, the cantonal services concerned and the tourism promotion bodies are responsible for promoting and communicating this tourist offer.

Germany is also encouraging its development, as the Ministry for Economics and Technology has published numerous documents aimed at facilitating the development of innovative health tourism. The development of tourism products is also recommended in Switzerland, particularly in the guidelines for health tourism proposed by the University of Applied Sciences in Chur. However, these studies and reports point to serious shortcomings in the proposed offer in terms of cooperation between tourism and medical players and under-utilisation of the potential for innovation. This is why the SanTour project aims to create favourable conditions for the creation of a modern and innovative product linking health and tourism and to evaluate its potential.

---

[2] Suisse Rando (2014): https://www.wandern.ch/de/downloads.

3   User Exploratory Study

In the context of the project, we launched an on-line questionnaire, targeted at hikers in Switzerland, with the goal of assessing their needs, and analyzing their behavior regarding hiking activities. The quantitative questionnaire is centered on the understanding the following aspects: behavior in outdoor/hiking activities, motivations for pedestrian walks, satisfaction regarding trail offer, support and information technologies. The questionnaire was responded by over 300 people, 91% Swiss, half of them of age between 51 and 70, 40% retired, and respecting gender equality. The results, as summarized in Fig. 2, show that the consulted users are active in hiking activities, either alone or in groups. Interestingly, the top reasons for hiking are reported to be (i) for general wellbeing, (ii) to be in contact with nature, and (iii) to be in good health. Therefore, it is clear that the health aspect is of special importance for the contacted users. Furthermore, there is actually a high interest in the concept proposed by San-Tour, and most users would agree to communicate their health information or physical capabilities to benefit from adapted recommendations.

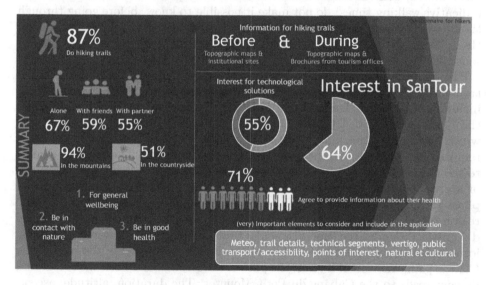

Fig. 2. SanTour. Results of an exploratory survey.

The results of this survey provide a strong indication that the concept proposed in SanTour touches relevant aspects for a population that is used to hiking and outdoor activities. Furthermore, it is evidenced that the health axis has a pivotal role in these activities, to the extent that users are generally open to share basic data about their conditions and limitations. Last but not least, users also consider important not to isolate the health aspect, but to link it to others such as points of interest, transportation, weather, and other types of information.

4   SanTour Knowledge Base

As described previously, SanTour recommendations are based on mainly two types of data: user health profiles and hiking trails. These two constitute the central knowledge base used by SanTour, and we briefly present them in the following sections.

4.1   Characterization of Trails

Although tourist offices, commune administrations and hiking associations make available information about trails and pedestrians paths, this only includes a general description, duration, distance, altitude, gradient and general difficulty of the route. Some applications, such as SuisseMobile, allow the journey time to be modulated according to the walking speed. In addition, some offer GPS navigation or statistics on the "performance" of the hiker (speed, time, etc.). However, there is still a lack of information linking the technical characteristics of a trail with the physical requirements necessary for a safe and enjoyable hike. Indeed, general indications of difficulty (signposts with a color code and indicative walking times) do not make it possible to know, before going through them, whether the proposed routes are adapted to the physical aptitudes of the hiker as well as to any limiting factors (for example, fear of emptiness or sensitivity to vertigo).

To fill this gap SanTour requires the implementation of a knowledge-base for trails, which includes this type of data. To do so, each trail needs to be cataloged, including its different features and difficulty points. The methodology followed the guidelines provided by the French Federation of Hiking (FFRandonnée[3]), which establishes three main types of difficulties. The first is related to the *effort* required for the trail, and its associated physical difficulty. The second is linked to the technical difficulty, and the third to the risks and psychological difficulties of a given point or segment. In order to test and prepare the data acquisition phase for the trail information, an series of on-site visits were effectuated to the region of Zinal, Valais, in partnership with the local tourism authorities of Val d'Anniviers[4]. Under the supervision of a trained guide, and the advice of a physiotherapist, an assessment of 5 different trails was performed in the region: the Clautis path, the trail of La Lée, the path of the Arolles, and both the ascent and descent roads to the Cabane du Petit Mountet. The duration, altitude, ascent, descent, length, description, and geographical information was provided by the tourist offices, and cross validated in the on-site visit. Furthermore, the GPS coordinates of the full paths was recorded using the hiking mobile application SNUKR[5], which is an external partner in the SanTour project. This information was necessary to construct the basic profile of each path, as exemplified in the Listing below. The data is represented using JSON-LD, annotated using mainly

---

[3] Fédération Française de la Randonnée Pédestre http://www.ffrandonnee.fr.

[4] https://www.valdanniviers.ch.

[5] SNUKR: http://snukr.ch.

the schema.org vocabulary. The example presents an excerpt of the description of the Clautis path, including its basic information details.

```
{
  "@context": "http://schema.org/",
  "@type": [ "HikingTrail", "TouristAttraction" ],
  "name": "Les Clautis",
  "description": "Randonee des Clautis",
  "touristType": {
    "@type": "Audience", "audienceType": "Beginners"
  },
  "address": {
    "@type": "PostalAddress",
    "addressCountry": "CH", "addressLocality":"Zinal"
  },
  "publicAccess": true,
  "altitude_max": 1720,
  "altitude_min": 1675,
  "duration": 1.5,
  "distance": 3.55,
  "image":"https://d25u9ndbhhiciz.cloudfront.net/points/59d8a48b798c500bf04bbf54-1-m.jpg"
}
```

However, as previously noted, this information is insufficient to create a profile that can be used for personalized recommendations according to health profiles. To complement the basic information, the data acquisition phase also contemplated the annotation of difficulty points. In each path, at least four people with different physical abilities and walking habits annotated the different difficulty points encountered in the way, such as rocks, roots on the path, steep climbs, bridges and obstacles, vertigo points, narrow passages, etc. Each of these points is associated to a particular geographical point, and is assigned a difficulty score. Examples of such difficulty points, represented as JSON-LD are presented in the Listing below. They represent respectively a rocky passage, and the presence of a bridge.

```
[
  {
    "@context": "http://schema.org/",
    "@type": [ "DifficultyPoint","Stone","Place"],
    "name": "ClautisPoint32",
    "description": "Gros cailloux",
    "difficulty": 10,
    "geo": {
      "@type": "GeoCoordinates","latitude": "49.8852515","longitude": "2.5106436"
    }
  },
  {
    "@context": "http://schema.org/",
    "@type": ["DifficultyPoint","Bridge","Place" ],
    "name": "ClautisPoint35",
    "description": "Small bridge",
    "difficulty": 5,
    "geo": {
      "@type": "GeoCoordinates","latitude": "49.777315","longitude": "2.6106436"
    }
  }
]
```

4.2   Health Profile

Having defined the methodology and the data model for the trails, the second elements to consider is the profile of the users, including their health profile, as well as physical abilities and/or limitations and preferences. Users may have different types of interactions within the SanTour environment. It may happen that they are foreign visitors and only require a single or sporadic recommendations. Or instead, they can be local hikers that regularly look for hiking options. For this reason, SanTour adopts a questionnaire-based data acquisition approach, which needs to be quick and simple to fill up, while comprehensive enough to gather the necessary information. In the example below we present an example of a person details in JSON-LD, using schema.org. The person has reported diabetes as a medical condition.

```
{
  "@context": "http://schema.org/",
  "@type": "Person",
  "name": "Marie Dupont",
  "healthCondition":
    {
    "@type": "MedicalCondition",
    "alternateMame": "Diabetes Type 2"
    "code": { "@type": "MedicalCode","code": "E11.9","codingSystem": "ICD-10"}
    }
}
```

The previous example is only for illustrative future purposes, as currently SanTour relies on anonymized surveys, and no personal identification data (e.g. names) are stored. Also, SanTour dos not currently take into account information about diseases. In the future this information can help further adapting the recommendations also according to limitations in this regard. Instead, SanTour requests mainly two types of data. The first is a self-assessment of physical and psychological capacity for aspects including: general physical activity, help needed to walk, walking speed and endurance, climbing capacity, balance, fear of falling, and of void, and pain. The questions are prepared in such a way that the user can self-describe her situation. There is unavoidable bias and/or degree of inaccuracy in this respect, but the approach was chosen in order to rely as much as possible on a self-controlled assessment. The example below is a representation of one of the questions in RDF Turtle format, using the MedRed ontology [3], whose purpose is to represent data acquisition instruments such as surveys, questionnaires, etc. The question in the example refers to the user's perceived speed in comparison with those of her peers.

```
ex:santourQ3 a medred:Question ;
  medred:isItemofSection ex:santourHealthSection1 ;
  dcterms:identifier   "santourQ3" ;
  dcterms:title        "Par rapport a la vitesse de marche moyenne (celle de vos proches),
        pensez vous marcher habituellement ..." ;
  medred:choices       ( ex:muchSlower ex:slower
                         ex:equalSpeed ex:faster
                         ex:muchFaster ) ;
  pplan:hasOutputVar   ex:santourQ3_var .
```

The other type of data requested to the user, is focused on preferences on types of features/elements present in a hiking trail. This is important in order to have an idea of the features (which can have certain degree of difficulty) that the user is comfortable with. For instance, a user may enjoy hiking in stony trails, but would prefer to avoid suspended bridges, because of vertigo. An example is presented in the listing below. It is represented in JSON-LD, and show a rating for stony trails. The preference is represented as a rating, using the schema.org vocabulary.

```
{
    "@type": ["Review","TrailPreference"]
    "author": "Laure",
    "datePublished": "2011-04-01",
    "@id": "laureCaillouxReview",
    "description": "Evaluer de -10 (je deteste), 0 (ca m'est egal), a +10 (j'aime).
        Cailloux.",
    "reviewRating": {
        "@type": "Rating",
        "bestRating": "10",
        "ratingValue": "7",
        "worstRating": "-10"
    }
}
```

5   Implementation

A first proof-of-concept implementation of SanTour has been developed, in order to evaluate and collect feedback, as well as to show the potential of this idea to stakeholders such as local tourist offices or hiking organizations. The implementation is a Web application, also available for mobile devices, which displays the health questionnaire as well as the hiking trail preferences form to the user. This part of the application serves as an entry point for the health profile and trail preferences described in previous sections. A screen-shot of the application can be seen in Fig. 3, displaying some of these questions. For the moment the application works on an anonymous fashion and no personal information is stored. In future versions of SanTour, it is expected that previous preferences can be combined with feedback information in order to provide more precise and tailored recommendations.

Fig. 3. SanTour application.

The application also provides visualizations of the health profile and the preferences, which can provide a quick idea of the type of user (Fig. 4). More advanced visualizations are planned in the future, especially for those cases that may require human intervention. This might be the case, for example, if health professionals are interested in using SanTour for their patients, in order to suggest them outdoor activities or specific trails adapted to their needs, therapies, rehabilitation, etc.

With this information, the application applies similarity measures between the entered information and the existing trail profiles, providing a score. The hiking trails are ordered according to the score, and if necessary, targeted suggestions or warnings are provided, e.g. a warning if the user reported to have pain in the knees, it can be suggested to be extra careful in steep descents. Figure 5 displays the recommendation panel, showing the ordered trails according to the score. For demonstration purposes the SanTour prototype only contains a handful of hiking trails.

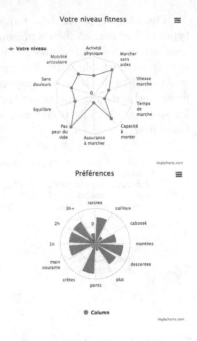

Fig. 4. SanTour charts.

Recommandations

parcours	distance	temps	lien	score
Les Clautis	3.55km	1h	Snukr	0.74 score
La Lee ⚠	3.73km	1h	Snukr	0.71 score
Attention si douleurs importantes	6.8km	2.75h	Snukr	0.46 score
Zinal-Petit Mountet chemin d'été ⚠	10.8km	3h	Snukr	0.41 score
Zinal-Petit Mountet Chemin d'hiver	12.6km	3.5h	Snukr	0.29 score

RECOMMANDATION

Fig. 5. SanTour recommendations.

6   Related Work

Hiking is a popular outdoor activity that requires little equipment, infrastructure, or even training in its simplest form. Maintaining or improving the physical fitness of hikers is a popular factor for this popularity, as confirmed in recent international studies [6,7]. Moreover, hiking also combines movement and social contacts, as well as appreciation of nature culture and landscape [8,10].

In terms of health and physical fitness, hiking allows significant improvements likely to break the undesirable effects of inactivity, including increased calories burned, decreased stress and increased well-being [8,17]. Despite its many advantages, hiking also carries risks not to be neglected. According to BPA (Swiss Accident Prevention office)[6], nearly 20,000 people are injured every year while hiking in Switzerland. In 2015, the Swiss Alpine Club counted some 1200 situations requiring the intervention of rescue organizations and 64 fatal accidents due to hiking[7]. A study carried out in the Italian Pre-Alps leads [5] notes the increasing rate of hikers requesting intervention due to late return, fatigue or bad weather. First aid reports also point out that poor assessment of physical abilities leads to excessive effort on the part of hikers whose physical fitness is insufficient, resulting in fatigue leading to falls.

The problem of the frequent subjectivity of the evaluation of hiking trails is highlighted in [9], proposing to evaluate their difficulty on the basis of the standardized energy expenditure they cause. In [4] a good overview of the methodology and difficulties in the characterization of hiking trails is presented. This work emphasizes that parameters such as altitude or slope are simple to calculate, while others are more complicated to characterize, or require the use of substitutes to do so. This work shows the interest and feasibility of crossing biophysical factors with pleasure or difficulty, by determining coefficients applicable to each biophysical factor whose addition establishes the expected level of difficulty. SanTour precisely goes into this direction, establishing a first concrete implementation.

In parallel with the characterization of the hiking trails, it is key to assess the physical fitness of the hiker. This can be estimated using a questionnaire, according to the transtheoretical model in [14]. More detailed methods have been studied for the evaluation of physical activity by self-reported questionnaires [2].

Concerning recommendation systems and algorithms, several choices exist, depending on the characteristics of the data [15], particularly those related to the user context [12]. Contextual aspects may include location, season, weather, etc. These systems also consider user preferences and profile, which create a model that can then be used by machine learning and artificial intelligence algorithms to generate tailored and personalized recommendations [1]. However, tourist recommendation systems do not take into account the health aspects of users or their psychomotor abilities.

Beyond the health dimension, hiking also has an economic role to play, particularly in mountain tourist regions. While the use of roads as such does not generate direct income because they are free, activities related to hiking represent an economic potential that is too often under-exploited. Yet, the exploitation of collaborations in tourism promotes the prosperity of the entire destination.

---

[6] http://www.bpa.ch/fr/Documents/03_Fuer-Fachpersonen/02_Betriebe/SafetyKit/Wandern/2016-05-11_factsheet_randonne_FR.pdf.

[7] http://www.sac-cas.ch/fr/en-chemin/securite/urgences-dans-les-montagnes.html.

The relevance of the industrial cluster model [13] to tourism has thus been noted [11,16]. This vision of the functioning of a destination highlights the need to develop strong interactions between the various companies or entities offering complementary tourism products in order to create a competitive advantage for the destination as a whole.

7   Discussion and Conclusions

The SanTour project aims at bringing the world of health and tourism closer together. Cooperation and mutual understanding between these actors is still largely lacking. An improvement in this area will increase the credibility of health tourism offers, starting with the one proposed by our project. Although this first step provides a concrete implementation of a proof-of-concept, there are still several open points that need to be explored in the near future, especially concerning the outreach and potential ways of exploitation:

- Determine what data are desired by tourism promotion organizations so that they can best adapt their offer to hikers and target them more precisely.
- Determine what data are useful for a better understanding of hiking for scientific purposes, and also for touristic destinations.
- Determine the expectations of the health-care community regarding accident prevention and the promotion of physical activity.

The mobile application developed in SanTour may also facilitate the sale of products related to hiking, such as the sale of local products or catering, by integrating them into its business model through partnerships with service providers. However, in order to identify clearly the potential opportunities in this respect, we intend to present the SanTour concepts to relevant potential partners, e.g. mountain guides, tourism promotion organizations, service providers of a partner destination, and actors in the health sector, including health promotion institutions.

In the near future, the SanTour project will launch pre-tests with a limited number of people to check the general functioning of the pilot and make the necessary corrections. Furthermore, satisfaction tests will be conducted by making the pilot available to visitors and mountain guides of the partner destination, then by gathering their opinions.

The SanTour project responds to the need for better prevention and personalized recommendations for hiking, by taking particular account of the physical fitness and limiting factors of hikers when proposing routes for them to follow. Our system of route proposals adapted to hikers aims to combine the beneficial effects of hiking and risk reduction. To achieve this, we base our approach on a dynamic and semantic knowledge-base that includes health profiles and characterization of hiking trails. The SanTour project is expected to increase the quality of the tourist offer, since the quality and credibility of the information play a key role in customer satisfaction, as does the match between the hikes on offer and the hiker's abilities.

Acknowledgements. We would like to thank Chloé Saas and Kinitic SA for thier support. Partially supported by the RCSO Project SanTour (64896) HES-SO Valais-Wallis.

References

1. Borràs, J., Moreno, A., Valls, A.: Intelligent tourism recommender systems: a survey. Expert Syst. Appl. **41**(16), 7370–7389 (2014)
2. Bülaa, C., Jotterandb, S., Martinc, B.W., Bized, R., Lenoble-Hoskoveca, C., Seematter-Bagnouda, L.: Activité physique et vieillissement: il n'est jamais trop tard!. Forum Médical Suisse **14**, 836–841 (2014)
3. Calbimonte, J.-P., Dubosson, F., Hilfiker, R., Cotting, A., Schumacher, M.: The MedRed ontology for representing clinical data acquisition metadata. In: d'Amato, C., et al. (eds.) ISWC 2017, Part II. LNCS, vol. 10588, pp. 38–47. Springer, Cham (2017). https://doi.org/10.1007/978-3-319-68204-4_4
4. Chhetri, P.: A GIS methodology for modelling hiking experiences in the Grampians National Park, Australia. Tour. Geogr. **17**(5), 795–814 (2015)
5. Ciesa, M., Grigolato, S., Cavalli, R.: Retrospective study on search and rescue operations in two prealps areas of Italy. Wilderness Environ. Med. **26**(2), 150–158 (2015)
6. Collins-Kreiner, N., Kliot, N., et al.: Particularism vs. universalism in hiking tourism. Ann. Tour. Res. **56**, 132–137 (2016)
7. Davies, N.J., Lumsdon, L.M., Weston, R.: Developing recreational trails: motivations for recreational walking. Tour. Plan. Dev. **9**(1), 77–88 (2012)
8. Ekkekakis, P., Backhouse, S.H., Gray, C., Lind, E.: Walking is popular among adults but is it pleasant? A framework for clarifying the link between walking and affect as illustrated in two studies. Psychol. Sport Exerc. **9**(3), 246–264 (2008)
9. Hugo, M.L.: Energy equivalent as a measure of the difficulty rating of hiking trails. Tour. Geogr. **1**(3), 358–373 (1999)
10. Hyun, M.Y., Park, Y.A., Kim, Y.G.: Motivations to walk Jeju "Ollegil", South Korea: development and validation of a walking motivation scale. Tour. Plan. Dev. **13**(4), 486–503 (2016)
11. Jackson, J., Murphy, P.: Tourism destinations as clusters: analytical experiences from the new world. Tour. Hosp. Res. **4**(1), 36–52 (2002)
12. Lamsfus, C., Alzua-Sorzabal, A., Martín, D., Salvador, Z., Usandizaga, A.: Human-centric ontology-based context modelling in tourism. In: KEOD, pp. 424–434 (2009)
13. Porter, M.E.: On Competition. Harvard Business Press, Boston (2008)
14. Prochaska, J.O., Diclemente, C.C.: Toward a comprehensive model of change. In: Miller, W.R., Heather, N. (eds.) Treating Addictive Behaviors. Applied Clinical Psychology, vol. 13, pp. 3–27. Springer, Boston (1986). https://doi.org/10.1007/978-1-4613-2191-0_1
15. Schumacher, M., Rey, J.P.: Recommender systems for dynamic packaging of tourism services. In: Law, R., Fuchs, M., Ricci, F. (eds.) Information and Communication Technologies in Tourism 2011, pp. 13–23. Springer, Vienna (2011). https://doi.org/10.1007/978-3-7091-0503-0_2

16. Weidenfeld, A., Butler, R., Williams, A.W.: The role of clustering, cooperation and complementarities in the visitor attraction sector. Curr. Issues Tour. **14**(7), 595–629 (2011)
17. Wolf, I.D., Wohlfart, T.: Walking, hiking and running in parks: a multidisciplinary assessment of health and well-being benefits. Landsc. Urban Plan. **130**, 89–103 (2014)

Electronic Word-of-Mouth (eWOM)
for Destination Promotion by Tourists

Prasad N. Samarakoon[1] and Nandana Mihindukulasooriya[2(✉)]

[1] Madrid, Spain
PrasadNSamarakoon@gmail.com
[2] Ontology Engineering Group, Universidad Politécnica de Madrid, Madrid, Spain
nmihindu@fi.upm.es

Abstract. As the social media has redefined how people communicate and contact their networks, the importance once held by interpersonal influence and word-of-mouth has shifted toward electronic word-of-mouth (eWOM). The influence of eWOM is prominent in the tourism industry. In such a context, this study aims to examine the viability of using tourists as ambassadors for promoting tourism in Sri Lanka using social media as the communication medium. For this study, we have created a semantic representation of an Instagram post and analyzed 82,771 public Instagram posts about Sri Lanka from 28,875 distinct users. The findings revealed that as a significant number of tourists use social media to share their experiences in Sri Lanka, the use of social media for destination promotion is a viable and timely choice. Although the Sri Lankan cuisine can be an enticing factor which has the capacity to open new tourism themes, our study unveiled that the promotion of the Sri Lankan cuisine is scarce.

Keywords: Tourism · Social media · Analytics · eWOM · Sri Lanka

1 Introduction

Perception of information as "the lifeblood of tourism" [1] gives ample evidence of the importance of correct, reliable and timely information for the tourism industry. The intangibility of the products related to the tourism industry increases the emphasis given to interpersonal influence and word-of-mouth when tourists make decisions in different stages ranging from planning to consuming [2]. With the exponential growth of the use of social media over the last decade [3,4], its impact is felt on all branches of society including family [5,6], government [7–9], marketing [10,11], *etc.* Many studies have been carried out to assess the opportunities and challenges presented on the tourism industry by the electronic word-of-mouth (eWOM) through social media [12–17].

The tourism industry in Sri Lanka is a crucial component of the island's economy. It is ranked as the third highest foreign exchange earner in the

© Springer Nature Switzerland AG 2018
C. Pautasso et al. (Eds.): ICWE 2018, LNCS 11153, pp. 251–259, 2018.
https://doi.org/10.1007/978-3-030-03056-8_24

country (14.20%) behind the worker remittances (29.20%) and textile industry (19.70%) [18]. In an era where eWOM has become an important medium to promote tourism industry globally, the authors of [19] state that the use of social media in Sri Lanka is still in its infancy.

With the expansion of social media and the understanding of its ability to influence the tourism industry, a number of studies have been published on many themes. Among them, the study of *Zeng and Gerritsen* on the studies carried out on social media in tourism industry is important as it recommends further comprehensive studies along four axes [20]. Namely, (1) community engagement, (2) comprehensive marketing strategies, (3) differentiated destination management, and (4) the legal and ethical issues arising from social media in tourism.

How social media community is engaged in all four stages of product life cycle (*i.e.* design and development, production, utilization, and disposal) is thoroughly explained in [21]. In the conception paper of [14], the authors describe how to use social media as an innovative marketing tool in the tourism industry while maintaining the sense of community belonging.

Tourists have shifted from believing in advertising of advantages and special features of potential destinations to a more personalized and interactive approach of promotion with the increased role played by social media in tourism [14]. This requires comprehensive marketing strategies. Understanding different clusters of social media users related to tourism [22] is of utmost importance in order to provide customized services and products. In the context of Sri Lanka, the lack of these strategies and at times the negative impacts of social media on the tourism industry is clearly portrayed in [19].

Generation of predictive models to reveal new potential touristic sights [23], using contextual information to propose personalized tourism attraction recommendations [24], understanding temporal and demographic tourist flows in order to device local and personalized strategies [25] are some of the efforts taken toward differentiated destination management through the use of social media.

As the moderation of social media posts is in an infant stage, one has to be aware of the fraudulent or misleading users in social media specially when the consumers are more interested in the content generated by the social media users but no so much about the authors of those content [17].

In this backdrop, our goal is to launch a discussion on how to use social media for tourism promotion in Sri Lanka and consequently discover hidden market potentials. We wish to explore the impact along the following two questions.

1. Is it viable to use social media for tourism promotion in Sri Lanka?

   In a setting where Sri Lankans are not considered to be avid social media consumers [19], it is necessary to verify whether the tourists can be employed as ambassadors for promoting tourism in Sri Lanka. Since word-of-mouth as well as electronic word-of-mouth are very important factors of tourist destination selection [12–17], such an approach would be highly effective. With an abundance of social media posts, we may discover useful patterns that could lead into exploitable knowledge that may help stake holders of tourism industry. We may also be able to discover eventual obstacles such as connectivity that limit the capabilities of social media postings.

2. Which tourism themes are consumed?

Tourism does not solely rely on sightseeing. The motivation to visit touristic sights is ranked at the 7th position according to the study of [26]. Discovery of traditional cuisine and exchange between locals can also be important aspects of tourism. Hence, we also want the tourists to perceive typical Sri Lankan experience with respect to culture, food, *etc.* We wish to analyze the social media to see if that is the case and if not, identify which aspects can be improved. Additionally, these aspects possess high market potentials as well.

For the purpose of this study we restrict ourselves only to Instagram as the selected social media among the numerous options possible. This decision was motivated by the type of content shared in Instagram. When we manually analyzed a sample of posts from Facebook, Twitter, and Instagram, the posts from Instagram were mostly related to tourism while the other social media were mixed with current local content related to current affairs. Specially when it comes to food, Instagram contained the most posts among the social media channels analyzed.

2   Semantic Representation of an Instagram Post

In this study, we limit our scope to the Instagram social media platform. For the purpose of analysing, we generate a semantic representation of Instagram posts using the RDF model as illustrated in Fig. 1. For representing the information

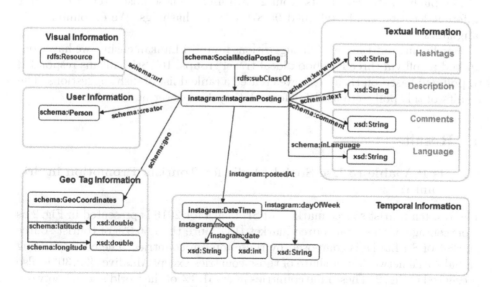

Fig. 1. Semantic representation of an Instagram post

in each post, we use the Schema.org vocabulary and a custom vocabulary for representing Instagram specific information.

An Instagram post contain both textual information such as description, comments and visual information such as the image or the video. The text can be parsed and processed to obtain information such as hashtags and the language. In addition, it contains the timestamp of the post which can be parsed to obtain information about month, day, day of the week, and hour the post was published. Instagram posts are geo-tagged and are associated with the information such as latitude, longitude of the place associated with the post and optionally name and address of the location. Finally, it also contains information about the user who published the post and her public profile information such as description and hometown. The goal of the paper is to use this information to answer the aforementioned questions.

3 Data Collection and Analysis

We restricted ourselves to using Instagram for this initial study due to many reasons. Being crowned as the most popular photo capturing and sharing application [27] and having more than 800 million active users per month [28] are two of the main reasons for our choice. As of March 2016, 98% of fashion brands having an Instagram profile [28] also vouches for its appeal in marketing and product promotion.

The information about the Instagram posts extracted using the *Instagram API*[1] using media search queries. The hashtag "srilanka" and its translations such as russian and japanese were included in the search queries. We analyzed 82,771 public instagram posts from 28,875 users. These posts were from 4,921 different locations and contained 95,876 distinct hashtags. We encountered 65 languages.

For finding out the top dish suggestions from Sri Lankan cusine, we have conducted a poll via three Facebook local travel groups. 167 Sri Lankans responded to poll and based on their votes we created a ranked list of dish suggestions. The results of this poll were used for formulating the answer in Sect. 4.2.

4 Results

4.1 Is It Viable to Use Social Media for Tourism Promotion in Sri Lanka?

The top ten tourist source markets of Sri Lanka for 2016 is presented in Fig. 2 as a percentage of the total source market [18]. More than 66.9% of tourist source market of Sri Lanka is composed by these top ten countries. The corresponding global social network user share of those countries except Maldives [29,30] is also presented in Fig. 2. These nine countries make 51.3% of the world's social network

---

[1] https://www.instagram.com/developer/.

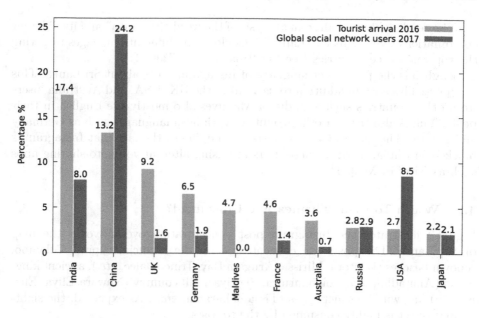

Fig. 2. Top ten tourist source markets of Sri Lanka for 2016 as a percentage of the total tourist market [18] and their corresponding social network user percentage partitioning for 2017 [29,30]. The number of social network users of Maldives could not be found.

user community. We observe a moderately positive correlation coefficient of 0.55 between the tourist source markets of Sri Lanka and the corresponding global social network user share.

If the tourists from those countries make a representative sample of their social network user population, it is indeed viable to use social media for tourism promotion in Sri Lanka with the aim of employing tourists as ambassadors for promoting tourism.

Table 1. Number of occurrences of hashtags concerning Sri Lanka in different languages.

Language	Country	Tag	Occurrence %
Hindi, Bengali, Telugu, Marati, Tamil	India	hi, bn, te, mr, ta	2.82
Chinese	China	ch	00.83
English	UK, German, France, Australia, USA	en	57.93
Dhivehi, Maldivian	Maldives	dv	00.55
Russian	Russia	ru	4.46
Japanese	Japan	jp	1.73

The results obtained after an analysis of the word "SriLanka" and its different combinations ("Sri_Lanka", "Lanka", "Ceylon") in different languages targeting the top ten source countries (see Fig. 2) is given in Table 1.

English is the prominent language of Instagram posts about Sri Lanka. This is expected because in addition to users from the UK, USA, and Australia, users from other countries such as India or Maldives also mostly use English in their posts. This is also true for other countries with latin languages such as Germany and France. The lack of Chinese posts can be due to the fact that Instagram is blocked in China. Most Chinese users are using alternative photo-sharing apps such as Nice[2] or Meipai[3].

4.2   Which Tourism Themes Are Consumed?

Figure 3 illustrates the Instagram post concentration overlaid over the map of Sri Lanka. The posts are concentrated on the financial capital Colombo, renown beaches (Bentota, Mirissa, Arugam Bay, Trincomalee, *etc.*), ancient kingdoms (Anuradhapura, Polonnaruwa, Sigiriya), hill country (Nuwara Eliya, Ella, Kandy) and wildlife sanctuaries (Tissamaharama, *etc.*). As expected, the sightseeing aspect is highly consumed by the tourists.

Among the top ten tourist source markets (see Fig. 2), the Sri Lankan cuisine is very different from those of eight countries excluding India and Maldives. As food related postings are among the top five categories of Instagram posts [27],

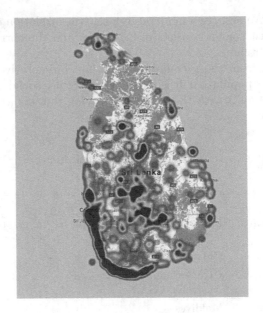

Fig. 3. A heatmap of Instagram posts about Sri Lanka

---

[2] http://www.oneniceapp.com.
[3] http://www.meipai.com/en.

one could expect to find a similar or more pronounced pattern in the postings of the tourists. After finding out the top dish suggestions for tourists as described in Sect. 3, we looked for the number hashtag occurrences of those dishes in our dataset. This number is only 0.33% of the total postings which implies either the tourists did not use the correct names of the dishes or that the actual number of photos containing food items is not that significant.

Relaxing the search criteria, we also included "food", "foods", "spices", "curry", "curries" as hashtags in the query along with the names of the top dishes. Then the number of relative occurrences increased up to 2.47%. This number can still be considered as insignificant compared to the total number of posts concerning Sri Lanka. Consequently, we could assume that tourists do not often post their interactions with Sri Lankan cuisine.

5   Conclusions and Future Work

With a moderately positive correlation coefficient between the top ten source markets and their corresponding global social network user share, we have demonstrated that using tourists' electronic word-of-mouth for destination promotion in Sri Lanka is a viable option. However, as the Instagram platform does not appear to be the correct social media for the Chinese source market, further investigation should be carried out in order to find the correct platform for them.

Through this study, we have also given empirical evidence that although the tourists highly consume the sightseeing aspect, they may not consume other aspects of tourism such as enjoying the Sri Lankan cuisine. This opens up further dialog on how to promote Sri Lankan cuisine among tourists and the related business opportunities.

Currently, we have performed the analysis on a limited number of Instagram posts and in the future, we not only plan to analyze a large volume of posts collected over a longer period of time but also include other popular social media platforms such as Twitter and Facebook.

At the moment, we only perform minimal natural language processing on the textual content for parsing hastags, language detection, *etc.* In the future, we plan to automatically analyze textual content using more advanced natural language processing techniques. Furthermore, we plan to analyze the images using image processing and machine learning techniques for example to estimate if a photo was taken during the daytime or at night, or identify the objects in a photo.

References

1. Buhalis, D.: Strategic use of information technologies in the tourism industry. Tour. Manag. **19**(5), 409–421 (1998)
2. Litvin, S.W., Goldsmith, R.E., Pan, B.: Electronic word-of-mouth in hospitality and tourism management. Tour. Manag. **29**(3), 458–468 (2008)

3. Kaplan, A.M., Haenlein, M.: Users of the world, unite! The challenges and opportunities of social media. Bus Horiz. **53**(1), 59–68 (2010)
4. Perrin, A.: Social media usage. Pew research center (2015)
5. O'Keeffe, G.S., Clarke-Pearson, K., et al.: The impact of social media on children, adolescents, and families. Pediatrics **127**(4), 800–804 (2011)
6. Cookingham, L.M., Ryan, G.L.: The impact of social media on the sexual and social wellness of adolescents. J. Pediatr. Adolesc. Gynecol. **28**(1), 2–5 (2015)
7. Ali, A.H.: The power of social media in developing nations: new tools for closing the global digital divide and beyond. Harv. Hum. Rts. J. **24**, 185 (2011)
8. Bertot, J.C., Jaeger, P.T., Hansen, D.: The impact of polices on government social media usage: issues, challenges, and recommendations. Gov. Inform. Q. **29**(1), 30–40 (2012)
9. Panagiotopoulos, P., Bigdeli, A.Z., Sams, S.: Citizen-government collaboration on social media: the case of Twitter in the 2011 riots in England. Gov. Inform. Q. **31**(3), 349–357 (2014)
10. De Vries, L., Gensler, S., Leeflang, P.S.: Popularity of brand posts on brand fan pages: an investigation of the effects of social media marketing. J. Interact. Mark. **26**(2), 83–91 (2012)
11. Felix, R., Rauschnabel, P.A., Hinsch, C.: Elements of strategic social media marketing: a holistic framework. J. Bus. Res. **70**, 118–126 (2017)
12. Bizirgianni, I., Dionysopoulou, P.: The influence of tourist trends of youth tourism through social media (SM) & information and communication technologies (ICTs). Procedia Soc. Behav. Sci. **73**, 652–660 (2013)
13. Sotiriadis, M.D., Van Zyl, C.: Electronic word-of-mouth and online reviews in tourism services: the use of Twitter by tourists. Electron. Commer. Res. **13**(1), 103–124 (2013)
14. Kavoura, A., Stavrianea, A.: Economic and social aspects from social media's implementation as a strategic innovative marketing tool in the tourism industry. Procedia Econ. Financ. **14**, 303–312 (2014)
15. Királ'ová, A., Pavlíčeka, A.: Development of social media strategies in tourism destination. Procedia Soc. Behav. Sci. **175**, 358–366 (2015)
16. Luo, Q., Zhong, D.: Using social network analysis to explain communication characteristics of travel-related electronic word-of-mouth on social networking sites. Tour. Manag. **46**, 274–282 (2015)
17. Narangajavana, Y., Fiol, L.J.C., Tena, M.Á.M., Artola, R.M.R., García, J.S.: The influence of social media in creating expectations. An empirical study for a tourist destination. Ann. Tour. Res. **65**, 60–70 (2017)
18. Sri Lanka Tourism Development Authority: Annual statistical report 2016. Technical report, Sri Lanka Tourism Development Authority (2016)
19. Sabraz Nawaz, S., Mubarak, K.M.: Adoption of social media marketing by tourism product suppliers: a study in eastern province of Sri Lanka. Eur. J. Bus. Manag. **7**(7), 448–455 (2015)
20. Zeng, B., Gerritsen, R.: What do we know about social media in tourism? A review. Tour. Manag. Perspect. **10**, 27–36 (2014)
21. Fan, W., Gordon, M.D.: The power of social media analytics. Commun. ACM **57**(6), 74–81 (2014)
22. Amaro, S., Duarte, P., Henriques, C.: Travelers use of social media: a clustering approach. Ann. Tour. Res. **59**, 1–15 (2016)
23. Mukhina, K.D., Rakitin, S.V., Visheratin, A.A.: Detection of tourists attraction points using Instagram profiles. Procedia Comput. Sci. **108**, 2378–2382 (2017)

24. Jiang, K., Yin, H., Wang, P., Yu, N.: Learning from contextual information of geo-tagged web photos to rank personalized tourism attractions. Neurocomputing **119**, 17–25 (2013)
25. Chua, A., Servillo, L., Marcheggiani, E., Moere, A.V.: Mapping cilento: using geo-tagged social media data to characterize tourist flows in southern Italy. Tour. Manag. **57**, 295–310 (2016)
26. Kozak, M., Rimmington, M.: Measuring tourist destination competitiveness: conceptual considerations and empirical findings1. Int. J. Hosp. Manag. **18**(3), 273–283 (1999)
27. Hu, Y., Manikonda, L., Kambhampati, S., et al.: What we Instagram: a first analysis of Instagram photo content and user types. In: ICWSM (2014)
28. Statista: Number of monthly active Instagram users from January 2013 to September 2017 (in millions)
29. Statista: Number of social network users in selected countries in 2017 and 2022 (in millions)
30. Statista: Number of social network users in Australia from 2015 to 2022 (in millions)

Building an Ecosystem for the Tyrolean Tourism Knowledge Graph

Elias Kärle[✉][iD], Umutcan Şimşek[iD], Oleksandra Panasiuk, and Dieter Fensel

Semantic Technology Institute, Universität Innsbruck,
Technikerstrasse 21a, 6020 Innsbruck, Austria
{elias.kaerle,umutcan.simsek,oleksandra.panasiuk,dieter.fensel}@sti2.at

Abstract. The introduction of the schema.org vocabulary was a big step towards making websites machine read- and understandable. Due to schema.org's RDF-like nature storing annotations in a graph database is easy and efficient. In this paper the authors show how they gather touristic data in the Austrian region of Tirol and provide this data publicly in a knowledge graph. The definition of subsets of the vocabulary is followed by providing means to map data sources efficiently to schema.org and then store the annotated content into the graph. To showcase the consumption of the touristic data four scenarios are described which use the knowledge graph for real life applications and data analysis.

Keywords: eTourism · Semantic web · Knowledge graph · schema.org

1 Introduction

The term knowledge graph has been coined by Google in 2012[1]. There is no formal definition for the term, however based on several definition attempts we consider knowledge graphs as "a knowledge base in graph form that mostly contains real-world entities and their relationships". Having the "knowledge" in graph form presents many advantages over relational data storage such as scalable growth, due to the lack of data and schema distinction. From an implementation point of view, standards and tools from the semantic web stack (e.g. RDF, SPARQL, Triple Stores) can be utilized, which accelerates the knowledge graph construction and consumption by automated agents like Intelligent Personal Assistants (IPAs). Tourism is a major economic sector in Tirol, generating around 20% of GDP in the region[2]. The Tyrolean tourism sector has been going through a extensive digitalization movement in the recent years. This movement includes making the valuable data hidden behind the walls of proprietary systems available on the web for automated agents like dialogue systems and

---

[1] https://googleblog.blogspot.co.at/2012/05/introducing-knowledge-graph-things-not.html.

[2] https://presse.tirol.at/de/daten-zahlen-zum-tourismus-in-tirol/pr335467.

C. Pautasso et al. (Eds.): ICWE 2018, LNCS 11153, pp. 260–267, 2018.
https://doi.org/10.1007/978-3-030-03056-8_25

intelligent personal assistants. Given the aforementioned factors, the most scalable way to achieve this is to enrich the data semantically and publish it on the web to facilitate the creation of a knowledge graph.

In this paper, we present the ecosystem we have been building for the creation of a Tyrolean Knowledge Graph that contributes to the digitalization of tourism in the region. We explain how we help various parties in the tourism sector publishing semantically annotated data with schema.org[3] and how we transfer the collected data into a knowledge graph. Additionally, we demonstrate various consumption scenarios for our knowledge graph.

The remainder of the paper is structured as follows: Sect. 2 gives an overview to the existing knowledge graphs and explains our motivation. Section 3 shows how we construct the knowledge graph and awaiting challenges. Section 4 presents various scenarios where the knowledge graph can be utilized. Section 5 concludes the paper with a summary and an outlook.

2 Related Work and Motivation

Following the semantic web [2] and linked data [3] research, many open knowledge graphs have been published. The initial prominent efforts aimed to cover as many domains as possible, therefore used Wikipedia as a source to construct the knowledge graphs. The DBPedia and YAGO knowledge graphs uses the infoboxes and categories in the Wikipedia website to extract triples. While Wikidata [16] follows a more collaborative approach and benefit from both bot and human contributions and focus on the provenance of the data. The NELL [17] project aims to extract triples from unstructured text by crawling the web. As for the tourism domain, the closest work to ours is the 3cixty [15] project. The project aims to create knowledge graphs for smart city applications. They use an ontology that heavily reuses schema.org to describe their data.

The Tyrolean Tourism Knowledge Graph contains static (e.g. phone number, address) and dynamic (e.g. accommodation offers) data based on schema.org annotations collected from different sources such as Destination Management Organizations (DMO) and Geographical Information Systems (GIS). In our previous work [1], we explained how we annotated the relevant data in the region with schema.org from different sources. Our knowledge graph consolidates these annotations and enables intelligent applications like chatbots to contribute the digitalization of tourism in Tyrol. Additionally, since we store the historical data, the knowledge graph allows data analytics to provide insights from the region.

3 Feeding the Graph

The quality of a knowledge graph is highly dependent on the data it contains. To build a sustainable, high quality tourism knowledge graph, reliable data sources have to be identified. The best source of frequently updated touristic data is

---

[3] https://schema.org/.

of course a hotel website. But an analysis of the distribution of schema.org amongst hotels [4] showed, that the current state of schema.org in tourism and especially in the accommodation business has too little adoption to be used as a data source. Yet, due to its growing uptake, driven by the big search engine providers, we still decided to work with schema.org, and to first extend the schema.org vocabulary for the accommodation sector [7] (released as part of schema.org 3.1[4]) and then fostering the distribution of schema.org in the whole tourism sector. Only having touristic websites annotated with schema.org would ensure the repeatability of the data aggregation process in the long run and at the same time help the touristic websites make their content more visible by implicitly applying semantic search engine optimization.

To simplify and unify the annotation process we started by defining sets of vocabularies for specific domains. The idea of the resulting domain specifications (DS) was first published in [14] and later applied to tourism in [9]. The DS are subsets of the schema.org vocabulary, each associated with required and optional properties. They provide the recommended patterns for annotating different touristic domains such as hotels, restaurants, ski schools and others and define the model of the structured data on the web. The domain specification can be consider as schema.org design patterns.

Instead of annotating the actual accommodation websites one by one we approached different Tyrolean destination management organizations (DMOs) and their IT service providers. For accommodation data, data about the regional events and infrastructure we worked with Feratel[5], a full stack touristic IT service provider, and Infomax[6]. For geodata we cooperated with General Solutions, a company specialized on visualizing geospatial information on web maps[7]. A generic source for touristic data we annotated was Outdooractive[8] and besides that also data about ski schools and ski lessons, provided by the company Waldhart Software[9]. Information not yet covered by the mentioned data sources was collected and annotated from the DMO's website directly.

For the annotation of web content we had to make a distinction between three different types of data. Static data is information about the core data of a business, like its address or a description. Dynamic data describes things like availabilities and prices and frequently changes. Active data describes software interfaces to interact with, like for example a booking API. The DS are sufficient for the manual annotation of static data. For dynamic data this is not an option. We decided to build wrapper software to allow automatic annotation. A wrapper defines different mappings from a data source to schema.org. Then the wrapper software reads the source, maps the data and stores the resulting file. To see the DS and the wrapper software in action we implemented these features in

---

[4] http://schema.org/docs/releases.html#v3.1.
[5] http://www.feratel.com/.
[6] https://www.infomax.de.
[7] https://general-solutions.eu/.
[8] https://www.outdooractive.com/.
[9] https://www.waldhart.at/.

semantify.it, a SaaS platform for creation, validation and distribution of semantic annotations. This platform stores the annotations as individual JSON-LD files in a MongoDB collection for more convenient publication on web pages. A detailed description of the semantify.it platform was published in [8]. Data sources we applied those wrappers to are, as mentioned above, Feratel, General Solutions, Infomax and Outdooractive. The wrapper made for General Solutions was also published in [10].

With that tools at hand we could start rolling out annotations into tourism. To have a maximum impact we approached different destination management organizations (DMOs) and applied our annotation process to their comprehensive websites. The results was the complete annotation of a DMO's static data and can be found in [1]. To ensure the quality of the annotations we also enhanced the DS to apply rules to touristic domains. Trough that extension a validator described in [14] can not only check the syntactic, but also the semantic correctness of annotations.

While with the mentioned solutions the annotation of static data was straight forward, the annotation of dynamic data raised some problems. Accommodation businesses, for example, offer several rooms, with different pricing- and catering options with different occupancy possibilities, being charge at changing rates at different seasons over the year, and on top with flexible stay durations. The result is a vast amount of booking options which goes, if expressed in schema.org annotations, into annotation file sizes of megabytes. To avoid this materialization of booking possibilities we developed the idea of publication heuristics to enable a representation of offers in schema.org for a website [6].

Finally, we needed to annotate the active data to allow bookings and purchases of touristic products and services by automated agents or third party software applications. Therefore we developed a way to annotated web APIs with the schema.org vocabulary and hence represent them as lightweight semantic web services [12]. The resulting "action wrapper" was applied to the internet booking engine software providers Easybooking, Feratel and Kognitiv. Both, the publication heuristics and the action wrapper were implemented as parts of the semantify.it platform.

To fill the knowledge graph with the curated data we replicated the data stored in semantify.it into the graph and added crawled schema.org annotations of already annotated touristic websites on the fly. For the replication process we tested two approaches. One used Java, taking the intermediate step of translating the data from JSON-LD to RDF and only then writing it into the graph. The other approach, which proofed to be the more efficient one, writes JSON-LD directly into the graph. Both approaches were using basic cleaning and identification measures on the data, where for example every website's crawl was stored in an explicit named graph for later reuse of legacy data for reasoning purposes. Later, more advanced data polishing measures will include the removal of duplicates, consolidation of entities and enrichment of data sets by adding information form trusted other sources.

We perform daily data migrations from semantify.it to the knowledge graph since December 2017. To build the knowledge graph, we use GraphDB[10], a product by Ontotext. Our knowledge graph currently contains 1.5 Billion statements of which 800 Million are explicit and 700 Million are inferred[11].

An overview of the knowledge graph creation life cycle according to our survey can be found in Fig. 1.

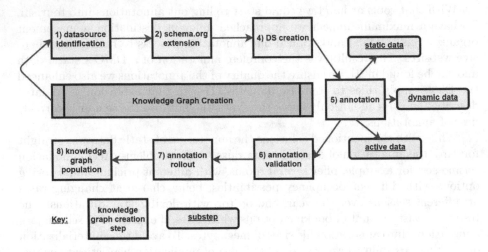

Fig. 1. The eight steps to create the Tirolean Tourism Knowledge Graph.

4   Use Case

The touristic data stored in the knowledge graph is reachable via a SPARQL interface[12] and open to everyone. For the purpose of demonstration and experimentation we applied four different use case scenarios on the graph's data.

4.1   Conversational Assistants

To demonstrate how the annotations, stored in knowledge graph, can be interpreted in a way accessible for users, we developed the conversation tourism assistant [11]. This agent extracts the core information items from the user's questions and maps them to schema.org types and properties. As dialog interface we used Google's Dialogflow[13] and develop the web service to discover requested information from the knowledge graph through SPARQL queries. The result is a fully functional chatbot-like assistant system on top of our GraphDB database.

---

[10] http://graphdb.ontotext.com/.
[11] April 2018 numbers.
[12] http://graphdb.sti2.at:8080/sparql.
[13] https://dialogflow.com.

Deployed to Amazon's Alexa for example it is possible to ask things like "Alexa, I want to do hiking in the region around Seefeld". The request is understood by Dialogflow and then forwarded to our web hook which does the mapping and the data retrieval from the graph.

Additional to the question answering type of application like mentioned above, active data annotations can enable conversational agents to complete tasks like booking a room without having coupled APIs [13]. We demonstrate how a dialogue system can process the semantic API descriptions to guide a dialogue to book a room through an annotated IBE in the next use case.

4.2 Active Data Consumption

As a show case for the use of active data we built an API layer on top of the knowledge graph[14]. This layer defines an entry point in form of a schema:SerachAction which points to the search API we provide. The response is a list of schema:Offers where the concrete manifestation depends on the type of search request. Every offer has another schema:Action attached which points to the action providers IBE. Trough that our graph acts like a broker between a user and the action provider where the business action is executed on the provider's side. Together with the action wrapper mentioned above, this allows the concept of "automatic direct booking" of hotel offers, which was published in [5]. The hotel data in the graph, together with the annotated booking APIs of Easybooking and Feratel becomes directly bookable trough the annotations pointing towards the hotel's own booking API.

4.3 Data Analysis

We store historical data in our knowledge graph as named graphs. This allows us to apply insightful analytics on the data. An example analysis is shown in Fig. 2. We analyzed the changes in average minimum and maximum accommodation prices per person per night in the regions of Mayrhofen and Seefeld between

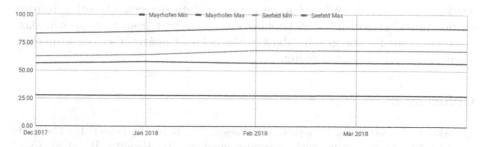

Fig. 2. Average minimum and maximum accommodation prices per person per night in Mayrhofen and Seefeld

---

[14] https://actions.semantify.it/api-docs/.

December 2017 and April 2018, based on the offer annotations we collected from the DMOs. The analysis shows that the prices in general are higher in Seefeld than Mayrhofen. There are no significant price fluctuations in Mayrhofen between different months. In Seefeld accommodation prices are visibly higher in February in comparison to other months.

5   Conclusion and Outlook

In this paper, we made a survey of our recent effort for building the Tirol Tourism Knowledge Graph from scratch. Starting with the definitions of schema.org subsets, we show how we then mapped touristic data sources and web APIs to schema.org and we present the idea of a publication heuristics for dynamic data. Finally we show four use cases where data from the knowledge graph is used by two different types of dialog systems, an eCommerce application and for statistical analysis over a time series of price development.

There are several learnings that can be taken from the survey we presented here. As already mentioned, the quality of a knowledge graph is highly depended on the quality of the data it contains. But the collection of touristic data frequently comes with lots of erroneous annotations. Importing the data from different source requires redundancies to be handled, hence a lot of data preprocessing before using the data. What we also learned is that the redundant storage of historical data in subgraphs makes sense for analysis of developments in tourism. Besides that, we learned that there are loads of use cases for knowledge graphs in tourism, most of which were not implemented in the course of that work but look promising.

Limitations of our approach are for example our method of mapping data sources to schema.org. Every source needs a own wrapper to be defined which is hardly scalable. The crawling of annotated content on websites is still very error-prone. But we are currently working on a more reliable crawler which performs validation and preprocessing by the time annotations are found, to improve data quality.

More future developments will improve data consolidation techniques when writing to the graph and add more incoming data sources, like other tourism service providers and internet booking engines. Apart from that we will show more use cases for the graph's data in the fields of assistant systems, machine learning and advanced reasoning.

References

1. Akbar, Z., Kärle, E., Panasiuk, O., Şimşek, U., Toma, I., Fensel, D.: Complete semantics to empower touristic service providers. In: Panetto, H., et al. (eds.) OTM 2017. LNCS, vol. 10574, pp. 353–370. Springer, Cham (2017). https://doi.org/10.1007/978-3-319-69459-7_24
2. Berners-Lee, T., Hendler, J., Lassila, O.: The semantic web. Sci. Am. **284**(5), 34–43 (2001)

3. Bizer, C., Heath, T., Berners-Lee, T.: Linked data - the story so far. Int. J. Semant. Web Inf. Syst. **5**(3), 1–22 (2009)

4. Kärle, E., Fensel, A., Toma, I., Fensel, D.: Why are there more hotels in Tyrol than in Austria? Analyzing schema.org usage in the hotel domain. In: Inversini, A., Schegg, R. (eds.) Information and Communication Technologies in Tourism 2016, pp. 99–112. Springer, Cham (2016). https://doi.org/10.1007/978-3-319-28231-2_8

5. Kärle, E., Fensel, D.: Annotation-based automatic action processing. In: Proceedings of the ISWC 2017 Posters & Demonstrations and Industry Tracks co-located with 16th International Semantic Web Conference (ISWC 2017), 23–25 October 2017, Vienna, Austria (2017)

6. Kärle, E., Fensel, D.: Heuristics for publishing dynamic content as structured data with schema.org. (2018, to appear)

7. Kärle, E., Simsek, U., Akbar, Z., Hepp, M., Fensel, D.: Extending the schema.org vocabulary for more expressive accommodation annotations. In: Schegg, R., Stangl, B. (eds.) Information and Communication Technologies in Tourism 2017, pp. 31–41. Springer, Cham (2017). https://doi.org/10.1007/978-3-319-51168-9_3

8. Kärle, E., Şimşek, U., Fensel, D.: semantify.it, a platform for creation, publication and distribution of semantic annotations. In: SEMAPRO 2017: The Eleventh International Conference on Advances in Semantic Processing, pp. 22–30. Curran Associates, Inc., New York, June 2017. http://arxiv.org/abs/1706.10067

9. Panasiuk, O., Kärle, E., Şimşek, U., Fensel, D.: Defining tourism domains for semantic annotation of web content. e-Rev. Tour. Res. **9** (2018). Research Notes from the ENTER 2018 Conference on ICT in Tourism

10. Panasiuk, O., Akbar, Z., Gerrier, T., Fensel, D.: Representing geodata for tourism with schema.org. In: Proceedings of the 4th International Conference on Geographical Information Systems Theory, Applications and Management - Volume 1: GISTAM, pp. 239–246. INSTICC, SciTePress (2018)

11. Panasiuk, O., Akbar, Z., Şimşek, U., Fensel, D.: Enabling conversational tourism assistants through schema.org mapping. In: Gangemi, A., et al. (eds.) ESWC 2018. LNCS, vol. 11155, pp. 137–141. Springer, Cham (2018). https://doi.org/10.1007/978-3-319-98192-5_26

12. Şimşek, U., Kärle, E., Fensel, D.: Machine readable web APIs with schema.org action annotations (2018, to appear)

13. Şimşek, U., Fensel, D.: Now we are talking! Flexible and open goal-oriented dialogue systems for accessing touristic services. e-Rev. Tour. Res. **9** (2018). Research Notes from the ENTER 2018 Conference on ICT in Tourism

14. Şimşek, U., Kärle, E., Holzknecht, O., Fensel, D.: Domain specific semantic validation of schema.org annotations. In: Petrenko, A.K., Voronkov, A. (eds.) PSI 2017. LNCS, vol. 10742, pp. 417–429. Springer, Cham (2018). https://doi.org/10.1007/978-3-319-74313-4_31

15. Troncy, R., et al.: 3cixty: building comprehensive knowledge bases for city exploration. Web Semant. Sci. Serv. Agents World Wide Web **46–47**, 2–13 (2017)

16. Vrandecic, D., Kroetzsch, M.: Wikidata: a free collaborative knowledge base. Commun. ACM **57**, 78–85 (2014)

17. Zimmermann, A., Gravier, C., Subercaze, J., Cruzille, Q.: Nell2RDF: read the web, and turn it into RDF. In: KNOW@ LOD, pp. 2–8 (2013)

Knowledge Base Evolution Analysis: A Case Study in the Tourism Domain

Mohammad Rashid[1]([envelope]), Giuseppe Rizzo[2], Marco Torchiano[1],
Nandana Mihindukulasooriya[3], and Oscar Corcho[3]

[1] Politecnico di Torino, Turin, Italy
{mohammad.rashid,marco.torchiano}@polito.it
[2] Instituto Superiore Mario Boella, Turin, Italy
giuseppe.rizzo@ismb.it
[3] Universidad Politécnica de Madrid, Madrid, Spain
{nmihindu,ocorcho}@fi.upm.es

Abstract. Stakeholders – curator, consumer, etc. – in the tourism domain routinely need to combine and compare statistical indicators about tourism. In this context, various Knowledge Bases (KBs) have been designed and developed in the Linked Open Data (LOD) cloud in order to support decision-making process in Tourism domain. Such KBs evolve over time: their data (instances) and schemes can be updated, extended, revised and refactored. However, unlike in more controlled types of knowledge bases, the evolution of KBs exposed in the LOD cloud is usually unrestrained, what may cause data to suffer from a variety of issues. This paper attempts to address the impact of KB evolution in tourism domain by showing how entity evolves over time using the 3cixty KB. We show that using multiple versions of the KB through time can help to understand inconsistency in the data collection process.

Keywords: Knowledge Base · Linked Data · Evolution analysis

1 Introduction

In the recent years much efforts have been given towards sharing Knowledge Bases (KBs) in the Linked Open Data (LOD) cloud[1]. Large KBs in the tourism domain are often maintained by organizations that act as curators to ensure their quality [9]. These KBs naturally evolve due to several causes: *(i)* resource representations and links that are created, updated, and removed; *(ii)* the entire graph can change or disappear. In general, KBs in the tourism domain are highly complex and dynamic in nature. For example, decision-makers in the tourism domain often rely on forecasting models to predict future requirements or on decision support systems to analyze stakeholders demands [9]. Whilst most datasets are published as open data, the data publishers continuously try to improve the quality of their data by updating ontologies and data instances or removing obsolete

---

[1] http://lod-cloud.net.

© Springer Nature Switzerland AG 2018
C. Pautasso et al. (Eds.): ICWE 2018, LNCS 11153, pp. 268–278, 2018.
https://doi.org/10.1007/978-3-030-03056-8_26

ones. However, unlike in more controlled types of knowledge bases, the evolution of KBs in the tourism domain may suffer from a variety of issues, both at a semantic level and at a pragmatic level (ambiguity, inaccuracies). This situation clearly affects negatively data stakeholders such as consumers, curators.

Taking into consideration a KB, we believe that understanding this evolution could help to define more suitable strategies for data sources integration, enrichment, and maintenance. One of the common tasks for KB evolution analysis is to perform a detailed data analysis, with data profiling. Data profiling is usually defined as the process of examining data to collect statistics and provide relevant metadata [1]. Based on data profiling we can thoroughly examine and understand a KB, its structure, and its properties before usage.

In this paper, we explored the impact of KB evolution in the tourism domain using the 3cixty KB [10]. The core idea in this work is to use dynamic features from data profiling results for analyzing the evolution of KBs. The main contributions of this work are: (1) a fundamental overview about the topic of KB evolution analysis; and (2) the presentation of the 3cixty KB as a use case to understand the impact of KB resource evolution. Furthermore, we used two entity types to explore the stability characteristics to identify any inconsistency present in the data extraction process. In this context, we created a set of APIs[2] for periodic snapshots generation and maintaining scheduled tasks for automatic and timely checks. We explored KB evolution analysis with *lode:Event*[3] and *dul:Places*[4] entity-type in the 3cixty KB, reporting the benefits of KB evolution analysis. These two entity types are the most common according to the total number of entities.

We continue by describing the details of our use case in Sect. 2, then we provide technical details about the KB evolution analysis in Sect. 3 and Stability characteristics in Sect. 4. Section 5 presents an experimental analysis. We outline the related works in Sect. 6 and conclude in Sect. 7.

2   Use Case: The 3cixty KB

3cixty is a knowledge base that describes cultural and tourist information. This knowledge base was initially developed within the 3cixty project[5], which aimed to develop a semantic web platform to build real-world and comprehensive knowledge bases in the domain of culture and tourism for a few cities. The entire approach has been tested first in the occasion of the Expo Milano 2015 [8], where a specific knowledge base for the city of Milan was developed, and has now been refined with the development of knowledge bases for the cities of Nice, London, Singapore, and Madeira island. They contain descriptions of events, places (sights and businesses), transportation facilities and social activities, collected

---

[2] The source code is available at https://github.com/rifat963/KBDataObservatory.
[3] http://linkedevents.org/ontology/Event.
[4] http://www.ontologydesignpatterns.org/ont/dul/DUL.owl.
[5] https://www.3cixty.com.

from numerous static, near- and real-time local and global data providers, including Expo Milano 2015 official services in the case of Milan, and numerous social media platforms. The generation of each city-driven 3cixty KB follows a strict data integration pipeline, that ranges from the definition of the data model, the selection of the primary sources used to populate the knowledge base, till the data reconciliation used for generating the final stream of cleaned data that is then presented to the users via multi-platform user interfaces. The quality of the data is today enforced through a continuous integration system that only verifies the integrity of the data semantics [10].

3   Knowledge Base Evolution Analysis

The evolution of a KB can be analyzed using fine-grained "change" detection at low-level or using "dynamics" of a dataset[6] at high-level. Fine-grained changes of KB sources are analyzed with regard to their sets of triples, set of entities, or schema signatures [5]. For example, fine-grained analysis at the triple level between two snapshots of a KB can detect which triples from the previous snapshots have been preserved in the later snapshots. Furthermore, it can detect which triples have been deleted, or which ones have been added. On the other hand, the dynamic feature of a dataset gives insights into how it behaves and evolves over a certain period [5]. Ellefi *et al.* [1] explored the dynamic features considering the use cases presented by Käfer *et al.* [2].

KB evolution analysis using dynamic feature help to understand the changes applied to an entire KB or parts of it. It has multiple dimensions regarding the dataset update behavior, such as frequency of change, changes pattern, changes impact and causes of change. More specifically, using dynamicity of a dataset, we can capture those changes that happen often; or changes that the curator wants to highlight because they are useful or interesting for a specific domain or application; or changes that indicate an abnormal situation or type of evolution [5,6]. The kind of evolution that a KB is subjected to depends on several factors such as:

- *Frequency of update:* KBs can be updated almost continuously (e.g. daily or weekly) or at long intervals (e.g. yearly);
- *Domain area:* depending on the specific domain, updates can be minor or substantial. For instance, social data is likely to be subject to wide fluctuations than encyclopedic data, which are likely to undergo smaller knowledge increments;
- *Data acquisition:* the process used to acquire the data to be stored in the KB and the characteristics of the sources may influence the evolution; for instance, updates on individual resources cause minor changes when compared to a complete reorganization of a data source infrastructure such as a change of the domain name;

---

[6] https://www.w3.org/wiki/DatasetDynamics.

– *Link between data sources:* when multiple sources are used for building a KB, the alignment and compatibility of such sources affect the overall KB evolution. The differences of KBs have been proved to play a crucial role in various curation tasks such as the synchronization of autonomously developed KB versions, or the visualization of the evolution history of a KB [6] for more user-friendly change management.

Taking into account above mentioned factors, the benefit of KB evolution analysis can be two-fold [3]: (1) quality control and maintenance; and (2) data exploitation. Considering quality control and maintenance, KB evolution can help to identify common issues such as broken links or URI changes that create inconsistencies in the dataset. On the other hand, data exploitation can provide valuable insights regarding dynamics of the data, domains, and the communities that explore operational aspects of evolution analysis [3].

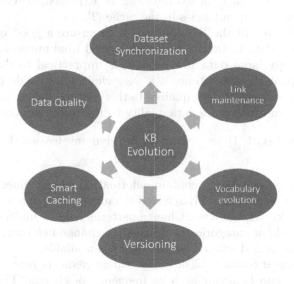

Fig. 1. Use cases of Knowledge Base evolution analysis.

Figure 1 illustrates common use cases [2] of knowledge base evolution using dynamic features. The use cases are explained in detail below.

– *Dataset Synchronization:* In any KB, large quantity of data need to be replicated and maintained at external sources. Furthermore, these data sources need to be in periodic synchronization with the original data sources [2].
– *Link maintenance:* In KB, data are made of statements that link between resources. Due to KB updates, often resources are erroneously removed or change semantics, without taking necessary steps to update their dependents resources. This creates the need to take appropriate action for link maintenance.

- *Vocabulary evolution:* Ontologies, vocabularies, and data schemata in a KB are often inconsistent and lack metadata information. Mihindukulasooriya *et al.* [4] present an empirical study of ontology evolution and data quality. They explicitly pointed out that changes in the ontology depend on the development process and on the community involved in the creation of the knowledge base. Furthermore, they also pointed the drawbacks of finding practical guidelines and best practices for ontology evolution.
- *Versioning:* It is relevant for ontologies, vocabularies, and data schemata in a KB, whose semantics may change over time to reflect usage [2]. Within this context, KB evolution analysis can show how changes propagate and help to design a stable versioning methodology.
- *Smart Cashing:* Query optimization and live querying approaches need a smart cashing approach for dereferencing and sources discovery. KB evolution analysis can help to identify which sources can be cached to save time and resources, how long cached data can be expected to remain valid, and whether there are dependencies in the cache [2].
- *Data Quality:* One of the key use case is to ensure a good quality of data in a KB. Since data instances are often derived from autonomous, evolving, and increasingly large data providers, it is impractical to do manual data curation, and at the same time, it is very challenging to do the continuous automatic assessment of data quality. In this context, using the KB evolution analysis, we can explore the data quality issues in tourism domain.

Based on Ellefi *et al.* [1], we present the key dynamic features for KB evolution analysis.

- *Lifespan*: knowledge bases contain information about different real-world objects or concepts commonly referred as entities. Lifespan measures change patterns of a knowledge base. Change patterns help to understand the existence and kinds of categories of updates or change behavior. Also, lifespan represents the period when a certain entity is available.
- *Update history*: it contains basic measurement elements regarding the knowledge base update behavior such as frequency of change. The frequency of change measures the update frequency of KB resources. For example, the instance count of an entity type for various versions.
- *Stability*: it helps to understand to what extent the performed update impacts the overall state of the knowledge base. Furthermore, the degree of changes helps to understand what are the causes for change triggers as well as the propagation effects.

4   Stability Characteristic

On the basis of the dynamic feature [1], a further conjecture poses that the growth of the knowledge in a mature KB ought to be stable. We define this KB growth measure as *stability characteristic*. A simple interpretation of the stability of a KB is monitoring the dynamics of knowledge base changes. This measure could be useful to understand high-level changes by analyzing KB growth patterns. Within this context, this measure explores two main areas: (1) evolution of resources and (2) impact of the erroneous removal of resources in a KB.

We argue that quality issues can be identified through monitoring lifespan of an RDF KBs. We can measure growth level of KB resources (instances) by measuring changes presented in different releases. In particular, knowledge base growth can be measured by detecting the changes over KB releases utilizing trend analysis such as the use of simple linear regression. Based on the comparison between observed and predicted values, we can detect the trend in the KB resources, thus detecting anomalies over KB releases if the resources have a downward trend over the releases.

We derive KB lifespan analysis regarding change patterns over time. To measure the KB growth, we applied linear regression analysis of entity counts over KB releases. In the regression analysis, we checked the latest release to measure the normalized distance between an actual and a predicted value. In particular, in the linear regression we used entity count (y_i) as dependent variable and time period (t_i) as independent variable. Here, $n = total\ number\ of\ KB\ releases$ and $i = 1...n$ present as the time period.

We start with a linear regression fitting the count measure of the class (C):

$$y(C) = at + b$$

The residual can be defined as:

$$residual_i(C) = a \cdot t_i + b - count_i(C)$$

We define the normalized distance as:

$$ND(C) = \frac{residual_n(C)}{mean(|residual_i(C)|)}$$

Based on the normalized distance, we can measure the KB growth of a class C as:

$$Stability(C) = \begin{cases} 1\ if ND(C) \geq 1 \\ 0\ if ND(C) < 1 \end{cases}$$

The value is 1 if the normalized distance between actual value is higher than the predicted value of type C, otherwise it is 0. In particular, if the KB growth measure has the value of 1 then the KB may have an unexpected growth with unwanted entities otherwise the KB remains stable.

5   Experimental Analysis

Experimental Settings: The 3cixty KB is continuously changing with frequent updates (daily updates). We target *lode:Event* and *dul:Places* class for Stability analysis. The distinct instance count for each class is presented in Table 1a. We manually collected 9 snapshots from 2016-03-11 to 2016-09-09. In addition,

Table 1. 3cixty KB dataset summary.

(a) *lode:Event* and *dul:Place* type.

Release	lode:Event	dul:Places
2016-03-11	605	20,692
2016-03-22	605	20,692
2016-04-09	1,301	27,858
2016-05-03	1,301	26,066
2016-05-13	1,409	26,827
2016-05-27	1,883	25,828
2016-06-15	2,182	41,018
2016-09-09	689	44,968

(b) Periodic snapshots of *lode:Event* class.

Release	Entity Count
2017-07-27	114,054
2017-07-28	114,542
2017-07-29	114,544
2017-07-30	114,544
other rows are omitted for brevity	
2017-09-14	188,967
2017-09-15	192,116
2017-09-16	154,745

we collected daily snapshots for *lode:Event* type starting from 2017-07-19 till 2017-09-27. Table 1b reports the entity count of *lode:Event* type using periodic snapshots generation.

Stability Characteristics: We applied a linear regression over the eight releases for the *lode:Event*-type and *dul:Place*-type entities (Fig. 2a and b).

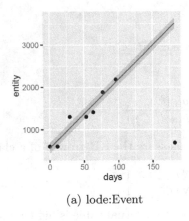

(a) lode:Event

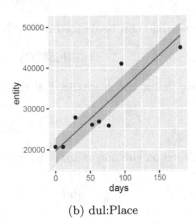

(b) dul:Place

Fig. 2. 3cixty two classes Stability measure.

From the linear regression, the KB has a total of $n = 8$ releases where the 8th predicted value for *lode:Event* $y'_{events_8} = 3511.548$ while the actual value = 689. Similarly, for *dul:Place* $y'_{places_8} = 47941.57$ and the actual value = 44968.

The residuals, $e_{events_8} = |689 - 3511.548| = 2822.545$ and $e_{places_8} = |44968 - 49741.57| = 2973.566$. The mean of the residuals, $e_{event_i} = 125.1784$ and $e_{place_i} = 3159.551$, where $i = 1...n$.

So the normalized distance for, 8th *lode:Event* entity $ND_{event} = \frac{2822.545}{125.1784} = 22.54818$ and *dul:Place* entity $ND_{place} = \frac{2973.566}{3159.551} = 0.9411357$.

For the *lode:Event* class, $ND_{events} \geq 1$ so the stability measure value $= 1$. However, for the *dul:Place* class, $ND_{places} < 1$ so the stability measure value $= 0$.

In the case of the *lode:Event* class, it clearly presents anomalies as the number of distinct entities drops significantly on the last release. To further validate our assumption we performed manual inspection on the last release of *lode:Event* entity type. We observed that entities that are present in 2016-06-06 are missing in 2016-09-09. Thus, it leads to a Stability Characteristics value of 1. We further investigated the value chain leading to the generation of the KB and we found an error in the reconciliation algorithm for 2016-09-09 release.

In Fig. 2a, the *lode:Event* class growth remains constant until it has errors in the last release. It has higher distance between actual and predicted value based on the *lode:Event*-type entity count. However, in the case of *dul:Place*-type, the actual entity count in the last release is near the predicted value. We can assume that on the last release, the 3cixty KB has improved the quality of data generation matching the expected growth. We further extended the stability characteristic analysis by monitoring *lode:Event* entity type.

To monitor any changes present for continuous updates, we collected 50 snapshots of *lode:Event* entity type from 2017-07-27 to 2017-09-16. Figure 3 illustrates the changes presents in the *lode:Event*-type due to KB growth. There are significant changes present in the last four releases (2017-09-13,2017-09-14,2017-09-15,2017-09-16) entity counts. In the 2017-09-13 release, we can see an exponential growth of entity count of 190,1867 compared to previous releases. Furthermore, on the next two releases (2017-09-14,2017-09-15) entity count remains stable due to fewer variation presents in the entity count. However, on the 2017-09-16 snapshots, we can observe a drop in the entity count which may lead to anomalies in the data integration pipeline. We further investigated the value chain leading to the generation of the KB, and we found an error in the external data acquisition process which leads to missing entities for 2017-09-16 snapshot.

6   Related Work

Taking into account changes over time, every dataset can be dynamic. In this context, Käfer *et al.* [2] design a Linked Data Observatory to monitor linked data dynamics. Umbrich *et al.* [11] present a comparative analysis on LOD datasets dynamics. In particular, they analyzed entity dynamics using a labeled directed graph based on LOD, where a node is an entity that is represented by a subject. In addition, Umbrich *et al.* [12] present a comprehensive survey based on technical solutions for dealing with changes in datasets of the Web of Data. Issues in curated RDF(S) have been addressed by Papavasileiou *et al.* [6]. They introduce a high-level language of changes and its formal detection and application semantics, as well as a corresponding change detection algorithm, which satisfies these needs for RDF(S) KBs. Ellefi *et al.* [1] present a comprehensive overview of the RDF dataset profiling feature, methods, tools, and vocabularies. They present dataset profiling in a taxonomy and illustrate the links between the dataset profiling and feature extraction approaches. It enables easy and efficient

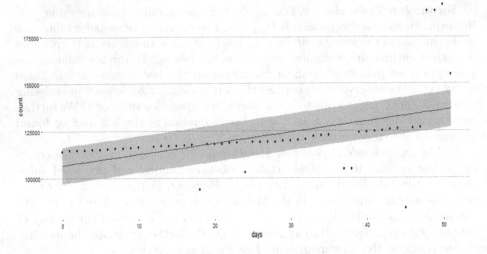

Fig. 3. KB Stability measure for 3cixty *lode:Event* class using periodic snapshots dataset.

navigation among versions, automated processing, and analysis of changes. They also include cross-snapshot queries (spanning across different versions), as well as queries involving both changes in schema and instance. Zabilith *et al.* [13] conducted an extensive work at the ontology level detection, representation, and management of the changes.

Pernelle *et al.* [7] present an approach that allows to detect and represent elementary and complex changes that can be detected only on the data level. In this work, we use linear regression for detecting changes present in the KB. However, instead of using a clustering technique [5] based on entities temporal pattern we mainly focus on presenting linear regression analysis to detect trend present in the KB. Clustering techniques can be of help to summarize the temporal changes in a dataset, but they are computationally expensive considering millions of entities present in a KB. In this regard, only using data profiling results as features we reduce the computational complexity of the task because we reduce the volume of data to process.

7   Conclusions and Future Work

We have focused on the use case of supporting tourist data producers and consumers using KB evolution analysis in their activities of data collection and integration process.

Knowledge about Linked Data dynamics is essential for a broad range of applications such as effective caching, link maintenance, and versioning [2]. However, less focus has been given towards understanding knowledge base resource changes over time to detect anomalies over various releases in the tourism domain. More specifically, we consider coarse-grained analysis as an essential requirement to capture any inconsistency present in the dataset. Although coarse-grained analysis cannot detect all possible inconsistencies, it helps to identify common issues such as erroneous deletion of resources in the data extraction and integration processes.

In this context, the focus of this work is to automate the timely process of KB change detection without user intervention based on evolution analysis. We have designed a set of APIs for monitoring KB evolution. More specifically, we explore the lifespan of an entity type using stability characteristics using simple linear regression model. In particular, it can help to detect unexpected growth or impact of the erroneous removal of resources in a KB. To verify our assumption, we discovered entities with anomalies in the 3cixty KB and performed further inspection. For *lode:Event* entities, we identified a large number of instances missing due to an algorithmic error in the data extraction pipeline. However, a further exploration of the KB evolution analysis is needed, and we consider this as a future research activity. We want to explore further *(i)* which factors are affecting KB growth and *(ii)* validating the stability measure.

Acknowledgments. This work was partially funded by the BES-2014-068449 grant.

References

1. Ellefi, M.B., et al.: RDF dataset profiling - a survey of features, methods, vocabularies and applications. Semant. Web **PP**, 1–29 (2018). https://doi.org/10.3233/SW-180294
2. Käfer, T., Abdelrahman, A., Umbrich, J., O'Byrne, P., Hogan, A.: Observing linked data dynamics. In: Cimiano, P., Corcho, O., Presutti, V., Hollink, L., Rudolph, S. (eds.) ESWC 2013. LNCS, vol. 7882, pp. 213–227. Springer, Heidelberg (2013). https://doi.org/10.1007/978-3-642-38288-8_15
3. Meimaris, M., Papastefanatos, G., Pateritsas, C., Galani, T., Stavrakas, Y.: A framework for managing evolving information resources on the data web. Comput. Res. Repository (CoRR) (2015). http://arxiv.org/abs/1504.06451
4. Mihindukulasooriya, N., Poveda-Villalón, M., García-Castro, R., Gómez-Pérez, A.: Collaborative ontology evolution and data quality - an empirical analysis. In: Dragoni, M., Poveda-Villalón, M., Jimenez-Ruiz, E. (eds.) OWLED/ORE -2016. LNCS, vol. 10161, pp. 95–114. Springer, Cham (2017). https://doi.org/10.1007/978-3-319-54627-8_8
5. Nishioka, C., Scherp, A.: Information-theoretic analysis of entity dynamics on the linked open data cloud. In: Demidova, E., Dietze, S., Szymański, J., Breslin, J. (eds.) Proceedings of the 3rd International Workshop on Dataset Profiling and Federated Search for Linked Data (PROFILES 2016) Co-located with the 13th ESWC 2016 Conference, CEUR Workshop Proceedings, Anissaras, Greece, 30 May 2016, vol. 1597 (2016). CEUR-WS.org
6. Papavasileiou, V., Flouris, G., Fundulaki, I., Kotzinos, D., Christophides, V.: High-level change detection in RDF(S) KBs. ACM Trans. Database Syst. (TODS) **38**(1), 1 (2013)
7. Pernelle, N., Saïs, F., Mercier, D., Thuraisamy, S.: RDF data evolution: efficient detection and semantic representation of changes. In: Michael, M., Marti, C., Erwin, F. (eds.) Joint Proceedings of the Posters and Demos Track of the 12th

International Conference on Semantic Systems - SEMANTiCS2016 and the 1st International Workshop on Semantic Change & Evolving Semantics SuCCESS 2016), CEUR Workshop Proceedings, Leipzig, Germany, 12–15 September 2016, vol. 1695 (2016). CEUR-WS.org

8. Troncy, R., et al.: 3cixty: building comprehensive knowledge bases for city exploration. Web Semant. Sci. Serv. Agents. World Wide Web **46–47**, 2–13 (2017). https://doi.org/10.1016/j.websem.2017.07.002

9. Sabou, M., Braşoveanu, A.M., Arsal, I.: Supporting tourism decision making with linked data. In: Proceedings of the 8th International Conference on Semantic Systems, pp. 201–204. ACM (2012)

10. Troncy, R., et al.: 3cixty: building comprehensive knowledge bases for city exploration. Web Semant. Sci. Serv. Agents World Wide Web **46**, 2–13 (2017)

11. Umbrich, J., Decker, S., Hausenblas, M., Polleres, A., Hogan, A.: Towards dataset dynamics: change frequency of linked open data sources. In: Christian, B., Tom, H., Tim, B.-L., Michael, H. (eds.) Proceedings of the WWW2010 Workshop on Linked Data on the Web(LDOW), CEUR Workshop Proceedings, Raleigh, USA, 27 April 2010, vol. 628 (2010). CEUR-WS.org

12. Umbrich, J., Villazón-Terrazas, B., Hausenblas, M.: Dataset dynamics compendium: a comparative study. In: Proceedings of the First International Workshop on Consuming Linked Data (COLD2010) at the 9th International Semantic Web Conference (ISWC2010), CEUR Workshop Proceedings, Shanghai, China, vol. 665 (2010). CEUR-WS.org

13. Zablith, F., et al.: Ontology evolution: a process-centric survey. Knowl. Eng. Rev. **30**(1), 45–75 (2015)

Type Prediction of RDF Knowledge Graphs Using Binary Classifiers with Structural Data

Nandana Mihindukulasooriya[✉] and Mariano Rico

Ontology Engineering Group, Universidad Politécnica de Madrid, Madrid, Spain
{nmihindu,mariano.rico}@fi.upm.es

Abstract. Type information, which is useful for responding many queries, plays a key role in Semantic Web. Nevertheless, it is common that type information of some instances is not present in knowledge graphs. Thus, type prediction of a given instance using background knowledge is an important knowledge graph completion task. To this end, the objective of this paper is to propose a data-driven type prediction approach using the structural information of the given instance utilising machine learning techniques. The experiments presented in the paper demonstrate that a binary classifier with structural information as features can be effectively used for type prediction of RDF knowledge graphs with high accuracy. The accuracy of the classifier is related to the diversity of training data as well as the how conceptually similar are the different classes in the training and test data. Further, the experiments demonstrate that it is possible to build universal classifiers to a given class, *i.e.*, a model training on one dataset can produce good predictions for another dataset in cases where training data contains conceptually different classes. For example, a model training on the English DBpedia can be used to predict types of the Spanish DBpedia.

Keywords: Linked Data · RDF · Knowledge graph · Data quality

1 Introduction

In the Semantic Web vision paper [1], Berners-Lee et al. identify the value of having access to structured collections of information with their associated explicit semantics and inference rules that can be used for automated reasoning. Semantic Web has come a long way since then and a large number of Semantic Web standards have been developed and a huge volume of data is available as a part of the Linked (Open) Cloud. Such data is generally expressed using ontologies or vocabularies and is represented using the RDF model. We refer to such datasets as knowledge graphs (KGs) from here onwards.

Naming things using globally identifiable URIs and providing their type information play an important role in making the data on the Semantic Web discoverable and reusable. For instance, such information allows a KG to answer the

© Springer Nature Switzerland AG 2018
C. Pautasso et al. (Eds.): ICWE 2018, LNCS 11153, pp. 279–287, 2018.
https://doi.org/10.1007/978-3-030-03056-8_27

query, "What is *La Tomatina*?" by looking at its type declaration. Further, such information enables exploratory queries such as "Find all scientists in a given knowledge graph". For instance, if a knowledge base contains a type declaration *e.g. Albert Einstein* is a *Scientist*, this will allow him to be included in the aforementioned query. Nevertheless, type information is not always available for all instances in a KG due to various reasons such as deficiencies in the data generation or transformation process (*e.g.*, lack of mappings) or deficiencies in source data (*e.g.*, missing type information).

In the Linked Open Data cloud, DBpedia [2] stands out as the central hub of Linked Open Data (LOD) because it provides a vast amount of information and most other datasets in the LOD cloud link to DBpedia. DBpedia data is extracted from Wikipedia and transformed to RDF using the mappings. While being a useful source of information containing more than 6.6 million entities (English DBpedia, 2016-10 version), DBpedia also contains large number of entities without type information (or only typed as *owl:Thing* which does not add much information value). Specifically, for the aforementioned DBpedia, 1.1 million entities do not have type.

To this end, the objective of the work presented in this paper is to propose a data-driven type prediction approach that predicts the type of a given instance using its structural information in the KG. More concretely, we propose a machine learning based binary classifier that uses the presence of a set of properties encoded as binary features to predict if a given instance belongs to a certain class or not. While the proposed approach this study is generic and applicable to any knowledge graph, the experiments are carried out using the English DBpedia and the Spanish DBpedia datasets. We chose DBpedia as it a large and a high-relevant dataset in the Linked Data Cloud. The Spanish DBpedia is the second largest DBpedia in size, after the English DBpedia, and around 40% of its content is exclusive, that is, cannot be found in the English DBpedia [3].

In order to provide a reproducible environment, all the datasets and experiments are publicly available as an OpenML [4] study at http://www.openml.org/s/109 and at the website[1].

The rest of the paper is structured as follows: Sect. 2 defines the research questions addressed in the paper; Sect. 3 presents the proposed approach; Sect. 4 presents the experiments to evaluate the hypotheses; Sect. 5 discusses related work; and finally Sect. 6 provides some conclusions and outlines future work.

2   Problem Definition

The research questions of this work are motivated by the fact that type information are not complete in datasets. Thus, the main objective of this work is to propose techniques for completing type information and evaluating such methods. The main research questions addressed in our work is:

– **RQ1.** Is it possible to build a model that can predict if a given instance belongs to a type using the properties the instance has?

---

[1] http://tourismkg.linkeddata.es.

- **RQ2.** How does the accuracy of the model change based on the diversity of the data? (e.g., the number of distinct classes)
- **RQ3.** Is a model trained from one dataset valid for another dataset?

In this context, we have formulated 3 hypotheses, related to the research question, that are evaluated in this paper. Those are: (a) Hypothesis 1 - A Machine Learning binary classifier can be used for type prediction with the presence of properties as features with high precision. (b) Hypothesis 2 - The accuracy of the aforementioned classifier will depend on the diversity of data (i.e., the number of different types of instances in data) (c) Hypothesis 3 - A model learned from one dataset can be used to predict types of another dataset. (e.g., learning from Spanish DBpedia and predicting on English DBpedia or vice versa).

3 Proposed Approaches

In this work, we propose an approach for predicting the type of an instance resource based on its structural characteristics, *i.e.*, the properties it has. We formulate this type prediction problem as a binary classification problem where, for each class in the corresponding ontology (*e.g.*, DBpedia ontology in this case). Thus, each class will have a prediction model that will predict if a given instance belongs to that class or not based on the properties a given instance resource has. For instance, we can build a binary classifier model for *dbo:Holiday* class, which predict if a given instance is a holiday or not based on the properties it has.

3.1 Feature Engineering

In the approach, each feature is binary and is associated with a given property. If the corresponding property is present in the instance, the value is 1 and 0 otherwise. The next decision is which properties to include as features. Trivially, all properties in a given ontology can be included as features. But this will lead to sparse feature matrix with most features having all zeros because they are not related to any of the classes in our training/test data. Thus in our experiments, we limit the features to a subset of properties *i.e.* all properties that are present in at least a single triple in the training data.

3.2 Training

The next step is to preparing data for training the binary classifier model of each class. For this, we need a set of a positive training data as well as a set of negative training data. Positive training data can be easily generated by querying all instances of a given class. For instance, for the classifier model for *dbo:Holiday* class, that will be all *Holiday* instances. Nevertheless, negative training data generation can be done in several different ways. For instance, a class that is disjoint with *Holiday* can be chosen, *e.g.*, *Person*, and all instances of that class can be used as negative training data. However, this will create a more simpler setting than the real world data where only instances of two classes are present. By adding more classes to the negative training data, we can make this setting more realistic. If the training data contains representative sample of instances of all classes, we can assume the learned models to be representative.

Further, if the dataset contains some noisy data, a manual inspection of the selected instances is needed because some of the type information can be wrong. For example, in the DBpedia dataset there were several erroneous types in its resources. In this manual analysis, we identified few common errors, for instance, pages with lists of people being typed as person.

Table 1. Datasets used in the experiments

Source	ID	Feat.	Labelled instances		ID	Feat.	Labelled instances	
Spanish DBpedia	ES-1	132	Positive	Holiday(809)	ES-2	144	Positive	Holiday(809)
			Negative	Person(1000)			Negative	Person(500), Event(500)
	ES-3	299	Postive	Holiday(809)				
			Negative	Activity, Agent, AnatomicalStructure, Award, Biomolecule, ChemicalSubstance, Colour, Currency, Device, Disease, Event, Food, Language, MeanOfTransportation, Species, SportCompetitionResult, TopicalConcept, Work - 50 each, Place(100)				
English DBpedia	EN-1	132	Positive	Holiday(1175)	EN-2	144	Positive	Holiday(1175)
			Negative	Person(1175)			Negative	Person(588), Event(587)
	EN-3	299	Positive	Holiday(1175)				
			Negative	Activity, Agent, AnatomicalStructure, Award, Biomolecule, ChemicalSubstance, Colour, Currency, Device, Disease, Event, Food, Language, MeanOfTransportation, Place, Species, SportCompetitionResult, TopicalConcept - 65 each, and Work(70)				

4   Evaluation

4.1   Experiment 1

The objective of the first experiment is to evaluate the hypothesis 1, that a machine learning classifier can be used to predict the type of a resource using as features the presence of properties. In this experiment, we build a supervised type predictor for *Holiday* class using as features a set of 132 properties of the DBpedia ontology (*i.e.*, all the properties found in training data). All the features are binary (0/1) nominal attributes, that is, a given resource has (or has not) a given property, not considering the value or the property.

For this experiment we used the dataset ES-1 extracted from the Spanish DBpedia (Table 1), which contains 809 instances of Holiday (labelled as positive) and 1000 instances of *Person* (labelled as negative). We selected the class *Person* because it is conceptually different from *Holiday*, as a first test to distinguish between instances of *Holiday* and *Person*.

Using the dataset ES-1, we ran a 10-fold stratified cross validation, achieving an accuracy of **99.06%** for method J48 [5] (only 17 instances were incorrectly classified in 1,809), and **99.28%** for Random Forest [6]. We can visualise the relation between instances computing the distance between instances as its euclidean distance in the vector space defined by its features. In this way we can compute a distance matrix and create a graph. Applying a force-directed layout such as Fruchterman-Reingold algorithm [7] we get the graph show in right side of Fig. 1. In that figure we can see a clear separation between *Holiday* instances and *Person* instances, with only a few instances of *Person* in the cluster of *Holiday*, in concordance with the high accuracy of the prediction.

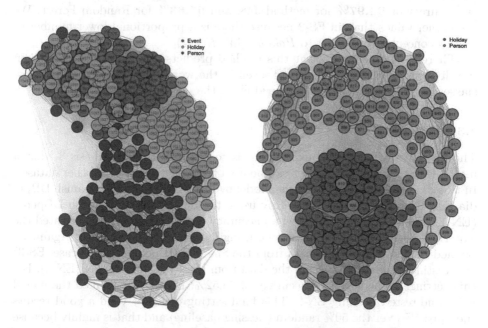

Fig. 1. Identifying Holidays in a knowledge graph. (Right) in a mix of Holidays and Persons, and (Left) in a mix of Holidays, Persons and Events. Notice that the colors for instances of Holiday and Person differ in each graph. (Color figure online)

4.2   Experiment 2

The objective of the second experiment is to evaluate the hypothesis 2, that the accuracy of the aforementioned classifier depends on the diversity of the knowledge graph. For this experiment, in addition to dataset ES-1, two other datasets were used. In all these three datasets, the positive training data remained the same, *i.e.*, in each of the three datasets there are 809 instances of *Holiday*. However, the negative training dataset ES-2 includes 500 *Person* instances and 500 *Event* instances. By including instances of *Event*, which are conceptually closer to *Holiday*, we increase the complexity of the training/test data.

The 10-fold stratified cross validation achieves an accuracy of **91.49%** for method J48, and **91.21%** for Random Forest. Notice the high values despite *Event* is the closest class to *Holiday* from the 162 classes (considering all levels not just first level) with instances in the Spanish DBpedia.

The knowledge graph, using the previously explained method, is the left graph in Fig. 1. In this graph we see a clear separation between instances of *Holiday* and *Person*, but there is a mix between *Holiday* and *Event*.

In dataset ES-3, the negative training data includes instances of all ten 1st level classes (*i.e.*, direct subclasses of *owl:Thing*) from the Spanish DBpedia. These classes are listed in Table 1. The 10-fold stratified cross validation achieves an accuracy of **94.97%** for method J48, and **95.63%** for Random Forest. We get higher values than in ES-2 because there is a proportional lower number of classes conceptually similar to *Holiday* (like *Event*).

Therefore we conclude that this method predicts with high accuracy when the diversity of classes is high and, even in the worst case, when there are few classes but very similar to the trained class, the achieved accuracy is high.

4.3   Experiment 3

The objective of this third experiment is to evaluate the hypothesis 3, that a model learned from one dataset can be used to predict types of another dataset. In this case, we first we trained the model by using data from the Spanish DBpedia (ES-1) and testing the model by using the data from the English DBpedia (EN-1). For this case we achieved an accuracy of 98.63%. Then, we repeated the experiment with more diverse setting using datasets ES-3 and EN-3. Again, we trained the model by using data from the Spanish DBpedia (in this case, ES-3) and testing the model by using the data from the English DBpedia (EN-3). For this setting, we achieved an accuracy of 75.52%. Finally, we trained the model ES-2 and tested it using EN-2. This final setting does not yield a good results (i.e., just 5% over the 50% random guessing baseline) and that is mainly because the conceptual similarity between *Holiday* and *Event*. We plan to further investigate how to improve such cases in the future. A summary of all experimental results are presented in Table 2.

Table 2. Summary of the experimental results.

Experiment	Dataset (See Table 1)	Performance
EXP - 1	ES-1	99.28% (Random Forest), 99.06% (J48)
	EN-1	98.38% (Random Forest), 98.64% (J48)
EXP - 2	ES-2	91.21% (Random Forest), 91.49% (J48)
	EN-2	93.06% (Random Forest), 92.60% (J48)
	ES-3	95.63% (Random Forest), 94.97% (J48)
	EN-3	92.77% (Random Forest), 91.70% (J48)
EXP - 3	ES-1 (Training)/EN-1 (Testing)	98.63% (Random Forest)
	ES-2 (Training)/EN-2 (Testing)	55.72% (Random Forest)
	ES-3 (Training)/EN-3 (Testing)	75.52% (Random Forest)

5 Related Work

Several approaches have been proposed for the type prediction problem in large datasets. Most of these approaches are tested on DBpedia because its relevance as the central hub of the Linked Data cloud.

One of the most prominent approaches in the area is the SDType [8] system, which has been applied to DBpedia both for its evaluation as well as for the dataset itself when being published. SDTypes exploits the information about the statistical distribution of properties over types to infer new ones. That is, in a nutshell, if a resource has the same properties as another one of a given type, then it can be inferred that such resource should be typed with the given type. We follow a similar line of thought in the work presented in this paper. However, unlike SDType, we use binary classifiers for each given class, compared to the multilabel classifiers in SDType.

More recent studies have proposed the use of machine learning techniques, like the one used to identify wrong mappings in DBpedia [9]. Specifically focused on improving the types of resources in a dataset, some contributions have been explored, using multilabel approaches [10,11], varying on the algorithms applied and how the training data is selected. In general, all of them define the process of assigning types as a multilabel classification problem, as several types are expected for each resource. In our work, we formulate the type prediction as a binary classification problem by generating a model for each of the classes in the given ontology.

Taxonomy-based classification approaches for multilabel process, which use the ontology to divide the training data into different subsets according to different criteria, has been also proposed [12]. Melo et al. [13] provide a comprehensive discussion on the state of the art.

6   Conclusions

In this paper, we have presented an approach for type prediction of instances based on the structural information, *i.e.*, the properties the instance has. The experiments that were carried out demonstrate that a binary classifier model can be built with high accuracy for type prediction using structural information as features and also the accuracy of the model depends on the diversity of the training knowledge graph. Further, the experiment demonstrate that a model that is trained on one dataset can be used for type prediction in a different dataset.

As future work, on the one hand we plan to extend this study to analyse the effects of diversity and KG complexity by using further granular levels of classes in the ontology (such as more deeper levels of subclasses, e.g. 2nd, 3rd, 4th levels) as well as testing the generated models with other multilingual datasets such as the French DBpedia, Italian DBpedia, German DBpedia, etc. On the other hand, we plan to extend this study to compare the performance of the approach proposed in this paper with other NLP-oriented approaches for type prediction to see the effectiveness of type prediction based on structural information and based on NLP features. Our intuition is that the ensemble approach that uses both structural features and NLP features will yield even a better performance.

Acknowledgments. This work was funded by the Spanish Ministry of Economy and Competitiveness (MINECO) with the BES-2014-068449 FPI grant, DATOS 4.0: Retos y soluciones (TIN2016-78011-C4-4-R) and esTextAnalytics (RTC-2016-4952-7) projects.

References

1. Berners-Lee, T., Hendler, J., Lassila, O.: The Semantic Web. Sci. Am. **284**(5), 34–43 (2001)
2. Auer, S., Bizer, C., Kobilarov, G., Lehmann, J., Cyganiak, R., Ives, Z.: DBpedia: a nucleus for a web of open data. In: Aberer, K., et al. (eds.) ASWC/ISWC -2007. LNCS, vol. 4825, pp. 722–735. Springer, Heidelberg (2007). https://doi.org/10.1007/978-3-540-76298-0_52
3. Mihindukulasooriya, N., Rico, M., García-Castro, R., Gómez-Pérez, A.: An analysis of the quality issues of the properties available in the Spanish DBpedia. In: Puerta, J.M., et al. (eds.) CAEPIA 2015. LNCS (LNAI), vol. 9422, pp. 198–209. Springer, Cham (2015). https://doi.org/10.1007/978-3-319-24598-0_18
4. Vanschoren, J., van Rijn, J.N., Bischl, B., Torgo, L.: OpenML: networked science in machine learning. SIGKDD Explor. **15**(2), 49–60 (2013)
5. Salzberg, S.L.: C4.5: programs for machine learning. Mach. Learn. **16**(3), 235–240 (1994)
6. Breiman, L.: Random Forests. Mach. Learn. **45**(1), 5–32 (2001)
7. Fruchterman, T.M., Reingold, E.M.: Graph drawing by force-directed placement. Softw. Pract. Exp. **21**(11), 1129–1164 (1991)
8. Paulheim, H., Bizer, C.: Type inference on noisy RDF data. In: Alani, H., et al. (eds.) ISWC 2013. LNCS, vol. 8218, pp. 510–525. Springer, Heidelberg (2013). https://doi.org/10.1007/978-3-642-41335-3_32

9. Rico, M., Mihindukulasooriya, N., Kontokostas, D., Paulheim, H., Hellmann, S., Gómez-Pérez, A.: Predicting incorrect mappings: a data-driven approach applied to DBpedia. In: Proceedings of SAC (2018)

10. Tsoumakas, G., Vlahavas, I.: Random k-Labelsets: an ensemble method for multilabel classification. In: Kok, J.N., Koronacki, J., Mantaras, R.L., Matwin, S., Mladenič, D., Skowron, A. (eds.) ECML 2007. LNCS (LNAI), vol. 4701, pp. 406–417. Springer, Heidelberg (2007). https://doi.org/10.1007/978-3-540-74958-5_38

11. Zhang, M.L., Zhou, Z.H.: Multilabel neural networks with applications to functional genomics and text categorization. IEEE Trans. Knowl. Data Eng. 18(10), 1338–1351 (2006)

12. Ristoski, P., Paulheim, H.: Feature selection in hierarchical feature spaces. In: Džeroski, S., Panov, P., Kocev, D., Todorovski, L. (eds.) DS 2014. LNCS (LNAI), vol. 8777, pp. 288–300. Springer, Cham (2014). https://doi.org/10.1007/978-3-319-11812-3_25

13. Melo, A., Völker, J., Paulheim, H.: Type prediction in noisy RDF knowledge bases using hierarchical multilabel classification with graph and latent features. Int. J. Artif. Intell. Tools 26(02), 1760011 (2017)

Semantic Network Visualization
of Cultural Heritage Data

Shaban Shabani[1,2(✉)], Zhan Liu[1], and Maria Sokhn[1]

[1] Institute of Information Systems, HES-SO Valais-Wallis, Sierre, Switzerland
{zhan.liu,maria.sokhn}@hevs.ch
[2] Department of Mathematics and Computer Science, University of Basel,
Basel, Switzerland
shaban.shabani@unibas.ch

Abstract. Advancement of digital technologies have helped the cultural heritage (CH) organizations such as archives, libraries, and museums to digitize their data collections and improve the accessibility to them. Over the past years various approaches have been developed to enable the visualization of the CH data. In this paper, we present a use case on annotation, linking, visualization and browsing of CH data and suggest some directions to achieve tangible visual analysis. We introduce the semantic linked data search and the method of connected concepts to enhance the users experience when searching for historical data.

Keywords: Network visualization · Cultural heritage
Semantic search · Linked data

1 Introduction

The role of documenting cultural heritage is a crucial element for preserving the culture for future generations and it has been long recognized. The digitization of cultural collections is changing our perception to cultural organizations. Over the past years, cultural organizations intensively digitize their collections and make them publicly accessible [2]. Digital CH data has importance in fields such as tourism, as it helps to promote regions and cultural diversity [1].

In the cultural heritage, a quick access to the right information has an important role. Visualizing the data in a meaningful representation is a more recent concept used for accessing data, deriving meaning and acquiring knowledge from the data [4]. Data visualization has an incredible power to attract people's attention, consequently it enables users to derive concrete conclusions.

This work aims at finding new approaches of visualizing the CH data to enhance users search experience through semantic search. The aim of semantic technologies is to provide more visually appealing data, by enabling graphical representations of the semantically structured data. Furthermore, it enables meaningful relations of data entities. The meaningful and labeled clustering of data in form of semantic concepts enable new ways to visualize data. As a

C. Pautasso et al. (Eds.): ICWE 2018, LNCS 11153, pp. 288–291, 2018.
https://doi.org/10.1007/978-3-030-03056-8_28

motivating scenario, we consider the following use case: a user visiting a historical and tourism attraction site in Valais, uses the City-Stories application to find meaningful relations of data entities about Zermatt. Based on his search, the application recommends to the user the relevant information over Zermatt and it visually displays the most important concepts such as: related locations, people, events and historical sites. In this paper we present an extension of our previous work within the City-Stories project [6]. The rest of this paper is organized as follows: in Sect. 2 we provide details about the datasets, Sect. 3 is the main part and it describes the three components: data annotation and linking, semantic linked data search and connected concepts visualization, and Sect. 4 concludes.

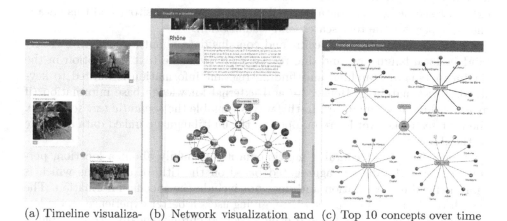

(a) Timeline visualization   (b) Network visualization and browsing   (c) Top 10 concepts over time

Fig. 1. Screenshots of the front-end application

2   Data Collection and Experimental Setup

Obtaining cultural heritage datasets has a crucial importance for implementing and testing our proposed approach. Hence, in this work we use digital archives datasets obtained from Mediatheque[1] and data collected via the Digital Valais[2] project, summing up to about 45 thousands records. These datasets contain a multi-format content (images, videos, audio and text) including media metadata (title, subject, description, author, date) and span on multi-disciplines such as culture, tradition, archeology, history etc. Part of our previous work focuses on cleaning, integration and alignment [6] of the data. In addition to collecting data from archival and memory institutions, we use data that has been collected via a crowdsourcing application [5], which enables local people to share valuable data and information they have about the cultural heritage of their region.

---

[1] http://www.mediatheque.ch/.
[2] http://www.valais-digital.ch/.

3   Semantic Linked Data Search and Network Visualization

Multimedia items in the dataset contain different information in the metadata, including text description, which can be in three languages (mainly French and German, and partially in English). In the first phase, we run the *data annotation and linking*. As there are different languages in the dataset, initially we detect the language used on the text description using the language identification tool[3]. Next, we run the entity linking [3] which automatically annotates mentions of DBpedia[4] resources in the text, and for each entity retrieved, we query the DBpedia SPQARL endpoint[5] to get additional information such as: label name, abstract description, thumbnail and image. The list of extracted entities and external knowledge base data is saved on the dataset repository and this data is the core part for the text search and visualization.

Because the dataset is specific and contains data about a region in Switzerland in local languages, and due to the short available text description in the media metadata, searching and finding relevant information is limited to keywords strict matching. Hence, we add external knowledge base information (if available) in three languages. In this way, we enable the *semantic text search*, i.e. the text search keywords are mapped to the multilanguage linked data available in the dataset.

Since the dataset contains multimedia items mainly about a location, person or event, the data is aggregated based on the title of the items which is more general representation and does not include the specific information. The search results are *timeline visualized*, giving users a better experience on exploring how these places, things and events evolved chronologically. An example of the timeline visualization is depicted in Fig. 1a, in which the user is searching for "Carnival of Sierre", and images and videos are visually represented and ordered by time.

Extracted concepts within the text description of the multimedia items are highlighted in distinguishable color. On the same page, users can read more about these concepts: image, description and links to the corresponding Wikipedia and DBpedia webpages are provided. The main part of the visualization is the *network of connected concepts*. The network consists of top k nodes and edges, where the nodes represent the strong concepts related to the chosen concept. An example is illustrated in Fig. 1b, where the user is interested to learn more about "Sierre". On the user interface (UI) the network of 10 connected concepts is generated around the chosen concept "Sierre". Size of the circular nodes depends on the importance, i.e. number of occurrences of the concepts with respect to the chosen concept. By clicking on each node, users can read more about other concepts in the network. Additionally, exploring more information about the displayed multimedia is available, allowing users to expand and collapse the

---

[3] https://pypi.python.org/pypi/langdetect.
[4] http://dbpedia.org.
[5] https://dbpedia.org/sparql.

network. Moreover, the feature of visualizing in a network the trend of connected concepts over period of time is available, enabling users to explore the change of important and relevant things for the chosen place, event or person they are interested in. This is shown in Fig. 1c.

4 Conclusion and Future Work

The overall objective of this paper is improving user search experience on CH related data, by understanding user's search context and enabling quick access to the relevant information. This is achieved by retrieving data to generate relevant results as well as visualizing the search results. Our approach based on connected concepts and network visualization, makes the search process easier for the users by showing them the most relevant data on one single UI and it provides better experience when searching for data. Additionally, linking with external knowledge bases, we provide more information about things they are interested in.

In our future work we intend to increase the size of the collections from several archival institutions and touristic locations, and test the performance of the overall system. Moreover, we aim to apply crowdsourcing for improving the accuracy of the semantic connected concepts approach.

Acknowledgement. This work was partly funded by the Hasler Foundation in the context of the project City-Stories. We are grateful to "Mediathque Valais", "Digital Valais Wallis" and "Archives de l'Etat du Valais" for providing the data.

References

1. Liu, Z., Shan, J., Balet, N.G., Fang, G.: Semantic social media analysis of Chinese tourists in Switzerland. Inf. Technol. Tour. **17**, 183–202 (2017)
2. Lynch, C.: Digital collections, digital libraries & the digitization of cultural heritage information. Microform Imaging Rev. **31**, 131–145 (2002)
3. Mendes, P.N., Jakob, M., García-Silva, A., Bizer, C.: Dbpedia spotlight: shedding light on the web of documents. In: Proceedings of the 7th International Conference on Semantic Systems, pp. 1–8. ACM (2011)
4. Nazemi, K., Burkhardt, D., Ginters, E., Kohlhammer, J.: Semantics visualization-definition, approaches and challenges. Procedia Comput. Sci. **75**, 75–83 (2015)
5. Shabani, S., Sokhn, M.: Gaming as a gateway: ensuring quality control for crowd-sourced data. In: Luo, Y. (ed.) CDVE 2017. LNCS, vol. 10451, pp. 73–76. Springer, Cham (2017). https://doi.org/10.1007/978-3-319-66805-5_9
6. Shabani, S., et al.: City-stories: a multimedia hybrid content and entity retrieval system for historical data. In: Proceedings of the 4th International Workshop on Computational History (HistoInformatics 2017) (2017)

Adaptation Process in Context-Aware Recommender System of Accessible Tourism Plan

Jose L. Jorro-Aragoneses[1](✉) and Susana Bautista-Blasco[2](✉)

[1] Universidad Complutense de Madrid, Madrid, Spain
jljorro@ucm.es
[2] Universidad Francisco de Vitoria, Madrid, Spain
susana.bautista@ufv.es

Abstract. In this paper, we propose an adaptation process to generate accessible plans based on the retrieved plans by the recommender system. In our case, if one of the activities of the retrieved plan does not apply the user preferences or contextual information, we change it for another activity to adapt the plan. We use a taxonomy based on the open data of the Madrid's council to adapt the plan and achieve an accessible tourism plan.

Keywords: Context · Accessibility · Tourism · Open data Adaptation

1 Introduction

Traditional recommender systems rely mainly on the relation between users and items. There is an active research area in context-aware recommender systems [2], where contextual and dynamic information from the environment is used to enrich the system knowledge and to personalize the recommendation to the specific situation like the location, the weather or social. Contextual information is very important in the tourism domain where any change in the context can change the activity to carry out, for example, if it is raining the user does not go to an outdoor activity. There are different previous works focusing on tourism recommenders [3] and different approaches based on contextual features [5]. Contextual information adds information to obtain a list of proper relevant activities to tourist. For example, the user location or weather state at the recommendation moment [1].

In this paper we propose an extension of MadridLive, a context-aware recommender system of tourism plan in Madrid based on a Case Based Reasoning (CBR) system [4]. Using CBR we obtain implicit information from the case base. In our case, the activities have an order in the plan, the sequence is logic and

Supported by the Spanish Committee of Economy and Competitiveness (TIN2014-55006-R); the funding provided by Banco Santander in UCM (CT17/17-CT17/18).

C. Pautasso et al. (Eds.): ICWE 2018, LNCS 11153, pp. 292–295, 2018.
https://doi.org/10.1007/978-3-030-03056-8_29

coherent based on the user preferences. This information is difficult to deduce using other approach. We include accessibility, handicaps and special needs as contextual features in the system. This accessibility context is used to adapt the system recommendation to avoid, for example, unaccessible locations and transports. This is important in order to guarantee the social inclusion for all kind of people. Given a query describing the user context and preferences, a CBR system [4] retrieves and reuse previously stored plans that fullfill the query requirements. Each case in the case base is a previously stored plan that has been performed and ranked by other users. The main contribution of this paper is an adaptation process to generate accessible plans based on a set of similar plans. Next sections describe the knowledge sources and the retrieval and adaptation processes.

2 Knowledge Sources

The system reasons with two knowledge sources: a case base of previous plans and a taxonomy of tourist activities categories based on the open data set of the Madrid's council[1]. The first one is used to recover the initial plan and, the second one is used to adapt the plan and achieve an accessible tourism plan.

We use a case base that contains 500 real tourism plans in Madrid. Each case has two main components: the case description (CD) and the case solution (CS). The CD includes tags for the categories of all the activities in the plan and the contextual knowledge associated to this plan described by the following features:

- **Time:** Time when start and finish a plan.
- **First Location:** Location of the first activity in a plan.
- **Location Type:** the place type (indoor or outdoor) of an activity.
- **Economic Cost:** An estimated cost to realize the plan.
- **Public Transport:** A boolean value to define if all activities can be visited using public transport.
- **Accessible Plan:** A boolean attribute to indicate if the plan is accessible to people with special needs.

The second knowledge source is the taxonomy. It lets classify all leisure activities that there are in Madrid in the next around 100 days. The system uses this taxonomy to search a new activity to insert in the plan. In this dataset there are around 1000 restaurants, more than 300 POIS (monuments, buildings, etc.) and nearly 1300 events. These numbers are updated daily by the council. The process of plan adaptation to achieve an accessible tourism plan uses a taxonomy of tourist activities categories. It is based on leisure categories from the activity classification in the open data of the Madrid's council. In this case, each available activity is classified using this taxonomy. Figure 1 presents a little example of our taxonomy of categories.

---

[1] https://datos.madrid.es/portal/site/egob/.

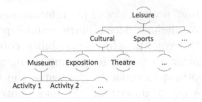

Fig. 1. An example of activity categories.

3 Retrieval

The recommendation process is based on retrieve and reuse plans previously performed and evaluated as positive experiences by other users. The CBR module retrieves the most similar case based on the query Q. It contains the conditions that the user wants in a leisure plan. Q contains the *user preferences* and the *contextual information* at the moment of the recommendation: time, location, weather, budget and handicaps. To do that, it uses a similarity function that compares each query attribute with its corresponding description attribute. The solution of the case retrieved is the plan that the system offers to the user. MadridLive is explained in detail in [4]. Similarity based retrieval maximizes the plan adequacy although the selected plan could not satisfy the user preferences or the contextual information. Next section describes how the plan is adapted to improve the final solution.

4 Plan Adaptation

The selected plan ($\mathcal{P}$) is adapted by reviewing and substituting some of the activities using the Algorithm 1. The algorithm replaces any activity (a_i) that does not satisfy the contextual information ($\mathcal{C}$) or the user preferences ($\mathcal{U}_p$) defined in the query by other similar activity that respects the user preferences. We recover a similar activity using the taxonomy. For example, if the best plan retrieved has got one unaccessible activity, the system will replace this activity by other accessible activity.

The algorithm searches for an activity using the taxonomy of categories of activities (see Fig. 1). Considering the activity to replace as a query to search the similar activity, the first step is to filter all activities that not apply the contextual restrictions of the original activity. The system classifies the candidate activities in the taxonomy of categories and recovers the activities with the most similar categories. In addition, these recovered activities apply all the restrictions of the original activity. The function selects one of them and return it to the adaptation algorithm. Finally, the system returns an adapted plan based on the contextual restrictions and user preferences.

For example, the best plan obtained contains the activity to visit *the Reina Sofia museum* but it is not accessible. The next step is substitute this activity. Firstly, the system filters all activities that are unaccessible. Next, it classifies

Data: $\mathcal{P} = [a_1, .., a_n], \mathcal{U}_p, \mathcal{C}$
Result: $\mathcal{R} = [b_1, .., b_n]$
$i \leftarrow 0$;
$\mathcal{R} \leftarrow []$;
while $i < \mathcal{P}.len$ **do**
    if $\neg respectContex(a_i, \mathcal{C}) \vee \neg respectPreferences(a_i, \mathcal{U}_p)$ **then**
        $R[i] \leftarrow getSimilarActivity(a_i, \mathcal{U}_p)$;
    else
        $R[i] \leftarrow a_i$;
    end
end

Algorithm 1: Adaptation algorithm

these filtered activities using the taxonomy. Finally, the system changes the original activity by another with similar categories, in our example, the activity proposed will be *the Prado museum.*

5 Working Progress

In this approach, we explain a novel idea in order to adapt real leisure plan for people with special needs. In our case, we focus on the feature of accessibility to modify the original plan. We consider using a taxonomy of categories to obtain the best activity from the open data source. Some difficulties that we found is that there are not enough of accessible activities in the open data used in some categories or the retrieved activities do not apply the user preferences. In addition, the system could return an activity out of the logical route between the previous and next activities in the original plan. For example, an activity so far. In these cases, we need to consider to apply a new filter less restrictive in order to recover a bigger set of candidate activities. Another possible solution to replace the original activity could generate an accessible walking tour between the previous and next activities considered in the original plan.

References

1. Achmad, K.A., Nugroho, L.E., Djunaedi, A.: Tourism contextual information for recommender system. In: 7th AES 2017, pp. 1–6. IEEE (2017)
2. Adomavicius, G., Tuzhilin, A.: Context-aware recommender systems. In: Ricci, F., Rokach L., Shapira, B. (eds.) Recommender Systems Handbook, pp. 191–226. Springer, Boston (2015). https://doi.org/10.1007/978-1-4899-7637-6_6
3. Borrás, J., Moreno, A., Valls, A.: Intelligent tourism recommender systems: a survey. Expert Syst. Appl. **41**(16), 7370–7389 (2014)
4. Jorro-Aragoneses, J.L., Díaz-Agudo, B., Recio-García, J.A.: Madrid Live: a context-aware recommender system of leisure plans. In: ICTAI, pp. 796–801 (2017)
5. Vansteenwegen, P., Souffriau, W.: Trip planning functionalities: state of the art and future. Inf. Technol. Tour. **12**(4), 305–315 (2010)

Author Index

Printed in the United States
By Bookmasters